WITHDRAWN

VOX POPULI

VOX POPULI

Popular Opinion and Violence
in the Religious Controversies
of the Fifth Century A.D.

Timothy E. Gregory

Ohio State University Press: Columbus

BR
219
G73

Copyright © 1979 by the Ohio State University Press
All Rights Reserved.

Library of Congress Cataloguing in Publication Data

Gregory, Timothy E.
  Vox populi

  Bibliography: p.
  Includes index.
    1. Church history—Primitive and early church, ca. 30-600. 2. Public opinion—Rome. 3. Violence—Moral and religious aspects. I. Title.
  BR219.G73   270.2   79-16885
  ISBN 0-8142-0291-8

FOR MY PARENTS

CONTENTS

Preface ix
Abbreviations xi

CHAPTER I   INTRODUCTION   3

CHAPTER II   THE URBAN CONTEXT
  The Late Roman City   15
  Decline or Expansion?   18
  Organizations and Institutions   26
  Constantinople, Ephesus, and Alexandria   31

CHAPTER III   THE EPISCOPACY OF JOHN CHRYSOSTOM: CONSTANTINOPLE
  Early Years and the Episcopal Election of 397   31
  Chrysostom as Bishop   45
  The Council of the Oak and First Exile   50
  Second Exile and Schism   58
  The Aftermath   64

CHAPTER IV   NESTORIUS AND THE COUNCIL OF EPHESUS: CONSTANTINOPLE AND EPHESUS
  Nestorius, Bishop of Constantinople   81
  The Christological Controversy   85
  The Outbreak of the Quarrel   88
  The Council of Ephesus, 431   100
  Constantinople after the Council   108

CHAPTER V   THE LATROCINIUM: CONSTANTINOPLE AND EPHESUS
  The Controversy Continued   129
  The Council of 448   131
  The Second Council of Ephesus   143
  The Aftermath in Constantinople   150

CHAPTER VI THE COUNCIL OF CHALCEDON: CONSTANTINOPLE AND ALEXANDRIA

Toward a New Policy	162
The Meeting of the Council	170
Opposition to Dioscorus	175
Revolt in Alexandria	181

CHAPTER VII CONCLUSIONS 203

Bibliography	229
Index	243

PREFACE

This is a study at the crossroads of social and religious history. It involves complex theological issues, but its focus is the way that theology appeared to ordinary people. Likewise, it discusses political and ecclesiastical events in some detail, but it shows how popular opinion was affected by these events and how this, in turn, played a role of its own. In a study such as this, one cannot ignore the phenomenon of violence, and violence touches our analysis at many points.

Two things led me to write this book. One was a seminar in comparative medieval urban history taught by professors Paul J. Alexander, Andrew Ehrenkreutz, and Sylvia L. Thrupp. In that seminar, students were exposed to issues and approaches that were new and exciting, and it was there that I first began to investigate the urban crowd in its medieval setting. The methodologies and interests of the three instructors were different, yet complementary, and I hope that I have learned from each of them.

The second consideration which led to the present book, I must confess, was the domestic—particularly urban—turmoil in America during the late 1960s. I was struck by the interrelationship between the ideology which was preached by the various sides and the resulting, sometimes violent, actions which often followed. Did people really believe what their leaders said? Why did peaceful protest turn into violent confrontation? What was the role of "outside agitators"? Now, some years later, I am not certain that I have found the answers to these questions, but I think I understand a good deal more.

Essentially, this book is an attempt to write the history of those who normally are excluded from historical consideration. A primary difficulty in such an undertaking is that the sources simply tell so little about the majority of mankind, at least in the premodern period. In the absence of quantitative material, the historian has to look for "the people" in the ordinary historical documents: narrative histories, letters, sermons, and the minutes of councils. By far the most common reference to "the people" in these sources concerns riots and other disturbances. This is the main reason for the focus on such phenomena in this book: they are some of the few events we know anything about. This should not suggest that I am interested in violence for its own sake or that I believe that the early Byzantine period was more violent than any other. It is simply a useful historical approach to the people I wish to study.

This book could not have been written without the advice, assistance, and personal inspiration of Professor Paul J. Alexander. In addition, I received valuable help from professors John W. Eadie, Ramsay MacMullen, and others. Obviously, I, not they, am responsible for any errors in the material. Membership in the American School of Classical Studies in Athens has allowed me to spend a considerable time in Greece, an experience I consider essential in any attempt to understand the Greek people in their historical context. Finally, I must thank my wife, Gail, for encouragement, patience, and for help in seeing things the way they really are.

ABBREVIATIONS

The following abbreviations are used for works frequently referred to in the end-of-chapter notes and the Bibliography.

AASS	*Acta Sanctorum*
ACO	*Acta Conciliorum Oecumenicorum.* Edited by Eduard Schwartz. 4 vols. in 12. Berlin, 1914–74.
Anal. Bolland.	*Analecta Bollandiana*
BZ	*Byzantinische Zeitschrift*
CAH	*Cambridge Ancient History*
CSCO	*Corpus Scriptorum Christianorum Orientalium*
CSEL	*Corpus Scriptorum Ecclesiasticorum Latinorum*
CSHB	*Corpus Scriptorum Historiae Byzantinae*
C. Th.	*Codex Theodosianus.* Edited by Theodore Mommsen and Paul Mayer. 2 vols. Berlin, 1905.
DTC	*Dictionnaire de théologie catholique*
DOP	*Dumbarton Oaks Papers*
FGH	*Fragmenta Historicorum Graecorum*
GCS	*Die griechischen christlichen Schriftsteller der ersten Jahrhunderts*
GRBS	*Greek, Roman, and Byzantine Studies*
Hefele-Leclercq	Karl Josef von Hefele. *Histoire des Conciles.* Translated by Henri Leclercq. Paris, 1907.
HJC	Chrysostomus Baur, *Der heilige Johannes Chrysostomus und seine Zeit.* 2 vols. Munich, 1929–30. Translated as *John Chrysostom and His Time.* 2 vols. Westminster, Maryland, 1959.
JEA	*Journal of Egyptian Archaeology*
JRS	*Journal of Roman Studies*
JTS	*Journal of Theological Studies*

Mansi	*Sacrorum conciliorum nova et amplissima collectio*
MGH	*Monumenta Germaniae Historica*
PG	*Patrologiae cursus completus. Series graeco-latina.* Edited by J. P. Migne. 161 vols. in 166. Paris, 1857–66.
PL	*Patrologiae cursus completus. Series latina.* Edited by J. P. Migne. 221 vols. Paris, 1844–55.
RAC	*Reallexikon fur Antike und Christentum.* Edited by Theodor Klauser. Stuttgart, 1950–.
RE	*Realencyclopädie der klassischen Altertumswissenschaft.* Edited by A. Pauly, G. Wissowa, and G. Kroll. Stuttgart, 1893–.
TU	*Texte und Untersuchungen zur Geschichte der altchristliche Literatur*

VOX
POPULI

I

INTRODUCTION

If you ask for your change, someone philosophizes to you on the Begotten and the Unbegotten. If you ask the price of bread, you are told, "The Father is greater and the Son inferior." If you ask, "Is the bath ready?" someone answers, "The Son was created from nothing."[1]

These words of Gregory of Nyssa describe one of the most characteristic phenomena of the later Roman Empire: popular concern for difficult theological questions. If we are to believe only a fraction of what the sources tell us, laymen in all the great cities of the East were deeply involved in the religious controversies of the time. And their interest did not always end with opinions and words. On many occasions words led to deeds and churches and whole cities were engulfed in bloodshed. Christians attacked one another in the streets, imperial soldiers rushed willfully upon unarmed believers, and groups of dissidents set fire to the churches of their enemies in the dead of night. Religious violence became endemic—on one occasion over 3,000 lives were lost in an assault on a church—and the emperor frequently had to turn away from political and military affairs to deal with the problem of factionalism in the cities. Ultimately whole groups of the faithful openly disobeyed the orders of the emperor and the "truths" of orthodoxy, thus paving the way for the partition of the empire and important geographical losses to the Arabs.

The present study is an analysis of these interrelated phenomena of violence and popular sentiment in the religious controversies of late antiquity. More specifically, it asks four basic questions:

1. Why did presumably uneducated laymen become so passionately involved in the complicated theological issues of the day?

2. Why did some individuals support one theological position rather than another?

3. What effect, if any, did popular religious opinion and action have on the ultimate resolution of the controversies?

4. What was the role of violence in these events?

The ancient authors themselves realized the importance of urban unrest, and they attempted to explain it in their own terms. Most authorities, perhaps taking Thucydides or Tacitus as their models, felt that it was in the "nature" of the crowd to rebel and cause violence: the *sordida plebs* acted perversely or from a selfish and shortsighted desire to make their lives more pleasant and luxurious. On rare occasions the ancient authors praised the motives of the crowd as noble and enlightened, but this was simply when the author approved its actions. In other words, for the ancient sources—pagan and Christian alike—the motivation of the crowd was a simple question. If, as was normally the case, the crowd did something that was disliked by the upper-class literary observers, its motive was base; if, on the other hand, the result of popular involvement was good, then the crowd was praised as reflecting collective wisdom and a love of the truth. The judgment was always a moral one and deeper analysis was rarely sought.

It is a truism that our historical inquiry is limited by the information provided by our sources and in the present instance the difficulty is particularly acute. In the first place, the sources were frequently hostile to popular opinion. We can, perhaps, trust a source when it tells us that a crowd did a particular thing; but we are on terribly shaky ground when we try to analyze the motivation for that action, since we have at best only a secondhand account of that motivation, usually from an authority who was far removed, both educationally and temperamentally, from the individuals involved. One has to rely on circumstantial evidence and follow a complex argument based on probabilities and one's own idea of how people in the fifth century actually thought. Obviously, the danger of error and misinterpretation is great: the minds of the "ordinary people" of antiquity are normally far removed from our own. The opportunity for understanding, however, is also great and worth the difficulties involved.[2]

Until the beginning of this century, historians had not advanced much beyond the simplistic views of the ancient authorities. In fact, it has only been relatively recently, in part as a result of Marxist thought, that historians have paid any really serious attention to the crowd in antiquity: the powerful in society, almost by definition, were the ones who made history "happen," and they were the proper subject of historical inquiry. In describing the religious controversies of the early church, for example, Edward Gibbon assigned little importance to the urban crowd, and he described their motives as base superstition, fanaticism, and blind obedience to unscrupulous leaders.³ But Gibbon, just like the authors he followed, made some exceptions to this general condemnation. For the most part, the actions of the crowd were base—because he did not agree with them—but Gibbon admired Athanasius, and he praised those who wisely followed the popular bishop of Alexandria.

In the late nineteenth and early twentieth centuries the great political historians, such as Bury and Seeck, were simply not interested in the actions of the crowd. When the course of events forced them to mention popular involvement in religious questions, they evaded the issue by observing that the crowd was moved by a concern for correct religious belief and practice.

At the beginning of this century, a few historians became more interested in the actions of the crowd. Scholars such as E. L. Woodward agreed with their predecessors that the majority of the people of, say, Alexandria in the fifth century cannot have understood the theological issues clearly. However, Woodward argued, this did not mean that they were acting irrationally or perversely. Instead, he saw the phenomenon of popular involvement in the theological disputes not in religious terms, but as a symptom and an outlet for more secular concerns, particularly a growing nationalism and discontent with Roman rule. Thus, the Bagaudae in Gaul, the Donatists in North Africa, and the Monophysites in Egypt and Syria were acting from a desire to identify themselves as culturally and nationally distinct and to overthrow the oppression of Rome in favor of local custom and government.⁴

In the years since its formulation, Woodward's thesis has been subject to much skepticism and opposition, and no one today would accept it without considerable modification. Yet, like many other attractive theories which have been "disproved," the ideas of Woodward have remained current not only in textbooks and college lectures but in the works of such responsible scholars as Ernst Stein, J. Maspero, E. R. Hardy, and the authors of volume 4 of Fliche-Martin's *Histoire de l'Église*. Proceeding independently, W. H. C. Frend arrived at similar conclusions in his influential study of *The Donatist Church*.

Nevertheless, most research carried out in the years since the Second World War has generally moved away from the theory of Woodward. In part, this is because of the greater sympathy which has developed for the essentially religious attitude of the later empire. Scholars in the past, affected by the rationalism of the Enlightenment, were hesitant to believe that religion could play any positive role except perhaps on the level of developed theology or ethics; popular religion, equated with base superstition, was to be despised or ignored. Such an attitude meant that secular motives and explanations were to be preferred whenever they could be found. Today, perhaps because of the failure of the social sciences to live up to expectations or becase of the ultimate irrationality of much of modern life, historians are much more willing to perceive the importance of religion in other ages. Reasonable men could, indeed, have been moved by religious sentiments. Most significant and influential in this regard was an article by A. H. M. Jones in which he discussed the work of Woodward and Frend and suggested important methodological guidelines for the evaluation of heresy as a social or political phenomenon.[5] In the end he concluded that heresy in the early church was genuinely religious in orientation and that it could not be explained by supposedly secular motives.

Nevertheless, even if we accept Jones' arguments, as most authorities have done, we must still be bothered by the original questions: Why did most people become passionately interested in these complex theological disputes? Did they really understand the issues? Furthermore, why did different individuals support different theological positions? In other words, while he was certainly correct in rejecting Woodward's simplistic social and political analysis, Jones did not fully come to terms with the question in all of its aspects.

It is unfortunate, but completely understandable, that historians have not taken advantage of the vast sociological and anthropological literature dealing with religious belief and practice. For example, even a superficial reading of Durkheim suggests applications of his theories to the religious developments of the early Christian period. In general terms, Durkheim argued that religious experience is conditioned and formed by the society in which it exists.[6] Weber and more recent authorities, such as Smelser and Bryan Wilson, have gone far beyond Durkheim to suggest how religious changes can be linked to specific changes in society. Wilson, for example, has claimed that changes in religion are to be explained by changes in the economic and social status accorded to certain groups and by the failure of society to accommodate the needs of these groups.[7] Such a "maladjustment" model has become widely accepted, not only among scholars, but even among the general public. Some authorities, however, have found reason to question this hypothesis, and, while not denying the basic conclusions of Durkheim, they explain the evolution of religion by reference to different aspects of the social system.

Mary Douglas is one of the most influential of recent proponents of this view, and she has made a persuasive case in arguing that religious phenomena (stability as well as change) are to be explained as results of the characteristics and innerworkings of the individual social system.[8] In addition, she has made some extremely important observations about the nature of belief and the ways in which symbols (both verbal and nonverbal) conceal or reveal differences in attitudes among people. Although she has not adressed herself to the controversies of the fifth century, one can easily see the usefulness of her approach. For example, one of the primary difficulties in our understanding of the phenomenon of crowd involvement in the christological disputes is the complexity of the theology involved. We find it hard to see how ordinary people could have understood the issues clearly enough to have an opinion. Douglas has shown, I think, that "understanding" the issues is not always the point of importance. Theological positions, like all forms of communication, are powerful symbols which stand for a person's own identity or aspirations. Theologians and historians have all too often seen these positions as a "system of ideas, corresponding to some determined object.... nature, the infinite, the unknowable, the ideal, etc.,"[9] while Douglas would argue that they should correspond only to how the individual sees himself in the (mostly social) universe around him.[10]

These are all reasonable ideas and they raise important issues for consideration, but how is the historian to take advantage of them, particularly in dealing with a society that is so imperfectly known as that of late antiquity? Social scientists, of course, normally examine contemporary societies in an attempt to discern the universal tendencies behind human behavior, while the historian must often approach such issues from an *ad hoc* basis in which he is pleased if only he can determine what happened in a particular instance. In the present study, I have tried to be aware of current thinking about the nature of religious change, but I will approach the material with no particular hypothesis about the nature of the religious experience and, hopefully, with no more bias than any other citizen of the twentieth century.

In looking at the phenomenon of crowd behavior (as opposed to religious change) historians have increasingly profited from the work of sociologists and political scientists. Further, the immediacy of contemporary terrorism, urban violence, and popular political action has naturally stirred our interest in similar phenomena in the past. In particular, the pioneering work of George Rudé has set the study of the crowd on a new level of understanding and significance.[11] Clearly, the approach of the ancient historian must be shaped by the nature and the quantity of the evidence available, and he is not so fortunate as to have court records or accurate demographic information. For this reason much of the methodology developed in modern studies of the crowd is of little value in dealing with premodern phenomena, nor should we expect analysis that is so detailed or conclusions that are so secure.

Nevertheless, Rudé's overall approach to the crowd and the kinds of questions that he asks are useful starting points for historians of any period. More specifically, the historian should set out to examine the crowd as he would any other historical group—without prejudice or monumental misconception—and he should be prepared to find that a given crowd acted reasonably, and perhaps according to a set purpose, in response to certain historical circumstances. This would counter the view of the crowd as essentially senseless (and thus historically unknowable), a formless mass which had no direction or purpose other than a love of faction, a group blown in one way or another by deceitful leaders or outside agitators. On the other hand, one should probably be suspicious of any simplistic view of the crowd and its motives. While admitting the possibility of rational popular behavior, the historian should not fall into the error of thinking that each individual within a given group felt exactly the same about all issues. Even more should he avoid the temptation to assume that "the people" as a whole acted according to some ideological preconception: unless there is evidence to that effect, one should not assume that the historical crowd represented the proletariat struggling consciously against an unjust social and political system.

The analysis of Rudé has taught us what we should have known long before: many different individuals with many different, and possibly conflicting, motives and goals made up the historical crowd. It should, therefore, be our purpose to investigate what Rudé calls "the faces in the crowd," to discern as far as possible, the kinds of persons who expressed themselves on the various issues of the day and to distinguish the motives of different groups and the bonds which held them together.

Largely because of the paucity of the evidence, few students of the ancient world have attempted to come to terms with the phenomenon of crowd behavior, although a few important works have made contributions in this direction. A. W. Lintott's *Violence in Republican Rome*, for example, deals primarily with the question of why the Romans of the late Republic (especially the *nobiles*) were willing to resort to violence, which ultimately destroyed their own political system.[12] Lintott frequently mentions the urban crowd, but his treatment is legalistic and political rather than social, and few of the larger questions of concern here (for example, the motivation of the crowd) are discussed fully. Z. Yavetz's *Plebs and Princeps* is more instructive for the present study.[13] Yavetz is concerned with problems such as the composition of the crowd, its relationship to the emperor in the Julio-Claudian period, and its motivation. He analyzes several events in considerable detail and then draws useful conclusions from them, much in the style of Rudé. He concludes that the Roman *plebs*, while not motivated by any particular ideology, normally had some purpose to its actions, which were thus not merely capricious. Moreover, he observes, the successful early Roman emperor took the *plebs* into account and made some provisions to appease it.

The works of Lintott and Yavetz deal with the Republic and the early empire, and they do not concern themselves with religious questions. On the urban crowd of late antiquity, Wolfgang Seyfarth's *Soziale Fragen der spätrömischen Kaiserzeit im Spiegel des Theodosianus* presents some brief but useful analysis. More specific is Hans Peter Kohns' *Versorgungskrisen und Hungerrevolten im spätantiken Rom*. As the title suggests, Kohns is concerned with a particular phenomenon—the food riot—which is well documented in the writings of Ammianus Marcellinus and Symmachus. Although he does examine a number of events in some detail, the nature of his problem frequently led him to say more about the food supply of the city than about the crowd and its actions. Finally, Ramsay MacMullen, in his *Enemies of the Roman Order*, devotes an interesting chapter to urban unrest but says little about religious questions.[14]

Before proceeding further, it will be useful to provide a few working definitions. First, the subjects of our inquiry—the people of the cities of the late Roman East. The problem in arriving at a definition of the crowd is twofold, having to do with semantic confusion in both English, on the one hand, and Greek and Latin on the other. All of these languages have a number of words which can roughly be translated as "the people." How are we to distinguish among them and which are we to use? More importantly, whom do we wish to identify, for such an identification sets the conceptual form for the whole of the study. Generally speaking, I wish to set my sights as wide as possible, so as not to exclude any individuals or groups that might be important.

Most investigations of the religious controversies of this period have approached the topic either by examining the development of theology or by tracing the political maneuverings of the great secular and ecclesiastical figures. The present study, however, will focus on those individuals who were not leaders, who were distinguished from the leaders in that they had no institutionalized large-scale authority (which is power that society defines as legitimate). Thus, while obviously admitting the historical importance of such individuals as the emperor and his court, the commanders of the army, and the bishops, we should focus our attention on all those other persons who had no obvious means to change the course of events in any direct way.

In my use of the term, most of "the people" in any city would, of course, be poor, but economic or social status is not the most important criterion. In fact, many wealthy individuals would have to be grouped as members of "the people" simply because they had no effective institutionalized authority. For example, an imperial official who had been removed from power, to the extent that he could not depend on former ties of friendship and/or loyalty, would find himself without authority. In a similar way, many women, even though their husbands might have important posts, must (as individuals) have been relatively powerless. In most cases, it will be relatively easy to distinguish between "the people" and the leaders of society, but the monks and the leaders of popular organizations (such as the guilds and the circus factions) are more difficult to categorize. The question is probably whether the authority they possessed was of sufficient magnitude to allow them to influence events as a matter of course. In the interests of simplicity, the leaders of popular organizations are normally classed along with "the people," while the monks are accorded a kind of special status. Clearly, an important abbot was a leader of society whose words and actions carried special weight; an ordinary monk, on the other hand, normally had little power (although even he might influence events in a special way). Because of the difficulty in placing the monks in any particular category and because of their importance in forming popular opinion, I will discuss their actions fully wherever appropriate.

All this is not to ignore the actions of the leaders of society or to attempt to write history "from the bottom," by *assuming* that the actions of the people really caused events to happen in the way they did. Instead, the study analyzes the dynamic interactions between the institutionalized leaders of society and those whom they tried to lead. Furthermore, a term such as "the people" does not imply any value judgment; it has no favorable or perjorative connotations nor does it indicate anything significant about the composition of any group. Likewise, it should not be assumed that all of the people of any city had to agree on any given issue or that popular opinion has any simple general definition. On the contrary, various groups of people in any city might support different religious positions and this was, in fact, more often the case than not. Indeed, it is one of the primary goals of this study to attempt an understanding of the divisions of opinion which frequently arose. It will be particularly instructive to see whether these divisions of opinion corresponded with other known social, economic, or political groupings within the city.

In the terminology of this study "the people" and "the crowd" are nearly synonymous in that neither is meant to have social, economic, or ideological overtones. "The crowd," however, often has a more specific, particular meaning. Thus, while one can speak of certain "people" thinking this and others that, the implication is vague (and is meant to be so); to say that one "crowd" did something while another did something else is more specific—there were observable collections of individuals which engaged in some specific acts.

The problem of definition is further complicated by the language and the literary conventions of the sources. As we have said, Greek and Latin have a number of words which can be translated as "the people" or "the masses," or "the many," and it is extremely difficult to know exactly what a given author had in mind in a particular passage.[15] This problem ultimately involves the sociological perceptions of the ancient authors and further lexical analysis may someday contribute to an understanding of both the thought-world and the social reality of late antiquity. But the problem is confused by the traditions of classical literature which often demanded the use of a word for reasons of style rather than content or meaning. Thus, an author might suddenly switch terms simply because he wished to vary his vocabulary or to avoid using the same word twice in a row. When faced with a passage such as this (as we often are in the pages that follow), the historian is tempted to throw up his hands in dismay: did the author mean to indicate some change in the composition of the crowd, or was he merely trying to write better Greek? The choice of terms might also reflect moral judgments rather than historical or sociological differences; thus *demos* was generally neutral or slightly favorable, while *ochlos*—which might be translated as "the mob"—had definite perjorative connotations. In fact, the greatest difficulty probably surrounds the meaning of *demos*, which has been translated (in both the singular and the plural), as "the people," "the city," "the circus factions," "the urban militia," and a host of similar words or terms. Context sometimes helps in determining what meaning to assume, but the problem frequently remains. At a number of points in the study we will pause to reconsider this problem as it relates to a specific event, and I will regularly include a transliteration of the original terms, along with an English approximation, so the reader may have an independent opportunity to judge.

Similar difficulties arise in connection with the words for "riot" or "disturbance." Generally speaking, *tarache* refers to some kind of a disturbance, which might range from a confusion of mind to a violent riot, and it is frequently difficult to tell exactly what a particular author meant. Thus, when a text reads that a sermon or a certain teaching caused a great *tarache* in a city, does this mean that people actually went into the streets to give vent to their feelings, or was there outward calm disturbed only by mental confusion and concern? Normally a *stasis* seems to have referred to a more serious incident, but it is difficult to be more specific without additional information from the context.

Finally, whenever violence is mentioned in this study, it refers simply to any action which threatened or actually resulted in bodily harm. This violence may have been carried out by the crowd against the leaders of society or by one crowd against another. Likewise, individual leaders may have employed violence against other leaders or, by calling in the soldiers, against the crowd itself.

In an analysis of the role of violence and popular sentiment in the religious controversies of late antiquity, two approaches are possible. The first involves a narrative or synthetic treatment of all the evidence from all of the religious disputes of the fourth, fifth, and sixth centuries. This approach, which has been used by most of those who have examined this question before, is attractive in that it will yield neater, more generalized conclusions based (hopefully) on a full analysis of all the information. The difficulty, of course, is that there are many incidents of popular involvement ranging over a wide geographical and chronological span.

Any synthetic approach will, at best, overlook the peculiarity of individual events, while at worst it will present conclusions based upon what is, in fact, incomplete evidence. In other words, the volume and disparity of the evidence almost preclude a synthetic approach to the problem.

Instead, I have decided to analyze as fully as possible a limited number of events, all of which took place in the cities of the East in the first half of the fifth century. The advantage of this approach besides making the material manageable, is that specific actions are placed in their appropriate historical contexts, and the conclusions are based on a firm body of evidence. The disadvantage of such a "case study" approach, of course, is that, even if the material is carefully selected, there is a danger that the particular events chosen for study were not representative, thus making the generalizations questionable. Further, because of the unevenness of our information, the conclusions may frequently be negative; that is, we may not always be able to answer the appropriate questions as fully as we would like. Nevertheless, the great strength of history as a discipline is that it considers the particular first and it bases its generalizations, not upon a preconceived model, but upon the accumulated data from specific individual events. Even though such an approach involves difficulties, it appears to be the only methodologically sound way to tackle the problem. In addition, the focus on the cities of Constantinople, Alexandria, and Ephesus gives the study a certain rational unity by allowing us to concentrate on the dynamic urban world of early Byzantium, while excluding the interesting, but very different, conditions in the late Roman countryside and the struggling Western population centers.

The first event involves the episcopacy of John Chrysostom (A.D. 397-404), and more particularly his deposition, when a large section of the population of Constantinople strongly demonstrated their affection for the bishop. From the time of Chrysostom the focus advances a number of years to the episcopacy of Nestorius and the Council of Ephesus (428-431). Throughout this period, both in Constantinople and in Ephesus, Nestorius and his teaching met with considerable popular opposition. Later, confusion and political maneuvering characterized the dispute over the teaching of Eutyches (448-449), which ended in violence at the so-called Latrocinium in Ephesus. Finally, by the time of the Council of Chalcedon (451) popular opinion in Constantinople appears to have come to favor the new policy of the emperor Marcian against the views of Eutyches and Dioscorus of Alexandria. The deposition of Dioscorus by the council, however, met with determined popular resistance in Alexandria: although the bishop never returned to Egypt, his followers resolutely defended his memory against the troops of the emperor and a series of Chalcedonian bishops.

Three of these events were important episodes in the christological controversy, while the fourth (the deposition of Chrysostom) had little theological significance. This contrast allows us to trace the development of popular attitudes toward contemporary theology, while reserving one event as a kind of "control." Further, it is possible to compare the growth of popular opinion in a complicated theological dispute with that when the issues were clear and simple (involving only moral and canonical questions). In each instance, Constantinople is a major focus, while events in Alexandria and Ephesus encourage comparison. From this evidence, the study examines the extent to which people in different cities were influenced by the same concerns. Then, since we will investigate popular opinion in Constantinople over a period of fifty years, it is possible to identify and analyze consistency and change over this time: did the people of Constantinople maintain a single theological position throughout this period, or did they vacillate? Ultimately, the answers to some of the questions will have significant consequences for our understanding of the nature of late Roman Christianity and the ultimate division of the empire between the Monophysites and the Chalcedonians.

1. Gregory of Nyssa, *De Deitate Filii et Spiritus Sancti* (PG 46, 557). All translations are by the author unless otherwise specified.

2. On these considerations see the illuminating comments of Cyril Mango, *Byzantine Literature as a Distorting Mirror* (Oxford, 1975).

3. Gibbon said that the people of Constantinople opposed Nestorius because of a superstitious veneration of Mary, while the supporters of Dioscorus were simply fanatics (*The Decline and Fall of the Roman Empire*, 47.5). "A chosen society of philosophers, men of a liberal education and curious disposition, might silently meditate, and temperately discuss in the gardens of Athens or the library of Alexandria, the abstruse questions of metaphysical science. But after the *Logos* had been revealed as the sacred object of faith. . . the mysterious system was embraced by a numerous and increasing multitude in every province of the Roman world. Those persons who, from their age or sex, or occupations, were least qualified to judge, were the least exercised in the habits of abstract reasoning, aspired to contemplate the economy of Divine Nature: and it is the boast of Tertullian (Apol. 46) that a Christian mechanic could readily answer such questions as had perplexed the wisest of Greek sages" (*Decline and Fall*, 21.1). See also the comments of Miriam Lichtheim, "Autonomy Versus Unity in the Christian East," in *The Transformation of the Roman World*, ed. Lynn White, Jr. (Los Angeles, 1966), pp. 119-22.

4. E. L. Woodward, *Christianity and Nationalism in the Later Roman Empire* (London, 1916); cf. the earlier comments of J. Leipoldt, *Schenute von Atripe und die Enstehung des national-ägyptischen Christentums*, TU vol. 25 (Leipzig, 1903).

5. A. H. M. Jones, "Were Ancient Heresies National or Social Movements in Disguise?" *JTS* 10 (1959), 280-96. See also P. R. L. Brown, "Religious Dissent in the Later Roman Empire," *History* 46 (1961), 83-101; and W. Liebeschuetz, "Did the Pelagian Movement Have Social Aims?" *Historia* 12 (1963), 227-41.

6. Emile Durkheim, *The Elementary Forms of the Religious Life*, trans. Joseph Ward Swain (London, 1915), pp. 415-47.

7. Bryan R. Wilson, ed., *Patterns of Sectarianism* (London, 1967), passim, cf. p. 31.

8. Mary Douglas, *Natural Symbols* (London, 1970), and *Implicit Meanings* (London, 1975).

9. Durkheim, *Elementary Forms*, p. 416.

10. Douglas, *Natural Symbols*, pp. 24-39.

11. George Rudé, *The Crowd in History, 1730-1848* (New York, 1961). See also E. J. Hobsbawm, *Primitive Rebels* (Manchester, 1959); E. Canetti, *Crowds and Power* (London, 1962); and N. J. Smelser, *Theory of Collective Behavior* (New York, 1963). For an influential but outdated view see G. LeBon, *The Crowd* (London, 1909).

12. A. W. Lintott, *Violence in Republican Rome* (Oxford, 1968). On this period there is also the older study of J. W. Heaton, *Mob Violence in the Late Roman Republic* (Urbana, 1939); A. N. Sherwin-White, "Violence in Roman Politics," *JRS* 46 (1956), 1-9; and A. W. Lintott's "The Tradition of Violence in the Annals of the Early Roman Republic," *Historia* 19 (1970), 12-19.

13. Z. Yavetz, *Plebs and Princeps* (Oxford, 1969); see also P. A. Brunt, "The Roman Mob," *Past and Present* 35 (December, 1966), 3-27; and Thomas W. Africa, "Urban Violence in Imperial Rome," *The Journal of Interdisciplinary History* 2 (1971), 3-21.

14. J. R. Martindale's "Public Disorders in the Late Roman Empire, Their Causes and Character," (B.A. thesis, Oxford 1960) is comprehensive and useful, although by nature it is shallow and not analytic; David Daube, *Civil Disobedience in Antiquity* (Edinburgh, 1973), on the other hand, is too general and suffers from serious conceptual problems.

II

THE URBAN CONTEXT

The Late Roman City

Before investigating individual cases of urban unrest, we should look briefly at the cities and the characteristics of urban society in the later Roman Empire.[1] In particular, it is important to understand and appreciate the "quality and flavor of life" in the urban centers of the period, something which is difficult for any historical time and place, but which is especially complicated for a period such as this where literary sources are few and frequently disappointing. From the late empire, however, a good deal is known about the physical aspects of cities: archaeological excavations have revealed the plans of streets and the foundations of monumental buildings, contemporary laws allow further insights into the administration of the cities and the regulation of everyday life, and orators, letter-writers, and historians provide tantalizing glimpses into contemporary urban society. Even though they are often colored by a biased attitude toward the poor, who form an important subject of the present study, such narrative vignettes are most useful sources for capturing the spirit of daily life in a late Roman city. A good example is the well-known passage from Ammianus Marcellinus:

> Let us now turn to the idle and slothful commons. . . . These spend all their life with wine and dice, in low haunts, pleasures, and the games. Their temple, their dwelling, their assembly, and the height of all their hope is the Circus Maximus. You may see groups of them gathered in the fora, the cross roads, the streets, and their other meeting-places, engaged in quarrelsome arguments with one another, some (as usual) defending this, others that. . . . As soon as the longed-for day of the chariot races begins to dawn, before the sun is yet shining clearly they all hasten in crowds to the spot at top speed, as if they would outstrip the very chariots that are to take part in the contest; and torn by

their conflicting hopes about the result of the race, the greater number of them pass sleepless nights. . . .

In another passage the same author described a singularly unpleasant eating establishment in late fourth-century Rome:

> The greater number of these gentry, given over to over-stuffing themselves with food, led by the charm of the odor of cooking and by the shrill voices of the women, like a flock of peacocks screaming with hunger, stand even from cockcrow beside the pots on tip-toe and gnaw the ends of their fingers as they wait for the dishes to cool. Others hang over the nauseous mass of half-raw meat, while it is cooking, watching it so intently that one would think that Democritus with other dissectors was examining the internal organs of dismembered animals and showing by what means future generations might be cured of internal pains.[2]

The reaction of Ammianus to the plight of the poor was a familiar one. The only mark of condescension is when he made them the butt of jokes and it is revealing that he was able to laugh at the destitute waiting anxiously for their unappetizing fare. Some of the other perils and pleasures of the urban poor are illustrated in a story told by the church historian Socrates:

> Now the bake-houses were built below ground level so they constructed taverns at the side of each, where prostitutes were kept. By this means [the bakers] entrapped many of those who went there, either for the sake of refreshment or to gratify their lusts. They used a certain mechanical contrivance to precipitate people from the tavern to the bakery below. This was done primarily to strangers; and those who were caught in this way were forced to work in the bakery, where they were imprisoned until old age. Their friends, meanwhile, concluded that they were dead.[3]

In this case, the bakers made a mistake and caught a soldier, who proved to be more than the kidnappers had bargained for. He drew his dagger and the bakers fled. Afterwards the soldier reported his adventure to the emperor, who put an end to the practice.

These anecdotes, while accurate reflections of some aspects of late Roman urban life, clearly do not tell the whole story. Despite its harshness and occasional brutality, life in a late Roman city must have had an attractive side. Christianity made an important contribution along these lines, at very least by providing a common unifying experience for most members of society. Another example from Socrates may illustrate this point and provide a balance to the passages quoted above. While he was attending the spectacles in the hippodrome in Constantinople, Theodosius II learned that the tyrant John had been overthrown. He immediately asked the people if they would be willing to leave the entertainment and go to the church to offer thanksgiving to God.

> The spectacles were forgotten at once and all the people filed out of the hippodrome singing praises together with him, as with one heart and voice.

When they arrived at the church the whole city became one vast congregation and they spent the rest of the day in prayer.[4]

In fact, the Roman state was normally concerned about the welfare of the urban poor, if only for political reasons: people do not normally starve to death peacefully. Also, the virtue of *philanthropia* had long been of importance as part of the imperial ideal and a good emperor was bound to take great pride in care for his subjects. This concern was practically reflected in the state control of the basic necessities of life.

Central to this was the free distribution of bread to the poor. This practice, or the forerunner of it, had begun in Rome in the time of Gaius Gracchus, and Constantine introduced it to Constantinople in 332.[5] Shortly thereafter the dole appears to have begun in other cities of the East.[6] Those who qualified because of their poverty were given a bronze ticket (*tessera* or *titulus*) with their name and the amount of bread they were to receive inscribed upon it. We do not know exactly what the requirements of poverty were, but a law of Valentinian I restricted the free bread to those "who have no other means of support."[7] Originally the alienation of *tesserae* was strictly forbidden, but this must have been impossible to prevent, and by the end of the fourth century large numbers of *tesserae* were being bought and sold openly.[8] In Constantinople 80,000 people were originally entitled to free bread; by any reckoning this was a large proportion of the population and perhaps as many as one-quarter of the inhabitants of Constantinople were supported by this form of state "relief."[9] At a designated time, the prefect of the city ordered all those who held *tesserae* to assemble and the bread was distributed from a series of steps. The daily ration was six half-pound loaves, which was probably enough to sustain life at a minimum level, even if the individual had to support a small family.[10]

The desperately poor were not the only urban residents to benefit from the state largesse. In Constantinople and some of the other large cities of the empire, the government guaranteed the quantity and the price of grain. Those who did not qualify for the bread dole were assured that the price of bread would not rise above a certain level even in times of shortage. Granaries were built in the cities, and care was taken to organize and protect the shipment of grain from the centers of production to the centers of consumption. In the early fifth century, a special fund, administered by the *praefectus urbi*, was established in Constantinople to purchase grain in times of emergency.[11] Shortages of bread were still all too common, but it must have been reassuring to city dwellers to know that the emperor had taken measures to assure their survival.

The great cities of the empire provided other necessities and amenities. The prices of oil, wine, pork, and fish appear to have been controlled and some cities may have distributed these items free to the poor.[12]

Monumental aqueducts supplied the cities with water, most of which was gathered in huge cisterns scattered throughout the neighborhoods or piped directly to where it was to be used; this water was apparently available free to all the citizens.[13] The great public baths were also normally free of charge, and the luxury of these places of relaxation and refreshment must have added considerably to the quality of life for the urban dweller. The magnificent colonnaded streets, public squares, and official buildings which characterized all Roman cities reached the peak of their refinement and luxury in the later empire. These were a source of pride for the emperor and the local aristocracy; but they also provided air and open spaces amid the overcrowded residential areas, and they occasionally afforded temporary shelter for the indigent until they found more permanent housing.

As is generally known, the theatre and the hippodrome were important centers in any late Roman city, but increasingly the churches came to play a greater role in contemporary urban social and economic life. The churches, we should remember, were not merely places of worship, but large complexes where people might assemble for a variety of reasons, not least of which were refreshment and fellowship. It also remained for the Christians—John Chrysostom, Basil, John the Almsgiver, and many others—to make concern for the poor, the sick, and the aged a personal human virtue. They also institutionalized their concern, as bishops and monasteries founded poorhouses, hospitals, hostels, and orphanages on a large scale. These institutions must have done much to relieve the most serious social and economic problems of the urban poor, and in some ways such individuals must have been better off in late antiquity than they had been before.[14]

Decline or Expansion?

The political and economic crises of the third century had serious consequences for the Roman city, and the urban centers which emerged into the early fourth century were much changed. Cities remained the basic element of social and political organization, but they appear no longer to have been the dynamic, restless, independent entities of earlier years. As Jones has pointed out, in the early empire the Roman government had to exercise all of its authority to control the independence of the cities, while in the later empire the state had to struggle just to keep the cities alive and functioning.[15]

Part of the difficulty of the cities was that the weight of the financial crisis fell particularly heavily on the urban aristocracy, the *curiales*, who had long been the mainstay of local municipal life. They were forced to bear the burden of the new system of taxation, and if the countryside could not meet its financial obligations, the *curiales* had to make up the deficit from their own resources. As a result, many *curiales* could no longer contribute lavishly to the public life of the cities, and some of them even fled civilized society, abandoning the estates which could no longer meet the demands placed upon them. The state devised a number of expedients, none of them entirely successful, to restore the *curiales* to their traditional place as the leaders of local society, but in many cities the only alternative was imperial intervention, either by the appointment of government officials (such as the *defensor civitatis*) or by direct subsidy, especially in the construction of civic buildings.

Developments such as these have naturally led scholars to the conclusion that the cities of the later empire were "in decline," both in a qualitative and a quantitative sense. Support for this view may easily be found in the contemporary literary sources, but such laments should not be accepted without reservation. In the first place, many of the passages which seem to document the demise of urban life refer, not to the size and prosperity of the cities, but to the survival of classical urban forms and institutions. Certainly, no one would claim that the ancient city-state survived the third century with all of its parts unchanged and, as we have seen, the old aristocratic institutions such as the *curia* suffered the greatest. Nevertheless, this says little about the vitality of the cities as they emerged in a new form. In addition, much of the literary evidence comes from the period of crisis in the third century rather than from the period after Constantine.

Thus, a passage from Eusebius frequently used to document the decline of the city notes that in Alexandria: "those people between forty and seventy were then so numerous that the full total of the number is not to be reached now, when those from fourteen to eighty years have been registered and counted together for the public food ration."[16] This information must originally have been based upon the official register for the grain dole of Alexandria, but the passage itself was not written by Eusebius but was a portion of a letter (from Dionysius, bishop of Alexandria) incorporated in the text of his history. The letter, thus, referred not to the situation in the fourth or fifth century, but to the middle of the third century. It shows that the population of Alexandria had declined in the third century, but it says nothing about the later period.

Now, as it happens, we have some information about the population of Alexandria in the late Republic: Diodorus (17, 52, 6), reports that about 60 B.C. the city could boast of 300,000 inhabitants. A. H. M. Jones, basing his calculation on the size of the grain supply and a statement of Procopius, estimated the population of the city at the time of Justinian as between 250,000 and 375,000 persons.[17] In other words, if we accept this evidence, the population of Alexandria was of roughly the same magnitude in the sixth century as it had been at the time of Caesar. The city may well have declined in size during the third century, but if this was the case, the fourth and fifth centuries witnessed recovery and rapid population growth rather than stagnation or decline. In fact, some of the literary authorities refer quite clearly to the efflorescence of cities under the later empire.[18]

The archaeological record is difficult to assess, although it holds considerable promise for future research. Throughout the period under consideration, many of the cities of the empire responded to the barbarian threat by building defensive circuits for the first time in centuries. Frequently these late Roman walls were quite small by comparison with their classical predecessors, and they normally enclosed a settled area that was only a fraction of that from an earlier period. This would appear to be good evidence of population decline: either the urban area was actually less, or the cities of the later empire were simply unable to muster the manpower necessary to defend the expansive classical walls and so opted for shorter defensive circuits.[19]

But let us examine a few examples in some detail. Athens was all but destroyed by the Herulian invasion of 267.[20] Shortly after this disaster, the Athenians began construction of the so-called Late Roman Fortification, which enclosed a small area of about forty acres to the north of the Acropolis. For "perhaps as much as a century," life in the city was constricted within these narrow limits, and the old urban center of the Agora lay deserted and desolate, serving only as a garbage dump.[21] Toward the beginning of the fifth century, however, Athens witnessed a remarkable building boom, as fine public structures and impressive private dwellings sprang up outside the late Roman wall. The circuit of the Themistoklean Walls may even have been restored, perhaps as early as the time of Julian.

From the evidence of Athens and many other sites, it seems clear that the function of the wall had changed during the late Roman period, and we may not simply use the reduced circuit walls as evidence of population decline. Generally speaking, the walls built after the third century A.D. were not constructed to enclose the entire settled area, but rather to provide an easily-defended citadel and civic center to which the urban and suburban residents could flee in times of danger. The Late Roman Fortification in Athens was an example of such a structure, and it "seems to have enclosed an inner city, always ready for refuge...."[22]

While a constricted fortification circuit is not necessarily evidence of population decline, the construction of enlarged walls must certainly indicate population growth. Antioch is a case in point. According to Glanville Downey, the growth of the city into vacant regions and considerable building activity "suggest that there was some expansion of the occupied area during Theodosius I's reign."[23] A short time later, possibly at the time of Eudocia's visit to the city in 438, the city wall was extended some distance to the south, enlarging the area of the city by a noticeable degree. It is not certain whether this new portion of the wall was built to accommodate growing population, or whether it was done to enclose an area which had already been built up, but the conclusion to be drawn is the same: the population of late Roman Antioch was not stagnant, but rather increasing.[24] This is confirmed by Libanius, who stated that in his own time the city was being swollen by a steady flow of immigrants.[25]

In all the great cities of the eastern part of the empire, the situation seems the same. In Corinth, Ephesus, Gerasa, and Alexandria, the urban population was constant or increasing, and the causes are not difficult to understand. The late fourth and early fifth centuries were, on the whole, a time of prosperity for the East, as the reforms of Diocletian and Constantine began to take effect. Although contemporaries cannot have known it, the worst of the civil wars and the barbarian invasions were over, and the prosperity of the cities had begun to return. Under such conditions it is likely that a certain amount of natural population recovery took place. In addition, there was undoubtedly substantial migration from the countryside and from the smaller cities less able to defend themselves, and it is a paradox that the unsettled conditions of the age may actually have contributed to the concentration of population in the larger urban centers. Further, the growth of the bureaucracy and its centralization in the main cities must have stimulated their growth, as the various bureaus, offices, warehouses, and factories drew large numbers of workers, traders, and litigants to the cities.

The most obvious case of urban expansion during this period was Constantinople itself. The legend of the founding of the city is a familar tale: after his defeat of Licinius at Chrysopolis, the first Christian emperor, guided by an angel, led his astonished courtiers around a huge circuit, enclosing a territory three times that of the Roman city of Byzantium. By the time of the dedication of the city in 330, Constantinople was complete with most of the amenities of urban life and, lured by the presence of the imperial court and the prospect of employment (and perhaps the security of the Constantinian walls), people began to flock to the new capital. Within less than a century, the population of Constantinople had grown so large that built-up areas spilled out across the walls into the countryside. In order to accommodate this population and to protect the new suburbs, the Theodosian Walls were constructed in 413, increasing the area of the city again by at least one-third.[26]

Any study involving early Byzantine cities and the people who lived in them will have to consider the phenomenon of general population growth, along with its attendant problems of crowding and social tension.

Urban Society

Within the large, bustling cities of the late Roman East, society was complex and not easily characterized. Nevertheless, many authorities have written as though three distinct classes could be discerned. Such an analysis is based partly upon the law codes which do make a relatively clear distinction between the top and the bottom of contemporary Roman society, between the *honestiores* and the *humiliores*.[27] *Humiliores*—the lower classes—were subject to torture during inquisition and they might receive capital punishment for comparatively light offenses. *Honestiores*, on the other hand, were usually not tortured, and exile with confiscation was normally the most severe punishment they might expect. Furthermore, it has been argued that the shopkeepers formed a kind of middle class between the *honestiores* and the *humiliores*.[28] The fiscal regulations of the state separated the merchants from the rest of the *humiliores* since they were required to pay the *collatio lustralis* (or *chrysargyron*).

Such a simplistic division of late Roman urban society is based in reality, but it raises many questions and says little that is really significant about contemporary life. It is clear that there was a group at the top of society which was allowed to maintain a privileged status through legal consideration. But this, after all, does not tell us very much: who were the *honestiores* and how large a portion of society did they comprise? The codes, unfortunately, do not give us a precise definition of the "more honorable" men—a suggestion that clear-cut distinctions did not exist. To be sure, senators, decurions, bishops, and important members of the army and the civil service were *honestiores*, but one does not know how far down the ranks such status went. Did, for example, "professional men" (teachers, lawyers, physicians), the lower ranks of the army, the civil service, and the church possess upper-class prerogatives? The answer seems to be: "sometimes"—"much was no doubt left to the discretion of the judge," and the ability of the individual to bribe him.[29] Presumably, an individual in any given situation knew where he stood before the law, but this seems rather imprecise evidence upon which to reconstruct the class structure of the later empire. Also, there must be some objection to labeling the *honestiores* as a "class." Certainly, a low-ranking imperial official who was born and served in eastern Syria or upper Egypt would have little in common with one of the great senators of Constantinople—except his share in a legal distinction.

Concerning the shopkeepers and merchants, there is little reason to view them as a kind of middle class. As has frequently been pointed out, there were considerable differences in the economic standing of the shopkeepers; some were relatively wealthy, while others were almost desperately poor.[30] The criteria used in formulating class distinctions must, at least, be consistent: in the case of the *honestiores* the distinction was in treatment before the law, while with the shopkeepers it was the payment of a special tax. If distinctions of class are to have any meaning, they must go beyond single attributes: merchants and *honestiores* must each have been significantly similar within their own group and dissimilar to all other groups in order for us to call them separate classes.

The whole question of social division in the later empire needs to be discussed in more sophisticated terms.[31] Considerable evidence is available for such a study, and interesting results would surely be obtained. This is not the place to attempt a full investigation of this question, but some observations may be mentioned.

In the first place, one should focus on the reality of late antiquity regardless of any preconceived model. In this regard the simplistic expectation of a "three-class society" should probably be discarded and a distinction made between "class" and "social strata." The former term, which is more restricted in scope, refers to groups in society "which have developed or should develop some 'consciousness of kind,' that is, some sense of existence as a group attribute of society. Stratification, on the other hand, refers to a more complex differentiation which may or may not involve specific groups."[32]

Identification of class appears to depend on several criteria: objective status (for example, economic standing), accorded status (the perception of others), and subjective status (a person or group's view of itself).[33] Using these criteria, it is easy to identify one true class in late Roman society: the aristocracy, or perhaps better, the traditional senatorial aristocracy.[34] By all measurements, this very small group formed a class at the top of society. The senators possessed wealth and standing, they defended their own position and realized their own importance, and others throughout society generally accorded them the same prerogatives of honor. Entrance to this class was closed to those who did not already possess the appropriate wealth, heritage, and educational background.

Beyond this readily identifiable class—which was insignificant in terms of numbers—the "class" system of the later empire is difficult to reconstruct. We are forced, it seems, to go to one or the other extreme. Either we oversimplify and say that there were two classes: the aristocracy and everyone else, or we immediately find ourselves faced with many (perhaps scores) of classes. Possibly most significant in this regard were those individuals who rose to positions of power, but who remained outside the traditional aristocracy: generals of barbarian or provincial origin, eunuchs, monks, administrators, and many of the emperors themselves! Surely no one would group these people together with the senators, but some of them may have formed a class which would rank on a slightly lower level. Similarly, the *curiales,* the local urban aristocracy, formed a class which was clearly defined in legal theory and practice.[35]

Given the present state of knowledge, it is reasonable to guess that many other classes existed in late Roman society: members of the army, day laborers, the lower clergy, the unemployed, widows, free peasants, *coloni*, slaves, and many more. Each of these groups presumably had their own place in society, and their members shared certain attitudes and legal and extralegal rights and obligations. When we examine particular events in Constantinople and the other cities of the empire, we should keep in mind the complexity of society and avoid the temptation to see social strife in a simple way as merely the rich against the poor. Among the rich, indeed, there were a number of different "classes," each of which must have viewed the same issues in very different ways.

The complexity of late Roman society was in part a result of the economic and social mobility which characterized the period. While not every peasant's son might "grow up to be emperor," a surprising number did just that. In many ways, of course, society under the later empire was rigid and there was a tendency for people to remain in the occupations of their fathers, but many individuals found that the autocratic power of the emperor, the growth of the imperial bureaucracy, the spread of Christianity, and the shift of emphasis from the West (with its old aristocratic traditions) meant the opportunity for economic and political advancement.[36]

At least as important as the horizontal divisions of late Roman society were the vertical ties which frequently bound diverse segments of the population into various communities of interest. Specific issues, of course, often cut across class lines: the poor of Constantinople, for example, joined with the educated aristocracy in perceiving a "Germanic threat" against which they had to act quickly and decisively. Likewise, a fear of natural disaster and a concern for Christianity served to tie different elements of society together and to prevent polarization along horizontal lines.[37]

The age-old institution of patronage also played an important role in this regard.[38] Throughout the ancient world much had always been accomplished through influence, and the situation did not change in the later empire. Nearly everyone without a position of power needed a patron of one kind or another and this was particularly true in dealing with the highly structured and hierarchically regimented imperial government. Furthermore, the recourse to a patron as a means to escape the demands of the tax collector is a familiar story, and whole towns and villages fell under the influence of powerful individuals. The reaction of the government to this development shows how pervasive and all-encompassing patronage really was, for to neutralize the power of private patrons, the emperor could do no better than to appoint a *defensor civitatis*, who was to act as a kind of public patron. Even this expedient failed, however, and private patronage continued to be a normal part of everyday life.

We know most about patronage in the rural areas, but it existed in the city as well. The phenomenon served frequently to bind the interests of the rich and poor closely together, perhaps one reason why anything resembling class antagonism was all but unknown. An interesting example of urban patronage may be found in the institution of the bread dole. It is well known that the Roman state, from a very early time, used the distribution of foodstuffs as a means to establish and maintain a clientele among the urban poor. In the late Republic the dole had served the interests of the great party politicians. But in the course of time the institution had come to represent the emperor alone, and he was able to increase his popularity by lavish distributions and to hold out the threat of reduction if the people did not behave in the proper way.

Nevertheless, it is possible that some private patrons were able to use the distribution of bread for their own purposes. When Constantine founded his city and wished to have it graced by a large number of noble houses, he offered inducements for important people to make their homes in the new capital. Among these attractions was the so-called *panis aedium*, which was soon paralleled in other great cities.[39] This institution provided free bread for those who built great homes (*domus*) in the city. Now, one may wonder why anyone rich enough to build a substantial house would need free bread. The homeowner might, of course, use the bread to help maintain his household, but we know that the right to receive the *panis aedium* might be assigned to others—an obvious opportunity for patronage. Probably the attraction of the *panis aedium* for the wealthy individual was not that it put bread on his own table, but that it allowed him an effective means to build up and strengthen his clientele.

We must ask what the urban patron hoped to gain from his clients. The prestige of having a large following was probably still important, but it is likely that, just as in former times, the patron hoped to gain something more concrete from his clients. It was no longer possible for clients to support their patrons with votes, but they may have discharged their obligation with their voices and their bodies. In examining the actions of the urban crowd, it is well to be aware of the possible effects of patronage, which would tie members of the "lower classes" more closely to the interests of their "upper class" patrons than to those of their peers.

In the later empire a new group of important patrons arose: the clergy and the monasteries. The bishops, especially, came to be very important patrons since they had significant judicial powers, and many commanded vast economic resources. One thinks immediately of the large number of charitable institutions—poorhouses, hospitals, hotels—belonging to the church of Constantinople, and the economic power of the bishops of Alexandria was probably even greater. Many individuals came to work for the great institutional churches, and perhaps a larger number came to depend on their charities. In the hands of ambitious prelates, this power of patronage must have been considerable. Monasteries, too, shared in this development, as they began to acquire land and to build their own charitable institutions. A powerful abbot might rival a bishop in the size and importance of his clientele.[40]

One should be careful, however, not to overemphasize the economic aspects of patronage in the later empire. Just as the citizen needed a powerful protector to allow him to approach the court of the emperor, the ordinary believer often felt he needed a powerful spiritual patron to allow him to draw near to the throne of God. In this way bishops and monks and independent "holy men" played an important role in society, and many of them attracted large and devoted bands of followers.[41]

By his bodily mortification, the ascetic had become detached from life as others lived it and had in fact entered into a unique relationship of familiarity with God (*parrhesia*).[42] The power which he possessed, both in his own person and as a result of his closeness to God, allowed the holy man to play the role of protector and patron (*prostates*) of ordinary persons. The intervention of a holy man to prevent a natural disaster or to cure a hopelessly ill individual are the more spectacular forms of this phenomenon. But perhaps more characteristic were the beneficient advice the holy man frequently gave to both emperor and simple farmer and the effective intervention he was able to offer with the terrible God of judgment. With considerable insight and significance for the present study, Peter Brown has connected the rise of the holy man with the decline of traditional forms of secular patronage, and he has shown how classical institutions were replaced by individuals as the intermediaries between the known and the unknown in human experience. In this way, the holy man played an important role in the difficulties which beset the late Roman countryside, but the situation was much the same in the city. In fact, the farmer at least had the security of an attachment to the land he had always known, despite the fluctuations in human society. For the urban dweller, especially one who had recently come to a great city such as Constantinople, everything was new, and life itself depended on building and maintaining favorable relationships with others. In this regard, we should expect the ascetic to play an important role as patron in an urban environment.

Organizations and Institutions

Organizations of various kinds characterized life in the cities of the later empire, and some of these may have served as catalysts in urban unrest. The best known of these organizations were the *collegia*, or guilds.⁴³ Occupational groups of merchants and craftsmen had been common throughout antiquity, but they attained a particular importance in the period of the later empire, when they were organized to serve the needs of the state. In a time of fiscal insecurity, the state needed to be certain, first, that the taxes would be collected and, second, that essential public services would be maintained. Guilds of weavers, bakers, cattle dealers, shipowners, ragpickers, and many others served the state in a variety of ways. They collected the *chrysargyron* from their members, they manufactured and distributed essential goods (such as weapons, cloth, bread, and wood for the public baths), and they provided important public services (such as dredging rivers and repairing buildings). Often these services were provided free by the guilds, as a kind of corvée, and even when compensation was allowed, prices were carefully controlled.

Since the state depended on the *collegia* for these tasks, it was imperative that they be regulated in some way, and the codes provide detailed evidence of how this was done. All workers in a particular industry were required to belong to the appropriate guild, and membership was probably hereditary. At times, membership in a guild must have been restrictive for the individual, especially when it required financial loss or personal hardship. For example, the guild of the breadmakers was required to provide bread at a certain fixed price regardless of the market price of the grain; if the price of grain rose, the baker had to absorb the loss with his own resources. This must have caused some hardship and possibly even antagonism against the state, but we should not assume that the *collegiati* were an oppressed group only waiting for the opportunity to rebel against authority. Most of the repressive legislation concerning the guilds comes from the Western part of the empire, and there is little evidence of general dissatisfaction from the East.

Nevertheless, individual issues must clearly have affected the *collegiati*, and their organization gave them a unity and a power which must have been formidable. Unlike most other urban dwellers, the members of the *collegia* had become accustomed to dealing with the state on a collective basis, and although there was probably little general dissatisfaction among them, in a situation of stress the *collegiati* might well have provided leadership and organization for popular protest. Normally the function of the guild was to serve the interests of the state, but in certain circumstances the relationship might have been reversed, and the members of the guild had the ability to exert pressure on the government.⁴⁴

Other organizations which also will warrant the closest scrutiny are the circus factions and the theatre claque; both have often been cited in connection with urban unrest in the later empire.[45] Historians have long paid attention to the circus factions—the Blues and the Greens—especially because they were the instigators of the Nika Revolt in 532. The factions originated as the corporations which supplied the horses, chariots, and charioteers for the circus in Rome, and in the first century A.D. they numbered six. As time wore on, the number of factions was perhaps reduced to two, and the membership and composition of the factions became more difficult to estimate and describe. At their core, the factions were made up simply of the individuals who earned their living by supplying the necessities for chariot racing. They gained many loyal adherents, however, who did not actually work for the corporation, but who banded together to support the drivers by cheering at the races. These individuals, who may have numbered in the thousands, were mostly young. We know that by the middle of the sixth century, at least, they identified themselves in public by their strange appearance, which, according to Procopius, they called the "Hunnic look."[46] They let their hair grow on their face and their head, except in the front where they cut it short across the forehead. The sleeves of their tunics were very full so that their appearance in the hippodrome made an impressive theatrical display as they clapped their hands in unison. The cheers and applause of the factions were carefully planned and staged, so a certain amount of organization was essential. Significantly, the members of the factions went about the city armed.

The leaders of these groups, experienced as they were in the techniques of crowd manipulation and slogan-shouting, might provide a nucleus around which popular discontent could rally for support and organization. Beyond that, some scholars have claimed that the factions represented different social and ideological groups. According to G. Manojlović, the Greens attracted the poor sections of society, the urban tradesmen and the unemployed, while the Blues were identified with the upper classes. Manojlović further argued that the Greens supported "oriental" ideas, including monophysitism, and the Blues maintained "western" traditions and eventually upheld the decisions of the Council of Chalcedon. The factions have also been equated with the demes (*demoi*), who were perhaps a kind of militia organized to defend the walls of the cities in the troubled times of the fourth and fifth centuries.

The views of Manojlović have won surprisingly wide acceptance, and they are repeated, with some minor variations, in many general texts. Perhaps the most extreme statement in this respect is the work of Jacques Jarry, who has seen factions and their supposed social and economic divisions behind most of the important phenomena in this period.[47] The recent studies of Alan Cameron, however, have shown convincingly that the factions always were primarily sporting organizations which provided an outlet for the rowdy behavior of young inhabitants of early Byzantine cities. As time went on, the factions became an integral part of ceremonies at court, and they were certainly involved in many of the disturbances which characterized the later fifth and sixth centuries. But there is little evidence for their activity in the early fifth century, the period encompassed by the present study.[48]

An institution similar to that of the factions was the theatre claque. This organization came into being as a result of the custom of providing regular rhythmic applause at the theatre. Actors paid the members of the claque for their support, and the claque responded by greeting performances with enthusiastic applause and long, drawn-out expressions of praise and admiration. The phenomenon, which probably originated in Alexandria, was brought to Rome by Nero, and by the time of the later empire the practice was widespread and all the notable cities of the empire had their own professional claques. Even some bishops, it is said, possessed a claque which responded loudly to the prelate's sermons.[49] The claques were probably rather small in number (that of Antioch numbered 400), but like the factions, their organization and experience in dealing with the crowd might give them a position of leadership in a situation of difficulty and discontent. In Antioch, especially, the theatre claque has been held responsible for a number of disturbances in the late fourth century.[50]

Just as the cities of the empire were being exposed to new and increasing social and economic strains, the old measures for maintaining public security began to appear inadequate, and simple physical danger became one of the characteristics of the age. Not least important in this regard were the external threats to the city. Throughout the empire, cities which had been safe from foreign enemies suddenly found themselves face-to-face with Goths, Huns, and Vandals. As we have seen, smaller circuit walls and powerful bastions were thrown up, giving the city at times the appearance and the mentality of a fortress.[51] Outlaws and bandits, sometimes organized into formidable bands, roamed various areas of the countryside, apparently at will.[52]

Within the city one should expect redoubled efforts to maintain public order: the city was the obvious place of refuge for much of society, and strong measures were called for to control the divergent interests of contemporary urban society. Nevertheless, police protection in the late Roman city seems to have been completely inadequate. Why this was so is something of a mystery. Indeed, the old means of security which had, more or less successfully, protected the inhabitants of Rome and the cities of the empire during the principate were disbanded during late antiquity, and no satisfactory replacement for them was provided.[53]

In every city there was apparently a kind of amateur night watch which patrolled the streets and which may have contributed to the prevention of crime. Their main function, however, was probably more symbolic than real: according to John Chrysostom, the night watchmen of Constantinople "go around in the cold, shouting greatly and walking through the narrow streets."[54] They proclaimed the reality of the power of the state to the denizens of back alleys and tenement houses, and they broke the spell of the night with their voices and the light of their lamps. But this force—whose members were normally conscripted from among the guilds—was clearly impotent in the face of organized violence or massive revolt. The Notitia of Constantinople tells us that one *curator* (who was probably a senator) was appointed for each of the thirteen urban regions of the city. These *curatores* were to maintain some kind of order in their district, but they were aided only by one public slave and five *vicomagistri*, who were "entrusted with the care of the city at night."[54]

In Rome and Constantinople the *praefectus urbi* had overall responsibility for the maintenance of public order, and he was often forced to act when the night watch proved unequal to the task. Yet, the prefect himself was hardly any better equipped to deal with violence or crime. Like the *curatores*, the *praefectus urbi* was normally an aristocrat or a professional administrator with no training or experience in military or police duties. In addition, again like the *curatores*, the *praefectus* had no real police force at his disposal. At most he could hope for support from his *officium*, which was made up largely of clerical workers.[56] On many occasions the prefect might be reduced to dire straits in the face of urban violence. Leontius, the prefect of Rome in the mid-fourth century dealt quickly with a difficult situation by riding bravely into a crowd of rioters and arresting their leaders, despite the trepidation of his *officium*. Other prefects were not so courageous or successful, and one was reduced to offering his children to the crowd as hostages, while another simply fled the city and sought safety in his suburban villa.[57]

Beyond all this, of course, the state had an ultimate solution to urban crime and violence: the army. Whenever the situation got completely out of hand, soldiers would be summoned to put an end to the difficulty. The presence of the emperor in Constantinople, with the necessary bodyguards and palatine troops, increased public security in the capital. Likewise, the augustal prefect in Alexandria, because of the reputation of the city for unruliness, had some soldiers at his disposal. Other authorities (such as provincial governors and civic magistrates) were less fortunate. They probably possessed a few soldiers, but these could not hope to deal with large-scale violence. Detachments of soldiers were, as a rule, not stationed permanently within the cities themselves, and in the case of serious disturbance, troops had to be summoned from outside. It seems clear that the state could apply overwhelming force when this was necessary but it is noteworthy that this was done only as a last resort and in response to a serious situation. In most cities, everyday peacekeeping forces were singularly inadequate.

Constantinople, Ephesus, and Alexandria

The cities of Constantinople, Ephesus, and Alexandria form the background for the events discussed in this study. They, along with Antioch, were the great cities of the Eastern empire, and all were important administrative, economic, and ecclesiastical centers which extended their influence far into vast hinterlands.

Ephesus was undoubtedly the smallest of the three; in the fifth century perhaps 50,000 people lived within the walls of Lysimachus, although many others probably made their homes in the immediate area, as a number of scattered villas and residential areas show.[58] Nevertheless, Ephesus was an important city, and it had an impressive history as a point where the culture of the classical world met that of Anatolia. It was the site of a famous sanctuary of Artemis, to whom—as St. Paul learned to his discomfiture—the citizens of the city had been passionately loyal. The Artemesion had perished, perhaps in the Gothic incursion of A.D. 263, but the city found other patrons in Mary the mother of Jesus, and the Apostle John, both of whom were said to have been buried in or near Ephesus. The church of St. John—the Apostolion—had, in fact, replaced the Artemesion as an important religious center, and pilgrims visited it for oracular dreams.

Administratively, Ephesus was the metropolis of the diocese of Asia and the residence of the proconsul, the most important civil official in western Asia Minor. In the fourth and fifth centuries, the city was a bustling center of trade and communication. It was the entrepôt for all the produce of the rich Meander and Cayster valleys, and the important "southern highway," linking the Greek cities of the coast with the hinterland of Anatolia and distant Syria, began at Ephesus. Likewise, the harbor of the city was filled with ships from all over the empire, with the route between Alexandria and Constantinople probably being most important. As one might expect in such a situation, Ephesus was also a manufacturing center (in the sense that concept can be applied to any ancient city), and its silversmiths and cloth workers had a wide reputation.[59]

The city may have suffered in the difficult times of the third century but the subsequent years witnessed substantial prosperity and monumental building.[60] A visitor to the Council of 431, for example, would have seen not only the Apostolion and the conciliar church of St. Mary, but also impressive secular and civic buildings. Perhaps most striking were the broad, straight marble-paved streets, lined with colonnades and statues, as cleared by the Austrian excavators over the past eighty years. The so-called Arcadiane, for example, extended some 600 meters from the theatre to the harbor; it was eleven meters wide, and on both sides there were colonnades with rows of shops behind. In the southern part of the city another monumental street, the Embolos, ran from the Library of Celsus (transformed into a fountain), past the Square of Domitian, to the Magnesian Gate. Like the Arcadiane, the Embolos was eleven meters wide, and it was lined with numerous buildings restored in this period: the Basilica, the Pryteneum, and the Baths of Scholasticus (to which was joined a particularly sumptuous brothel). Scattered throughout the city were houses, some of them obviously for the poorer residents, while others were lavishly decorated with frescoes and mosaic floors. Not far from the harbor were the spacious Baths of Constantius, constructed in the mid-fourth century as one of the many indications of imperial beneficence toward the city. Statues of emperors and proconsuls were everywhere to be seen, as were honorific dedications, and it is difficult to know whether to attribute the obvious vitality of Ephesus during this period more to economic factors or to imperial patronage.

By the reign of Theodosius I, Ephesus had become a predominantly Christian city, and that character was reinforced not only by the association with Saint Paul and Saint John and the Virgin, but also by the miracle of the Seven Sleepers, in which Christian young men escaped persecution in the third century by falling asleep in a cave and awakening during the reign of Theodosius II. Throughout the city, excavators have found crosses scratched on walls and gates (and even on the foreheads of a number of statues), and a surviving inscription commemorates the erection of a monumental cross over one of the busiest intersections. Ecclesiastically, the bishop of Ephesus was the metropolitan of Asia and thus an important ecclesiastical figure who had jurisdictional claims to a wide geographical area. In the fifth century, however, his position was to be challenged more and more by the growing strength of the bishops of Constantinople.

Alexandria was, like Ephesus, one of the great cities of the empire, but it was larger and even more grand. From the time it was founded by Alexander, the city had been a showplace of culture and center of untold wealth based on the agricultural richness of the Nile Valley. Nowhere else in the dry Mediterranean world was there an area so well-watered and thus so productive as Egypt, and because of the geography of the country, Alexandria was predestined for a centralized control that was likewise unique. Even in the Pharaonic period, cities in Egypt did not develop in the normal sense, and the small villages along the river were administered by a strong government located in Thebes or Memphis or Amarna. With the founding of Alexandria in the fourth century B.C., this situation changed; a huge metropolis was established at the mouth of the Nile. Nevertheless, Alexandria never enjoyed the normal development or the typical institutions of a city in another part of the empire: it was always a capital city, the seat of the governor or king who administered the rich countryside from that point.[61]

Thus, in a very real sense, Alexandria was not an Egyptian city. It was, from the beginning, a Greek city and Greek-speaking people made up the bulk of the population. Native Egyptians, of course, moved to Alexandria, but they probably remained a minority, and they lived in different quarters of the city away from the Hellenized inhabitants. Hostility naturally developed between the Greeks and Egyptians, and this frequently gave way to violent clashes. In addition, the settlement of large numbers of Hellenized Jews in Alexandria added another important element to the ethnic mix in the city, and the Jews frequently played a significant part in the turmoil which seemed to characterize life in Alexandria from an early date. Frequent riots and other confrontations gave the city a reputation for instability, just as its wealth created the impression of opulence, luxury, and wanton extravagance.

As we have seen, the economic basis of Alexandria was the agricultural produce of the Nile valley, and this was funneled to the city by means of taxation and the function that the city served as the entrepôt for the transport of Egyptian grain to Rome, Constantinople, and even the distant provinces of Gaul. Thus, the city was always full of traders and merchants, some of them operating on a very large scale, as well as sailors and others involved with long-distance trade. Furthermore, Alexandria was unlike most other cities of the ancient world in that it developed a considerable industrial base. In words attributed to the emperor Hadrian by the author of his life in the *Augustan History*,

> The people are most factious, vain, and unruly; the city is rich, wealthy, and prosperous. Some are glass blowers, some are making paper, and others are engaged in weaving linen; everyone at any rate seems to be engaged in some occupation. The gouty, the circumcised, the blind, all have some trade. Not even the maimed live in idleness. They have only one god—money. Christians, Jews, everyone worship this divinity. Would that this city were endowed with better morals, a city which has the primacy of all Egypt in view of its size.

This document mentions industries in which the factories of Alexandria were preeminent: the manufacture of glass, paper, and linen cloth. Other centers of industry, particularly in Syria, Gaul, and Germany, competed with Egypt for markets in these products, but Alexandria remained the primary place of manufacture, especially for the Eastern trade. In large measure, this was because of the skill which Egyptian artisans had attained, but it was also connected with the resources which were plentiful in the Egyptian countryside. In addition, Alexandria was famous for its production of luxury goods, such as ointments, perfumes, and oils, and we may be certain that it possessed an important industry in jewelry, metalworking, sculpture, and the other arts.[62]

34   Vox Populi

In fact, the economic difficulties of the later empire appear only to have improved the position of Alexandria as the leading city in the Greek East. During this period, the Nile continued to rise and fall and every year it renewed the agricultural wealth of the countryside. Everywhere throughout the empire, even in times of difficulty, people needed grain, and Alexandria could supply it. Likewise, the economic problems of the age clearly did not destroy the taste for luxury goods on the part of the substantial number of peole who could afford them, and again, those in the markets and workshops of Alexandria were willing and able to meet the demand. Thus, by concentrating their production on either end of the financial scale—the cheapest (and most necessary) of goods on the one hand, and the most expensive on the other—the merchants, shipowners, and workers of Alexandria survived the crises which had plagued other areas.

During the later empire, the people of Alexandria found an important source of unity in the bishop of the city, and this naturally increased as Christianity spread among the citizens. Paganism had been strong in Alexandria, and its supporters offered a desperate resistance to the new religion; but by the beginning of the fifth century Christianity had all but triumphed. At the turn of the century, Judaism was still an important religion in the city, but the Jews also felt the power of the "pope" of Egypt, and they were expelled from the city. Thus, the antagonisms which had rent Alexandrian society from the time of its foundation seemed resolved, although violently, in the person of the patriarch. It is true that there was probably some animosity between the inhabitants of the city and the population of the rest of the countryside, but, with the support of the powerful monastic community, the patriarch commanded the allegiance of nearly every Egyptian. He personally controlled much of the economic productivity of the country (through the vast ownership of the church and its fleets of grain transport ships), and he rivaled and often overshadowed the authority of the Roman governor. It was thus with good reason that contemporaries frequently referred to the bishop of Alexandria as "Pharaoh."[63]

Constantinople was in many ways different from Alexandria and Ephesus. It had only recently become a great city, and it had no tradition of a long and glorious local history. The imperial city was certainly the heir of Rome, and it inherited most of the institutions and many of the traditions of the older capital. But the population of Constantinople was "new," and many of the residents were immigrants from various parts of the empire who had (by the end of the fourth century) little opportunity to develop emotional ties to Byzantium. As we have seen, in the fourth and fifth centuries the population of the city was constantly increasing, and there must have been considerable social instability. On the other hand, the continuous construction activity must have provided much of the employment necessary to support this increasing population. Probably by the beginning of the fifth century Constantinople had outstripped the other urban centers of the empire, and it had as many as 400,000 inhabitants.[64]

Like Alexandria, Constantinople was a center of trade and manufacturing. But, so far as we can tell, industry was fairly light since much of the heavy manufacturing which supplied the capital was located in the other cities of the vicinity: Heraclea, Cyzicus, Nicomedia. Constantinople was instead a center of small, luxury-oriented industry (textiles, jewelry, metal work), although many of the inhabitants must have been employed in supplying the basic necessities of daily life: bread and other foodstuffs, tiles, pottery, and tools.

The city and its economy were dominated by the presence of the imperial court. From the death of Theodosius the Great in 395 through the middle of the sixth century, few of the emperors of the East were warriors, and they rarely left Constantinople for any extended period. This brought large numbers of administrators, courtiers, and bureaucrats to the city, not to mention the throngs of litigants and petitioners who came to make their case before the court. In addition, as the emperors assembled famous relics in the city and built magnificent churches to grace the capital, Constantinople became an important center of pilgrimage, thus attracting thousands more people to the area. Many of the residents must have made their living in feeding, housing, entertaining, and robbing these visitors. Everywhere throughout the city there were inescapable reminders of the power of the emperors: towering columns, statue-lined streets, great churches, and frequent imperial processions. These physical accoutrements of power, as well as the burgeoning population and the new sense of self-assurance which accompanied the birth of the Byzantine world, must have contributed to the atmosphere in the city in the early fifth century.

The church of Constantinople, just as the city itself, was a newcomer in the ranks of high ecclesiastical politics. The bishop of Byzantium had earlier been subject to the bishop of Heraclea in Thrace, but he now found himself among the most important religious leaders of the empire. It was an established custom that the rank of a particular church was dependent upon the political importance of its city, and the status of the bishop of Constantinople—and his ambitions—increased along with the power and prestige of the capital. By the end of the fourth century, the bishop of Constantinople ranked second only to the bishop of old Rome, and he began seriously to encroach on the territory and prerogatives of his ecclesiastical rivals of the East, most notably the bishops of Alexandria and Ephesus.

36 Vox Populi

1. On the cities of the later empire see the standard works of A. H. M. Jones, *The Greek City from Alexander to Justinian* (Oxford, 1940), and *The Cities of the Eastern Roman Provinces*, rev. ed (Oxford, 1971). P. Petit, *Libanius et la vie municipale à Antioche au IVe siècle après J-C.* (Paris, 1955), D. Claude, *Die byzantinische Stadt im 6. Jahrhundert* (Munich, 1969), J. H. W. G. Liebescheutz, *Antioch* (Oxford, 1972), and Clive Foss, "Byzantine Cities of Western Asia Minor" (Ph.D. diss., Harvard University, 1972).

2. Ammianus Marcellinus *Res Gestae* (Rolfe translation), 28. 4, 28-34. Cf. the comments of Sir Ronald Syme, *Ammianus and the Historia Augusta* (Oxford, 1968), pp. 146-53.

3. Socrates *Historia Ecclesiastica* 5. 18.

4. Ibid. 7. 23.

5. *Chronicon Paschale* (ed. Bonn) p. 531; A. H. M. Jones, *Later Roman Empire*, pp. 696-701.

6. Jones, *Later Roman Empire*, p. 735; Liebeschuetz, *Antioch*, pp. 126-32.

7. *C. Th.* 14. 17, 5 (369, Rome).

8. Jones, *Later Roman Empire*, pp. 696-97.

9. At the time of its inauguration the grain dole must have been available to nearly half of the inhabitants of the city, but it is interesting that the number of recipients did not grow significantly as the population increased; so far as we can tell, approximately the same number of people were supported by state grain in 550 as in the fourth century, although the city was certainly much larger. See the interesting discussion in Gilbert Dagron, *Naissance d'une capitale* (Paris, 1974), pp. 530-41.

10. *C. Th.* 14. 15, 5. This regulation was given for Rome and it may not have been valid for Constantinople. Further, J. Le Gall, "Rome, ville de fainéants?" *Revue des Études Latines* 49 (1971), 226-77, and others, have claimed that the distribution of bread was not enough for a family to live on. The argument, however, is based on the evidence for the early empire when the amount seems to have been less.

11. *C. Th.* 14. 16, 1 (409); 14. 6, 3 (434).

12. Jones, *Later Roman Empire*, pp. 701-5.

13. Ibid., pp. 705-6.

14. D. J. Constantelos, *Byzantine Philanthropy and Social Welfare* (New Brunswick, 1968), pp. 19-41; 152-84 (hospitals); 185-221 (hostels); 257-69 (poorhouses). See also Dagron, *Naissance,* pp. 509-17.

15. Jones, *The Greek City*, p. 155.

16. Eusebius *Historia Ecclesiastica*, ed. Eduard Schwartz, vol. 3 (Leipzig, 1909), 7. 21.

17. Jones, *Later Roman Empire*, pp. 698, 1040.

18. Ammianus Marcellinus *Res Gestae* 15. 11.

19. See, for example, the arguments of J. C. Russell, *Late Ancient and Medieval Populations* (Philadelphia, 1958), pp. 7-8, 71-88.

20. Kenneth Setton, "The Archaeology of Medieval Athens," in *Essays in Medieval Life and Thought Presented in Honor of Austin Patterson Evans* (New York, 1955), pp. 227-58; Homer A. Thompson, "Athenian Twilight," *JRS* 49 (1959), 61-72; and John Travlos *Poleodomikē Exelexis Tōn Athēnōn* [Urban Development of Athens] (Athens, 1960), pp. 125-34.

21. Thompson, "Athenian Twilight," p. 65.

22. Setton, "Archaeology of Medieval Athens," p. 241.

23. Glanville Downey, *A History of Antioch in Syria from Seleucus to the Arab Conquest* (Princeton, 1961), p. 434.

24. Ibid., pp. 452-53; see also Downey's article, "The Size of the Population of Antioch," *Transactions and Proceedings of the American Philosophical Association*, 89 (1958), 84-91; and Liebeschuetz, *Antioch*, pp. 92-100.

25. Libanius, *Orationes* 2. 66; 10. 25; 11. 163-69, cited by Liebeschuetz, *Antioch*, pp. 96-97.

The Urban Context 37

26. R. Janin, *Constantinople Byzantine*, 2nd ed. (Paris, 1964), pp. 32-33; Dagron, *Naissance*, pp. 518-44. Cf. Russell's statement: "By this time it [Constantinople] had surpassed Rome more probably because Rome was declining rapidly than because Constantinople was increasing much in the fifth century."

27. See, for example, the views of E. Stein, *Histoire du Bas-Empire*, ed. and trans. Jean-Remy Planque, vol. 1 (Paris, 1959), pp. 16-17; A. Piganiol, *L'empire chrétien, 325-395* (Paris, 1947), p. 286; and Stewart Irving Oost, *Galla Placidia Augusta* (Chicago, 1968), pp. 11-12. On the *honestiores* and the *humiliores*, see Jones, *Later Roman Empire*, pp. 17-18, 518, and, for the earlier empire, Peter Garnsey, *Social Status and Legal Privilege in the Roman Empire* (Oxford, 1970). For an introduction to all the issues discussed below see Ramsay MacMullen, *Roman Social Relations, 50 B.C. to A.D. 284* (New Haven, 1974), pp. 57-127.

28. Liebeschuetz, *Antioch*, pp. 52-54: ". . . there was a great social gulf between the tradesmen as a whole and the upper classes," although "Libanius would always include the shopkeepers among the sound and respectable citizens as opposed to the riff-raff. . ." On the issue of class in the Roman world, see MacMullen, *Roman Social Relations*, pp. 88-120.

29. Jones, *Later Roman Empire*, p. 519.

30. Liebeschuetz, *Antioch*, p. 59; MacMullen, *Roman Social Relations*, pp. 89, 98-99.

31. There have been some notable works in this direction. See, for example, A. F. Norman, "Gradations in Later Municipal Society," *JRS* 48 (1958), 79-85; Wolfgang Seyfarth, *Soziale Fragen der spätrömischen Kaiserzeit im Spiegel des Theodosianus* (Berlin, 1963); H. G. Beck, "Konstantinopel," *BZ* 58 (1965), 11-45; and Franz Tinnefeld, *Die fruhbyzantinische Gesellschaft* (Munich, 1977).

32. Seymour M. Lipset, "Stratification, Social: Social Class," in *International Encyclopedia of the Social Sciences*, vol. 15 (New York, 1968), p. 298. For a useful discussion of many aspects of class and social stratification see Reinhard Bendix and Seymour M. Lipset, eds., *Class, Status, and Power: Social Stratification in Comparative Perspective*, 2nd ed. (New York, 1966).

33. Lipset, "Stratification, Social," p. 310.

34. Beck, "Konstantinopel," p. 20; M. T. W. Arnheim, *The Senatorial Aristocracy in the Later Roman Empire* (Oxford, 1972), pp. 8-12.

35. See MacMullen, *Roman Social Relations*, pp. 89-92.

36. A. P. Rudakov, *Orcherki vizantiyskoy kul'tury po dannym grecheskoy agiografii* [Essays on Byzantine culture from the evidence of Greek hagiography] (Moscow, 1917; rp. London, 1970), pp. 140-41; Ramsay Macmullen, "Social Mobility and the Theodosian Code," *JRS* 54 (1964), 49-53; W. Ceran, "Stagnation or Fluctuation in Early Byzantine Society," *Byzantinoslavica* 31 (1970), 192-203.

37. See the interesting study of Martin Hengel, *Property and Riches in the Early Church*, (Philadelphia, 1974).

38. Libanius *de patrociniis, Or.* 47; Beck, "Konstantinopel," p. 34; Liebeschuetz, *Antioch*, pp. 53-54, 192-208; and Arnheim, *Senatorial Aristocracy*, pp. 148-52.

39. *C. Th.* 14. 17, 11-13; 14. 26; Victor Martin and Denis van Berchem, "*Le panis aedium d'Alexandrie,*" *Revue de philologie de littérature et d'histoire anciennes*, 3rd ser. 16 (1942), 5-21; Jones, *Later Roman Empire*, p. 697. Martin and van Berchem realized the difficulty implicit in a bread dole for the wealthy and they suggested, without any real evidence, that they received their "bread" in gold. On the *domus* see Christine Strube, "Der Begrif domus in der Notita urbis Constantinopolitanae," in *Studien zur Frühgeschichte Konstantinopels*, ed. H. G. Beck (Munich, 1973), pp. 121-34.

40. The subject of ecclesiastical patronage is a large one, but it is perhaps best illustrated in the evidence from Egypt. See George R. Monks, "The Church of Alexandria and the City's Economic Life in the Sixth Century," *Speculum* 28 (1953), 349-62; and A. Steinwenter, "Die Stellung der Bischöfe in der byzantinischen Verwaltung Ägyptens," in *Studi in onore di P. Francisci*, vol. 1 (Milan, 1954), pp. 77-99.

41. Peter Brown, "The Rise and Function of the Holy Men in Late Antiquity," *JRS* 61 (1971), 80-101, and the literature cited there. A striking example of the preference given to

an ascetic as bishop is the refusal of the inhabitants of Cyzicus to accept a bishop chosen for them by the bishop of Constantinople. They preferred a monk instead (Socrates *Hist. Eccl.* 7.28).

42. On the subject of *parrhesia* in a Christian context, see Arnoldo Momigliano, "La Libertà di Parola nel Mondo Antico," *Revista Storica Italiana* 83 (1971), 499-524, and the bibliography cited there.

43. A. Waltzing, *Étude historique sur les corporations professionnelles chez les Romains depuis les origines jusqu'à la chute de l'empire d'Occident*, 4 vols. (Louvain, 1895-1900); and A. Stöckle, *Spätrömische und byzantinische Zünfte* (Leipzig, 1911).

44. Ramsay MacMullen, *Enemies of the Roman Order* (Cambridge, Mass., 1966), pp. 173-78; Liebsechuetz, *Antioch*, pp. 222-23.

45. The literature on the circus factions is considerable. Until recently the standard studies were G. Manojlović, "Le peuple de Constantinople," *Byzantion* 11 (1936), 616-17; and A. Diakanov, "Vizantiiskie dimy i fakcii v V-VII vv" [Byzantine demes and factions in the 5th-7th centuries], *Vizantiskii sbornik* (1945), 144-227. Now see Alan Cameron, "Demes and Factions," *BZ* 67 (1974), 74-91, and *Circus Factions* (Oxford, 1976).

46. Procopius, *Anekdota*, ed. Jacob Henry (Leipzig, 1963).

47. Jacques Jarry, *Hérésies et factions dans l'Empire byzantine du IVe au VIIe siècle*. (Cairo, 1968).

48. Cameron, *Circus Factions*, pp. 221-29.

49. Socrates *Hist. Eccl.* 7.13.

50. R. Browning, "The Riot of A D. 387 in Antioch," *JRS* 42 (1952), 13-20; Liebeschuetz, *Antioch*, pp. 211-17; Cameron, *Circus Factions*, pp. 193-229.

51. On the nature of the "fortress mentality" see Lewis Mumford, *The City in History* (New York, 1961), pp. 66-68.

52. Like the restrictions placed on the guilds, rural violence may have affected the West much more than the East. E. A. Thompson, "Peasant Revolts in Late Roman Gaul and Spain," *Past and Present* 2 (1952), 11-23; MacMullen *Enemies of the Roman Order*, pp. 192-241, 255-68.

53. Constantine disbanded the praetorian guard in 312; the demise of the cohorts of *vigiles* and the urban cohorts probably followed soon after. There is no evidence that such bodies were ever established in Constantinople. On the lack of public security in the later empire see Hans Peter Kohns, *Versorgungskrisen und Hungerrevolten im spätantiken Rom. Antiquitas* (Bonn, 1961), pp. 102-9; Jones, *Later Roman Empire*, pp. 692-95; MacMullen, *Enemies of the Roman Order*, pp. 336-37; and Dagron, *Naissance*, pp. 108-13.

54. John Chrysostom *hom in Act. Ap.* 26. 4 (*PG.* 60, 202-4).

55. Jones, *Later Roman Empire*, p. 694.

56. W. G. Sinnigen, *The Officium of the Urban Prefect during the Later Roman Empire* (Rome, 1957), pp. 94-99; Dagron, *Naissance*, p. 109.

57. Ammianus Marcellinus *Res Gestae* 15. 7, 2-5; 19. 10, 2-3; 27. 3, 11-13.

58. On late Roman Ephesus see Franz Miltner, *Ephesos* (Vienna, 1958), and Foss, "Byzantine Cities," pp. 136-202, where much of the otherwise scattered material is gathered together. The guide to the site, Josef Keil, *Führer durch Ephesos* (Vienna, 1964), provides a good introduction and there are now important articles in *RE*, supplemental vol. 12 (Stuttgart, 1970), "Ephesos," 248-364 and 1588-1704. See also W. Brockhoff, *Studien zur Geschichte der Stadt Ephesos vom 4. nachchristlichen Jahuhundert bis zu ihrem Untergang in der ersten Hälfte des 15. Jahrhunderts* (Dissertation, Jena, 1905), and Hermann Vetters, "Zum byzantinischen Ephesos," *Jahrbuch der österreichischen byzantinischen Gesellschaft*, 15 (1966), 273-87. The archaeological material is collected in *Forschungen in Ephesos*, ed. Österreichischen archäologisches Institut 6 vols. (Vienna, 1906-51). On the population of Ephesus in the later empire, see Russell, *Late Ancient and Medieval Populations*, pp. 80-81.

59. David Magie, *Roman Rule in Asia Minor*, 2 vols. (Princeton, 1950), pp. 46-47 (industry and commerce of Ephesus) and pp. 705-6 and 1566-67 (Goths); T. R. S.

Broughton, "Roman Asia," in *An Economic Survey of Ancient Rome*, ed. Tenney Frank, vol. 4 (Baltimore, 1938); and Dieter Knibbe, "Ephesos," *RE*, supplemental vol. 12, 287-89.

60. Much of this description is dependent on Foss, "Byzantine Cities," pp. 170-98.

61. On Alexandria in general, see P. M. Fraser, *Ptolemaic Alexandria*, 3 vols. (Oxford, 1972), and W. Schubert, "Alexandria," *RAC*, vol. 1, 271-83. See also H. I. Bell, "Alexandria," *JEA* 13 (1927), 171 ff., and *Egypt from Alexander the Great to the Arab Conquest* (Oxford, 1948). On the rebelliousness of the Alexandrians, see H. I. Bell, *Jews and Christians in Egypt* (London, 1924), and H. Mursurillo, *The Acts of the Pagan Martyrs* (Oxford, 1954).

62. On the economic situation of Alexandria under Roman rule, see J. G. Milne, *A History of Egypt under Roman Rule* 3rd ed. (London, 1924), A. C. Johnson, *Roman Egypt* in *An Economic Survey of Ancient Rome*, ed. Tenney Frank, vol. 2 (Baltimore, 1936), and M. Rostovtzeff, *Social and Economic History of the Roman Empire*, 2nd ed. (Oxford, 1957).

63. For the church of Alexandria, see E. R. Hardy, *Christian Egypt* (New York, 1952), and Bell, *Jews and Christians*. On the economic position of the partiarch of Alexandria, see the *Vita Johannis Eleemosynarii, Anal. Bolland* 45 (1927), 19-73, trans. Elizabeth Dawes and Norman H. Baynes (Oxford, 1948); and George R. Monks, "The Church of Alexandria," pp. 349-62. On the political, military, and economic organization of late Roman Egypt, see M. Gelzer, *Studien zur byzantinischen Verwaltung Ägyptens* (Leipzig, 1909); H. I. Bell, "The Byzantine Servile State in Egypt," *JEA* 4 (1917), 86 ff; E. R. Hardy, *The Large Estates of Byzantine Egypt* (New York, 1931); A. C. Johnson and Louis C. West, *Byzantine Egypt* (Princeton, 1949); J. Maspero, *Organisation militaire de l'Égypte byzantine* (Paris, 1912); Germaine Rouillard, *L'Administration civile de l'Egypte byzantine*, 2nd ed. (Paris, 1928); and Ernst Stein, "L'administration de l'Egypte byzantine," *Gnomon* 6 (1930), 401-7.

64. For Constantinople see R. Janin, *Constantinople byzantine*, 2nd ed., Jones, *Later Roman Empire*, pp. 687-711; and Dagron, *Naissance*. Popular in scope and approach, but sometimes useful, are Glanville Downey, *Constantinople in the Age of Justinian* (Norman, 1960); and Dean A. Miller, *Imperial Constantinople* (New York, 1969). Concerning the population of the city see A. Andreades, "De la population de Constantinople sous les empereurs byzantines," *Metron* 1 (1920), 1-56; D. Jacoby, "La population de Constantinople à l'époque byzantine: un problème de démographie urbaine," *Byzantion* 31 (1961), 81-109; and Dagron, *Naissance*, pp. 518-41.

65. On the development of the church of Constantinople see Dagron, *Naissance*, pp. 367-517, and N. H. Baynes, "Alexandria and Constantinople," *JEA* 12 (1926), 145-56, rpt. in his *Byzantine Studies and Other Essays* (London, 1955), pp. 97-115.

III

THE EPISCOPACY OF JOHN CHRYSOSTOM: CONSTANTINOPLE

Early Years and the Episcopal Election of 397

John Chrysostom was born in Antioch in the middle of the fourth century, probably about 354.[1] Like many other bishops of the period, he was from a wealthy family. His father, Secundus, had been an important military officer in Syria and the family was able to provide for John's thorough education without using his inheritance.[2] Although he received an excellent classical training and had the renowned sophist Libanius as one of his teachers, John abandoned whatever plans he may have had for a secular career when he was about eighteen years old.[3] Instead, he became a disciple of Miletius, the orthodox bishop of Antioch, and spent much of his time learning monastic "philosophy" from the famous ascetics Carterius and Diodorus.[4] He became a monk and after three years was ordained a lector in the church of Antioch.[5]

Burning with the ardor of youth, however, he found the duties of a minor cleric in the city could not compete with the spiritual attractions of the ascetic life, and he went into the desert. There he lived in common with others for several years but, finding his spiritual strength growing, he "withdrew by himself into a cave, so as to be completely undisturbed and unknown. Here he lived for two years. . . . During this time he learned the New Testament entirely by heart, in order not to stagnate spiritually."[6] He passed the night standing in prayer and often went without sleep for days at a time. Indeed, his biographer asserts that he spent this whole period of his life without lying down, either by day or night.

John's quest for the solitary life was, however, less than successful. As a notable "holy man," he appears to have been beset with visitors, presumably including both those seeking spiritual advice and those concerned with more secular advantages.[7] Finally, the severity of his life and the harshness of the climate weakened his health and he nearly died. As a result, John was persuaded to return to Antioch, but he never forgot his training in the desert, and he continued his ascetic practices amid the more active ecclesiastical life.

After his return to the city John served the church of Antioch for about five years as deacon. Owing to the nature of this office, which involved the distribution of much of the official charity of the church, he was fully exposed to the needs—and affections—of the urban poor, and it is not unreasonable to suppose that it was then that he developed his remarkable social conscience. In any case, we are told that the poor found contact with John a source of "sweetness amid the bitterness of life."[8] At the end of this service, probably in 386, John was ordained a priest, and he began to preach the sermons which brought him so much fame.

During this period, Chrysostom was witness to the notorious "riot of the statues," and his sermons provide us with an insight into his ideas about the causes and results of such a disturbance.[9] He made no attempt to conceal his disapproval of what had happened and of those whom he considered responsible for it:

> A people (*demos*) so well-ordered and quiet... always obedient to its rulers (*archontes*) has now suddenly turned against us. I mourn and lament now, not because of the greatness of the approaching wrath, but because of the excess of the madness which was shown.... Behold, the crimes were the work of a few, but the indictment is for all. Because of them we all fear and suffer the punishment for their deeds. But if we had seized them and had driven them from the city, and corrected them and healed the sick member, we should not have the present terror. I know the character of the city has always been noble, but certain strangers and men of mixed race, accursed and worthless, heedless of their own salvation, attempt reckless deeds. For this reason I have been crying out and bearing witness, "Let us punish the madness of the blasphemers."[10]

Chrysostom clearly blamed these blasphemers, "strangers and men of mixed race," as the instigators of the violence. He even seems to imply that they had actually organized and led the demonstration. It is tempting to equate these persons with the partisans of the theatre and the hippodrome, and this identification is probably correct.[11] Nevertheless, it is important to note that John stressed their blasphemy and disregard of salvation. Devotees of the "spectacles" might fit this description, but it is even more appropriate of heretics.

> Earlier I told you, "Let us control their spirit and secure their salvation. Even if we should die in the attempt, the action would bring us great gain. Let us not overlook the insult done to our common lord. Ignoring such things will bring some great calamity to our city." These things I foretold and they have come to pass and we are suffering from our inertia. You ignored the insult which was done to God and he has allowed the emperor to be insulted and a great danger to hang over us all as a penalty for our lack of action.... Now, since we are

being chastened by our present calamity, let us finally restrain the disorderly madness of these men.[12]

In the last analysis, John was not primarily concerned with the historical or political aspects of the disturbance, but rather with moral questions. The people of Antioch had not listened to his advice to rid the city of impious individuals who angered God by their sinful behavior or beliefs. Accordingly, they had brought divine displeasure and vengeance upon themselves. When we have occasion to investigate John's attitude toward popular demonstrations, we should remember that in 387 his reaction was largely that of a moralist who categorically deplored the violence which had occurred. He did not even consider the possibility that the demonstrators had some justification for their actions.[13]

While John was performing his priestly duties in Antioch, events were developing in Constantinople which were soon to change his life. Before we consider these, however, it is necessary to examine briefly the episcopacy of Nectarius, Chrysostom's predecessor, for this seriously affected the election of 397 and the reception John was to receive in Constantinople.

Nectarius became bishop in 381 when the Fathers of the Council of Constantinople included his name on a list of candidates they presented to the emperor to succeed Gregory of Nazianzus. To the surprise of all, Theodosius selected Nectarius, even though he was as yet an unbaptized layman.

Perhaps because of his lack of theological training, or because of a genuine desire to avoid difficulties, Nectarius managed to spend sixteen years on the episcopal throne of Constantinople without taking any active role in the pressing ecclesiastical or political issues of his time. Arian insurgents, for example, burned his palace, but when the emperor requested him to prepare a defense against the heretics, he could do no better than to ask the bishop of the Novatians for advice. He allowed accused criminals to remain in ecclesiastical office, and he ignored the request of St. Ambrose that he censure a runaway deacon who had become a bishop in the East.[14] Despite the bishop's inactivity in controversial matters, the power of the see of Constantinople grew, and the religious policy of the government continued successfully under the direction of Theodosius, who may have been quite content to have a silent bishop.[15]

As a result, something approaching religious harmony existed in Constantinople for the first time since the foundation of the city some half-century before. Although the power and the number of the Arians should not be underestimated, the orthodox hierarchy was able to make a substantial recovery from the persecution of the Arian emperors.[16]

The death of Nectarius on September 26, 397, was followed by a particularly hotly contested election, the first to be held since the restoration of orthodoxy. The election of a bishop at any time under the later empire was an event of singular importance, comparable only to the selection of a new emperor, but the situation in 397 was especially volatile after years of Arianism and the weak administration of Nectarius.[17] Furthermore, under Nectarius, we may suppose that a large number of higher clerics (the various officials of the episcopal administration) had been given wide latitude for action. These individuals had tasted episcopal power, and they undoubtedly felt they had demonstrated their executive ability. It is not surprising that many of them sought their own election to the vacant episcopal throne and that some of them confidently expected success in the undertaking.

The situation was further complicated by the growing jealousy of the bishops of Alexandria and their readiness to interfere in the internal affairs of their upstart rivals in Constantinople.[18] The Alexandrian "popes" had been secure in their ecclesiastical leadership of the East so long as an Arian sat on the episcopal throne in Constantinople, but when Theodosius restored the churches to the orthodox and the Council of Constantinople increased the honor of the imperial see, the position of Alexandria was threatened. As early as 380, Peter, the bishop of Alexandria, had interfered in the election of a bishop of Constantinople, and when this strategem failed, Peter's successor, Timothy, led the opposition which resulted in the bishop's resignation.[19] Clearly, Alexandria would be a force to consider in the election of 397.

As soon as the death of Nectarius became known, men of every condition presented themselves as candidates to succeed him: "men who are not men [eunuchs], priests unworthy of their position, some trying to influence the imperial officials, others offering bribes, and still others kneeling in supplication before the people (*demoi*)."[20] Theophilus, the bishop of Alexandria, intervened by nominating Isidore, a priest of his own church, as a candidate.[21]

In the counsels of the emperor Arcadius, where the decision would ultimately be made, opinion was divided among the supporters of various candidates.[22] Meanwhile, groups of people assembled outside the palace and importuned the emperor to select a man experienced in priestly duties.[23] Obviously there was considerable sentiment that the choice be made for other than political reasons.

John had apparently not been under general consideration, but ultimately he was chosen, not it would seem by the emperor, but by the powerful eunuch Eutropius, who was at that time virtual regent for the young Arcadius.[24] Palladius says that Eutropius had met John in Antioch and was impressed by his character and ability,[25] but it is not difficult to read more secular motives into the choice. The eunuch naturally disliked the machinations of Theophilus, and he may have felt that a stranger who had taken no part in the factional politics of the capital and who owed his election to himself might prove a more willing tool in his own manipulation of official matters.[26]

The government was aware of the popularity of John in Antioch, and special arrangements were made to bring him to Constantinople. According to Sozomen, the *comes orientis* who was responsible for this task feared popular uprisings (*staseis*) should the people of Antioch learn what was about to happen.[27] Accordingly, the official devised a plan to convey the unsuspecting priest secretly from his native city to the capital, and on February 26, 398, he became bishop of Constantinople.[28]

Chrysostom as Bishop

Sozomen, who exalted the memory of John, claimed that the laity (*laos*) and the clergy of Constantinople were unanimous in their support of Chrysostom's candidacy and that the emperor only concurred in their preference.[29] To the degree that the laity of Constantinople knew of John's reputation (which is very doubtful), they may have welcomed his election, since he was certainly a man "experienced in priestly duties." However, the intense feelings involved in the election cannot have been quickly suppressed, and no unanimity of support for John was likely, even after the decision of the court was announced.[30] A large number of candidates had been disappointed, and they lacked even the satisfaction of knowing that the ultimate victor came from within their ranks. Instead, the new bishop was a "stranger" brought from the metropolis of Syria.[31] Clearly, the clergy which faced John when he first arrived in Constantinople was already partly hostile to him. Not least of his enemies were the supporters of Theophilus of Alexandria, who cannot have accepted their defeat lightly.

John's first actions as bishop of Constantinople must have caused considerable alarm. Shortly after his consecration, he initiated a thorough reform of the administration of the see. He deprived several clerics of their positions for immoral or even criminal behavior, and he undertook a sweeping campaign against clerical avarice, injustice, and immorality; singled out for particular condemnation were the priests who kept women as "housekeepers" (συνείσακται).[32] Further, he introduced new night vigils and other strenuous forms of public prayer.[33] Naturally not all the clergy were pleased with these reforms, and their wrath was increased by Serapion, John's hotheaded archdeacon, whom many considered the instigator of the disagreeable measures. According to one account, Serapion advised John that "You can rule these people only if you chastize them all with the same whip." The rumor of this spread among the clergy, and Socrates says that much of the abuse earned by Serapion fell upon John.[34]

Further, John reformed the expenditure of the episcopal account. He stopped all spending on onecclesiastical matters and drastically cut the budget of the episcopal residence, eliminating banquets and other lavish entertainments. He used the savings to build and staff hospitals for strangers in the city, but he earned a reputation for being cold and unfriendly toward his ecclesiastical colleagues.[35]

John also found enemies outside the clergy of the city. He was an ardent opponent of heresy and paganism, and the enmity was presumably mutual. On a trip to Asia, he closed the churches belonging to the Quartodecimans and the Novatians,[36] but the Arians were his principal adversaries, and his first sermon after becoming bishop was directed against them.[37] When the Arians organized elaborate nocturnal processions designed to glorify God and to attract the believer through a direct appeal to the senses, John feared the effect on the orthodox, and he countered with processions of his own. He secured imperial assistance for these and, when the efforts of the orthodox surpassed those of the heretics in splendor and popular favor, the Arians reacted with violence. One can easily imagine the scene as the heretics attacked their opponents, and the incense and singing were dispersed by missiles and sticks. Several people were injured on both sides, including a eunuch of the empress who was struck in the head with a stone. As a result of this confrontation the emperor forbade the Arians to hold their nocturnal assemblies, but the processions of the orthodox were so successful that they continued as a regular part of the worship of the church of the capital.[38] The people (*demos*) of Constantinople enjoyed the spectacle of the processions, full of light and music, and they attributed their institution to John. But the Arians, from this point at least, must have regarded the bishop as their bitter enemy, and they may have been ready to support the machinations of his enemies.

We know little of John's direct contact with pagans,[39] but we can be sure that he created many enemies among the monastic community of the capital.[40] Although he praised the monks who remained piously in their desert solitudes, he had nothing but harsh words for those who came to the cities to enjoy the pleasures and benefits of urban life.[41] Naturally, some of the monks who had recently arrived in Constantinople resented this, and Isaac, the leader of the monastic community in the city, became one of the foremost of John's enemies.[42]

In a recent important study, Gilbert Dagron has pointed out the peculiar nature of early Constantinopolitan monasticism.[43] He argues that the movement there was particularly "urban" in form, and that the monks were more concerned with social and economic questions than were their brothers in the desert. Community life was more open, and the monks were used to considerable independence from episcopal authority. Dagron traces the origins of this phenomenon to the period of Arian

The Episcopacy of John Chrysostom 47

domination in Constantinople, and he maintains that this form of monasticism remained strongly Macedonian in sentiment for years to come. Thus, John could expect only growing opposition from the monks of the city. They must have been irritated not only by his weak support of the monastic life, but also by his rigid orthodoxy and his desire to impose tight episcopal control over ecclesiastical institutions and charitable services previously administered independently by the monks themselves.

Thus, John had many enemies. But he also found many devoted admirers; indeed, the popular support which Chrysostom enjoyed is one of the most characteristic features of his episcopacy. In fact, as we shall see, the affection many people felt for the bishop outlasted his official condemnation and deposition and played an important role in the ultimate restoration of his memory.

It is not difficult to propose reasons for the remarkable popularity of the new bishop. In the first place, for all his ferocious morality, John appears to have been kind and understanding and easily accessible to the humble as well as the great. (Indeed, the refusal of John to devote all his time to personages of importance was the cause of much irritation and the source of some of the more serious charges against him.) Further, we should assume that the reforms in the administration of the bishopric—as much as they angered some—pleased many others who had been upset by the lax administration of Nectarius. Clearly, if we are to believe the sources, there had been popular sentiment for a bishop who would act in such a manner at the time of the election of 397.

The content of John's sermons, as well as their style, had an obvious appeal to many of the inhabitants of Constantinople, particularly the poor. He had, of course, been popular in Antioch, and the manner in which his sermons were received in Constantinople provides an interesting measure of his popularity there. When it was known that the bishop would be speaking, people flocked to the church in such numbers that they threatened to crush one another. In order to be heard and to ensure his own safety, John had to place himself in the *bema*.[44] Loud applause frequently interrupted his sermons, and it is interesting that his sermon condemning this practice was itself periodically interrupted by applause.[45] On one occasion, he disappointed the crowd by allowing a guest to preach instead of himself; everyone in the church cried out in disappointment, and many simply walked out of the building.[46] John attracted not only the ordinarily pious members of society; he also found support among the more disreputable elements, and "even the lovers of the hippodrome and the theatre left the courtyards of the devil" and attended his sermons.

We should not assume that brilliant oratory appealed only to the highly educated. They alone might have appreciated an obscure classical reference or a subtle rhetorical maneuver, but this was an era in which eloquence was generally respected and oratorical ability won praise of a more popular sort.[47] We have already seen how the sermons of John attracted large and enthusiastic crowds, and Socrates specifically states that much of his popularity was a result of the people's (*laos*) love of his oratory.

> John gained the support of the people (*plethos*) because he openly condemned wrongdoers in the church and complained strongly against the unjust, as though he himself had been injured. This was pleasing to the majority of the people (*polloi*), but it angered the wealthy and the powerful, who are in any case guilty of the greater part of the crimes committed.[48]

Fortunately, the practice of transcribing the sermons of great ecclesiastical orators has preserved the texts of many of John's sermons, and we are able to read the passages which appealed to the crowds which packed the church whenever the bishop spoke. Some of these are deeply moving, and they provide a clear example of Chrysostom's social consciousness. Perhaps the most evocative of these was inspired by what the bishop saw on a cold winter morning. He began the sermon:

> I come to you today as an ambassador from the poor of the city, not because of the decrees or speeches, but because I have seen their terrible sufferings. . . . It is right to speak of mercy at any time, but especially now, when such great cold prevails, when no one can find work, nor spend the night in the open. . . . Many people examine the poor man closely before giving him anything: where he comes from, how he lives. . . . why isn't he working even though he is strong enough. . . Thus, many of the poor mutilate themselves, hoping to melt your hard hearts. But some of you complain that the poor are only deserters, foreigners, and good-for-nothings, people who run away from their homes, and pour into the city. But it is an honor for us if all the poor people expect help and safety from us. . . . Whether they are worthy or not you will be rewarded just the same.[49]

On another occasion, he discussed the different treatment which was, in fact, accorded the rich and the poor. He objected that such a distinction should not be made among Christians, all of whom were equal in the sight of God.

> In the church I accept no vain striving for position, but preach to all alike . . . for He who calls all alike does not allow one to be puffed up by pride while another is crushed under foot[50]

Finally, in the following words, one can feel John's outraged sense of justice as he thundered from the pulpit of the cathedral:

> "Let the moth eat, but do not let the poor eat; let the worm devour, but do not clothe the naked; let all perish with time, but do not allow Christ to be fed when he lacks these things." "Who says this?" it will be asked. But it is terrible to relate that it is said with deeds rather than with words. . . . And do you not fear that a thunderbolt from heaven will fall on you as a result of these words! Excuse me, for I am bursting with anger. . . . You demand a strict accounting

from the poor and miserable, who are nearly dead, but do you not fear the terrible tribunal of Christ?[51]

Beyond this thorough accusation and condemnation of the rich, Chrysostom's sermons contained other attractions for the downtrodden among his audience. While he pointed out the injustices of this world, the bishop also promised the certainty of redress in the world to come. The poor inhabitants of Constantinople must certainly have found consolation in John's frequent assertion that their future life would be as happy as their present life was wretched.[52]

Nevertheless, Chrysostom's purpose was clearly not to encourage antagonism between the rich and the poor, but to promote moral reform. He was in no sense a revolutionary or demagogue, and the references to the crimes of the rich (which may have delighted the poor) were directed solely at the rich themselves in an attempt to produce a change in their behavior. They were not intended to produce a hatred of the wealthy. On the other hand, many of the things John said in his sermons cannot have pleased all of the poor. He continually complained, for example, that the people of Constantinople, while they were willing to fill the church to hear him speak, rarely put into practice the essentials of what he taught them. In particular, he complained that they paid little attention to his condemnation of the spectacles. These institutions—the hippodrome and the theatre which Chrysostom considered so detrimental to Christian morality—were, according to all sources, passionately supported by the inhabitants of all the great cities of the empire, the poor even more than the rich.[53] Chrysostom's attitude toward the spectacles may have alienated some of his potential supporters, especially those closely connected with the theatre or the racecourse (for example, *factionarii*, charioteers, actors), and one can only wonder at the power of John's oratory that even some of these people found their way to the church to hear him speak!

We must, however, not ascribe John's popularity only to the content and style of his sermons and his general concern for social justice. His manner of life also contributed to his reputation. As we have seen, John was an ascetic, and he brought his strict religious exercises with him to the episcopal residence of the capital. It was true that he was now a bishop and had many worldly concerns, but the severity of his past and present life set him apart from contemporaries. He was, in fact, a "holy man" in the midst of an urban setting.

We have already briefly examined the importance of the holy man in chapter 2. As a person with a special relationship to God, the holy man could be expected to intervene in any number of spiritual and secular concerns, and he became a patron with extraordinary powers. As a bishop, of course, Chrysostom could also act as a more traditional patron. His concern for charity and his control of the wealth of the church, as well as his opportunity to approach the emperor and members of his court, made Chrysostom a man of considerable importance. Indeed, the fact that a bishop was an ascetic would only serve to increase his effectiveness as a traditional patron. Ascetics were often on familiar terms with the powerful of the world, and no one could think that an ascetic who owned little or no personal property would seek a favor for personal gain. This removal of the ascetic from the normal rules of society—which, it must be remembered, involved constant and severe personal mortification—further enhanced his efficaciousness as a negotiator among equals, since all could turn to him as a person removed from ordinary ties, and even from ordinary passions.[54]

As with so many other aspects of this study, I can never hope to give a definitive explanation of Chrysostom's remarkable popularity among the inhabitants of Constantinople; each individual undoubtedly had his or her own personal attitude toward the bishop, and the sources only provide a dim reflection of these. Nevertheless, there were many aspects of Chrysostom's life and personality which might reasonably have been attractive to many people, and the sources, even those hostile to him, are united in their description of the extraordinary affection with which the bishop was regarded. His enemies, who had never reconciled themselves to John's election, would clearly have to take this popular support into consideration as they schemed against him.

In fact, Socrates reported that at an early date John's opponents made some public accusations against him in hopes of diminishing his popular following. Unfortunately, we have few details of this maneuver; presumably they condemned his supposedly antisocial behavior in one or more sermons. "The faithful, however, applauded vehemently and loved the man [Chrysostom] because of what he had said in the church, and they paid little attention to those who had accused him."[55]

The Council of the Oak and First Exile

Meanwhile as John continued to "correct the rich and teach them humility," conflict developed between the bishop's erstwhile patron Eutropius and the powerful barbarian general Gainas. The exact course of events is unclear, but Gainas ultimately secured the disgrace and death of the eunuch, and by the end of 399 he "was master of the government of the east."[56] Opposition to growing Germanic dominance of the city began to develop, however, and Gainas was forced to chance everything in a desperate attempt to seize the government by force. This was a failure, as a great tumult (*thorybos*) arose in the city, and all the inhabitants began to assail the barbarians with whatever weapons were at hand.[57] Only seven thousand Germans survived the onslaught, and these sought sanctuary in the church which had been provided for their worship. The emperor rejected their plea for mercy and sent soldiers to the church. They set fire to the building and burned the barbarians alive.[58]

Chrysostom played only a secondary role in these events, but his action revealed his ability to rise above the divisions of party or faction to appeal directly to men of different persuasions.[59] Thus, when the fall of Eutropius was imminent and the eunuch fled to the church for sanctuary, John delivered two sermons at the unfortunate man's expense, pointing out the vanity and uselessness of riches and power. Ultimately he did, however, make an unsuccessful attempt to save Eutropius' life.[60] Later, when Gainas demanded that the Arian Goths be given a church within the city, John persuaded Arcadius not to yield to the threats of the heretics. But he did provide for the worship of the orthodox Goths by giving them a church near the imperial palace and ordaining priests who were proficient in their language. Finally, when the barbarians were besieging the capital, John is reported to have gone, "by universal desire," to the camp of the Goths in an attempt to conciliate Gainas.[61]

Throughout these difficult events, John maintained a position of strict morality and orthodoxy; politics or party feelings apparently played no part in his actions. However, what may most have impressed the people of Constantinople, both rich and poor alike, was John's opposition to Gainas and his Arian Goths. Clearly, there was considerable unanimity of feeling on this question, and John's actions are likely to have increased the esteem in which the bishop was held. As we have seen, the rich are unlikely to have been generally pleased by John's outspoken attacks on their greed and callousness. His action in opposing Gainas, and making a spectacle of Eutropius, however, may have won him some support among the wealthy and members of the court, who were the greatest enemies of both men.

From these complicated developments the empress, Eudoxia, emerged as the most important person in the palace. Unfortunately, John soon earned her enmity, probably through some undiplomatic reference to her greed and love of luxury.[62] The animosity of the empress gave Theophilus of Alexandria the opportunity for which he had been waiting and John's reception of the so-called Tall Brothers, Egyptian monks accused of Origenism, provided an occasion to unite the bishop's enemies in an attempt to rid the church of his domination.[63]

The main points of their plan are clear. Theophilus and his supporters in Constantinople maintained that Chrysostom had behaved arrogantly and even violently, especially toward church property and the clergy. By his reception and defense of the Tall Brothers, moreover, he had implicated himself in the heresy of Origen and interfered unlawfully in the affairs of another bishop. This campaign was directed primarily toward important members of the court and the bishops who would eventually judge the case, and most of the individual accusations and the methods of persuasion demonstrate this design.[64] Yet, we should remember that John's opponents had earlier tried to discredit him in the eyes of the people of Constantinople, and the visit of Epiphanius to the capital shows that another attempt was made at this time.

Epiphanius, bishop of Salamis (in Cyprus), was a famous opponent of all heresy, especially Origenism. When the affair of the Tall Brothers began, Theophilus, although he had formerly defended Origen, took care to have the heresy condemned at an Alexandrian synod and encouraged other bishops to do the same. Epiphanius, pleased at his colleague's change of heart, gladly complied and agreed to Theophilus' suggestion that he go himself to Constantinople, since the bishop of that city had become tainted with heresy.[65]

When Epiphanius arrived in Constantinople, he refused to have any dealings with John, implying that he already considered him guilty of heresy. Armed with earlier condemnations of Origenism, he assembled the bishops who happened to be in the city and inveighed against John, apparently without success. Finally, Chrysostom's enemies decided that on the next Sunday, when all the people were assembled in the church of the Holy Apostles, Epiphanius would publicly condemn Origen and the Tall Brothers. They hoped that, by association, John would lose prestige with the crowd (ᾤοντο γὰρ οὕτως συγκρούσειν αὐτὸν πρὸς τὸ πλῆθος).[66] Obviously, this popular support was of some concern to Chrysostom's enemies. John, however, learned of this plan and sent Serapion to intercept Epiphanius just as he was about to enter the church. The deacon advised the bishop not to carry out his plan, for he would surely be held responsible for any disturbance which resulted (εἰ ταραχῆς ἐν τῷ πλήθει ἢ στάσεως κινηθείσης αὐτὸς κινδυνεύσει ὡς αἴτιος γεγονώς).[67] Whether this meant that the authorities would hold Epiphanius responsible for a division of opinion among the people and resulting violence, or that the people themselves would take offense and attack Epiphanius, we cannot be certain. In either case, it is clear that Serapion and (as it turned out) Epiphanius realized that the condemnation of the Tall Brothers would be regarded by the crowd (*plethos*) as an attack on Chrysostom, and that this would lead to a riot, probably with violence.[68] We can only add that Epiphanius heeded the advice of Serapion; he made no further attacks on Chrysostom and soon left the city altogether.[69]

Theophilus, of course, did not abandon his designs so easily. Soon after the departure of Epiphanius, he arrived in Constantinople, armed with bribes and fortified by a company of Egyptian bishops (even though the emperor had requested his presence alone). None of the clergy of the city was waiting for the Alexandrian "pope" when his ship landed, but a great throng of Egyptian sailors enthusiastically greeted their bishop.[70] From the harbor, Theophilus went directly to his lodgings, deliberately ignoring the customary visit to the great church and the episcopal residence of the city.[71] He spent the next three weeks preparing his case against John, securing false accusations and bribing important people. Chrysostom tells us that his adversary was so successful—or at least confident—that he acted as though all the clergy were won over to his side and the church were already without a bishop.[72] Throughout this time, there is no evidence that Theophilus again attempted to secure the support or even the neutrality of John's numerous nonclerical supporters.

Finally, early in 403, all was ready and Theophilus summoned a number of previously selected bishops to attend the gathering known as the Council of the Oak.[73] This synod assembled at the residence-monastery of Rufinus, the former praetorian prefect, in the vicinity of Chalcedon. The property belonged to the state, and its use by the enemies of Chrysostom indicated that opinion at the court had turned against the bishop.

Realizing what the outcome of the council would be, John refused to answer the summons sent him. He replied that he would appear only before a larger council which was not dominated by those openly plotting his deposition. In Chrysostom's absence, his enemies proceeded to accuse him of various crimes, ranging from the illegal sale of church property to gluttony. The abbot Isaac unwittingly provided evidence of the popular mood during the council by charging that John "encouraged the faithful to revolt against the synod" (τοῖς λαοῖς ὑποβάλλει στασιάζειν κατὰ τῆς συνόδου).[74] Nevertheless, no mention was made of the charge of heresy, and Theophilus even went so far as a public reconciliation with the Tall Brothers. The bishops unanimously declared John deposed from his episcopal position—not for any of the crimes mentioned by his accusers, but simply because he had failed to answer the summons of the council. The bishops sent the emperor a notice of the deposition and added a plea that John be declared guilty of treason as well (presumably for insulting Eudoxia). Arcadius willingly agreed to this.[75]

What happened next might easily have been predicted. John's popularity was well-known, as the incident involving Epiphanius clearly showed, and his supporters were obviously upset by the proceedings of the council, the only explanation which would give any credence to Isaac's charges that the bishop had stirred up the people to revolt. As Sozomen described the scene:

> When the people (*plethos*) of Constantinople learned of these things it was toward evening; they immediately rose up in sedition (*stasis*). At day-break they assembled hurriedly at the church [Hagia Sophia] and, among other

54 *Vox Populi*

things, they shouted that a greater council should be called to judge him. The emperor sent men to carry John away into exile, but the crowd would not let them pass.

There was a standoff and violence seemed likely, but the confrontation was avoided by the action of John himself, for he

> feared that another accusation might be made against him—either that he disobeyed the command of the emperor or that he incited the people (*demos*) to riot. Accordingly, on the third day after his deposition, at about noon, he slipped out of the church, eluding the distraught people.[76]

The account of Palladius contains a letter supposedly written by John to Pope Innocent describing, among other things, the events surrounding his first exile.[77] In detail, this letter differs considerably from the account of Sozomen, but it agrees that there was grave concern among John's supporters as soon as the sentence of deposition was known and that some of these supporters expressed their concern with action:

> Late at night, when all the people (*demos*) were following me, I was seized by the urban *curiosus* in the middle of the city. I was led away by force to the harbor, put in a boat, and we set sail that night; and all this while I was in the process of calling a synod for a just trial.[78]

If the condemnation of Chrysostom led to popular demonstrations in his favor, the bishop's exile led to even more serious disturbances:

> When he had gone into exile, the faithful rose in violent revolt (χαλεπῶς ὁ λαὸς ἐστασίαζε). And they heaped abuse on the emperor, the synod, and especially on Theophilus and Severianus, whom they regarded as the instigators of the plot.[79]

Severianus, the bishop of Gabala, who had been one of Theophilus's most important allies, happened to be giving a sermon at the time of the disturbance. He took the occasion to praise the sentence against John, saying that at least he was guilty of the sin of pride. This set off the final episode. In the account of Sozomen:

> These words angered the people (*plethos*) and the disturbance became completely uncontrollable. They could not be kept quiet in the churches and market places, and they carried their lamentation and complaint for the return of John even to the palace of the emperor.

There the supporters of John finally received some satisfaction:

> Yielding to the petitions of the people (εἴξασα δὲ ταῖς ἱκεσίαις τοῦ δήμου), the empress persuaded her husband to agree. Quickly she sent her trusted eunuch to bring John back... maintaining that she had taken no part in the machinations against him.[80]

Socrates added to this account the information that "many" (*polloi*)—

The Episcopacy of John Chrysostom 55

he does not identify them further—who had previously called for John's deposition now considered him wronged and joined the others in demanding his return. He says also that the anger of the crowd intensified when it learned that Theophilus had abandoned the charge of Origenism and had been reconciled with the Tall Brothers. Socrates agreed with Sozomen that the petitions of the people brought about the recall of John, but he claimed that it was the emperor who was persuaded, rather than the empress.[81]

Theodoret, on the other hand, reported that an earthquake shook the palace during the night of John's exile. Eudoxia regarded this as a sign of God's displeasure and, fearing worse calamities, recalled the bishop as soon as morning arrived.[82] Palladius wrote only that "a certain disturbance (θραῦσιν) occurred in the bedroom," and that this caused so much alarm in the palace that messages were dispatched a few days later to return John to the capital.[83] What this "disturbance" may have been is difficult to say; the term could be used to describe an earthquake, and it could conceivably refer to the empress' reaction to the demonstration outside the palace. Baur, however, suggested that Eudoxia suffered a miscarriage.[84] It is possible, of course, that two or more events combined to change the minds of the court. Eudoxia may have suffered a miscarriage, but in such a case the petitions of the turbulent crowd outside her window must have contributed to her distress.

In fact, the emperor and the empress may not have been firmly committed to John's disgrace. It is possible that they sent him only a short distance from Constantinople in order to test the immediate reaction to his exile—either on the part of God or the people of the city. When this was ascertained, they quickly dispatched messages to recall the bishop.

According to the sources we have examined, those involved in the disturbances following John's deposition understood the situation, and they articulated their demands clearly. They placed the blame for the bishop's exile squarely on the shoulders of those they thought responsible, and they made clear to the emperor and the empress that they would be satisfied only by his return. We hear of no leaders among the crowd, and the sources imply that the demonstrations developed spontaneously; nevertheless, the clarity of the petitions presented to the emperor suggest some kind of leadership. Furthermore, it is interesting to find that the crowd demanded that a greater council should be called to judge the case, something echoed in John's own letter to Pope Innocent. Finally, we are not told how the crowd presented its petitions, but we should suspect some kind of chanting or coordinated shouting: otherwise the points would have been lost in the general confusion of different voices.[85] Unfortunately, the sources tell us nothing about the social composition of the crowds or about their numbers. If we accept the account of Sozomen, however, we must assume that the active supporters of John were fairly numerous, for they were able to withstand for three days the efforts of the emperor to remove John from the church by force.

It would seem that the demonstrations which immediately followed the exile of Chrysostom were serious and noisy, but that no violence or the destruction of property actually resulted. In part this was because the emperor's men—presumably soldiers—who were sent to carry out the sentence apparently did not attack the crowd. The sudden disappearance of John, however, and, most importantly, the willingness of the court to acquiesce in the demand of the demonstrators were undoubtedly crucial in calming the situation.

Considerable time elapsed between the decision to recall the bishop and his actual return to the city.[86] In large measure, this was because of John's own hesitation about taking up his episcopal duties while he was, formally at least, still deposed. During this time, tension grew in the city and tempers occasionally flared. A particularly striking example of this is provided by Zosimus. After telling of John's voluntary exile, he added that

> the people (*plethos*) were disturbed by this [his exile], for the man was a great leader of the unreasonable mob (ἦν γὰρ ὁ ἄνθρωπος ἄλογον ὄχλον ὑπαγαγέσθαι δεινός), and the city was filled with disturbances. The church of the Christians [Hagia Sophia] was seized by those who are called monks. ... Laying hold of the churches, these men prevented the people (*plethe*) from entering for their accustomed prayers. This angered both the people (δημοτικοί) and the soldiers, and together they demanded authority to put an end to the audacity of the monks. On a given signal they attacked without restraint and continued the slaughter until the church was full of corpses. Those who ran away were pursued and anyone who happened to be wearing dark clothing was cut down.[87]

The situation can easily be imagined. The monks of Constantinople, under the leadership of Isaac, dismayed by the decision to restore the bishop, seized the churches and prevented the followers of Chrysostom (whom Zosimus identifies as *ta plethe*) from meeting for prayer. The latter, undoubtedly exhilarated by their recent success, finally became impatient and joined with the soldiers—sent by a court temporarily friendly toward them—in the attack on the monks.[88]

These events show how far enmity had developed between the supporters of John and the monastic community. They also reveal how fine the line might be between a peaceful demonstration and acts of violence and even bloodshed. Moreover, once a beginning of violence had been made, it might be difficult to contain. We should perhaps connect another incident with this attack on the church.

After the decision had been made to restore Chrysostom, Theophilus wished to prepare a counterstroke. He did not dare to attack the bishop openly fearing a court which was then favorable to John.[89] Instead, the Egyptian chose to discredit Chrysostom by making accusations against Heraclides, his former deacon who was then bishop of Ephesus.[90] A dispute arose over the legality of Theophilus' charges, since Heraclides was not present to defend himself, and the two parties quickly came to blows:

> Becoming very angry, the company of those Alexandrians and Egyptians who remained [in the city] and the faithful of Constantinople attacked one another, so that many were wounded and some killed.[91]

Apparently the people of Constantinople had rather the better of the battle, for the bishops who had opposed John became fearful and fled the city. Theophilus, too, took ship for Alexandria, accompanied by Isaac, the leader of the monastic community. Palladius summed up this incident simply and added a graphic detail saying that "Theophilus and the Egyptians sought safety in flight, for the populace (*polis*) wished to drown him in the sea!"[92]

In the account of the battle between the Egyptians and the people of Constantinople, it is perhaps natural to assume that the Egyptians were the bishops who had accompanied Theophilus to the Council of the Oak. In this case, however, one would have expected Sozomen to remark on the spectacle of bishops giving and receiving wounds. In any case, the bishops of Egypt, regardless of how many of them had come along, would hardly have been a match for the populace of Constantinople. Although Theophilus and his colleagues obviously did not consider themselves exempt from bodily harm, it is probable that the bulk of the actual fighting was carried on by less exalted personages. To judge by the practice of his successors, it is likely that Theophilus brought a band of roughnecks with him to Constantinople. Further, we know that at just this time large numbers of Egyptian sailors were in Constantinople, and they had already on another occasion demonstrated their support of Theophilus.[93] As the events showed, even these willing allies of the bishop of Alexandria were not able to prevent the recall of Chrysostom, but we should not forget that behind the scenes, on the docks and in the streets and churches of Constantinople itself, the agents of Alexandria were constantly at work.

As John slowly made his way back to the city, the sea was filled with boats carrying great numbers of the faithful who had come, bearing lighted torches, to welcome their bishop's return.[94] A party of thirty bishops—supposedly loyal to Chrysostom—headed the jubilant party, which landed at Marinanae, a village just outside Constantinople.[95] There John stopped, refusing to go farther until another council should annul the sentence against him. But "the faithful (*laos*) were annoyed by this and when they began to insult the court he was forced to enter [the city]. The people (*demos*) then came to greet him and, singing psalms and bearing lighted candles, they led him to the church." Here again John hesitated, but "they forced him to give the greeting of peace to the faithful and sit upon the episcopal throne."⁹⁶

Chrysostom then delivered an extemporaneous sermon which began with a comparison between Theophilus and his Pharaonic predecessors:

> Those things happened then to Abraham, but today they happened to the church: pharaoh had his shieldbearers, while Theophilus had his spearbearers.⁹⁷

The main theme of the sermon was, however, the loyalty of the people of Constantinople: "We prayed and they fled; you have stood firm as a rock." Significantly, John felt that the support of the people had caused the empress to change her mind and order his recall: "You have secured the cooperation of the empress. . . . As someone concerned for her child, she went about everywhere, not of course in person, but through her personal bodyguard." "But what shall I call you: sheep or shepherds? governors or soldiers and generals?" The people had clearly taken the initiative and provided the moral leadership which had been lacking. But John was careful in his praise for the actions of the crowd. He had earlier in the sermon condemned Theophilus for violence, and he did not want the same charge to apply to his own followers.⁹⁸ "I say these things not to lead you into insurrection; for theirs is the insurrection, while yours is zeal." According to both Socrates and Sozomen, the sermon was well received by the people, who continuously interrupted it with loud applause.⁹⁹

Second Exile and Schism

After his return from exile, John was even more popular with the faithful.¹⁰⁰ Sixty bishops assembled in Constantinople and annulled the decrees of the Council of the Oak.¹⁰¹ The old enemies of John were still powerful, however, and they soon began to win the support of the court, again probably because of John's undiplomatic remarks about the activities of the empress.¹⁰² Seemingly at a loss as to how to proceed against the bishop, these men once again turned to Theophilus, telling him that he could advise them from a distance if he feared the people of Constantinople. Remembering his recent hasty departure (εἰδὼς ὅπως διέφυγεν), Theophilus answered that he would indeed rather remain in Egypt. He did send along, however, three of his own bishops and suggested that John's enemies refer to a canon which forbade the appeal of an ecclesiastical sentence to the secular power—which, they could claim, John had done.¹⁰³

The events of the next few months are extremely difficult to reconstruct, and even their chronological sequence is far from certain. Only the broad outlines may be described with confidence. This whole period, from Chrysostom's return to Constantinople to his second exile, was characterized by a curious conflict and lack of resolution within the court itself. On the one side was the uncompromising hostility of John's enemies—apparently including the empress herself—who would accept nothing less than the final deposition and exile of the bishop. On the other hand there was fear lest this act again be followed by catastrophe, perhaps in the form of popular sedition. The emperor himself hesitated, and he was persuaded to agree to the condemnation of John only by degrees.

Within a month or two after John's return, another council assembled in an attempt to declare Chrysostom deposed by virtue of the canon mentioned above. But this synod was unable to achieve its purpose because of the strength of John's episcopal supporters and the uncertainty of the emperor and his court.[104] Around Christmas of 403, Leontius of Ancyra and Acacius of Beroea, who had fled the city after the Council of the Oak, felt safe enough to return to Constantinople. Their encouragement of the emperor was not without effect, and Arcadius refused to hold further communion with John.[105] The stalemate continued through a tense Lent; the clergy hostile to John continued to strengthen the resolve of the court, and Chrysostom met with some forty-two bishops who supported him. Throughout these difficulties, we are told, the faithful (*laos*) continued to enjoy his sermons.[106]

Finally, not long before Easter of 404, John's enemies further gained the confidence of Arcadius. They appear to have done this by suggesting that the bishop be encouraged to leave the city voluntarily. This was a compromise which would suit the weak emperor: neither John's followers nor God could be angry with the emperor, and there would be no dispute concerning his successor's election. Any further reluctance to act on the part of the emperor was overcome by the assertion that John was already regarded as a heretic by the populace of the city; almost no one supported him, his adversaries claimed.[107]

The approaching feast of Easter was suggested as the best time to force John to "resign" from his position.[108] Arcadius wrote simply to the bishop "Leave the church!" (ἔξελθε ἐκ τῆς ἐκκλησίας). But John refused, saying that he would not go voluntarily. Accordingly, an official was dispatched to remove John to the episcopal residence and confine him there. This was probably done in an attempt to intimidate John into resigning, but it reminds one of the other half-measures taken by the court in the affair. The imprisonment of the bishop would test popular reaction and determine whether another exile would incur the wrath of God.[103]

As Holy Week drew to a close, Arcadius sent John another message, again demanding that he leave the church—here obviously meaning that he should leave the city. John refused, as before, and the emperor was thrown into confusion; he wished John to be out of the city by Easter, but he did not want to defile the holiday with violence, and the city was already in turmoil as a result of John's imprisonment.[110] Hurriedly, Arcadius consulted with Antiochus of Ptolemais and others who opposed

John. They reassured the emperor and comforted his conscience by offering to take all the responsibility for John's deposition upon themselves. Matters had clearly come to a head, and all the city awaited the violence which seemed certain to follow. Forty of John's followers approached the empress and begged that the holy festival not be dishonored by bloodshed.[111]

Throughout this period, Chrysostom's enemies continued their attempt to convince the court that John had lost his popular support, although they apparently did nothing to reduce that popularity. Thus, just before Easter they closed the churches to all of John's clerical supporters, hoping that the faithful would assemble as usual, even though the clergy they found in the churches would be universally hostile to John. Instead of this, however, John's followers, under the leadership of the clergy loyal to him, gathered to celebrate the Resurrection in the Baths of Constantius.[112]

The enemies of John had been watchful, however, and by means of their spies they learned of this assembly. A group of bishops begged the *magister officiorum* to disperse the gathering lest the emperor find the church empty and learn of John's popularity.[113] The magistrate refused at first, saying that it was night; because of the size of the crowd, something unexpected might happen. Finally, he unwillingly ordered a certain Lucius, reputed to be a pagan, to go to the Baths.[114] He was to command the faithful to disperse and proceed to the church, but he was not to resort to violence. The supporters of John refused to obey his command, and Lucius returned to the bishops—not, significantly, to the *magister officiorum*. They persuaded Lucius, by holding out the promise of promotion, to agree to use whatever force was necessary to prevent the festival from being celebrated outside the church.

> He set off immediately, in the second watch of the night, accompanied by the clergy of the party of Acacius.... He had with him four hundred newly-enlisted Thracian swordsmen, completely reckless individuals. With them and with the clergy as guides, he eagerly attacked the crowd (*ochloi*). With his flashing sword he cut his way through to the blessed waters. He prevented the celebration of the Savior's resurrection and, seizing the deacons, he poured out the sacramental elements. Priests, already advanced in age, he beat about the head with clubs, and the font was stained with blood.... Women ran away naked at the sides of their husbands, forgetting their shame in fear of murder or dishonor. Here a man flees, crying and with a wounded hand, there another drags off a virgin, tearing off her clothes as he goes. They are all carrying away the booty they have collected.[115]

The supporters of John apparently made no attempt to resist the uncontrolled violence of the soldiers. They were unprepared for the attack, and they could only flee in disarray. The choice of Lucius by the *magister officiorum* may have been purely arbitrary or necessitated by his rank as tribune, but it was perhaps not accidental that a pagan held such a position in a city torn by feuds among Christians. Further, the soldiers used in the attack were undoubtedly also pagans who enjoyed the discomfiture of Christians: they were from outside Constantinople and thus had no ties or loyalties to individuals or groups within the city. Perhaps many of the soldiers who had been stationed in and around Constantinople for some time had become supporters of Chrysostom, and their use in this particular mission would not have been practical.

The clergy seized during the attack were imprisoned and the officers among the faithful (ἀξιωματικοὶ τοῦ λαοῦ) expelled from the city.[116] As news of the incident spread throughout the city, many people joined in the lamentation; even heretics, Jews, and pagans are said to have sympathized with the injured.[117]

The next day the supporters of John—who from this time were called Johannites—assembled outside the city in the area called the Pempton, there to celebrate Easter Sunday. The emperor, on an early morning ride, chanced upon them and was amazed by the large number of newly baptized, supposedly about 3,000. John's enemies, who were accompanying the emperor, were quick to assure him that they were heretics and sent the most reckless of their company to disperse the assembly. The newly baptized, "instructed in peace by John," did not resist, and many of the clergy and laity were arrested, including the wives of distinguished men (ἀνδρῶν ἐπισήμων).[118]

In all this confusion and violence, the attempt to remove John from his see had failed, although he remained a virtual prisoner in the episcopal residence, and his followers had openly broken with the other ecclesiastical authorities. A new stalemate had been reached, but tension was in the air, and the dispute spread beyond Constantinople.[119] Further, at least two attempts were made on John's life. A voluntary guard formed to protect the bishop thwarted these, but two passers-by were killed in the melée. The officials, meanwhile, took no measures to protect the life of John until forced to do so by the public outcry against his continual harrassment.[120]

For two months, Chrysostom remained in the episcopal palace, and during this time the emperor must surely have become aware of the support which he continued to enjoy among the inhabitants of the city. Nevertheless, just after Pentecost, John's enemies again approached Arcadius and reiterated their willingness to take full responsibility for the bishop's expulsion. At this time, they also advanced the argument which was at last to end the indecision of the emperor. They claimed that John was the cause of the popular unrest which had been disturbing the city. This would not end, they argued, unless John were expelled from the city.[121]

Persuaded by this, the emperor sent a *notarius* with a message to John telling him again to prepare to leave. Meanwhile a "certain pious influential man"—that is, a friend of John's at court—informed the bishop that Lucius, the tribune, was with his soldiers at the public bath—perhaps the Baths of Zeuxippos—waiting to drag him from the church by force. He further advised John to slip away unnoticed so that the people (*demoi*) would not come into conflict with the soldiers. John realized that the long period of uncertainty had ended, and he made his preparations. He bade farewell to the deaconnesses and had them hidden from the crowds outside—who were still guarding him from violence—so that their discomfiture would not betray his departure. He then escaped the notice of the crowd and went voluntarily into exile.[122]

Profiting from their earlier experience, John's enemies realized the danger of the hostile popular mood, and they made the first move against his supporters, probably even before it was generally known that John had departed the city. Palladius reported that as soon as John left the church, soldiers rushed upon it and, amid the cheers of Jews and pagans, they cruelly beat many people.[123] Sozomen, moreover, says specifically that John's enemies feared that the faithful (*laos*) would "go forward and try to bring John back again by force."[124] Accordingly, they locked the doors of Hagia Sophia, where many of John's supporters were kept immobilized.

When John's departure was discovered, the news spread quickly throughout the city. Everywhere people feared that a general persecution of the Johannites would follow. A great panic seized the populace, and many tried to reach the sea and flee the city in boats. Meanwhile, those inside Hagia Sophia were at first unable to force their way out of the building, since they all rushed toward the exits and threw themselves against the doors, which opened inward. Finally some of the stone work around the doors broke loose, and those within escaped. But just at this time, the church suddenly broke into flame.[125]

The conflagration raged the whole of the night following John's expulsion, and it was extinguished the next day only after it had completely destroyed the great church of Constantinople, the Senate house, and many nearby buildings. In the view of Palladius, the fire was an act of God, divine retribution against the enemies of Chrysostom.[126] Some of the Johannites, however, accused their enemies of setting the fire in an attempt to burn them at the same time.[127] It is not impossible that the opponents of the Johannites thought of such an expedient; the supporters of John were trapped in the church, and a similar example had occurred only four years earlier in the burning of the Gothic church.

Nevertheless, the weight of the ancient testimony suggests that it was the Johannites themselves who started the fire. According to Zosimus, the purpose of the Johannites was not simply to burn the church, but to destroy the city as a whole:

Disturbed at this [John's exile] and resolved that no one would succeed him as bishop of the city, they decided to destroy the city by fire. In this way they secretly set fire to the church at night.[128]

These are the feelings of desperate men: if John was not bishop, there would be no more church and no more city! One is reminded of the actions of certain heretical groups when faced with condemnation and the destruction or conversion of their churches: they gathered solemnly in their religious buildings, set fire to them, and burned themselves to death.[129] In this connection, we should remember that the fire began just as, or possibly before the doors of Hagia Sophia were forced. Perhaps the more extreme among the Johannites planned their own martyrdom.

After describing the exile of John, the Paschal Chronicle reports that:

Suddenly the great church burned, together with the Senate house. The fire was set by the so-called Xylokerketes, who had seized it. . . .[130]

Fortunately, we can identify these mysterious Xylokerketes, or "wooden circus people," since the followers of Chrysostom, after they had been driven from the Baths of Constantius, assembled in the area of the old wooden hippodrome built by Constantine outside the walls of the city.[131] Thus, from this evidence, we are once again to assume that the Johannites —or at least a part of them—were responsible for the fire. Indeed, there is some reason to think that the fire was set by a small group of the Johannites, perhaps carrying out a coordinated plan. In explaining his story of the supernatural origin of the fire, Palladius stated that the blaze broke out in the Senate house on the side *away* from the church, while Socrates said that the fire started in that building because there was a strong wind from the east. If we accept the testimony of Palladius, it is difficult to see how a windborne fire could have sprung up on the far side of the building. Further, no modern reconstruction of this area places the Senate house to the west of Hagia Sophia;[132] if the wind were coming from the east the flames would have spread inland toward the center of the city and away from the Senate. The conclusion seems to be that the fire was set simultaneously at several different points.

Later, when the confusion had subsided, Optatus, the *praefectus urbi* and a pagan who delighted in the difficulties of the Christians, accused some of the leaders of the Johannites of setting the fire. Nevertheless, despite his frequent resort to violent means, he was unable to secure a single confession or conviction.[133] Finally the attempt was abandoned, and an imperial edict ordered the inquiry closed.[134] The failure of the investigation might suggest that the Johannites were innocent of any crime in the matter of the fire, but it may just as well show that the emperor's men simply questioned the wrong individuals.[135] If those who set the fire comprised a small, possibly even separate group—perhaps the Xylokerketes as opposed to the Johannites as a whole—they might all

64 *Vox Populi*

have perished in the conflagration. In any case, we may assume that the peace-loving clerics who led the Johannites probably told the truth when they answered that they knew nothing about the origin of the fire.

The Aftermath

Immediately after John's second expulsion, his enemies made a concerted attempt to divide his supporters and to induce them to accept new leadership. Many of the clergy loyal to John were arrested and exiled, and the methods used in the investigation of the fire served to deplete the number of John's most loyal supporters. Further, only five days after John left the city, Arsacius, the aged brother of Chrysostom's predecessor Nectarius, was consecrated bishop of Constantinople. The Johannites, however,

> refused to hold communion with him or even pray with him since he associated with the enemies of John. When they continued to... assemble in the farthest part of the city, he [Arsacius] consulted with the emperor about the matter. A tribune was ordered to attack those gathered together and, by means of stones and clubs, he soon put the multitude (*plethos*) to flight. The most distinguished and most ardent in their support of John (τοὺς δὲ ἐπισημότερον καὶ προθυμότερον τὰ Ἰωάννου ζηλοῦντας) were imprisoned.

The soldiers, "as they often do," exceeded their orders and began to rob the women of their jewelry. "The city was full of turmoil and lamentation (ταραχὴ καὶ οἰμωγή), but still they did not abandon their love for John."[136]

Some months later, an extraordinary hailstorm, followed four days later by the sudden death of the empress Eudoxia, strengthened the resolve of the Johannites. Quite naturally, they regarded these events as proof of God's displeasure with the empress' part in the exile of John and a confirmation of the justice of their own schism.[137]

As for John himself, he first crossed the straits to Chalcedon, then proceeded to Cucusa, in Armenia, where he spent most of his exile, writing warm and comforting letters to many of his friends. At length, the court decided to make his residence more remote still, and he was ordered to Pityus, on the Black Sea. During the long and difficult journey he died, on September 17, 407.[138]

Several laws directed against the Johannites provide us with valuable information about the state of affairs in Constantinople and elsewhere during the months immediately following the second and definitive exile of the bishop. The first of these shows that the dispute spread outside the capital and that groups of Johannites sprang up as far afield as Egypt.[139] As in Constantinople, these provincial Johannites were characterized by their refusal to assemble in the churches controlled by the officially recognized hierarchy. Although the emperor admitted that the Johannites were orthodox, he ordered the provincial governors to forbid their gatherings.

Another law ordered the prosecution of those in Constantinople who sheltered *clericos nova ac tumultuosa conventicula extra ecclesiam celebrantes*.[140] It further required all "foreign" (*perigrini*) clerics and bishops to be expelled from the city, lest there be a *seditio*. Yet another law warned masters not to allow their slaves, and guilds (*corpora*) not to allow their members, to participate in "tumultuous gatherings" (*tumultuosa conventicula*), threatening each group with heavy fines in gold for disobedience.[141] Baur has used these latter two laws as evidence for his hypothesis that the Johannites turned to violence after the expulsion of their bishop.[142] These *tumultuosa conventicula*, however, were simply the religious assemblies of the Johannites, held, as one law states, outside the city and "in the farthest part of the city." There is no need to assume that *tumultuosus* suggested any violence, since the term might have a political or moral, as well as a more literal, significance. The emperor and his court did not like the religious services of the Johannites; therefore, they were *tumultuosa*. In addition, of course, the very existence of these dissident gatherings was a disturbance to the official church. The *seditio* mentioned in one of the laws would seem to refer more directly to violence, but instead of providing evidence that the Johannites had resorted to violence, the text shows clearly that, as of the date of the law, a *seditio* had not yet occurred: the clerics and bishops were to be expelled so that such an event would not take place.

Sozomen, as we have seen, noted that the city was filled with *tarache*. But again, this does not seem to mean that the Johannites engaged in violence, for taken in context the word must refer either to what the soldiers did to the Johannites or to the fear and uncertainty experienced by the latter in such circumstances. In sum, apart from the incident of the burning of Hagia Sophia, which was isolated and unique, there is no evidence of any violence committed by the Johannites in the period after the second exile of the bishop. Clearly, the emperor feared violence from the supporters of John, but the Johannites do not appear even to have presented their desires openly to the court. Their attitude was one of passive resistance characterized by a firm refusal to participate in the worship of the official church.

As time went on, the government continued to issue edicts against the Johannites, ordering them to hold communion with the regular hierarchy. It enforced these demands with periodic persecution, so that "many (*polloi*) feared to frequent the market place and the baths." Some even considered flight from the city in order to save their lives.[143] Despite these difficulties, the Johannites flourished. When Atticus succeeded Arsacius as bishop, sometime in 406, he complained that none of the faithful of the city would hold communion with him.[144] Yet, during all this time, there is no indication that the Johannites met for other than religious purposes. Regardless of the persecution, their meetings did not turn into violent protests against the religious policy of the state.

Atticus was an astute ecclesiastical politician, and he undoubtedly took measures to restore the Johannites to communion; but they remained firm in their loyalty to Chrysostom. Ultimately, probably about 415, Atticus admitted defeat and restored John's name to the diptychs of Constantinople. In a letter to Cyril of Alexandria, he excused himself by saying that he was forced to act by the insistence of the emperor and the people.[145] Almost certainly, in light of the intransigence of the Johannites, he saw this as the only way to heal the schism. Further, John was already dead and the restoration of his memory was not a threat to Atticus; indeed, it would only add to his reputation.[146] Veneration of Chrysostom continued to be popular after the restoration, and in 428 Nestorius introduced a feast in honor of his predecessor in Constantinople.[147] Finally, ten years later, Theodosius II had John's remains brought to the capital amid popular rejoicing that impressed contemporaries and posterity alike.[148]

Several distinctions may be made between the disturbances which characterized the first exile of Chrysostom and the events which accompanied his final expulsion. In the first instance, John's enemies appear originally to have attempted to alienate the bishop's popular support: Theophilus tried to discredit John by accusing him of defending the errors of Origenism. When this failed, all plans to separate John from his popular support appear, strangely, to have been abandoned. Perhaps the enemies of the bishop underestimated the affection with which John was regarded, and the reaction to his exile seems to have taken the court completely by surprise. The authorities made little or no attempt to stop or even control the demonstrations, and the officials sent to seize John and carry him into exile were not able to complete their mission. In the face of unified and resolute popular opinion, the court found itself unable to maintain its decision, and John was recalled from exile. The demonstration in John's behalf, while not the only factor involved, was probably the most important consideration leading to the reversal of imperial policy. Victorious after the capitulation of the emperor, John's supporters engaged in violent confrontations with the monks and Egyptians, and they greeted the bishop's return *en masse* by forcing him immediately to resume his episcopal duties.

The second series of events was significantly different. It may even be doubted that the Johannites took the initiative in protesting the second exile. The difference stemmed from the determination of John's enemies to prevent a repetition of the earlier disturbances, which had had an unfortunate (from their point of view) effect on the emperor. Instead of trying to separate John from his popular support, they planned simply to neutralize any demonstration by an overwhelming use of force. When violence came, it was directed by John's enemies, and the supporters of the bishop had no opportunity to organize themselves or even resist. When John went into exile, they were shut up in the church; and when they reassembled later, they were attacked by soldiers and their leaders were arrested. The only active protest which the Johannites managed was a desperate one: the fire which destroyed Hagia Sophia and an important part of the city.

It is unlikely that the enthusiasm of John's followers had weakened significantly between the two events; in the second they were simply powerless to effect their wishes. Moreover, the personality and moral philosophy of John himself must have affected the popular response to his deposition. As we have already seen, John was an opponent of violence, and he took every opportunity to avoid involving his followers in a confrontation with the state. In the first case, events moved swiftly and John was out of the city (and hence his direct influence with the crowd reduced) within a relatively short time—at most three days. Thus, his followers gave way to their own feelings, and ultimately resorted to violence and even bloodshed in his behalf. In the second case, the open confrontation began well before John left the city, and there is ample evidence to show that he used his authority with the crowd to restrain their anger and opposition to the policy of the court. Thus, by the time John went into exile for the second time, his supporters had been cowed by the soldiers, and the moment for resistance, or even protest, had been lost. In such a situation, the Johannites could hardly dare more than the passive resistance which they offered. This hopelessness, however, led to despair among a few of the faithful, and they set the fire which destroyed Hagia Sophia.

The poor of Constantinople were among the most ardent of John's followers; to them the bishop's social and moral philosophy appealed most directly. His support for their needs, his condemnation of the rich, and his willingness to stand against the powerful of the world—as John the Baptist stood against the court of Herod—must have appealed powerfully to simple men. But his oratory, strict morality, and asceticism were attributes that were appreciated not only by the poor; many people of more elevated status supported Chrysostom.

Thus, the *Codex* mentions slaves as potential Johannites,[149] but it also points to other supporters whom we would perhaps place in the middle of society: members of the guilds and government bureaucrats.[150] In addition, men and women of the highest situation were attracted by the teaching and the personality of John. These were the officers and distinguished men, as well as the bishops who remained loyal to John and who provided leadership for the Johannites after Chrysostom went into exile. Among these people were Nicarete, a woman from an illustrious family in Bithynia, and the deaconness Olympiadae. The former was noted for her charity toward the poor and her knowledge of medicine, while the latter proved to be an intellectual match for the prefect Optatus who supported John in his exile from her own funds.[151]

This social and economic mixture among John's supporters suggests that there were no "hidden" social or economic motives involved in these events. Despite the fondness of the poor for Chrysostom, we cannot, except in the most restricted sense, regard the outburst of popular fervor in his behalf as socially or economically oriented. The followers of John expressed their anger at his deposition simply because they actually supported their bishop, not because they wished to use the opportunity to strike at the rich or express any other secular concern.

As is normally the case, it is impossible to say much about the numbers of those who openly displayed their opposition to the two condemnations of Chrysostom. Obviously, we should not take the sources literally when they imply that all the people of Constantinople rose to support their bishop. Yet, we know of absolutely no popular opposition to John's episcopacy and the one figure we have gives the number of newly baptized Johannites in 404 as 3,000! His enemies, on the other hand, included members of the court, monks, Egyptian sailors, and a handful of ecclesiastics from within and outside Constantinople. From all we can tell, popular sentiment in the capital was overwhelmingly in favor of the bishop, to the point that he could, on occasion, count on the sympathy if not the support of pagans, heretics, and Jews.

Aside from his apparent holiness, the most important factor in explaining John's popularity was his ability to appeal to a wide body of public opinion. As we have seen, he remained above politics and followed a course of strict and outspoken morality. Those chastized by the moralizing bishop became his implacable enemies, but even they could not deny the basis on which the charges were made, while a more objective observer might feel that John had acted correctly, if perhaps unwisely, since honest morality is rarely good politics.[152] Support for John was thus a very simple matter: to many people he was a kind and saintly bishop who was persecuted for having dared to speak the truth about the powerful of the world.

John's enemies made a serious miscalculation when they decided to ignore his popular support. In particular, they missed an opportunity by failing to sustain a charge of heresy. Only by following such a course are they likely to have confused the issues sufficiently and brought people to question the desirability of supporting his cause. The government, as we have seen, found it had to consider public opinion. It could, when properly prepared, expel John from the city and overwhelm his supporters with superior force, but the moral position of the Johannites was unassailable, and they remained an embarrassment to the church and proof that the emperor had failed in his responsibility to preserve the unity of orthodox Christianity.

1. The best sources for the life of John Chrysostom are, of course, his own works, found scattered throughout *PG*. They must be supplemented by the *Dialogus* of Palladius (*Palladii Dialogus de Vita S. Johannis Chrysostomi*, ed. P. R. Coleman-Norton [Cambridge, 1928], which is almost contemporary but was written for the purpose of redeeming the memory of the deposed bishop, and the ecclesiastical historians, particularly Socrates (*PG* 67) and Sozomen (*GCS* 50). The most important secondary source is Chrysostomus Baur, *Der heilige Johannes Chrysostomus und seine Zeit* (hereafter cited as *HJC*), 2 vols. (Munich, 1929–30), translated as *John Chrysostom and His Time* by M. Gonzaga, 2 vols. (Westminster, Md., 1959), which has an extensive bibliography and discussion of sources. See also Louis Duchesne, *Early History of the Christian Church*, trans. Claude Jenkins, vol. 3 (London, 1924), pp. 40-75. On the date of John's birth, see Baur, *HJC*, vol. 1, pp. 3–4.

2. Palladius says that Chrysostom's father was *stratelates* of Syria (*Dialogus*, p. 28). It is not certain what the rank of *stratelates* signified. John himself states that the *stratelates* ranked third in the province (*Hom.* 3.3 *in Act. Ap., PG* 60, 37–38). Socrates called Gainas *stratelates* after he became the supreme commander of the eastern army. Thus, it might mean anything from *dux* to *magister militum*. Little consistency apparently attended the use of the term. See O. Hirschfeld, "Die Rangtitel der römischen Kaiserzeit," in his *Kleine Schriften* (Berlin, 1913), pp. 646–81. On John's inheritance, see his *De Sacerdotio* 1.5 (*PG* 48, 624).

3. Socrates says that John had planned to become a lawyer, but that he found this calling unsuitable to his spiritual temperament (*Hist. Eccl.* 6.3) and while Socrates says merely that it was expected that John would become a lawyer (*Hist. Eccl.* 8.2), Palladius indicates that John had always intended to devote himself to the service of God (*Dialogus*, p. 28). Chrysostom himself is also contradictory: cf. *De Sacerdotio* 1. 4 (*PG* 48, 624) and 1. 1 (*PG* 48, 623). Baur, (*HJC*, vol. 1, pp. 60-61) makes a good point when he says that John displayed no knowledge of legal procedure in his writings, but he presses the evidence far more than it will bear in maintaining that he never considered a secular career. On the relationship between Chrysostom and Libanius see Socrates *Hist. Eccl.* 7.3; Sozomen *Hist. Eccl.* 8.2. But cf. P. Petit, *Essai sur la vie et la correspondance du Sophiste Libanius* (Paris, 1955), pp. 131–23, and P. Mass, "Libanios und Johannes Chrysostomus," *Sitzungsberichte der preussischen Akademie der Wissenschaften*, 2 (1912), 1123–26.

4. Socrates *Hist. Eccl.* 6.3; Sozomen *Hist. Eccl.* 8.2. A study of Scripture and theology may have occupied some of Chrysostom's time (see Baur, *HJC*, vol. 1, pp. 69–81), but if Socrates is to be believed, training in the ascetic life was the primary concern of Carterius and Diodorus. On this see Franz Dölger, *Byzanz und die europaische Staatenwelt* (Ettal, 1953), pp. 197–208. It is interesting that two other members of this *asketerion* were Theodore of Mopsuestia and Nestorius!

5. Palladius *Dialogus*, p. 28.

6. Ibid. The first four years of his desert life were spent under the direction of a certain old man named Syrus.

7. Sozomen *Hist. Eccl.* 8.2.

8. Palladius *Dialogus*, p. 29. On the office of deacon see Theodor Klauser, "Diakon," *RAC*, 3 (1957), pp. 888–909.

9. Theodoret *Historia Ecclesiastica* 5.20; Sozomen *Hist. Eccl.* 7.23; Zonaras *Epitome Historiarum* 13.18, 30; Libanius *Or.* 19.25; 20.4; 22.4; Zosimus *Historia Nova* 4.41; Chrysostom *Hom. de Statuis ad Pop. Ant.* (*PG* 49, 15–222). Robert Browning, "The Riot of A.D. 387 in Antioch," 13-20, gives modern bibliography. What the tax was is uncertain.

Sozomen says that it was levied to pay for protracted war. Its affect on the city population might at first suggest the *collatio lustralis*, but it disturbed so many *viri illustres* that it might have been the *aurum coronarium*, which would have affected many rich landowners living in the city. See Browning, "The Riot of A.D. 387," pp. 12-15. The date of the riot is also controversial; Theodoret and Zosimus place it in 392, but see Baur, *HJC*, vol. 1, pp. 279-80.

10. *Hom.* 2 *de Statuis ad Populum Ant.* (*PG* 49, 33-37).

11. John often spoke about the people of the hippodrome and the theatre in these terms; see *Hom* 2 *de Statuis ad Pop. Ant.* (*PG* 49, 58), *Hom. contra Ludos et Theatros* (*PG* 56, 26370). See B. H. Vandenbert, "Saint Jean Chrysostome et les spectacles," *Zeitschrift für Religion und Geitesgeschichte* 7 (1955), 34-46; Robert Browning, "The Riot of 387," pp. 11-20.

12. *Hom* 2 *de Statuis ad Pop. Ant.* (*PG* 49, 37).

13. See *Hom.* 6 *de Statuis ad Pop. Ant.* (*PG* 49, 82), where Chrysostom used the event to stress the necessity of obedience to duly constituted authority.

14. Socrates *Hist. Eccl.* 5.10; 13; Sozomen *Hist. Eccl.* 7.12; 14; 8.6.

15. Socrates *Hist. Eccl.* (5.10; 20-21; 23-24) describes the efforts against heretics and the dissensions which arose in various heretical groups, no doubt partly as a result of persecution. Cf. Sozomen *Hist. Eccl.* 8.12; 17-18.

16. P. Batiffol, *La Siège apostolique* (359-451), 3rd ed. (Paris, 1924), p. 282, and E. Gerland, "Die Vorgeschichte des Patriarchates von Konstantinopel," *Byzantinisch-neugriesche Jahrbucher* 9 (1932), 226-28, stress the importance of the episcopate of Nectarius in the development of the patriarchate. See also E. Stein, "Le dévelopment du pouvoir du siège de Constantinople jusqu'au concile de Chalcédoine," *Le Monde Slave* 3 (1926), 80-108.

17. On episcopal elections see H.-G. Beck, *Kirche und theologische Literatur im byzantinischen Reich*, 12 Abetilung, 2 Teil, 1 Band of *Handbuch der Altertumswissenschaft* (Munich, 1959), pp. 69-70. A. H. M. Jones, *Later Roman Empire*, pp. 915-20. Chrysostom himself speaks of the disputes attendant upon episcopal elections in *De Sacerdotio* 3.15 (*PG* 48, 652). Cf. Gregory of Nazianzus *Orationes* 43.27 (*PG* 36, 546); Palladius *Dialogus*, pp. 93-97 (dispute in Antioch); Socrates *Hist. Eccl.* 4.29 (Damasus and Ursinus); 30 (Ambrose). Theodosius II made arrangements for the swift election of a successor to Maximian as bishop of Constantinople "so there would not again be a disturbance (*tarache*) in the church."

18. See N. H. Baynes, "Alexandria and Constantinople."

19. Sozomen *Hist. Eccl.* 7.7; 9.

20. Palladius *Dialogus*, p. 29.

21. Sozomen *Hist. Eccl.* 7.2; Socrates *Hist. Eccl.* 6.2. Isidore had been a monk in the Nitrian desert and in 397 he was in charge of strangers and the poor for the Alexandrian church. Sozomen says that Theophilus nominated Isidore out of gratitude for some earlier service and only after John arrived in Constantinople and was ready for consecration. Although it seems that Theophilus himself came to the city only at this time, it is most unlikely that he kept his candidate unknown until then. Cf. Baur, *HJC*, vol. 2, pp. 10-11.

22. Sozomen *Hist. Eccl.* 8.2.

23. Palladius *Dialogus*, p. 29.

24. Eutropius had carried out a similarly surprising plan in marrying Arcadius to Eudoxia, a daughter of a Frankish general, just a short time earlier. On Eutropius and the situation at the court during this period see Alan Cameron, *Claudian: Poetry and Propaganda at the Court of Honorius* (Oxford, 1970), pp. 124-55.

25. Palladius *Dialogus*, p. 29. Baur, *HJC*, vol. 2, p. 13, suggests the influence of Caesarius, one of the ambassadors from the court to Antioch in 387. He had been appointed consul for 397 and his religious concern is suggested by his foundation of a church to St. Thyrsos in Constantinople (Sozomen *Hist. Eccl.* 9.2); Theodoret says (*Hist. Eccl.* 5.27) that the emperor chose John. Arcadius certainly agreed with the selection, but considering all we know about the relations among the members of the imperial court at this time, it is much

The Episcopacy of John Chrysostom   71

more likely that Eutropius made the actual decision. Cf. O. Seeck, *Geschichte des Untergangs der Antiken Welt*, vol. 3 (Berlin, 1895-1921), pp. 338-39.

26. Baur, *HJC*, vol. 2, p. 13.

27. Sozomen *Hist. Eccl.* 8.2; Palladius *Dialogus*, pp. 29-30; Theodore of Trimithus (*PG* 47, 62). The title and name of the officer differ in the sources, but all agree on the secrecy of the mission and the reason for it.

28. Socrates *Hist. Eccl.* 6.2. The *synaxaria*, however, give December 15, 397. The discrepancy may be resolved by assuming that the earlier date refers to his arrival in the city, the latter to his actual enthronment. See Baur, *HJC*, vol. 2, pp. 19-20.

29. Sozomen *Hist. Eccl.* 8.2.

30. Rarely were defeated candidates for an episcopal election content with the decision. Such men were always a threat to a bishop. Cf. Sozomen *Hist. Eccl.* 7.11; Socrates *Hist. Eccl.* 7.40; Palladius *Dialogus*, p. 64.

31. For a discussion of the problem of the "stranger" as bishop, see below, chapter 4.

32. Sozomen *Hist. Eccl.* 8.3; Theodoret *Hist. Eccl.* 5.28; Socrates *Hist. Eccl.* 6.4; Palladius *Dialogus*, pp. 31-32. It is probable, as we have indicated above, that much laxity had developed during the administration of Nectarius.

33. Palladius *Dialogus*, pp. 31-33.

34. Socrates *Hist. Eccl.* 6.4. That these stories about John continued to circulate into the mid-fifth century shows that a tradition hostile to him must have existed (even though it could be turned to the bishop's own advantage by Sozomen). Part of this may have stemmed from the pagan Eunapius who was openly antagonistic toward Chrysostom, but there may have been a hostile Christian source as well.

35. As is well known, Chrysostom ate alone; this was later to be one of the charges brought against him. In eliminating episcopal entertainment he offended the many who had come to expect it (Palladius *Dialogus*, pp. 79-80), and he undoubtedly earned the displeasure of the cooks, grocers, butchers, entertainers, etc. who had become the clients of the bishop and depended on the lavish outlays that were frequent during the time of Nectarius.

Apparently there was already one hospital in Constantinople and Chrysostom founded others. Palladius *Dialogus*, pp. 33; 69-71. He may have been influenced in this by the example of his friend St. Basil (cf. Basil, *Ep.* 94, *PG* 32, 448). About 400 a certain Florentius (or Florus) built a hospice in Constantinople and later a whole series of hospitals opened. See Baur, *HJC*, vol. 2, pp. 55-56. Cf. *C. Th.* 12.3,8 (370), which established a public physician for all but two of the regions of Rome. There must have been a similar institution in Alexandria, of which Isidore may have been the director. J. Pargoire, "Les débuts de monachisme à Constantinople," *Revue des questions historique* 65 (1899), 92; Ad. d-Alès, "L'Hospitalité chrétienne aux IVe et Ve siècle," *Études* 189 (1926), 75-76; A. Philipsborn, "Der Fortschritt in der Entwicklung des byzantinischen Krankhauswesens," *BZ* 54 (1961), 338-65. Cf. G. Dagron, "Les moines et la ville," *Travaux et Mémoires*, 4 (1970), 229-76.

36. Socrates *Hist. Eccl.* 6.19.

37. *Hom* 11 *contra Anomoeos* (*PG* 48, 796-98). Even though Arianism was not to be a serious threat to the East after 381, there were still many Arians in Constantinople. They obviously still felt strong enough and devoted enough to engage in violence with the orthodox on several occasions. As late as 415 the government had to threaten the Eunomian clergy with the confiscation of their property if they continued to use their house in Constantinople for heretical worship: *C. Th.* 16.5, 58 (415).

38. Socrates *Hist. Eccl.* 6.8; Sozomen *Hist. Eccl.* 8. 8. The Arians probably sang short additions to or parodies of orthodox hymns (such as the Monophysites' addition to the Trisagion)—e.g., their mocking rhetorical question: "Where are those who say the three have one power?" The importance of songs and slogans as vehicles of religious propaganda should not be underestimated and we will have occasion to discuss them again. During the period of Arian ascendency similar practices developed in Antioch (Sozomen *Hist. Eccl.* 4. 28). An earlier attempt to express theological opinion in popular songs was the *Thalia* of

Arius, a collection which was "loose and dissolute, similar in style and metres to the songs of Sotades" (Socrates *Hist. Eccl.* 1.9). The sources do not say how the violence in Constantinople ended: whether one side "won" or if official force had to be used to restore peace.

39. Sozomen (*Hist. Eccl* 8.5) says generally that he converted many pagans (perhaps Goths?) and Theodoret (*Hist. Eccl.* 5.29) reports that he had various temples destroyed in Phoenicia; further, he supported as best he could the petition of Porphyry against the pagans in Gaza (Marcus Diaconus *Vita Porphyrii* 37, ed. H. Grégoire and M. A. Kugener, p. 32). It is unlikely that many pagans would have liked such a fiercely Christian bishop (cf. Zosimus' attitude), but none of Chrysostom's recorded confrontations with pagans were of an extraordinary nature and it is not certain that any of them took place in Constantinople.

40. The monks regarded him as "difficult and passionate, crude and arrogant" (Sozomen *Hist. Eccl.* 8.9). On the early history of Constantinopolitan monasticism see E. Marin, *Les moines de Constantinople depuis la foundation de la ville jusqu'à la mort de Photius, 330-898* (Paris, 1897), which must be seriously modified by the studies of J. Pargoire, "Les Débuts de monachisme," and more recently Gilbert Dagron, "Les moines et la ville."

41. *De Compunctione* 2.2 (*PG* 47, 413); *De Sacerdotio*, 6.6-8 (*PG* 48, 682-85); *De Virginitate* 4 (*PG* 48, 536); *Hom* 44.1 *in Matt.* (*PG* 57, 463ff.); *Hom.* 21, 6 *in Gen.* (*PG* 53, 182-83); *Hom.* 7. 4 *in Heb.* (*PG* 63, 67-68); cf. Quasten, *Patrology*, vol. 3 (Utrecht, 1960), pp. 463-64.

42. There is, to my knowledge, no really satisfactory modern treatment of St. Isaac. He was a Syrian monk who came to Constantinople late in the fourth century. He is now generally considered the "founder" of Constantinoplitan monasticism. According to Callinicus, the author of the *Vita S. Hypatii* (ed. and trans. G. J. M. Bartelink, Paris, 1971, p. 74) there was in 384, when Hypatius came to Constantinople, only one monastery in the city, that of Isaac. Pargoire ("Les Débuts du monachisme") shows that there were no permanent monastic establishments in Constantinople before the time of Isaac. A holy man named Isaac accosted the emperor Valens and requested that he return the churches to the orthodox. When he refused, Isaac predicted his approaching death. The emperor then rode off to Adrianople (Sozomen *Hist. Eccl.* 6. 40). It is possible that this was the same Isaac. It is much more difficult to be sure that the Isaac who opposed Chrysostom and left for Alexandria with Theophilus (see below) was the same person as the founder of monasticism in Constantinople. The chief difficulty lies in the fact that the *vita* of St. Isaac (*AASS*, 30 May, vol. 7, pp. 246ff.) indicates that he died during the reign of Theodosius the Great. Pargoire ("Les Débuts du monachisme," pp. 122-24) identifies the two Isaacs and discounts the evidence of the *vita* by citing the nearly contemporary *vita* of St. Hypatius, which indicates that Isaac was still alive in 406. See also J. Pargoire, "Date de la morte de St. Isaac," *Échos d'Orient* 2 (1898-99), 138-45. That Isaac was not fondly remembered—and thus may have opposed Chrysostom—may be suggested by the fact that his monastery was not named after him but after his successor Dalmatius. This monastery—*ta Dalmatou*—was located just outside the Constantinian walls near the Xerolophos and the porta Satorninou (Janin, *Constantinople byzantine*, 2nd ed., pp. 86-89).

43. Dagron, "Les moines et la ville."

44. Socrates *Hist. Eccl.* 8.5.

45. *Hom* 30.4 *in Act. Ap.* (*PG* 60, 226-28); *Hom. in Pater meus usque Modo Operatur* (*PG* 63, 511).

46. Sozomen *Hist. Eccl.* 8.5.

47. Socrates *Hist. Eccl.* 6.4. Cf. Paul Albert, *St. Jean Chrysostome considéré comme orateur populaire* (Paris, 1858).

48. Socrates *Hist. Eccl.* 6.5; Palladius *Dialogus*, p. 33.

49. *Sermo de Eleemosyna* (*PG* 51, 251-72). In the 90 sermons on the Gospel of St. Matthew, Baur counts 40 sermons on the theme of almsgiving. John himself admitted that it was a favorite topic: "Perhaps someone will object that day after day I preach on almsgiving and love of one's neighbor. Of course! And I will continue to speak about it. For if you were perfect in this virtue, even then I would not dare stop for fear of making you negligent"

(*Hom.* 88.3 *in Matth.*, *PG* 58, 779). Bury says (*History of the Later Roman Empire*, 2nd ed., vol. 1 of 2 vols. [London, 1923], p. 139) that Chrysostom was "almost a socialist." Even in exile in remote Armenia John was popular and loved by all around him, not only because of the money he dispensed, but also because of his kind words and advice (Sozomen *Hist. Eccl.* 8.27).

50. The Biblical text upon which this was based is Ecclesiasticus 13.27-28; Chrysostom *Expositio in Psalmum* 48 (*PG* 55, 221).

51. *Hom.* 21 *in Epist. I ad Cor.* (*PG* 61, 176-77). This sermon is particularly interesting. In it John blamed the rich for the existence of robbers, traitors, informers, and tramps. Ordinary people, he claimed, had fallen to such positions because the rich had made them covetous by constantly making a show of their wealth in the sight of the poor. The poor, then, without any other means to attain wealth, turned to crime. He advised the rich to make no show of their wealth and to bestow gifts freely on the poor before they arrived at such terrible expedients.

52. *Hom.* 9 *in Epist. II ad Cor.* (*PG* 61, 461-64). John says on many occasions that the poor were happier in this life than the rich. This, however, was probably meant for the consideration of the rich rather than the poor. Cf. *Hom.* 1 and 2 *de Statuis ad Pop. Ant.* (*PG* 49, 15-48).

53. *Hom* 14 and 15 *ad Pop. Ant.* (*PG* 49, 153 and 159); *Hom.* 3. 1 *de Diablo Tent.* (*PG* 49, 263-64); *Hom.* 3. 1-2 *de David et Saul* (*PG* 54, 695-97); *Hom. contra Ludos et Theatros* (*PG* 56, 263-70). For the popularity of the spectacles, see Ammianus Marcellinus *Res Gestae* 14. 6, 25; 28. 4, 29; Ludwig Friedlaender, *Darstellungen aus der Sittengeschichte Roms*, 10th ed., vol. 2 (Leipzig, 1922), pp. 1-20; and Alan Cameron, *Porphyrius the Charioteer* (Oxford, 1973).

54. Peter Brown, "The Rise and Function of the Holy Man," pp. 80-101, and the literature cited there.

55. Socrates *Hist. Eccl.* 6.4.

56. Bury, *Later Roman Empire*, vol. 1, p. 133; Stein, *Histoire*, vol. 1, pp. 235-37; Synesius *de providentia seu Aegyptus* (*PG* 66, 1209-82); Alan Cameron, *Claudian*, pp. 124-55; Claudian *in Eutropium*; *C. Th.* 9.40, 17 (399); Philostorgius *Historia Ecclesiastica* 9.6; Socrates *Hist. Eccl.* 5.6; Sozomen *Hist. Eccl.* 8.7; Zosimus *Historia Nova* 5.12-18. Socrates says that the city was full of barbarians and that the citizens felt as they they were captives.

57. Zosimus *Historia Nova* 5.19, ed. Mendelssohn. Manojlović ("Le peuple de Constantinople") interpreted this event as one of the first examples of the use of the δῆμοι\as a militia to defend the city, but cf. Cameron, *Circus Factions*, pp. 105-125.

58. Sozomen *Hist. Eccl.* 8.4; *Chron. Pasch.*, ed. Bonn, p. 567; Socrates *Hist. Eccl.* 6. 6; Zosimus *Historia Nova* 5. 19, pp. 238-39; Theodoret *Hist. Eccl.* 5. 32-35; Marcellinus Comes *Chronicon*, ed. Mommsen, p. 66. According to Sozomen the soldiers of the emperor set fire to the church "so that they could not flee because the gates (πύλαι) were closed." What gates were closed? The context would appear to suggest the gates of the city, but they might be the doors of the church. The *Paschal Chronicle* dates this to July 12, 400 and says that a large number of Christians (i.e., presumably orthodox Romans) were burned also. If this were the case, we should have to interpret the effect of this incident somewhat differently. Zosimus reports that a large number of Christians were disturbed by the burning of the barbarians, presumably because their murder in a church—in the center of the city at that—was a sacrilege. It is unlikely, however, that Chrysostom was implicated in any way with the death of the Goths in the church.

59. This was one of the primary characteristics of John's personality, as the sources time and again reveal. He was not a politician but a moralist who could be honest with all conditions of people. This earned for him powerful enemies and devoted followers from various factions and segments of society. Cf. Socrates *Hist. Eccl.* 6.3.

60. Chrysostom *In Eutropium* and *De Capto Eutropio* (*PG* 52, 391-414).

61. Theodoret *Hist. Eccl.* 5.32-33, is the only mention of the embassy to Gainas. For Chrysostom's opposition to Gainas, see Theodoret *Hist. Eccl.* 5.32-35; Socrates *Hist. Eccl.* 6.5; Sozomen *Hist. Eccl.* 8.4.

74   Vox Populi

62. Socrates *Hist. Eccl.* 6.15; Sozomen *Hist. Eccl.* 8.16; Zosimus *Historia Nova* 5.23; Palladius *Dialogus*, p. 45. Eudoxia was certainly not ill-disposed toward John from the beginning. For example, she aided him in the campaign against the Arian processions.

63. The reasons given for the quarrel between the monks and their bishop are extremely interesting and valuable as information on ecclesiastical relationships in Egypt. See Palladius *Dialogus*, pp. 34–39; Socrates *Hist. Eccl.* 6.7; Sozomen *Hist. Eccl.* 8.11. Sozomen says that certain Egyptian monks thought of God as a corporeal being and when Theophilus condemned them for this "they rose in revolt (ἐστασίαζον) and they wanted to kill Theophilus as impious. The patriarch confronted the insurgents simply by reversing his former position. He condemned Origen and so pacified the monks. Theophilus then accused certain monks, whom he disliked for other reasons, of Origenism. One of the monks, when he learned the Theophilus had denied the idea that God had a body (arms, legs, and all) just as a man, cried out, "They have taken away my God!"

64. The charges made by the deacon John and the monk Isaac at the Council of the Oak demonstrate the policy of Theophilus. See Photius *Bibliotheca* 59 (ed. and trans. René Henry, vol. 2 [Paris, 1960]. pp. 52–57).

65. Sozomen *Hist. Eccl.* 8.14; Socrates *Hist. Eccl.* 6.14. Baur, *HJC*, vol. 2, pp. 188–91.

66. Sozomen *Hist. Eccl.* 8.14. The technique of claiming that a person is a heretic by comparing or associating him with a known heretic was a common one and we will meet it again. What is significant in the present instance is that the attempt was unsuccessful.

67. Sozomen *Hist. Eccl.* 8.14; Socrates *Hist. Eccl.* 6.14.

68. Socrates says that Serapion also advised Epiphanius that his actions were in violation of canons which forbade the interference of one bishop in the affairs of another.

69. Just before Epiphanius left Constantinople the two bishops supposedly met and Epiphanius predicted the deposition of John and John the death of Epiphanius. Sozomen *Hist. Eccl.* 8.15; Socrates *Hist. Eccl.* 6.14.

70. Sozomen *Hist. Eccl.* 8.15–16; Socrates *Hist. Eccl.* 6.15–16. Cf. Sozomen *Hist. Eccl.* 8.17: "the fleet of the Alexandrians, those who happened to be present, both from the other ships but especially from the grain ships, gathered together and praising him enthusiastically they received him." By the sixth century at least the bishops of Alexandria had a very close relationship with the Egyptian fleets, especially the grain fleet, and this text suggests that the Egyptian sailors could be relied upon as strong supporters of the bishop at an earlier date. See the *Vita Johannis Eleemosynarii, Anal. Bolland.* 45 (1927), 19–73, and George R. Monks, "The Church of Alexandria," pp. 349–62.

71. Sozomen *Hist. Eccl.* 8.17; Socrates *Hist. Eccl.* 6.15. Theophilus probably stayed at an imperial palace, identified by Socrates as *ta Plakidias*. There were at least two palaces of this name, one in the first region, the other in the tenth region, in the northwest area of the city toward the Constantinian walls: Janin, *Constantinople byzantine*, 2nd ed., pp. 135–36. John "himself" says that Theophilus stayed outside the city (Palladius *Dialogus*, pp. 8–9). This reference, like many others, is from a letter included in Palladius' *Dialogus* and supposedly written by John to Pope Innocent, explaining the situation up to the time of his second exile. This letter is probably authentic, for Sozomen has a copy of Innocent's reply. But it was almost certainly edited by Palladius, even though he has allowed some inconsistencies between the letter and the rest of his narrative to slip by. See note 112 below and the Introduction to Coleman-Norton's edition of the *Dialogus*, where this problem is discussed. See also J. F. D'Alton, *Selections from St. John Chrysostom* (London, 1940), pp. 289–312, which contains a text and commentary of this passage. D'Alton maintains that this letter is authentic because it is so different in style from Palladius (p. 295).

72. Palladius *Dialogus*, pp. 9. 44.

73. Sozomen *Hist. Eccl.* 8.17; Socrates *Hist. Eccl.* 6.15; Palladius *Dialogus*, pp. 10, 45-51; Photius *Bibliotheca* 59 (Vol. II, pp. 52–57); and Baur, *HJC*, vol. 1, pp. 202–19.

74. Photius *Bibliotheca* 59, vol. 2, p. 56. A similar situation had occurred in 342 when Constantius II ordered the general Hermogenes to expel Paul from his episcopal throne. This disturbed the populace and they burned the house of Hermogenes, dragged the helpless

general through the streets, and murdered him! Constantius had to come from Antioch himself to quell the riot, and he punished the people by cutting the bread ration in half (Socrates *Hist. Eccl.* 2.13).

75. Palladius *Dialogus*, p. 51.

76. Sozomen *Hist. Eccl.* 8.18. On these events see also my comments in "Zosimus 5.23," pp. 61–83.

77. There is some difficulty here: neither Palladius himself (p. 51) nor John's letter preserved in Palladius refer to disturbances at this time. Furthermore, their account of the time and manner in which John left the city differs from what Sozomen says. Naturally, since the *Dialogus* was written near the time of the events described and both Palladius and John were participants in these events (see Coleman-Norton, lx–lxiii), their silence would count heavily against the account of Sozomen. Perhaps Sozomen confused the disturbances which happened in 404 with those events a year earlier. Yet, Sozomen's account of the episcopacy of Chrysostom is carefully done, and both it and the report of Socrates (who supports Sozomen on these points) may be based independently on the contemporary *Christian History* of Philip of Side. (See "Zosimus 5.23," pp. 63–64.) Moreover, the only positive contradiction in the sources is that Palladius says John was taken at night and by force, while Sozomen says that he went at noon and willingly. The account of Sozomen is supported by Zosimus, an unlikely ally of the church historian, who says that after John learned of the sentence of deposition he left Constantinople willingly (ἑκών). (Zosimus *Historia Nova* 5.23.)

78. Palladius *Dialogus*, p. 11.

79. Socrates *Hist. Eccl.* 6.16; Baur, *HJC*, vol. 2, pp. 134–42.

80. Sozomen *Hist. Eccl.* 8.18. Later he says that those at court were moved by the petition of the people (*demos*) (8.19).

81. Socrates *Hist. Eccl.* 6.16.

82. Theodoret *Hist. Eccl.* 5.34.

83. Palladius *Dialogus*, p. 51.

84. Baur, *HJC*, vol. 2, pp. 226–27.

85. This assumes that the sources understood the demands of the demonstrators and reported them accurately. It is always possible that the sources attributed motives to the demonstrators which they never had and secular motives may have been at work here. Nevertheless, at least three separate historiographical traditions bear on this question (including that represented by the pagan Zosimus) and none of them know anything of secular motivation.

86. Baur, *HJC*, vol. 2, pp. 227–29.

87. Zosimus *Historia Nova* 5.23 (pp. 244–45).

88. For a more detailed analysis of this event see my "Zosimus 5.23."

89. Sozomen *Hist. Eccl.* 8.19.

90. John's letter to Innocent (Palladius *Dialogus*, p. 11) and Sozomen (*Hist. Eccl.* 8.19) place this event before his return, while Palladius (*Dialogus*, p. 51) and Socrates (*Hist. Eccl.* 6.17) place it afterwards. The latter even dates the departure of Theophilus to the winter of 403. How this is to be related to the investigation of Heraclides by the Council of the Oak is not certain.

In 401 John had openly interfered in the affairs of the see of Ephesus and he even made a personal trip there to settle matters to his own satisfaction. According to Socrates *Hist. Eccl.* 6.11, John was delayed in Ephesus when the people of the city refused to accept Heraclides and rioted. This is the only incident I know in which John was the target of popular demonstrations. This, however, may easily be explained. The inhabitants of Ephesus did not have the opportunity to observe the qualities for which John was admired by the people of Constantinople, and, of course, they had reason to dislike the interference of any bishop of Constantinople. Before 381 the see of Ephesus, as the capital of Asia, was on at least an equal rank with Constantinople. But the council of Constantinople had raised the bishop of the capital above all the other eastern bishops. Perhaps the people of Ephesus felt that the "upstart" Constantinople should not precede their own city and that the bishop of Constantinople had no right to interfere in their own ecclesiastical affairs. Cf. Baur, *HJC*, vol. 2, pp. 119–34.

91. Socrates *Hist. Eccl.* 6.17; Sozomen *Hist. Eccl.* 8.19.

92. Palladius *Dialogus*, p. 51.

93. See note 70 above; Evagrius *Historia Ecclesiastica*, ed. J. Bidez and L. Parmentier (London, 1898), 2.4. (All subsequent references to Evagrius will cite this edition.)

94. Theodoret *Hist. Eccl.* 5.34.

95. Palladius *Dialogus*, p. 11. We do not know the identity of these bishops. They may have included some of those who had condemned him a little earlier, although there is every reason to believe a substantial number of bishops did remain loyal to Chrysostom throughout all these difficulties.

96. Socrates *Hist. Eccl.* 6.16. The location of Marianae is unknown, although it must obviously have lain along the coast of the Bosporus. Sozomen says it was near Anaplous, which is simply the right side of the strait, as one sails south (Janin, *Constantinople byzantine*, 2nd ed., pp. 468, 515).

97. *Hom. Post Reditum ab Exilio* (*PG* 52, 443–48). The authenticity of this sermon is not unquestioned, but the evidence cited here, at least, agrees with what we know about the situation from other sources.

98. Recall Chrysostom's reaction to the riot of 387 and his fear (Sozomen *Hist. Eccl.* 8.18) that he would be accused of provoking the people to riot.

99. Sozomen *Hist. Eccl.* 8.18; Socrates *Hist. Eccl.* 6.16.

100. Sozomen *Hist. Eccl.* 8.19; Zosimus *Historia Nova* 5.24.

101. Arcadius ordered Theophilus to attend this council, but he refused, "giving as his excuse the revolt of the people (στάσιν τοῦ δήμου), and the untimely zeal of those who were opposed to him there, even though this same *demos* had been full of insults against him before the [arrival of] the imperial letters" (Palladius *Dialogus*, p. 12). It is uncertain whether the *demos* here refers to that of Constantinople or Alexandria.

102. Sozomen *Hist. Eccl.* 8.20; Socrates *Hist. Eccl.* 6.18; Zosimus *Historia Nova* 5.24. Cf. V. A. Thierry, *St. Jean Chrysostome et l'Impératrice Eudoxie*, 2nd ed. (Paris, 1874); I. Gottwald, "La statue de l'impératrice Eudoxie à Constantinople," *Échoes d'Orient* 10 (1907), 274–76, and Baur, *HJC*, vol. 2, pp. 233–44.

103. Palladius *Dialogus*, p. 52. Canon 12 of the Arian synod of Antioch is quoted on p. 53 of the *Dialogus*.

104. Palladius *Dialogus*, pp. 53–53, ascribed the victory to Elpidius, a friend of John's, but it is clear from this passage and from later events that imperial policy was vacillating. Palladius says that the emperor was not to blame, "but others were changing what had already been wisely established."

105. Sozomen *Hist. Eccl.* 8.20.

106. Palladius *Dialogus*, p. 54: "the faithful (*laoi*) enjoyed his teaching with considerable enthusiasm." Cf. *C. Th.* 16.4, 4 (29 January 404), which forbade members of the various *officia* from attending the meetings of John's supporters, under penalty of loss of office and confiscation.

107. Palladius *Dialogus*, p. 54, says that Antiochus and his party persuaded the emperor. Sozomen *Hist. Eccl.* 8.20, and Socrates *Hist. Eccl.* 6.18, claim that a council actually condemned John a second time; Palladius knows nothing of this. Throughout all these events one cannot help being amazed at the ignorance of the emperor. This is perhaps one of the worst examples of the evil effects of the isolation of the emperor in the early Byzantine period. He relied on the word of his advisers and it was possible to lead him astray.

108. It is not clear why John's enemies wanted John out of the city by Easter. Perhaps they felt that another important holiday—during which the emperor would hold communion with the bishop—could not pass with things undecided. Another reason might be that they feared that the great crowds which would gather for the holiday would

The Episcopacy of John Chrysostom 77

demonstrate John's popularity to Arcadius. Herbert Moore (in his translation of the *Dialogus* [London, 1921], p. 78) suggests that less opposition might be encountered with the people in a holiday mood. This seems to me unconvincing. Bearing in mind the events which followed the first exile, one would think the last thing the plotters would want was the presence of large, idle crowds ready to object again to the exile of their bishop.

109. Palladius *Dialogus*, p. 55.

110. Palladius *Dialogus*, pp. 55–56: "the tumult (κλόνον), of the city." MS "G" adds "and of the faithful (*laos*)."

111. Palladius *Dialogus*, p. 59.

112. It is, unfortunately, all but impossible to untangle the sources at this important point. Socrates (*Hist. Eccl.* 6.18) says merely that they celebrated the festival in the baths, and Palladius (*Dialogus*, pp. 56–57) says essentially the same thing. In his letter to Innocent (Palladius *Dialogus*, pp. 12–13), however, John says that the assembly took place "in the churches" and implies that he was there at the time (which would be quite possible, if the celebration took place in a church near the *episcopeion*, where he was confined—*e.g.* Hagia Sophia or St. Irene). That he really means that the assembly was in a church building seems to be indicated by his mention of πάντα τὰ ἔνδον, which are almost certainly the sacred articles of the church. Finally, Sozomen (*Hist. Eccl.* 8.21) confuses things completely by mentioning two attacks: one in the church on Easter Eve and another in the baths the next day. His description of the attack in the church parallels the three other accounts, while his mention of the attack in the baths is limited to an observation that people were forced out of the baths and had to go outside of the walls for their assembly.

See Coleman-Norton, pp. 152–53, where the various scholarly opinions on this matter are discussed. If the letter of Chrysostom is authentic, its evidence should probably be given the most weight, since it was written just after the events described. But, as we have seen, there is considerable doubt about that. I must agree with Coleman-Norton, against the majority opinion, that a reconstruction involving just one attack seems preferable, but it is a difficult choice. One might reject Palladius' explanation of the cause of the attack (that the bishops hostile to John wished to drive the people into the church) and suppose that the soldiers were sent only to disperse the gathering of the Johannites. A second attack could then be explained—as John's enemies would certainly not tolerate another gathering, even outside the church. Another possible interpretation would be to reject the idea that Chrysostom claimed to have been present and that he meant to indicate that the assembly had been held outside the regular churches (by making another interpretation of πάντα τὰ ἔνδον).

Although the sources disagree about the site of the first (or only) attack, all of them seem to be describing the same event: the disturbance of the baptismal rites, the flight of the unclad women, the beating of the clergy. There is, however, no uniformity of terminology so it is impossible to say if there was a common source for all the extant accounts. It appears that all of the accounts we have were derived from separate (oral?) traditions. All but Chrysostom agree that something happened in the baths of Constantius and it would be rash to ignore this evidence.

If the soldiers were trying to drive John's supporters into the church for the "proper" celebration of Easter—as seems most likely—we should probably postulate a single attack which took place in the baths. In this case there would be no need to attack a gathering in the church—such an assembly was exactly what the opponents of John wanted. *Hai Konstantianai* takes its name from the large public bath begun in 345, but often attributed to Constantine the Great. The name was later applied to a large area of the city just to the south of the church of the Holy Apostles, including a palace, churches, and monasteries. But the sources here probably have in mind the more immediate area of the bath. This was not completed until 427 (*Chron. Pasch.*, pp. 580–81) and so the area was still under construction in 404—a suitable place for the semi-secret meeting and the confusion described by the sources. The proximity of the church of the Holy Apostles makes one wonder if this church played any part in this event. Perhaps this was the church used by many of the supporters of John. It will be remembered that Epiphanius had planned to preach his sermon against John in this church. Cf. Janin, *Constantinople byzantine*, 2nd ed., pp. 219–20, 372–73; and Gunter Prinzing and Paul Speck, "Fünf Lokalitäten in Konstantinopel," in *Studien zur Frühgeschichte Konstantinopels*, ed. H.-G Beck, pp. 179–227.

78   Vox Populi

113. The officer is simply called *magistros*, but this almost certainly is a reference to the *magister officiorum*, who theoretically commanded the *scholae*. Although the *magister* rarely exercised direct control over the *scholae*—this was usually done by the emperor—under a ruler like Arcadius and in the unusual situation, this would not be impossible. Further, the officer in question acted as though he was not quite sure of his position. If the officer was the *magister officiorum*, his name was Anthemius, who held office from January 29 to July 30, 404 (*C. Th.* 6.27, 14; 10.22, 5; 16.4, 4).

114. Lucius, who is otherwise unknown, may have been *tribunus Scutariorum* (probably the *syntagmatarchēs* of Sozomen *Hist. Eccl.* 8.23). If the troops he commanded were the *scutarii*, the quality of the recruits had seriously deteriorated since the time of Diocletian. At the time of Justinian each regiment of the *scholae* had 500 men. See Jones, *Later Roman Empire*, pp. 54, 613-14; Seek's *Geschichte des Untergangs*, vol. 5, pp. 583-84.

115. Palladius *Dialogus*, pp. 12-13 (John's letter) and 57-58; Sozomen *Hist. Eccl.* 8.21. As mentioned above, all the accounts agree in detail as to what happened, although they disagree as to time and place.

116. Palladius *Dialogus*, p. 58.

117. Palladius *Dialogus*, p. 13 (from John's letter).

118. Palladius *Dialogus*, pp. 58-59; Sozomen *Hist. Eccl.* 8.21; Socrates *Hist. Eccl.* 6.18. The Pempton was an area just outside the Constantinian walls (five miles from the center of the city, hence its name) to the northwest of the city, probably along the right bank of the Lycus. Janin, *Constantinople byzantine*, 2nd ed., p. 454.

119. Palladius *Dialogus*, p. 14.

120. Sozomen *Hist. Eccl.* 8.22.

121. Sozomen *Hist. Eccl.* 8.22; Socrates *Hist. Eccl.* 6.18; Palladius *Dialogus*, pp. 59-60.

122. Palladius *Dialogus*, pp. 60-61; Sozomen *Hist. Eccl.* 8.22; Socrates *Hist. Eccl.* 6.18; Theodoret *Hist. Eccl.* 5.34. Seeck, *Geschichte des Untergangs*, vol. 5, pp. 336-37, criticizes John for having left his see voluntarily. But, as we have seen, John tried to avoid violence wherever possible and he obviously did not feel justified in taking advantage of the power which the support of the masses gave him. It is interesting that Palladius uses the plural—*demoi*—to refer to the supporters of John. I cannot think that he means the circus factions.

123. Palladius *Dialogus*, pp. 61-62. The authenticity of this passage has been questioned. See Coleman-Norton, pp. 172-73. Part of the passage is drawn from Philo (*Legatio ad Gaium* 46) and part from Chrysostom himself (*Hom. post Reditum ab Exsilio Suo*, PG 52, 444), referring to his first exile. The passage may be suspect because of this apparent plagiarism and because there is no other source for this attack. Yet, it agrees rather well with the account of Sozomen, and we cannot reject the validity of such a passage simply because an author has used someone else's words.

124. Sozomen *Hist. Eccl.* 8.22. John himself may even have been in the church when the emperor's message reached him, although there is great difficulty on this point.

125. Sozomen *Hist. Eccl.* 8.22.

126. Palladius *Dialogus*, p. 62. Cf. Marcellinus Comes *Chronicon*, p. 68: *flamma ignis, quae de beati Johannis throno quondam episcopi nata fuit.* . . .

127. Sozomen *Hist. Eccl.* 8.22.

128. Zosimus *Historia Nova* 5.24. Socrates *Hist. Eccl.* 6.18, agrees that the Johannites were responsible.

129. For example, the Arians when threatened with the confiscation of their churches during the episcopacy of Nestorius (Socrates *Hist. Eccl.* 7.29) and the Montanists when forceably converted by Leo III in the eighth century (Theophanes, *Chronographia* A.M. 6214 [ed. de Boor], p. 401).

130. *Chron. Pasch.*, p. 568 (ed. Bonn).

131. Ibid.; Sozomen *Hist. Eccl.* 8.21. On the Xylokerkos, see Janin, *Constantinople byzantine*, 2nd ed., pp. 195, 440. Note that Palladius (*Dialogus*, pp. 58-59) says that the Johannites assembled in the Pempton, which is considerably to the north of the Xylokerkos. This may suggest that the two groups were in some way distinct.

132. E.g., Cyril Mango, *The Brazen House* (Copenhagen, 1959), p. 23 and *passim*.

133. Sozomen *Hist. Eccl.* 8.14; Palladius *Dialogus*, p. 63; Socrates *Hist. Eccl.* 6.18. Optatus did not become prefect until 405 and he may have begun the inquiry in another capacity.

134. *C. Th.* 16.2, 37 (August 29, 404).

135. Among others arrested, the lector Eutropius was tortured in an attempt to learn who had set the fire, but he was able to tell the authorities nothing, although he ultimately died from the treatment he received.

136. Sozomen *Hist. Eccl.* 8.23; Socrates *Hist. Eccl.* 6.19; Palladius *Dialogus*, p. 64; *Chron. Pasch.*, p. 468; cf. Palladius *Dialogus*, pp. 126–29; Sozomen *Hist. Eccl.* 8.24; 26.

137. Socrates *Hist. Eccl.* 6.19, and Sozomen *Hist. Eccl.* 8.17, both assert that the Johannites viewed these events in such a light.

138. Baur, *HJC*, vol. 2, pp. 350–62, and Duchesne, *Early History of the Christian Church*, vol. 3, pp. 73–75.

139. *C. Th.* 16.4, 6 (November 18, 404). Palladius seems to place this edict in 406 under Atticus.

140. *C. Th.* 16.2, 37 (August 29, 404). This is the law mentioned above which ordered the inquiry concerning the fire to be closed.

141. *C. Th.* 16.4, 5 (September 11, 404).

142. Baur, *HJC*, vol. 2, pp. 269–71.

143. Sozomen *Hist. Eccl.* 8.23.

144. Palladius *Dialogus*, pp. 64–65. Optatus tried persuasion, as well as violence in his attempt to reunite the Johannites, and he had some success (Sozomen *Hist. Eccl.* 8. 24).

145. Socrates *Hist. Eccl.* 7. 25; Theodoret *Hist. Eccl.* 5. 34; Cyril *Epist.* 75 (*PG* 77, 348–52). Cyril, on the other hand, complained that the restoration of Chrysostom was unnecessary, since he had been successful in winning converts from the Johannites (*Ep.* 76 [*PG* 77, 352–60]).

146. Socrates and Theophanes (A.M. 5912, pp. 83–84) say specifically that Atticus acted to heal the schism, Theophanes adding that he was moved to this by the sight of the Johannites assembling outside the churches of the orthodox.

147. Marcellinus Comes *Chronicon*, p. 77.

148. Socrates *Hist. Eccl.* 7.45; Marcellinus Comes *Chronicon*, p. 77; Theophanes A.M. 5930 (pp. 93–93). Theophanes indicates that the schism had continued after the restoration of John and was not completely healed until the removal of the remains to Constantinople.

149. *C. Th.* 16.4, 5.

150. *C. Th.* 16.4, 4; 5.

151. Sozomen *Hist. Eccl.* 8.23; 24; 27. At the time of one of the attacks on the Johannites the soldiers seized jewelry and golden girdles from the faithful, certainly an indication of wealth (Sozomen *Hist. Eccl.* 8.23).

152. In this regard John and the Johannites remind one of the Novatians, who were distinguished from the official church primarily by their uncompromising morality. They, too, were accorded considerable respect, even by their enemies, although the Novatians were, theoretically at least, heretics as well as schismatics and John was no lover of their theology of forgiveness. It is interesting to note, however, that the Novatian bishop Sissinius took the lead in honoring the Johannite martyr Eutropius.

IV

NESTORIUS AND THE COUNCIL OF EPHESUS: CONSTANTINOPLE AND EPHESUS

Nestorius, Bishop of Constantinople

Twenty-four years separated the final exile of John Chrysostom from the elevation of his compatriot Nestorius to the see of Constantinople.[1] By then, Theodosius II had succeeded his father, although, like Arcadius, he seems frequently to have been under the influence of some stronger personality at court[2]—first the praetorian prefect, Anthemius, and later his sister, Pulcheria, under whose domination "la Cour de Constantinople prit une allure monastique."[3] This situation apparently changed after 421, when Theodosius married Eudocia, the former Athenais, daughter of a pagan Athenian philosopher.

During the reign of Theodosius, the Germanic threat to Constantinople diminished as the barbarians turned their attention increasingly to the West. But they were replaced by an even more formidable enemy, the Huns, who devastated areas of Thrace in 395–98, 408–13, and again sometime about 422. Their presence so near to Constantinople must have made the inhabitants nervous, and the heavy tribute they demanded placed a sizable drain on the treasury.[4]

Sisinnius, the third successor of John Chrysostom as bishop of Constantinople, died late in 427, and the historian, Philip of Side, and Proclus, the deposed bishop of Cyzicus, were the principal candidates. The monks, the clergy, and the laity each supported different persons, and there was disagreement even within these groups. The emperor at first wished to select a monk—probably the archimandrite Dalmatius—hoping that an ascetic would arouse the least opposition. But Dalmatius refused, and no one else in the monastic community would agree to accept the responsibility. Finally, Theodosius determined to appoint an outsider as bishop, someone who was not a part of the strong rivalries and who could, hopefully, undertake the governance of the church without prejudiced opposition. Just as in the case of Chrysostom, a call went out to Antioch to bring a famous Syrian preacher to Constantinople.[5]

Nestorius was born, perhaps to Persian parents, in the military settlement of Germanikeia in Syria Euphratensis, about the year 381.[6] He came to Antioch and studied in the famous theological "school" of that city, quite possibly under Theodore of Mopsuestia.[7] He became a priest and entered the ascetic life in the monastery of Euprepios just outside the walls of the city. His speaking ability first gained for him the position of expounder of Scripture in his monastery; then, when a successor to Sisinnius was being sought, it brought him to the attention of the court, since Theodosius hoped that Nestorius' oratory would aid in the instruction of the inhabitants of Constantinople. The majority of the people of the capital (οἱ πλεῖστοι) we are told, applauded the choice of Nestorius because of his reputation for austerity and asceticism.[8]

Dionysius, probably the *magister militum per Orientem*, brought Nestorius to Constantinople, and he was consecrated bishop on the tenth of April, 428.[9] Despite his favorable reception, Nestorius was faced with immediate problems. The election in which he had been chosen was hotly contested, and Proclus and Philip of Side were not the kind of men to take defeat lightly. Both had been similarly passed over two years earlier, when the supporters of Sisinnius had prevailed, and Socrates wrote that Philip reacted to that setback by including some bitter remarks about Sisinnius in his *Christian History*.[10] We may also suspect that the followers of each of these men formed parties which remained strong throughout the reign of Nestorius, for after his deposition they once again competed for the vacant episcopal throne.[11] Besides these disappointed partisans, Nestorius may have found enemies among the clergy and laity of Constantinople simply because he was an outsider, a Syrian.[12]

More significantly, Nestorius appears immediately to have encountered the opposition of the monastic community of Constantinople. This is indicated by the actions of Hypatius, a Phrygian monk who had established himself in the old villa of Rufinus near Chalcedon. When Nestorius was on his way to Constantinople, Hypatius saw a vision in which Nestorius was enthroned by "laymen." Immediately Hypatius prophesied that Nestorius would remain in office for only three and onehalf years before being removed as a heretic. The authenticity of this particular scene may properly be questioned, but not, I think, the general hostility of Hypatius and many other monks toward Nestorius from a very early time.[13] The source of this opposition may have been the failure of the monastic party to control the election, but Nestorius' early indication that he intended to exercise strict control over the ecclesiastical establishment must have contributed to it.[14]

Like Chrysostom, Nestorius succeeded episcopal administrations notable for their laxity and near-inertia in difficult matters. The episcopate of Arsacius (404–06), the immediate successor of Chrysostom, for example, was "singularly mild and peaceful."[15] Atticus (406–25), probably the strongest of the intervening bishops, was praised by Socrates for his success in pacifying and governing the church; but it is clear that this achievement was based upon concession and compromise: according to Socrates "he was all things to all men."[16] One need only remember that Atticus had responded to popular pressure in returning John to the episcopal diptychs, and his charity was extended even to heretics. Further, in an age in which rhetoric was highly praised and valued, "his sermons were not such that they received much applause from his audience, nor did they deserve to be written down."[17] As for Nestorius' immediate predecessor, Sisinnius (425–27), Socrates wrote that he was personally pious and concerned for the poor, but added that his simple disposition "rendered him rather averse to practical affairs, so that by men of active habits he was thought indolent."[18]

No one could possibly accuse Nestorius of disinterest, and the spectre of another reforming Syrian prelate may have been enough to cause the alienation of the monks from Nestorius' camp. In any case, it is noteworthy that the monastic attitude toward the new bishop was in marked contrast to the popular support which he apparently enjoyed at the beginning of his episcopate.

From these considerations, one would expect the general reaction to the episcopacy of Nestorius to be much the same as that accorded to Chrysostom: support from most of the inhabitants of the city and decided opposition from many powerful groups and individuals. Nevertheless, within a short time after his arrival in the city, Nestorius had alienated all but the most loyal of his supporters. To explain this, it is not enough simply to assert that his "personality" was less attractive than that of Chrysostom. It is true that the sources describe him as hotheaded, stubborn, impolitic, and bellicose, but these are some of the same qualities that in Chrysostom were virtues. Chrysostom's ferocity seems to have been tempered by a kindness and charity that was apparently missing in Nestorius' character, and this may have been an important distinction between the two men, but it is a difficult thing to measure or discuss in historical terms. The ecclesiastical tradition was as uniformly hostile to Nestorius as it was favorable to Chrysostom, and it is not surprising that all aspects of Nestorius' character have been universally blackened. In fact, the real distinction between the two men lay in the failure of Nestorius' policy against the heretics and his involvement in theological controversy, something which Chrysostom had generally escaped. It is true that in 397 Arianism was by no means dead in Constantinople, and

John was accused of Origenism by his enemies; but theological debate played a negligible role in the events which led to his deposition. Such was not to be the case with Nestorius.

Probably on the occasion of his consecration, Nestorius announced publicly his plan regarding heresy in the empire:

> Speaking to the emperor before all the faithful, he said, "Give me, O emperor, the land free of heretics and I will give you heaven in return; help me destroy the heretics and I will help you destroy the Persians.[19]

As mentioned before, the immediate predecessors of Nestorius had been disinclined to persecute heretics, and even though the emperor had been the author of a number of laws against heretics before 428, none of them were particularly severe and their implementation was not prosecuted rigorously:

> The laws against heretics had formidable penalties associated with them, but these were not always carried out; for the emperor had no wish to persecute his subjects.[20]

Accordingly, it is not surprising that "some of the multitude" rejoiced at the statement of the new bishop, but others—including certainly the heretics themselves—realized that only trouble would come from this program. Nestorius had "revealed himself as an ardent persecutor."[21]

Only five days after his elevation, Nestorius began to put his plan against the heretics into action. Undoubtedly with the emperor's knowledge and approval, he dispatched men to destroy a chapel of the Arians.[22] The sight of this drove the Arians into a frenzy, and they set fire to the building themselves. The church burned to the ground and the fire spread to adjoining buildings. After the fire died out,

> a disturbance (*thorybos*) arose in the city and the Arians prepared themselves for revenge. But God, the guardian of the city (ὁ τὴν πόλιν φυλάσσων), did not allow the evil to be actualized in deeds. Nestorius, however, was from that time regarded as an incendiary not only by the heretics, but also by those of his own faith.[23]

But even this disaster did not dampen Nestorius' ardor, and he continued to disturb the city. He wished to attack the Novatians of Constantinople, but either because the emperor considered them harmless or because they had influential friends at court, Theodosius refused to cooperate and they escaped the wrath of the bishop. Nestorius then extended his persecution to the Quartodecimans in Asia, Lydia, and Caria; in Sardis and Miletus many people died in a riot (*stasis*) when they resisted the efforts of the bishop of Constantinople.[24] Nestorius secured a legal basis for his activities when, on May 30, 428, Theodosius issued an edict which renewed and strengthened the old penalties for heresy.[25] Nevertheless, we must suppose that even some of those who had originally supported Nestorius' attack on heresy developed reservations when they saw the violence and questionable results of his methods.

The Christological Controversy

This was only the beginning of Nestorius' difficulties, however, for he almost immediately became involved in the complexities of the christological controversy. At this point it might be well to examine briefly the history of this dispute before 428. This is a difficult undertaking and one which presents many opportunities for confusion and error. It must involve not only an examination of theology, but also a consideration of how this evolving theology appeared to those not trained to understand it fully.[26]

Questions concerning the relationship between the divine and the human elements in the person of Christ—and questions concerning relationships among the persons of the Trinity, for these are really parts of the same problem—were as old as Christianity itself.[27] The New Testament, particularly the Gospel of John, provided a tension between the Logos, who dwelt with God from the "beginning" and who became man, and the concept of a single monarchic God. How could the Trinity and the divinity of Christ be reconciled with monotheism? To some, the apparent contradiction inherent in the idea of the Trinity was simply a mystery to be accepted as impossible to understand. Others, however, turned to the methods and systems of classical philosophy for an explanation and solution of the dilemma. The Greek philosophical schools added their vocabularies and means of approach to the controversy, but they did not provide a generally agreed upon answer.[28]

It is impossible to do justice to the complexity of views which arose, but one may simplify and identify two opposing tendencies, each of which emphasized one aspect of the problem at the expense of the rest. One of these stressed the unity of the Godhead and the all-pervasive quality of the divine element in the Trinity.[29] This tendency, represented at its extreme by the theology of Origen, Docetism, and finally Gnosticism, could not fully deny the humanity of Christ, but it made this humanity at best a secondary attribute, something which was only incidental to the person of Christ. Generally speaking, this view was characteristic of the so-called Alexandrian "school" of theology. An opposing view was held by the theologians of the "school" of Antioch, who stressed the humanity of Christ at the expense of his divinity.[30] They emphasized the monarchy of the Father and resisted any tendency toward pagan polytheism by insisting on the absolute monotheism of the Christian God. In its extreme form, these tendencies led ultimately to Monarchianism, Modalism, and Adoptionism, heresies which exalted the Father but decreased the importance of the Son.

Both of these tendencies had long traditions and many particular variations, and one should not expect them to be always mutually exclusive or easily identifiable. Nevertheless, a distinction between the tradition stressing the humanity of Christ (and the monarchy of the Father) and that emphasizing his divinity is a useful generalization in attempting to understand how complicated theological systems appeared to the largely uneducated inhabitants of the cities of the late Roman East.

In viewing the conflict between these two traditions, which is the very essence of the christological controversy, one should always remember that the question was one of more than theoretical interest. For the believer, eternity was at stake.

> Behind the seemingly unending wrangle over whether Christ existed "in two natures" or "out of two natures" lay deep questions of human salvation, not least those embodied in the doctrines of the Eucharist and the Atonement.[31]

To put the situation very simply, if Christ is God, how does Christianity differ from paganism, with its multiplicity of divinities? But if Christ is not God, then how can he have effected our salvation?

It has been common to write about "popular religion" in the later Roman empire and to suggest that the lower-class residents of the empire tended almost naturally toward one or the other of the theological positions of the time. Thus, some have claimed that the inhabitants of the East always had a taste for despotic rulers and monarchic deities. Their ancestors worshipped the gods with a singleness of purpose and an excess of devotion matched only by their political subservience in entrusting their fate to a succession of autocratic kings and emperors. Thus, Eastern popular Christianity is supposed to have smacked of pagan intrusions in following the traditions of the school of Alexandria. The people worshipped a thoroughly divine Christ and ultimately became the fanatical Monophysites who rent the empire in their refusal to compromise their age-old beliefs.[32]

Others would see the "common people" of the empire in a different light. According to this view, they tended to accept Christianity in a simple form which stressed the humanity of Christ and the singularity of the divinity. They regarded the word of the Bible with special veneration and accepted literally its ethical teachings and its picture of Christ as a real man. They represented a simple—one might almost say Judaising—Christianity and regarded all who attempted allegorical or philosophical explanations of the mysteries of the faith as pagans. Such primitive Christians ultimately became the main force behind Arianism and Nestorianism.[23]

Obviously, neither of these views alone can explain the popular support for the various christological positions, and the attribution of diametrically opposite sentiments to "popular Christianity" by different authorities must cause some suspicion as to method. It may, however, be correct to point to the importance of pre-Christian traditions and the nature and extent of the conversion to Christianity in shaping popular response to the christological controversy. Nevertheless, in the complex urban environment of the East, this popular response is unlikely to have been simple, and we should not expect to find any easy answers. It is possible, of course, that popular opinion—in Constantinople and Alexandria, in Syria and throughout Egypt—was already formed before the beginnings of the controversy and that the history of Nestorianism and Monophysitism is merely the account of the separation of peoples already different by temperament and long tradition. But such a hypothesis must be demonstrated rather than assumed.

For example, it may be possible to find some of the antecedents of fifth-century christological thought in the Arian controversy. The issue is easily confused, however, for the christological position of Arius can be viewed in two ways. He and his followers taught that there is only one nature (perhaps semidivine) in the person of Christ. They accused their opponents of teaching two natures.[34] In this sense, the Arians appear to have been proto-Monophysites.[35] Yet, viewed from another perspective, Arius remained directly in the tradition of those who maintained a simpler form of Christianity and who rejected any compromise with paganism. In their strong antipagan sentiments and their desire to view Christ as somehow inferior to the Father, the Arians maintained principles which were to be very important to Nestorius.[36]

The christological controversy *per se* began only about the middle of the fourth century when Cappadocian theology proposed terms sufficiently exact to allow precise distinctions concerning the person of Christ. The teachings of Apollinarius of Laodicea (in Syria) provided the impetus for the new struggle.[37] The father of Apollinarius—he had the same name—came from Alexandria to Laodicea, where he taught grammar. Although both father and son were Christians, together they attended the lectures of the pagan sophist, Epiphanius, and for this they were excommunicated by the Arian bishop of Laodicea. From this time at least the two Apollinarii espoused the Athanasian cause, and by about 362 they had formed around themselves an orthodox community. The younger Apollinarius became the bishop of this group, but he was soon exiled by the Arians, and he opened a theological school in Antioch.

The theology of Apollinarius was based upon two propositions: that perfect God and perfect man cannot be united in one being, and that the fathers of Nicaea had been correct in accepting the *homoousios*. It followed from these propositions that Christ could not be fully human and that the divine element should predominate in the second person of the Trinity. Apollinarius suggested that the person of Christ had a human body (*sarx*) but that the place of a human mind (*nous*) had been taken by the divine Logos. In this way, Christ had a single divine nature, and his humanity was curtailed to preserve unity. As early as 377, Basil of Caesarea began to complain about the teachings of Apollinarius, and these were soon condemned, first by Pope Damasus in 379 and then by the Council of Constantinople in 381. After 383 the adherents of Apollinarius were included in the legal condemnations of heretics and various penalties were imposed upon them.[38] Nevertheless, just as had the Arians, many Apollinarians survived their official condemnation.[39] More importantly, the disciples of Apollinarius managed to conceal many of their ideas in spurious works attributed to orthodox Fathers, and these circulated throughout the East, gaining unsuspecting converts to the heresy.[40] From this time, Apollinarius' slogan "one is the incarnate nature of God the Word" (μία φύσις τοῦ Θεοῦ λόγου σεσαρκωμένη) became the formula which divided the two sides of the christological controversy.[41]

The Outbreak of the Quarrel

Later in his life, when he was justifying his involvement in the christological dispute, Nestorius wrote that he discovered the controversy already fully developed in Constantinople when he arrived there in 428:

> But in Constantinople, when I found that men were inquiring and in need of being taught, I yielded to their persuasions as the truth required. For factions of the people who were questioning this came together to the bishop's palace, having need of a solution of their questions and of arriving at unanimity. Those on the one hand who called the blessed Mary the mother of God they called Manichaeans, but those who named the blessed Mary the mother of a man Photinians. . . . But when they were questioned by me, the former denied not the humanity nor the latter the divinity, but they confessed them both alike, while they were distinct only in name: they of the party of Apollinaris accepted "Mother of God" and they of the party of Photinus "Mother of man." But after I knew they disputed not in the spirit of heretics, I said that neither the latter nor the former were heretics, (the former) because they knew not Apollinaris and his dogma while similarly the latter (knew) the dogma neither of Photinus nor of Paul (of Samosata).[42]

If we accept this statement, and there seems little reason to reject it totally, we must conclude that controversy over the nature of Christ had already become a subject of disagreement before 428. According to Nestorius, individuals without proper theological training were discussing complex issues which they could not quite understand.[43] Factions had arisen, he claimed, not over any real theological disagreement, but because of allegiance to different theological "schools" and the use of different terminology. From the very beginning the word *theotokos* (Godbearer or Mother of God) was seen as the basis for division, and both sides accused their opponents of espousing heresies which had been condemned years before. The christological significance of the title of Mary should be obvious: if one were to stress the divine nature of Christ, his mother should be styled *theotokos*; but if an emphasis were placed on his humanity, Mary should be called *anthropotokos*, the Mother of Man (the man Jesus).[44]

This was the first theological difficulty which Nestorius had to face as bishop of Constantinople, and it was settled quietly and privately. Nestorius suggested that the disputing factions would have no cause for disagreement if they made use only of the words found in the Scriptures and called Mary *Christotokos*, the Mother of Christ.[45]

> When they heard these things they said: "Before God has our inquiry been solved." And many praised and gave glory and went away from me and remained in agreement....

But the christological dispute was far from over, and soon it again became a public issue. How and why this happened is unclear. Socrates and the enemies of Nestorius claimed that christological questions were raised by the bishop himself, or at least by members of his clerical staff. Friedrich Loofs, however, supported by evidence from Nestorius, argued that the matter was considered settled until Cyril of Alexandria and his associates revived the difficult theological question, much as Theophilus raised the issue of Origenism against Chrysostom.[47] According to this view, Cyril's enemies had accused him of some irregularities in his administration of the see of Alexandria, and Nestorius either supported the accusers or at least did nothing to defend his episcopal colleague. Thus endangered, Cyril resorted to the old expedient of casting doubt on the orthodoxy of his enemies.

Whatever the ultimate origins of the conflict, the whole matter was brought to public attention by the Syrian presbyter Anastasius. This man, whom Nestorius particularly esteemed and to whom he entrusted matters of the greatest importance, gave a sermon in Constantinople, probably late in 428, in the course of which he said: "Let no one call Mary *theotokos*. For Mary was human and it is impossible for God to be born of a human."[48] The reaction to this sermon—and in particular to the condemnation of the *theotokos*—was immediate and unfavorable: "He disturbed many of the clergy and all of the laity in this matter" (πολλοὺς κληρικούς τε καὶ λαϊκοὺς ἐν αὐτῷ πάντας ἐτάραξεν).[49]

In the midst of this disturbance, Nestorius rose to defend Anastasius. The bishop preached a number of sermons in which he also condemned the use of the term *theotokos*.[50] But, instead of clarifying the matter and settling the dispute, the sermons of Nestorius only increased the disagreement. The church of Constantinople was split into factions that "resembled combatants in a night battle, each side uttering confused and contradictory statements."[51] The dispute spread quickly outside the capital, and it finally reached Egypt, where difficulties arose even among the monks of the Nitrian desert.[52]

Eusebius (later bishop of Dorylaeum), a *scholasticus* in the service of the empress (either Pulcheria or Eudocia), was the first to speak publicly against the teachings of Nestorius and Anastasius. He posted a written document "in public and in the church [Hagia Sophia]" which began as follows:

> I have sworn this statement by the Holy Trinity so that it may be made known to the bishops, priests, deacons, readers, and the faithful living in Constantinople... that the heresy of Nestorius is of the same kind as that of Paul of Samosata who was condemned 160 years ago by the orthodox fathers.[53]

The document continued with six sayings attributed to Paul, alongside of which Eusebius placed words of Nestorius which might be interpreted in a similar sense. The obvious purpose was to show that Nestorius was as much a heretic as Paul of Samosata:

> Paul said, "Mary did not bear the Word." Agreeing with this, Nestorius said, "My good man, Mary did not bear the divinity."

Eusebius then commented on the similarity of the views of the two "heretics" and concluded:

> If someone, then, would dare to say that the Son was not the only-begotten of the Father, born before the ages and that he was not born of the Virgin Mary, and that he is not the one Lord Jesus Christ, let him be anathema.

It is noteworthy that Eusebius did not merely prepare a learned theological attack on Nestorius. Instead, he drew up a document and had it posted where it might be read by all. This document was anything but subtle, and its reasoning, while ultimately questionable, was difficult to refute. The propaganda had its effect and, according to Theophanes, Eusebius stirred up many riots and disturbances (πολλοὺς θορύβους ἤγειρε καὶ ταραχάς).[54]

Possibly in the same year, Proclus, who, it will be remembered, had lost his bid to become bishop when the emperor chose Nestorius, preached a sermon in the great church of Constantinople.[55] The occasion was a feast of the Virgin (παρθενικὴ πανήγυρις), an appropriate time for public support of the *theotokos*. Although Nestorius was present in the church, Proclus took the opportunity to condemn his teaching soundly. The thrust of Proclus' argument was clear and simple: Christ was both God and man; if he were merely a man (ψιλὸς ἄνθρωπος) salvation would be impossible.[56] He also took care to connect this unity of natures in Christ with the Virgin, so that to deny honor to Mary would be seen as questioning the divinity of Christ.[57] If anyone was confused by the controversy, this sermon must have done much to clarify the difficult theological issues involved, since it stated the theological objections to Nestorius' teaching in simple terms understandable to most of its audience.

Proclus also took care to defend the honor of the Virgin and perhaps to play on the sympathies of those who venerated Mary in a special way. Christological concerns may have been paramount in the mind of Proclus, but one has the impression that the ringing praises of the Virgin had considerable effect upon his audience:

> Brethren, today a feast of the Virgin summons the tongue to praise. The present festival is an embassy of help to those gathered together; and it is especially fitting. For it is the demonstration of purity and the most perfect boast of the race of women, the glory of the female, because [Mary was] at the same time mother and virgin. The assembly is a beautiful one. . . . For, behold, the land and the sea have become spear-bearers for the Virgin. . . . Let nature leap for joy and women be honored; let mankind dance and virgins be glorified. . . . The holy Mary has called us here together, the stainless jewel of virginity, the rational paradise of the second Adam, the workshop of the unity of the natures, the festival of the saving covenant, the bridal chamber in which the Word espoused the flesh, the living bush which the fire of the divine birth did not burn. . . slave and mother, virgin and heaven, the only bridge between God and men.[58]

Proclus concluded his sermon by quoting a prophecy from Ezekiel concerning the closed gate through which only "the lord God Israel" should come in an go out. This prophecy was "an exact description of the holy and Godbearing (*theotokos*) Mary. Let all contrary teachings be dismissed, and let us all be enlightened by the instruction of the Scriptures, so that we may have a share in the kingdom of heaven in Christ Jesus. . . ."[59] The implication is clear: anyone who denied this title to the Virgin would miss his share in the kingdom of heaven.

Unfortunately, the narrative historians tell us little about the state of affairs in Constantinople between the outbreak of the controversy in 428 and 431 when the council was called. Although it is possible that much of what Socrates and Theophanes said about 428 is appropriate to the whole period, it is clear that they were more interested in describing the outbreak of the quarrel than its subsequent development. For much of this period we must, therefore, rely on letters and other such sources, which are difficult to use because of their obvious bias and the problems they present for chronological reconstruction.

Cyril, in his first letter to Nestorius, written probably toward the middle of 429, observed that conditions were then very disturbed in Constantinople. He claimed that there were even some people in the capital who denied that Christ was God.[60] Perhaps about this same time, Cyril wrote his first letter to Pope Celestine. In this letter the bishop of

Alexandria proposed his explanation of the origin of the controversy and added a description of the contemporary situation in Constantinople:

> And there occurred a great outcry and a desire to flee among all the faithful; for they did not wish to remain in communion with those who believed thus. So now the faithful of Constantinople have seceded, except for a few rather stupid people and some flatterers of his [Nestorius], and almost all the monasteries and their archimandrites, and many members of the senate do not meet together, fearing lest they be harmed because of their faith.[61]

In this letter we have important evidence for the division of the inhabitants of Constantinople into groups supporting or opposing the use of the *theotokos* and the teaching of Nestorius. Cyril admitted that a few people continued to support their bishop, but he insisted that most of the faithful, including the monks and the senators, opposed the teachings of Nestorius and went about in fear of persecution for their beliefs.

Other evidence supports Cyril's contention that the monasteries of Constantinople continued to be centers of opposition to Nestorius. This is perhaps best illustrated by the petition submitted to the emperor by "Basil, deacon and archimandrite, Thalassius, reader and monk, and the rest of the Christian monks."[62] This document began with a partial list of all the fathers who believed that Christ "is true God." It continued by mentioning the heresy of Paul of Samosata, through which occurred "schism among the people and revolts by the priests." Now, the monks claimed, Nestorius was stirring up the same trouble again. As a result, a number of priests had been persecuted for preaching against the doctrines of Nestorius "in the church of Irene by the sea."[63] After this violence, committed, we must presume, by the soldiers of the emperor:

> The faithful (*laos*) cried out, seeking the familiar teaching of orthodoxy. And they said, "We have an emperor, a bishop we do not have" (βασιλέα ἔχομεν, ἐπίσκοπον οὐκ ἔχομεν). Meanwhile, the faithful who were arrested by the *apparitores* underwent terrible suffering. They were variously beaten in the *dekanikon* of the capital. Such things have not happened even among the barbarian nations.[64]

Some persons, the monks claimed, supported the demands of the faithful, and they were made to suffer for this. A certain zealous monk denounced Nestorius in the midst of a church, and when he was arrested he had to be dragged away screaming. Also, some of the monks planned to assassinate their bishop should divine aid not be forthcoming. A party made up of monks, other members of the clergy, and laymen approached Nestorius, and he had them seized and treated badly. The monks concluded their petition and their tale of terror with a demand that Theodosius summon an ecumenical council to deal with the heresy and injustice of the bishop of Constantinople. By doing this, the monks argued, the emperor would unite the faithful under his rule.

Even Nestorius himself admitted that he had few supporters in the monasteries of Constantinople. Complaining to Cyril, he said, "You have filled all the churches and all the monasteries with disturbance against me so that even the unfeeling have been roused to feeling."[65]

Cyril took care to involve the church of Rome in the dispute, and in August of 430 a synod in Rome, on the advice of the bishop of Alexandria, condemned the teachings of Nestorius.[66] Soon after this, Pope Celestine wrote a letter "to the priests, deacons and clergy . . . and to the catholic faithful (*laos*) who live in Constantinople."[67] In this letter, Celestine warned against the errors of Nestorius, and he launched into a series of comparisons, measuring Nestorius against the standard of other well-known ecclesiastical figures. Obviously, Nestorius did not compare favorably with his predecessors Atticus and Sisinnius, for during their episcopates heresy was suppressed,[68] and the Christian faithful were well governed. But even more damning was the comparison made between Nestorius and the condemned heretics Arius and Paul of Samosata.

Meanwhile, Cyril himself did not leave the job of propagandist entirely to others. Two letters he sent to Constantinople give us further information about this. One of them, directed to the clergy and laity of the capital, was similar to the letter of Celestine. In it Cyril warned the people about the teachings of Nestorius and reminded them that both the church of Rome and that of Alexandria had recently condemned the heresy of their bishop.[69] He feared lest they suffer a "disturbance in their faith" and said that they must not act like "a great rioting herd" (θορυβουμένη ἀγέλη μεγάλη), but like good laymen and clerics (λαοὶ καὶ ἐκκλησιοί).

These two letters, and others like them, make us wonder to what extent they reflect propaganda directed toward the people of the city. At first sight, they appear to be in a different category from the placards erected, for example, by Eusebius of Dorylaeum: letters do not normally have a very wide circulation. However, there is evidence that letters written "to the faithful" of a given city were actually read to the assembled people at public gatherings. If we may gauge from the few examples we have, these public recitations may have been quite elaborate and even theatrical. In any case, this procedure undoubtedly allowed letters to serve as a means toward the manipulation of popular opinion, particularly among those who could not read, and they should be carefully examined.

In a letter Cyril wrote to his clerical envoys in Constantinople, he discussed the origin of the controversy and accused Nestorius of dividing the person of Christ (the heresy of the two sons: one divine, one human).[70] He then reproduced two statements which he attributed to Nestorius:

> I do not judge goodwill toward me by applause, but by a desire for [correct] dogma and by the maintenance of both the divinity and the humanity of the Master.

> And I take special care for our people (*demoi*), who have very much reverence and a warm piety, but who are imperfect because of their ignorance of divine teaching. But this is not a fault of the faithful (*laoi*), but—how shall I say it appropriately?—it is because the teachers do not have time to present you with the really correct doctrines.[71]

Cyril continued by comparing Nestorius unfavorably with Atticus. He then provided some important information about the supporters of Nestorius in Constantinople:

> Is it any wonder [that I have enemies there] if I am slandered by the dregs of the city, Chairemon, Victor, Sophronas, and that boy of the disturber-of-the-peace Flavian? For they are evil both in their own matters and in everything else. And let him who stirs them up know that I am not afraid of a long journey nor of making my defense against them.[72]

Cyril concluded by predicting that Nestorius would soon find himself judged by the bishop of Alexandria.

In a long article, Eduard Schwartz has shown that the Victor mentioned in this letter was an important Egyptian monk, perhaps from the Tabbenisian cloister near Alexandria.[73] He was in Constantinople, not as a supporter of Cyril, but as one of those who had accused him of wrongdoing in the administration of his see. He later returned to Egypt, and by the time of the council in 431 he had forgotten his antagonism to the bishop of Alexandria. We know nothing about the other individuals mentioned in this letter, although it would be reasonable to assume that they were Egyptians. It is tempting to identify Flavian as the young priest who was later to become bishop of Constantinople and face the accusations of Cyril's successor, but there is no evidence to support such a hypothesis. Finally, it is interesting to note that Cyril accused Nestorius of willfully stirring up opposition to him in Constantinople and warned him to desist or face the sudden appearance of the Egyptian bishop. This may be so much rhetoric, but it does suggest that Nestorius was active in attempting to build an ecclesiastical party favorable to himself and hostile to Cyril. Probably the actions of Chairemon, Victor, and Sophronas were directed toward the court and the various bishops assembled in the capital, and we have no indication that they attempted to sway popular favor in the direction of Nestorius.

Finally, we know of two other events which happened during the time before the assembly of the Council of Ephesus. How they might have influenced public opinion is difficult to say. First despite his violent persecution of heretics, and an earlier condemnation of their doctrines, Nestorius apparently became involved with some Pelagians who had sought asylum in Constantinople. He wrote a warm letter of support to Celestine, the leader of the Pelagians, and many in Constantinople regarded the bishop as the protector of these heretics.[74] As a result, the westerner Marius Mercator produced a tract against the Pelagians and sent it to the church of Constantinople, the monasteries, and the emperor.⁷⁵ This document and the subsequent exile of the Pelagians from the Eastern capital can hardly have improved the bishop's reputation there.

At about this same time, some barbarian servants of an important man of Constantinople fled to Hagia Sophia as suppliants after a disagreement with their master. They were armed and refused to leave the chuch. After killing one ecclesiastic and wounding another, however, they killed themselves. One source says that they had planned to burn the church and suggests that they killed themselves only by mistake.⁷⁶ An observer of this event predicted that the desecration of the church was an evil omen for the future and quoted an ancient poet to support his prophecy:

> For such signs are likely to happen
> Whenever defilement breaks out in the temples.⁷⁷

Socrates noted that subsequent events confirmed this prediction, "for, as was appropriate, it indicated a dissension among the faithful and the deposition of the author of the dissension."⁷⁸ The connection of this event with the affair of Nestorius is most tenuous: the "prophecy" sounds very much like something thought up or remembered well after the event. If, however, the story is genuine, it may reflect a feeling of tension and uneasiness about the teachings of Nestorius. In such a case, unusual and particularly unfortunate occurrences might have been seen as indications of divine disapproval of the bishop of Constantinople.

The sources hostile to Nestorius, as would be expected, tried to create the impression that all of Constantinople rose in opposition against its bishop. Nestorius, for his part, failed to give any indication that he had any large popular support, and we may infer that the greater part of those actively involved in the controversy did indeed support the party of Cyril of Alexandria. Also, all the evidence indicates that the opposition to Nestorius was widespread among the clergy of Constantinople and that he had few, if any, supporters among the monks.

Yet, from the words of Cyril himself we know that some people supported Nestorius. In his letter to Pope Celestine, Cyril conceded that a few flatterers and lightheaded people still remained loyal to their bishop, and in his letter to his envoys in Constantinople, he identified four of his own bitter opponents. Further, Socrates stated that there was a division of opinion "resembling a night battle," which suggests that at least a small number of people were on the side of Nestorius.⁷⁹

The most important ally of Nestorius was the emperor himself. Theodosius, once he finally selected a bishop for his capital, was determined to defend that choice so long as he was able. Thus, Nestorius had at his disposal all the coercive force of the government, and he did not hestitate to use this when he was attacked by various clerics and laymen.

We have evidence of this in the monks' complaint of violence at the hands of his supporters. Likewise, friends of Hypatius were distressed and feared for his safety when the monk publicly removed the name of Nestorius from the diptychs, "for Nestorius was at the height of his power in the city."[80] Cyril wrote separate letters to Theodosius, to Eudocia, and to Pulcheria, warning them against the teachings of Nestorius. The emperor replied, accusing Cyril of causing all the difficulties in the church and condemning him for his attempt to sow discord in the imperial family.[81] Nestorius claimed further that he had not only the support of the emperor, but also that of the "chief men . . . . and the episcopate of Constantinople (presumably members of the *synodos endemousa*)."[82]

Unforunately, the sources do not allow us to say much about the composition of groups supporting or opposing Nestorius. While a variety of terms were used to describe the crowds involved in the affair of John Chrysostom, in the case of Nestorius the sources almost universally use *laos* rather than any of its possible synonyms.[83] This use of *laos* may have been meant (by the sources hostile to Nestorius) to imply that the crowds who opposed Nestorius were made up of all classes of the population united in their dislike of the heresy of their bishop. Or, the sources might have used *laos* to indicate the orthodox population, in order to distinguish them from the heretics who supported their enemies.

The words of Cyril appear to give us some insight into the social composition of the partisans of Nestorius. However, we must expect some exaggeration when he described them as "lightheaded people and flatterers" and "the filth of the city." On this evidence, it would surely be rash to maintain that Nestorius' support was drawn from the lowest elements of society. Cyril's terminology undoubtedly was designed to attack his enemies rather than to provide us with objective information about them. On the other end of the social scale, both Cyril and Nestorius claimed that members of the aristocracy supported them.[84] It might be suggested that important members of the imperial court supported Nestorius (because the emperor did), while rich and powerful men who were independent of imperial favor opposed him. As has been mentioned, most of the monks of the capital appear to have opposed Nestorius, and some of the secular clergy did so as well. But Nestorius certainly had some supporters among the clergy, as is indicated by the party which remained loyal to him in Ephesus. Certainly, the Syrian priests (for example, Anastasius), whom he brought with him from Antioch, did not abandon the bishop.

The sources agree that there was a "disturbance" (*tarache*) from the time of the first sermon of Anastasius until the assembly of the council itself. This *tarache* may refer to a series of riots, or the term may mean no more than an unsettled condition, or a disturbance of the mind. More rarely the sources speak of a *thorybos*—which seems more serious than a *tarache*, and may indicate a riot, although it, too, may reflect only general

Nestorius and the Council of Ephesus 97

agitation or peaceful protest. The sources never mention a *stasis*, which in other contexts often implies violence of some kind. In fact, there is no evidence whatsoever that the opponents of Nestorius (as opposed to his supporters) ever resorted to violence to give weight to their demands. We know of only one event in which the "faithful" gathered to demonstrate their opposition to Nestorius. One might suspect that this incident, which was reported only by the petition of the monks to the emperor, was arranged by the clerical opponents of Nestorius, although it may have developed spontaneously as the result of the arrest of some popular priests. In any case, the demonstrators (*laos*) were well enough organized to chant an appropriate protest: "We have an emperor, a bishop we don't have." Anyone who has witnessed a political demonstration in Greece or the Near East, or even in America, will realize the emotive power of such a rhythmical slogan.

The most difficult question concerns the motivation of those who supported or opposed Nestorius. Why did they choose one theological position rather than the other? In our discussion of the origins of the christological controversy, we have suggested that there were basically two ways of viewing the person of Christ. The view which stressed the unity and divinity of Christ at the expense of his humanity was a theological position which many have equated with paganism and "intellectual" or "philosophical" Christianity. The view which stressed the humanity of Christ, on the other hand, was a straightforward, seemingly more Biblical form of the faith which might be more easily understandable to the less educated elements in the Christian population. From this analysis one might expect that a large segment of the population of Constantinople would favor the theology of Nestorius, since he represented a simpler, antipagan tradition of christological thought. Yet just the opposite was the case. Why was there such a strong reaction against the teachings of Nestorius?

Much of the controversy turned around the use of *theotokos*. As we have seen, christological questions had been connected with the title of the Virgin from a very early date, and anyone trained in elementary theology would have understood the primary issue: to refuse to call Mary *theotokos* was to question the divinity of Christ. Nevertheless, in the theologically charged atmosphere of Constantinople, can we expect that "all the faithful" understood this point, especially since Nestorius and his followers made an attempt to present their side of the controversy?

Constantinople, of course, had no theological "school" of its own, but from the time of Gregory of Nazianzus at least the bishops of the capital seem generally to have accepted the *theotokos* without question. Moreover, the *theotokos* was much more than a term of theological disputation. Unlike the *homoousios*, which was an emotionally sterile word designed originally to distinguish the Arians from the orthodox, the *theotokos* was a powerfully evocative term which belonged to the "language of devotion."[85]

One of the earliest attested uses of the *theotokos* is in a third or fourth century papyrus, which contains a prayer to the Virgin, beseeching her as though she could herself free the supplicant from danger.[86] The Fathers of the fourth and fifth centuries—with the notable exception of John Chrysostom[87]—continued to pay increasing honor to Mary. More and more she was set as the ideal after which women, and more particularly, ascetics should strive. In this period, the monastic movement took the Virgin as its special patron, and it is not surprising to find the monks as the strongest defender of her honor.[88] Artistic and liturgical studies unfortunately contribute relatively little to our understanding of growing Mariolatry; it is well known that the popular veneration of Mary increased greatly in the fifth century, but it is not at all certain to what extent this development preceded the Council of Ephesus.[89] Yet, the institution of at least one feast of the Virgin at Constantinople and the dedication of the cathedral church at Ephesus in her honor are indications of considerable veneration. Further evidence of this development is obvious in the elaborate praise of Mary in the sermon of Proclus, discussed above.

The tendency to regard the Virgin as important in herself—as opposed to her role as subordinate to her son—may well have been the Christianization of the pagan Great Mother. There is some evidence that such was the case in the neighborhood of Constantinople. Epiphanius, already mentioned in connection with his role in the deposition of Chrysostom, provides information about a sect which he called the Collyridians. Most of the devotees of this heresy, which was most prevalent in Thrace and Scythia, were women. On certain festival days they decorated a throne for the Virgin and ceremonially offered bread to her. Epiphanius regarded these practices as pagan survivals.[90]

Nestorius' vigorous attack on the *theotokos* was prompted, at least in part, by what he felt were current abuses of the term. Thus, while he did not object to the *theotokos* in principle, he feared that its public use would lead to the errors of both Apollinarianism and Arianism.[91] In particular, it is clear that Nestorius thought that the *theotokos* would encourage an inappropriate elevation of the Virgin and a return to pagan polytheism. Some people, he said, not only failed to understand the person of Christ, but they also made a goddess of his mother:

> Does God have a mother? Then we must excuse the pagans for giving mothers to the gods.[92]
>
> But there are also some who treat the virgin mother of Christ, together with God, as in some way divine.[93]
>
> I have already said many times that if any of you, or anyone else, be simple and

prefer to use the *theotokos* then I have no objection to the term—only do not make a goddess (*thea*) of the Virgin.[94]

Most authorities have maintained that the controversy concerning the *theotokos* was carried out on purely christological grounds: that when people defended or rejected the term they were defending or rejecting the divinity of Christ. Nevertheless, it is clear that some people worshipped the Virgin as more than the instrument through which the Incarnation came about: they venerated her directly for herself and for the assistance she might give mankind. These individuals undoubtedly opposed Nestorius because he appeared to question the honor which was due to Mary.

Despite this evidence, we must admit that the narrative sources almost universally ascribe the opposition to Nestorius to christological considerations. This is as we would expect it to be, since those hostile to Nestorius would hardly maintain that their party contained idolators. Nevertheless, we cannot simply dismiss the notion that many people understood at least the basics of the christological debate. As Socrates claimed:

> Nestorius had the reputation among the many of saying that the Lord was a mere man (ψιλὸς ἄνθρωπος).[95]

The monk Hypatius appears to reflect this same sentiment: Nestorius meddled in "forbidden things" and insulted God.[96]

From this evidence, it would appear that many people understood the christological significance of the controversy. This may be explained, at least in part, by the statement of Socrates that the laity had been "taught" and "persuaded" to accept certain dogmatic principles concerning the divinity of Christ. Questions which had puzzled theologians for some time and which were still not firmly resolved were presented to the faithful of Constantinople as established propositions. Undoubtedly proponents of both sides of the controversy gave sermons in the capital, but it appears that the supporters of Alexandrian theology had gained the upper hand over their rivals from Antioch. Sermons in the churches of Constantinople prior to 428 probably tended to emphasize the divinity of Christ.[97]

We are able to say something about the people who "taught" these things to the inhabitants of Constantinople. They were not all members of the local clergy, as Nestorius wrote:

> Now the clergy of Alexandria, who were in favor of his [Cyril's] deeds, persuaded them [the inhabitants of Constantinople] as persons deceived that they should accept the word *theotokos* and they were stirring up and making trouble and going around in every place and making use of everything as a help therein.[98]

These people were undoubtedly the envoys of the bishop of Alexandria, whom we have already met several times before. Nestorius further complained that Cyril had stirred up enmity against him by having his agents carry through the city the letter which he had written to the Egyptian monks.⁹⁹ This letter and others like it from Cyril and Pope Celestine, the sermon of Proclus, and the public notice of Eusebius set forth the objections to the theology of Nestorius clearly, if simply: he forbade a term which the Fathers had used, he denied the divinity of Christ, and he taught the same things as Paul of Samosata and other condemned heretics. Such a campaign, obviously designed to sway public opinion, apparently had its result.

Noteworthy in this campaign was the use of the term "mere man"—ψιλὸς ἄνθρωπος, a phrase taken to deny the divinity of Christ—something which had been connected with the heresy of Paul of Samosata and now attributed to Nestorius. It is all but certain that this did not represent the teaching of Nestorius, but this was how his views were presented to the public. This clever piece of propaganda is a good example of the skill of Cyril and his associates in molding popular opinion. It may be added, also, that Cyril had an easier position to defend. He had merely to reiterate that to deny the *theotokos* was to deny the divinity of Christ, while Nestorius had to explain his objection to the public use of the term while maintaining his loyalty to the divinity and the humanity of Christ—a difficult task, indeed.

Many people probably joined the opposition to Nestorius for reasons that were not theological. Cyril lost no time in enlisting the support of those who favored Proclus and Philip of Side in the most recent episcopal elections; they were naturally jealous of the new bishop.¹⁰⁰ We have already seen that Proclus was a leading spokesman in this opposition. Those who regarded their bishop as an arsonist and furious persecutor, a foreigner and unbending moralist, also may have joined the opposition.¹⁰¹ These probably included the greater part of the monastic community.

The reasons why some people remained loyal to Nestorius are not difficult to ascertain. Throughout this period the bishop received the support and assistance of the emperor, and an early observer of the controversy probably felt that Nestorius would defeat his Alexandrian rival. Also, it is certain that some people supported Nestorius because they agreed with his theology. Teachers from the "school" of Antioch had been active in Constantinople, and they may have won some adherents to their views. Some of Nestorius' followers may also have been adherents of an older, more primitive form of Christianity which, generally speaking, Nestorians represented. Nevertheless, by persecuting potential allies, such as the Arians, Quartodecimans, and Novatians, Nestorius alienated much of his support and stood alone.

The Council of Ephesus—431

All parties to the controversy were willing to settle the dispute by reference to general council. The monks, as we have seen, demanded that a council be convened to condemn Nestorius. Cyril, remembering the triumph of his uncle at the Council of the Oak and confident of his own theological ability and the support of Pope Celestine, was anxious to submit the matter to a council. Nestorius himself, perhaps trusting in his own innocence and the support of the emperor, may have been the first to press for a council.[102] Theodosius, on the other hand, resisted the idea. He had selected Nestorius as bishop of Constantinople, and he wished to defend him rather than have him examined by a council. The chronicler Malalas indicated that the emperor yielded only after much pressure was put upon him:

> When a disturbance occurred because of his [Nestorius'] sermons, Theodosius himself was forced to summon the council.[103]

There can be little doubt that by *tarache* the chronicler meant the general unrest we have been describing above. Finally, on November 30, 430, Theodosius yielded. He issued a letter to all the metropolitans of the empire, requiring them to appear in Ephesus, along with a few of their subordinate bishops, at Pentecost of 431.[104]

Nestorius arrived in Ephesus immediately after Easter and, although he was the first of the great metropolitans, he found many ordinary bishops already assembled in the city awaiting the opening of the council.[105] He was accompanied by what Socrates called "a powerful mob"(πολλὴ δύναμις ὄχλων).[106] This phrase probably refers to a group of ruffians Nestorius had recruited near the Baths of Zeuxippos before he left Constantinople.[107] The bishop thus came to Ephesus with a kind of popular bodyguard. Nestorius was also accompanied by his friends the *comes* Ireneus, and by Candidianus, the *comes domesticorum*. The emperor had commissioned Candidianus to preserve order in Ephesus so that the deliberations of the bishops might proceed in peace; he was to be especially concerned that outsiders not cause "riots" (*thoryboi*).[108] Ireneus had no official commission and went to Ephesus, apparently, out of friendship for the bishop. Each of these men undoubtedly brought a large contingent of soldiers with him. The party of Nestorius clearly expected some resistance in Ephesus, and they came prepared to meet it.

Not long after Nestorius had settled in the city, Cyril of Alexandria arrived, accompanied by about fifty-five bishops and a considerable number of monks and other hangers-on.[109] The two principals occupied their time before the beginning of the council by attacking each other verbally and making public appeals for support.[110] Much of this propaganda was directed at the bishops, but there undoubtedly was an attempt on the part of both sides to influence the populace of Ephesus. It was probably at this time that Nestorius delivered his famous, but unfortunate sermons in which he said that he would never call an infant (that is, the

Christ child) God.¹¹¹ One can imagine that the supporters of Cyril quickly spread this statement throughout the city, making the appropriate comments on it and emphasizing the heresy of the bishop of Constantinople.

Control over the ecclesiastical situation in the city was exercised by Memnon, bishop of Ephesus, who was an avowed enemy of Nestorius. Ephesus had been an extremely important see and it had, along with Alexandria, suffered most from the growth in importance of Constantinople. In fact, Ephesus probably had more to fear from Constantinople than had Alexandria, as the bishops of the capital had real interests in Asia: John Chrysostom, it will be remembered, became involved in the selection of the bishop of Ephesus, and Nestorius himself had encroached on the prerogative of Memnon in his persecution of the Quartodecimans in Asia. Probably because of this enmity, Memnon closed all the churches of Ephesus to Nestorius and his followers, gathered large groups of violent people and stirred them into a fury against the bishop of Constantinople.¹¹² Nestorius fled to the house which had been reserved for his use, and there he was protected by the soldiers:

> Seditious persons filled the city with idle and turbulent men, who were assembled together by Memnon, the bishop of Ephesus; and he was at their head and was making them run about armed in the city, in such wise that every one of us fled and hid himself and had resort to caution and saved himself in great fear.¹¹³

Although Nestorius came to Ephesus with his official and unofficial bodyguards, he was not safe against the violence controlled by Memnon and Cyril.

The story of the opening of the council is familiar enough.¹¹⁴ The day of Pentecost, June 7, which had been set for the opening ceremony, passed without the arrival of the Eastern bishops under the leadership of John of Antioch. The bishops already in Ephesus agreed to wait for some time, but on the twenty-first of June, Cyril proposed to open the council on the following day. In doing this, he relied on the commission given him by Pope Celestine (as "prosecutor" of Nestorius), and he claimed that further delay in the heat of the summer would cause more sickness and death among the bishops. The supporters of Nestorius realized that the exclusion of the oriental delegation would deprive them of their most influential support, and sixty-eight bishops signed a letter protesting the decision of Cyril and demanding that the council await the arrival of John of Antioch.¹¹⁵ The next day the delegation sent by these bishops was driven violently from the council, and Cyril paid no attention to the protests of Candidianus, who produced letters from the emperor requiring all metropolitans to be present before the beginning of the debate.¹¹⁶ Although Candidianus knew that Cyril's actions were in direct violation of the wishes of the emperor, he did not attempt to delay the opening of the council by force. As Nestorius wrote some time later:

> And, as I suppose, Candidianus knew them [the supporters of Cyril] and was frightened by them; and by words alone would he have hindered them; but he dared not proceed to deeds and to afflict those who did such things.[117]

One must wonder at Candidianus' restraint. Perhaps he did not feel that his orders authorized him to use force against the bishop of Alexandria, but his troops later attacked other ecclesiastics. More likely, and despite the preparations made by the supporters of Nestorius, Candidianus felt that his forces were no match for the armed "idle and turbulent men ... assembled by Memnon."

Cyril opened the council on June 22 "in the church called Mary."[118] The council then dispatched four bishops to summon Nestorius. When they returned, one of these, an Egyptian named Theopemptos, reported that they saw a number of soldiers with clubs in the house of Nestorius.[119] These soldiers told the bishops that they had orders not to allow anyone to enter the house. But some of the clergy in Nestorius' party came outside and told the bishops to wait. The tribune Florentius, a subordinate of Candidianus, reported that Nestorius would soon appear. After some time, however, Florentius returned and told the bishops that no one could see Nestorius. Another attempt was made to invite Nestorius to the council, but when the envoys arrived at the gate of his house, they found soldiers armed with clubs again barring their entrance. The soldiers shoved the bishops out of the shade and into the heat of the sun and otherwise bullied them. Despite the protests of the bishops, the soldiers told them that they would not be admitted even if they stood in the sun all day. John of Hephaestos, who reported these events to the synod, supposed that the soldiers took their orders "from him"—that is, from Nestorius.[120]

Nestorius did not deny that his dwelling was protected by soldiers or that the soldiers had mistreated the envoys of the council. Instead, he claimed that the messengers sent to his house had come not to convey him to the council, but to do away with him:

> Seditious persons ... came under the pretence of summoning me to the council ... but in reality they came to carry me off by assault and by violence and to spread the rumor that "he has surely perished." From the fact that you [Cyril] reproach us with posting soldiers, it is clear that if they had not first been posted around me and been a wall for me, I should have been destroyed by violent men.[121]

Since Nestorius did not answer his summons to attend the council, the supporters of Cyril moved quickly to his deposition. Many of the bishops uttered short statements condemning Nestorius, and some of his "blasphemous" words were read. Then, the bishops shouted "These are the

104 *Vox Populi*

opinions of all; we all say this; this is the universal prayer," and Nestorius was formally deposed.[122]

Meanwhile, many of the inhabitants of Ephesus had assembled outside the church where they anxiously awaited the decision of the council. Triumphantly, Cyril wrote back to the church of Alexandria:

> We bishops, more than two hundred of us, came out together. And all the faithful (*laos*) of the city remained from early morning to early evening awaiting the decision of the holy council. When they heard that the blasphemer had been deposed, all with one voice began to praise the holy synod and to glorify God, because the enemy of the faith has fallen. While we were coming out of the church, they went before us with lamps even unto our lodgings—for it was evening. And there arose much joy and illumination in the city, so that even the women went before us carrying censers. And the Savior revealed his glory to the blasphemers, since he can do anything.[123]

The assembly of such a crowd outside the church may well have influenced the decision of the council. Cyril and his followers probably took care to mention the arrival of the people to those bishops who had not yet abandoned Nestorius, and they may have taken that into consideration in casting their vote for the deposition. It is interesting to speculate what might have been the reception of the bishops had Nestorius not been condemned. Also noteworthy was the participation of the women of Ephesus in this demonstration.[124]

Some time after June 22, Cyril wrote another letter to the church of Alexandria. At that time, popular demonstrations were still continuing in Ephesus:

> For [there was] happiness among the teachers and leaders of the faithful (*laoi*) ... so that all agreed, saying with one mouth, "One Lord, one faith, one baptism."[125]

The formulaic quality of this slogan and its recollection of the words of Scripture (see *Ephesians* 4.5, a particularly appropriate book of the New Testament!) are obvious. Such a slogan and such uniformity are unlikely to have occurred without considerable organization.

The situation had not calmed appreciably when the Easterners, under the leadership of John of Antioch, finally arrived in Ephesus on June 26. They wrote to the emperor:

> Being commanded by your pious letters, we arrived in the metropolitan city of Ephesus. And we found the affairs of the church filled with civil war and all manner of confusion. Cyril of Alexandria and Memnon conspired together and assembled a crowd of countryfolk (πλῆθος ἀγροικικόν) .[126]
>
> He [Memnon] closed the holy churches, the holy *martyria*, and the church of St. John (τὸ ἅγιον ἀποστόλιον) , not allowing the feast of Pentecost to be celebrated ... and gathering together a crowd of country-folk, he disturbed the city.[127]

But it is Nestorius himself who gives us the fullest description of these disturbances:

> And the followers of the Egyptian and those of Memnon, by whom they were aided, were going round the city, girded and armed with rods, stiff-necked men, who rushed upon them [the supporters of Nestorius] with the clamor of barbarians and . . . breathing anger without self-control, with all pride, against those whom they knew not to be in agreement with the things which were done by them. They were taking bells around the city and were kindling fire in many places and handing round documents of various kinds; and all those things which were taking place were matters of astonishment and fear, so that they blocked all the ways and made everyone flee and not be seen, and they were behaving arbitrarily, giving way to drunkenness and to intoxication and to a disgraceful outcry. And there was no one hindering, nor even bringing aid, and thus men were angered. But all of it was being done against us, and for this reason we made use of the aid of the emperors and of the authority of the *strategoi*, who were angered at the things which were done, though they let them be.[128]

Thus, the followers of Cyril, including peasants from the surrounding countryside, Egyptian sailors, and various ecclesiastics, went around the city like travelling showmen. They displayed diverse documents describing the heresy of Nestorius, and they summoned crowds by ringing bells and lighting fires (if, indeed, the fires were not set for more destructive purposes). Against this, the armed force of Candidianus and Ireneus continued to do nothing.

The opponents of Nestorius had no intention of allowing popular excitement to dwindle. Soon after the close of the first session of the council, several bishops delivered a series of sermons which strongly defended Alexandrian theology.[129] Although these sermons were largely concerned with difficult questions of Christology, the presentation of these ideas was simple and easy to understand. Unlike most contemporary theological works, they made use of uncomplicated arguments and an almost commonsense appeal to scriptural authority. Of particular interest is the last sermon of Cyril, for it seems to advocate a veneration of the Virgin which considerably exceeds christological considerations: "Mary the *theotokos*, the holy ornament of all the universe, the unquenchable lamp, the crown of virginity, the sceptre, the container of the uncontainable, mother and virgin."[130] The similarity to the sermon of Proclus in Constantinople is striking. In both cases, the Virgin was praised for her own virtues as well as for her connection with the birth of Christ.

We must consider further evidence before we describe the party of Nestorius as the innocent victims of malicious violence, for the followers of Cyril accused Nestorius and his party of initiating much of the disturbance which followed the first session of the council. In a letter addressed to the emperor, the bishops of Cyril's council claimed that Nestorius had been in no danger in Ephesus, but that he had made the soldiers attack the bishops only to avoid having to make his defense before the council.[131] In their synodal letter to Pope Celestine, the bishops complained about "violence against the holy synod,"[132] and Cyril accused the soldiers of mistreating the envoys sent to John of Antioch.[133]

But it was Memnon who raised the most interesting charges against Nestorius and his supporters. Shortly after they reached Ephesus and learned of the condemnation of Nestorius, the oriental bishops assembled in council and promptly deposed Memnon and Cyril.[134] Memnon reacted by sending a letter to the clergy of Constantinople, listing the abuses he and his party had suffered during and after the council.[135] Candidianus and Ireneus, he complained, had ordered their soldiers to attack the bishops of the council, and they inflicted many wounds upon them. More specifically, Candidianus prevented supplies from reaching the council, organized "a great mob of country-folk from the ecclesiastical properties" (πολὺ πλῆθος χωρικοκῶν ἀπὸ τῶν ἐκκλησιαστικῶν κτημάτων),[136] encouraged the ruffians whom Nestorius had brought from the Baths of Zeuxippos, and "filled the city with disturbance." Ireneus, for his part, attempted to have someone else consecrated bishop of Ephesus. "All the orthodox of the city," however, resisted this, and by seizing the churches they prevented the replacement of their bishop.[137] Ταραχὴ γὰρ ταραχὴν ἀπαύστως διαδέχεται.

Violence was apparently carried out by the partisans of both sides. Cyril and Nestorius had come to Ephesus prepared for violence, and each party attempted to use the force at its disposal to best advantage. Cyril controlled the monks and sailors he had brought from Egypt and the local mobs assembled by Memnon; Nestorius was supported by imperial troops and bands of ruffians brought from Constantinople. An interesting element in these disturbances was the country population, members of which were brought into the city by both sides. Possibly these peasants did not have any strong ideological ties to either of the parties so that they could be easily manipulated.

Nevertheless, the people and clergy of Ephesus appear strongly to have supported the party of Cyril. This was in part occasioned by the propaganda of the Cyrillians (encouraged by Memnon, who closed the churches to the Nestorians), but simple loyalty to their bishop may also have played a part. That is, as in the cases we have examined already, nontechnical, almost simplistic presentation of complex theological issues and loyalty to a popular bishop counted for much in the determination of popular opinion.

Nevertheless, it can be argued that the faithful of Ephesus felt a particular veneration for the Virgin Mary and that they opposed Nestorius and his teachings for this reason.[138] Ephesus, it will be remembered, was in antiquity the site of the worship of Artemis of the Ephesians, who was herself also a virgin and mother, and St. Paul, in the first century, had occasion to experience the devotion of the Ephesians to their patron deity. Very early the tradition had become established that the apostle John had come to Ephesus late in his life and had died there. Since the New Testament indicates that the mother of Christ had been placed under the care of John after the Crucifixion, it is not surprising that a tradition developed which linked the Virgin with Ephesus. The earliest evidence of this tradition is Epiphanius' (late fourth century) denial that the Scriptures said anything about the death of the Virgin or her journey to Asia with John.[139] However, by the early fifth century the story of the death of the Virgin in Ephesus had become established, at least in that city, and Mary had become the patronness of the inhabitants. Thus, the church in which the council was held was "called Mary" (καλουμένη Μαρία), a designation which may indicate a popular appellation which had not yet received official sanction. Further evidence of the close connection between Mary and Ephesus is found in a letter written by Cyril's council to "the clergy and the faithful":

> Wherefore the impious Nestorius, the renewer of heresy, came first into the [city] of the Ephesians, that place where [are][140] John the Theologian and the holy Mary, the *theotokos parthenos*.

The sermon of Cyril, in which he praised the Virgin in terms of strong veneration, may very well have been intended to maintain the support of the people of Ephesus, for whom the honor of Mary was the primary concern of the controversy. Also, it is interesting to note that some of the women of Ephesus played an important part in the joyful procession after the deposition of Nestorius. It may be suggesting too much, but it should be remembered that women had characteristically been among the most ardent worshippers of the Asian Great Mother and of the Christian Mother of God (for example, the Collyridians mentioned above).

Memnon probably opposed Nestorius for reasons of ecclesiastical politics; Nestorius was bishop of Constantinople and he had already shown himself ready to meddle in the affairs of the bishop of Ephesus. One would like to know whether such a feeling of local patriotism, perhaps a survival of the local jealousies common in the classical period, was felt by the inhabitants of Ephesus. Did they regard Nestorius as an enemy simply because he was bishop of Constantinople? It would be reasonable to assume that they did, but there is no certain evidence to confirm or deny this hypothesis.[141]

Their uniformity of opinion allowed the people of Ephesus to play an important role at the Council of 431. As we have already mentioned, the presence of a large, probably vocal crowd outside the conciliar church may have influenced the votes of a few of the bishops. More importantly, the people of Ephesus posed a counterforce to the troops of Candidianus and Ireneus. As we have seen, the supporters of Nestorius planned to use violence to force the acquittal of the bishop of Constantinople, or at least to nullify the machinations of Cyril. They were able to do neither. The soldiers of Candidianus terrorized some of the bishops, but they stood by helplessly while the Cyrilians openly disregarded the wishes of the emperor and condemned his bishop. The forces brought to Ephesus by Nestorius may have been adequate to deal with Cyril's Egyptian troublemakers, but they could do nothing in the face of organized, unified popular opposition. Most of the violence mentioned by the sources was carried out by "outsiders," but in the background loomed the threat of massive popular rebellion. Candidianus might neutralize a few rebellious bishops or discontented monks, but he could not subdue the whole population of the metropolitan city of Asia.

Constantinople after the Council

While this was going on in Ephesus, the situation was not much calmer in Constantinople. Immediately after his deposition, Nestorius wrote to the emperor describing the violence and illegality committed by the followers of Cyril and Memnon.[142] Candidianus complained to Theodosius as well and, although his letter has not survived, we can be sure that it was bitterly hostile to the party of Cyril.[143] The council also addressed a letter to the emperor defending its actions, but either Theodosius never received this communication or he paid no attention to it, as he was still determined to support Nestorius.[144] On June 29, he dispatched the *agens in rebus* Palladius to Ephesus with a letter which specifically condemned everything that had been done there. He reproved the bishops for acting before the arrival of the oriental contingent, forbade any of the participants from leaving the city, and promised that he would send another imperial official to investigate the situation fully.[145]

Meanwhile, the agents of Cyril had been active in Constantinople during the absence of Nestorius. And the bishop of Alexandria, undoubtedly aware of the adverse reaction which the deposition of Nestorius would have on the emperor, was not slow to take advantage of the tense situation in the capital. Immediately after the condemnation of Nestorius, Cyril dispatched a letter to the clergy and *oikonomoi* of the church of Constantinople. This short letter announced the deposition of the bishop and concluded with a warning for them to watch over the property of the church in the city.[146] The news of the action of the council spread rapidly throughout Constantinople, and the agents of Cyril were quick to point out that the emperor's support of Nestorius was contrary to the decision of an ecumenical council. The result was predictable. In the words of Nestorius:

> When the followers of Cyril saw the vehemence of the emperor . . . they roused up a disturbance and discord among the people with an outcry, as though the

emperor were opposed to God; they rose up against the nobles and the chiefs who acquiesced not in what had been done by them and they were running hither and thither. And . . . they took with them those who had been separated and removed from the monasteries by reason of their lives and their strange manners and had for this reason been expelled, and all who were of heretical sects and were possessed with fanaticism and with hatred against me. And one passion was in them all, Jews and pagans and all the sects, and they were busying themselves that they should accept without examination the things which were done without examination against me; and at the same time all of them, even those who had participated with me at table and in prayer and in thought, were agreed . . . against me and were vowing vows one with another against me. . . . In nothing were they divided.

There is much to say on the subject of the dreams which they recounted, which they say that they saw concerning me, while others [saw] other things. And they amazed the hearers by the saints . . . whom they saw and by the revelations which were recounted by them and by a prophecy which was fabricated. For there was none of them who was unaffected nor [any] that was distinct from their communion; I speak not only of Christians but also [of] pagans. For they were persuading all men of the things which they were seeing, likening themselves to angels of light. . . . The emperor allowed everything to take place . . . for they were not frightened by him nor [feared] to cause sedition and to run about to all men.[147]

This testimony of Nestorius, written some years after the event, is most interesting, for it tells us not only something about the composition of the groups opposing him, but also gives us considerable information about the means they used to influence popular opinion. The original support of Nestorius seems to have disappeared. The emperor and the "nobles and chiefs," who were probably members of the imperial court,[148] still remained loyal to Nestorius, but the bishop admitted that even those who had previously been closest to him had now abandoned him—perhaps because of the decision of the council, perhaps because of the threats of the Cyrillians. More importantly, the opponents of Nestorius were united in everything. We may be suspicious of Nestorius' statement that among his enemies were Jews, pagans, and heretics, but it is not impossible that these disgruntled groups all found unity in opposition to the bishop of Constantinople.[149]

At the forefront of the opposition was the monastic community of Constantinople. It is interesting that Nestorius describes some of these monks as those who "had been separated and removed from the monasteries by reason of their lives and their strange manners." This would seem to support Dagron's hypothesis about the unique nature of urban monasticism in Constantinople and its antagonism toward the bishop of the city. Nestorius clearly represented a threat to the monastic movement, including those who had been removed for their unusual practices, and its leaders were outspoken in their opposition to the bishop.[150]

110 *Vox Populi*

The actions of the Cyrillians are reminiscent of the carnival-like atmosphere which prevailed in Ephesus somewhat earlier. They ran about the city, attracting adherents from all quarters and attacking their enemies openly. On this occasion, the Cyrillians added visions and prophecies as proof of their orthodoxy. Unfortunately, we cannot identify any of these supernatural occurrences specifically, except perhaps the earlier vision of Hypatius and the prophecy that Nestorius would be deposed after three and one-half years. We can imagine, however, that they took the form of the "appearance" of various saints warning against the heretical teachings of Nestorius.[151] Particularly interesting is Nestorius' assertion that his enemies likened "themselves to angels of light."

Theodosius, as would be expected, feared revolution in Constantinople, and he determined to prevent further communication between the council and the city. Guards were set over the principal routes of access, and the leaders of the clergy watched the sea and the roads in vain. Sometime in early July a letter arrived at the gates of Constantinople, addressed by the council to the bishops Komarios and Potamon, and the archimandrites Dalmatius, Timotheos, and Eulogios.[152] After some delay caused by the blockade, a beggar brought the letter into the city concealed in his cane.[153]

The anti-Nestorian bishops in Constantinople then drew up a statement, which they presumably sent to the fathers of the council, describing events in the capital:

> All the monasteries arose, together with their archimandrites, and they went out toward the palace singing antiphons. There was a certain holy Dalmatius,[154] one of the archimandrites; for forty-eight years he had not left his monastery, but had remained inside and the pious emperor had come to see him... While he was praying concerning this [the deposition of Nestorius], a voice came down from heaven and [ordered him] to go out. For God did not wish his flock to perish. There was with them a large number of the orthodox faithful (*laos*). When they went into the palace, the archimandrites were ordered by the emperor to go inside and the greater part of the monks and the faithful remained outside singing psalms.[155]

Nestorius also furnished a report of this scene:

> They held assemblies of priests and troops of monks and they took counsel against me.... And they had as helpers in these things all the ministers of the emperor.... As indeed the *schema* of the monks was very dear to him, so all of them were unanimous in the one purpose of persuading him... And all of the monks participated ... even those who in other things were without love among themselves, [some] being enemies and [others] envied, especially for the sake of the praise of them. And they took for themselves as organizer and chief, in order to overwhelm the emperor with amazement, Dalmatius the archimandrite, who for many years had not gone forth from his monastery; and a multitude of monks surrounded him in the midst of the city, chanting the office, in order that all the city might be assembled with them and proceed before the emperor and be able to hinder his purpose. For they had prepared

all these things in advance in order that there might not be any hindrance and they went in with [the chanting] of the office even to the emperor.[156]

After this elaborate procession reached the palace, Dalmatius was granted an audience with the emperor. Theodosius was astonished to see the retiring monk and asked him why he had left his monastery, since not even sickness in the imperial family or tumults in the city had moved him before. Dalmatius replied that God had commanded him to reprove the emperor for his defense of Nestorius. Theodosius answered that he found no fault in his bishop, and he reminded Dalmatius that he and all the other monks had refused the episcopal chair when it had been offered to them.

> "Neither do I find any cause of blame in this man; I and my empire and my race are guiltless of this impiety" [the deposition of Nestorius] ... And Dalmatius and those with him cried out: "On me let this impiety be, O emperor; I rebuke thee and thine on account of these things; I will make my defense for these things before the tribunal of Christ, as having done this very deed." And after he [had] received this promise [that the archimandrites would take the responsibility for the deposition of Nestorius] ... he decreed and confirmed the things which had been done against me.[157]

The letter which the clergy of Constantinople sent to the council in Ephesus described the scene after the confrontation between Dalmatius and the emperor:

> Then they came out, having received a just answer. And all cried out, "The orders of the emperor!" (τὰ μανδάτα τοῦ βασιλέως). Then they said, "Let us go off to the martyrion of the holy Mokios[158] to read the letter and learn of the order of the emperor!" Then everyone went away, both the monks and the laymen; for the road was an important one. Carrying candles and singing the last psalm in the last region of the city, the monks were joined by the faithful. When they saw the large number of people,[159] they cried out against the enemy. Then they came to the martyrion of the holy Mokios and the letter was read to them.[160]

After listening to the letter from the council, the faithful of Constantinople cried out with one voice: "anathema to Nestorius." Dalmatius then quieted the crowd and told them of his interview with the emperor. According to this account, the primary concern of Dalmatius was to secure Theodosius' assurance that messages from the council could reach the clergy of Constantinople without interference. And, as in the account of Nestorius, the emperor agreed.[161]

Nestorius presented another version of this scene:

> The impious band went forth from [his] majesty and some spread abroad [some things] and others other things against me; and they carried Dalmatius around, reclining on a couch which was spread with coverlets, and mules bore him in the midst of the streets of the city, in such wise that it was made known

to all men that a victory had been gained over the purpose of the emperor, amidst great assemblies of the people and the monks, who were dancing and clapping hands and crying out the things which can be said against one who has been deprived for inequity. But after it was known that the intention of the emperor had been overcome by them, all the heretics, who had formerly been deprived by me, took part with them, and all with one mouth were alike proclaiming my anathema, taking courage from anything that had taken place, in every part of the city, but especially in the parts by the sanctuary, in such wise that they added crowds of the people to themselves and committed inequity without reverence. Thus they took courage, clapping their hands and saying nothing except "God the Word died!" And there was not any distinction between heretics and orthodox ... and they were fighting without mercy against those who were not persuaded to predicate the suffering of the nature of God the Word. . . . The services in the churches and in the monasteries were forgotten and they were busied with sedition and persecution and affairs such as these. As for those who were furnishing them with money and supplies and provisions, by all these things which they were giving they were both preparing them and demanding of them to be ceaselessly engaged in these things.[162]

In this passage, Nestorius claimed that the monks and the people involved in the demonstrations against him were being paid for their actions and that whoever was supplying them with money and provisions required them to continue their demonstration. Although Nestorius did not make the accusation directly, he undoubtedly meant to imply that Cyril and Alexandrian cash were behind this apparently spontaneous outpouring of popular sentiment.

Socrates summed up his impression of events in Constantinople in these words:

After the deposition of Nestorius there arose a terrible disturbance (*tarache*) in the church of Constantinople. For, as I have already said, the faithful (*laos*) were disturbed by his exaggerated speech. By common agreement, however, all the clergy anathematized him.[163]

The dispute was not, of course, ended by the decision of the emperor to abandon his support of Nestorius.[164] Cyril and Memnon, as well as the bishop of Constantinople, had been deposed, and they were under arrest in Ephesus. The oriental delegation was still adamant, and a full imperial investigation had been promised. This latter, indeed, never came about, but both "councils" (that of Cyril and that of the Easterners) were invited to send delegations to present their cases to the emperor in Chalcedon. The dispute dragged on, and a full reconciliation was not achieved until 435.[165] But after the meeting of Theodosius and Dalmatius, all support for Nestorius effectively collapsed. Nestorius returned to his monastery in Syria, and a short time later Maximianus was elected his successor as bishop of Constantinople.[166]

Some time after the close of the council, Theodoret came to Chalcedon, representing views not far removed from those of Nestorius, and he was pleased to find considerable popular support for Antiochene theology.

According to his account, a veritable stream of people came to him, presumably from Constantinople.¹⁶⁷ He celebrated the liturgy among them, and they were so pleased by his preaching that they remained there, through the heat of the sun, until the seventh hour. In a similar fashion, Theodoret received "the whole of the clergy and the good monks," who assisted him in his struggle with the Cyrillians. The result was that many of "our people" (οἱ μεθ᾽ ἡμῶν λαϊκοί) were wounded, along with many of the false monks. The emperor, as might be expected, wondered that Theodoret was able to gather such popular support.

These people who flocked to Chalcedon to hear the preaching of Theodoret were undoubtedly supporters of Nestorius. Yet, so far as we can tell, they had made no effort in his behalf at the time of his deposition. Probably they were smaller in number than Theodoret would have us believe, and they were obviously without leadership until he arrived. This, plus the awesome organization prepared by the Cyrillians and the monks of Dalmatius, undoubtedly cowed the Nestorians and prevented them from aiding their bishop in his time of need.

The disturbances in Constantinople which followed the deposition of Nestorius were of a familiar kind. The alignment of forces on either side was the same as before the council, except that now the agents of Cyril had done their job effectively, and they could also point to the decision of a council to justify their action. We can identify no supporters of Nestorius outside those in the service of the emperor, and even some of these had now allied with Cyril.

The wealth of the bishop of Alexandria was proverbial, and Cyril did not hestitate to use the resources of his church in defense of the faith. He distributed 1,400 pounds of gold to various members of the imperial court shortly after the Council of Ephesus, and this large-scale bribery must have had some effect upon the outcome of the affair of Nestorius, especially since Cyril sought the support of the empress Pulcheria by this means.¹⁶⁸ The sources further stress the importance of the personal intervention of Dalmatius in changing the emperor's mind. These were probably the crucial factors involved, but we know that Theodosius altered his position during a massive popular demonstration designed explicitly to convince him that all the inhabitants of the city were united in their dislike of Nestorius. The sources tell us that the goal of that assembly of monks and laymen was to "hinder the purpose" of the emperor and to force him to change his mind. Before the council, the emperor knew that Nestorius was unpopular in Constantinople, but at least a few people supported him, and it could be hoped that popular antagonism might be overcome. The demonstrations which followed his condemnation must have convinced Theodosius that Nestorius could remain as bishop only at the cost of overwhelming public opposition. This is not to discount the role played by the personality of Dalmatius and the intrigue of Cyril; it is only to suggest that when Theodosius made his decision to abandon Nestorius, he probably considered the large, well-organized crowd just outside the walls of the palace.[169]

Also, we should note that, just as in earlier demonstrations in Constantinople and Ephesus, the emperor did not interfere with the expression of popular opinion, even though it ran exactly counter to his well-known wishes. Perhaps the emperor wanted to have a definitive statement of the popular will before he made a final decision on the fate of Nestorius.

As a last point, we should ask once again whether the disturbances which occurred during the episcopate of Nestorius can be explained in terms other than religious. That is, is it possible that some people opposed Nestorius for social, political, or economic reasons? In this connection, it is well to remember that Nestorius must have been regarded, in Constantinople at least, as the "emperor's man": Theodosius had selected him and supported him against the wishes of most of the clergy of the capital. It could be suggested, then, that some people saw in their opposition to Nestorius a way to indicate their disapproval of imperial policy in general.

This is an extremely difficult question, and the evidence for it is less than satisfactory. As we would expect, the sources give no indication that there were any social or political considerations involved, and they explain the affair exclusively in religious terms. There may, however, have been nonreligious factors which our sources (most of which are concerned with religious questions) simply did not report. The increased need for gold occasioned by the large payments made to the Huns in these years may well have created unrest among certain segments of the population, particularly the merchants, who had to pay the *chrysargyron*, and the senators, who were liable for the *collatio glebalis* and the *aurum oblaticum*.[170] But there is no certain evidence of such unrest at just this time. Much less do we have evidence that these people translated their dissatisfaction into a protest against the religious policy of the emperor.

One approach to this problem is to see whether any social or economic groups consistently supported one side in the controversy. In the case of Nestorius, we have seen that such divisions in the populations of Constantinople and Ephesus do not emerge clearly. The inhabitants of Ephesus unanimously supported their bishop, Memnon, and after the council the inhabitants of Constantinople almost unanimously called for the condemnation of Nestorius.

During his tenure as praetorian prefect and regent for the young Theodosius, Anthemius reorganized the administration of the food supply of Constantinople.[171] It has been generally assumed that this resulted in years of plenty for the inhabitants of the capital. Nevertheless, there was again a shortage of grain in Constantinople in 431, and the people apparently blamed the emperor:

At this time, when Theodosius was holding a procession to the public granaries, a shortage of wheat fell upon the *plebs* and the emperor was assailed by stones from the starving people.[172]

The sources do not tell us when during the year this event took place or whether it was before or after the disturbances described above. But it may be more than coincidence that the great demonstrations supporting the deposition of Nestorius and the dramatic change in the religious policy of the emperor occurred at about the same time as this severe administrative crisis in the city. Moreover, if we accept the testimony of Nestorius, the Cyrillians bribed the demonstrators with money and supplies. Such a policy would be particularly effective in a year of famine, and this may have contributed further to the willingness of the emperor to listen to the disaffected populace.

Many modern historians and theologians have denied that Nestorius was really a "Nestorian": the teachings of Nestorius were nothing more than "a presentation of the Antiochene Christology which is clearest, simplest, and nearest to the Church that we possess."[173] Even Socrates, who was a contemporary of Nestorius, assured his readers that Nestorius was not a heretic, but a simple Christian who spoke about things he did not understand.[174] Specifically, Socrates absolved him of the charge that he denied the divinity of Christ or that he taught the same things as Paul of Samosata. All this only increases our interest in contemporary popular opinion, which almost universally condemned the bishop as a heretic. If modern authorities generally agree that Nestorius—as opposed to some of his followers—was orthodox, how could the uneducated inhabitants of Constantinople and Ephesus be so certain of his heresy?

We can conclude that the disturbances which took place during the episcopate of Nestorius were basically religious in origin, but that the movitation of popular opinion was probably much more complicated than a casual reading of the sources would suggest. Although some persons (for example, the partisans of Proclus) undoubtedly had political reasons for opposing Nestorius, most people probably did so because they disliked his religious teachings. This opposition, however, was not entirely spontaneous; it was in part at least the product of the elaborate campaign directed by the supporters of Cyril of Alexandria.

Long before the controversy began, proponents of the Alexandrian school of theology had prepared the ground in Constantinople by teaching questionable doctrines as accepted points of faith. After the emergence of Nestorius, his enemies were quick to point out the bishop's errors to those who might not immediately recognize them: Nestorius, they said, taught that Christ was an ordinary man (ψιλὸς ἄνθρωπος); this teaching, they also pointed out, derived ultimately from Paul of Samosata, who had been condemned years before. The clerical envoys of Cyril, Egyptian monks and sailors, and discontented Constantinopolitans kept things in constant ferment and resorted to agitation or claims of divine assistance when ordinary persuasion failed. Thus, many of the demonstrations against Nestorius were clearly organized and directed by capable leaders. Important among these were the monks of Constantinople, who were from the beginning outspoken in their opposition to the bishop and who used their position of authority among the people to shape and direct popular sentiment against Nestorius. In this connection, it is important to note the increasing importance of the monastic community in Constantinople in the first half of the fifth century. The monks obviously had a more powerful position in 428 than they had held in 404, and this helps to explain their greater significance in the affair of Nestorius.[175]

Furthermore, Nestorius had attacked the term *theotokos* and had forbidden its use. The Cyrillians pointed out the christological significance of this word, but some people probably opposed Nestorius simply because he seemed to question the honor which was due to the Virgin.

In the end, the sources do not allow us to say much about the possible secular motivations of the inhabitants of Constantinople and Ephesus (as distinct from their leaders). It is reasonable to assume that disturbed conditions in Constantinople in 431 contributed to the tensions of that year, but it is impossible to say more than that. About the significance of popular opinion we may be more certain. Leaders of both sides took care to secure the support of the urban crowd. In both Constantinople and Ephesus the Cyrillians were more successful, and this popular support helped to secure the deposition of Nestorius by the council and the acceptance of that decision by the emperor.

---

1. The most important primary sources for the affair of Nestorius include the bishop's own apology, which has survived only in a Syriac translation: *The Bazaar of Heracleides*, ed. and trans. G. R. Driver and Leonard Hodgson (Oxford, 1925), and a French edition, *Le Livre d'Héraclide de Damas*, ed. and trans. F. Nau (Paris, 1910; rpt. 1969); the massive collection of conciliar records and associated documents compiled by Eduard Schwartz, *Acta Conciliorum Oecumenicorum* [ACO], vol. 1 (Berlin, 1927-32); and the *Ecclesiastical History* of Socrates (*PG* 67). Among the most important secondary sources are Karl Joseph von Hefele and Henri Leclercq, *Histoire des conciles* (hereafter cited as Hefele-Leclercq, vol. 2 (Paris, 1910), pp. 219–443; G. Bardy, P. de Labriolle *et al.*, *Histoire de l'Eglise de la mort de Théodose à l'élection de Grégoire le Grand*, vol. 4 of *Histoire de l'Eglise depuis les origines jusqu'à nos jours*, ed. A. Fliche and V. Martin (Paris, 1948), pp. 163-203; and Duchesne, Early History of the Christian Chuch, vol. 3, p. 219–70. On the secular history of the period, see Bury, *Later Roman Empire*, vol. 2, pp. 212–35; Stein, *Histoire*, vol. 1, pp. 255–309; and Jones, *Later Roman Empire*, pp. 170–216. See also the important dissertation of Kenneth G. Holum, "Aelia Pulcheria and the Eastern Roman Empire" (University of Chicago, 1973).

2. This, at least, is the view of most of the ancient sources, which modern scholarship has generally followed in evaluating Theodosius II. Caution should be used, however, in accepting such a verdict on his reign. Church historians, writing after his death, remembered Theodosius as one who had allowed the Latrocinium and encouraged the growth of Monophysitism, the bane of orthodoxy in the later fifth and sixth centuries. It was easy to

blacken the emperor's reputation by asserting his weakness. There can be no doubt that intrigue flourished at the court and that others, particularly at the beginning of the reign, frequently determined policy. But the view of Theodosius as an emperor without a policy and without a will must be seriously questioned. See the opinion of Sozomen (*Hist. Eccl.* Prologue 9) and W. H. C. Frend, *The Rise of the Monophysite Movement* (Cambridge, 1972), pp. 94–95.

3. Stein, *Histoire*, vol. 1, p. 276 (cf. Socrates *Hist. Eccl.* 7.22, from whom this is taken); see also Bury, *Later Roman Empire*, vol. 1, pp. 214–215.

4. Stein, *Histoire*, vol. 1, p. 289; E. A. Thompson, *A History of Attila and the Huns* (Oxford, 1948), pp. 24–31; F. Altheim, *Attila und die Hunnen* (Baden-Baden, 1951), pp. 5–107; J. Otto Maenchen-Helfen, *The World of the Huns* (Berkeley, 1973). St. Hypatius speaks of a "large fort" which he and his fellow monks had to build in Thrace to defend themselves against the Huns—evidence, incidentally, that the government was unable to defend its subjects so close to Constantinople (Callinicus *Vita Sancti Hypatii* (ed. Bartelink) 3.10–11 (pp. 82–84).

5. Socrates *Hist. Eccl.* 7.29; Nestorius *Bazaar* (ed. G. R. Driver and L. Hodgson), pp. 274–76. Unfortunately, the sources do not tell us who was the candidate of the "people," who of the clergy and so on. Such information would be most valuable here, but it may be significant that the clergy and the monks were apparently divided in their interests and that the laity supported a third candidate. Socrates called Nestorius ἔπηλυς, "a newcomer, stranger, foreigner," which I have translated "outsider." Socrates' term may have come from contemporary reference to the new bishop as an interloper or newcomer.

6. J. Rucker, "Nestorius," *R.E.* 17, pt. 1 (1936), 126–36. Socrates *Hist. Eccl.* 7.29, calls him γένος Γερμανικεύς, while Theophanes, *Chronographia*, A. M. 5923, ed. de Boor, p. 88, says Γερμανικεὺς τῷ γένει. Cf. M. Brière, "La légende syriaque de Nestorius," *Revue de l'Orient chrétien*, 2nd series, 5 (1910), 1-25, for the story of Nestorius' Persian parents.

7. *ACO*, I, i, 6, pp. 152–53; Evagrius *Historia Ecclesiastica* 1, 2; Brière, "La légende syriaque," pp. 17–18.

8. Socrates *Hist. Eccl.* 7.29. "He was proclaimed by the people (πλεῖστοι) because of his sobriety (σωφροσύνη)."

9. Socrates *Hist. Eccl.* 7.29; Callinicus *Vita Hypatii* 32, 1, p. 208 (ed. Bartelink). Dionysius was *stratelates* of the East (see chap. 2, n. 2).

10. Socrates *Hist. Eccl.* 7.26.

11. Socrates *Hist. Eccl.* 7.35, 40. The party of Proclus appears to have been the more influential or greater in number (perhaps because of Proclus's oratorical ability?), and, although the ascetic Maximanus was chosen to succeed Nestorius, Proclus finally became bishop of Constantinople in 434.

12. See note 5 above. Such a feeling of antagonism toward the outsider is more likely among the clergy than the laity of Constantinople. The clergy, of course, had hoped for promotion from among their ranks and they must have disliked the "importation" of a bishop, especially when he brought along his own staff of priests and other servants. As for the laity of the city, we must remember that Constantinople was a new city and many of its inhabitants had themselves arrived relatively recently. On the other hand, they may have distinguished themselves from Syrians, who were traditionally considered culturally inferior.

13. Callinicus *Vita Hypatii* 32, 2, p. 210 (ed. Bartelink). The Council of Ephesus also congratulated Dalmatius for his early condemnation of Nestorius. Cf. Dagron, "Les Moines et la ville," p. 266, n. 173. We may doubt the veracity of these accounts because of Nestorius' later condemnation: it was obviously in the interest of the monastic community to claim that their enmity toward the heretical bishop dated from the earliest time. Also, three and one-half years is a standard time span in biblical and apocalyptic literature; often it is the rule of Antichrist on earth. See Paul J. Alexander, *The Oracle of Baalbek* (Washington, D. C., 1967), p. 115, n. 61. Nevertheless, I am inclined to accept the general truth behind these stories, for example, Hypatius' dream in which he saw Nestorius being enthroned by "laymen" (presumably the emperor and his court). In view of the later charges against Nestorius, this is an insignificant matter, but it might have been an important point in 428 when members of the monastic community had hoped for control of the church. The *Vita*

Hypatii adds that Nestorius was concerned enough about Hypatius' prediction to send an emissary to him about it; this might suggest that the monk's prophecy was rather widely known.

14. If one accepts Dagron's identification of the monastic community in Constantinople as Macedonian in sentiment, it is significant that Nestorius was especially harsh toward the Arians (Dagron, "Les moines et la ville," p. 266, n. 172).

15. Socrates *Hist. Eccl.* 6.19.

16. Socrates *Hist. Eccl.* 7.2.

17. Socrates *Hist. Eccl.* 7.2.

18. Socrates *Hist. Eccl.* 7.26; 28.

19. Socrates *Hist. Eccl.* 7.29.

20. Socrates *Hist. Eccl.* 7.21; *C. Th.* 16.5, 48; 5, 57; 6, 6; 5, 25; 5, 24; 5, 36; 5, 49; 5, 58–59; 6, 7. Colm Luibhéid, "Theodosius II and Heresy," *Journal of Ecclesiastical History* 16 (1965), 36–37, and most other authorities seem to have overlooked the statement of Sozomen, which is strongly supported by the evidence of the other sources. Heretics were all but tolerated during the early years of the reign of Theodosius II.

21. Socrates *Hist. Eccl.* 7.29.

22. Socrates *Hist. Eccl.* 7.29. The fact that the Arians still had a church in Constantinople further demonstrates the relative toleration of heretics. The location of the church is unknown.

23. Socrates *Hist. Eccl.* 7.29. It is possible of course that the Arians did not intend to burn their church but that they set fires in some nearby buildings in revenge or as a diversion and that the wind carried the flames to their place of worship.

24. Socrates *Hist. Eccl.* 7.29. At 7. 31, he says that Antony of Germa (on the Hellespont) was induced by Nestorius' example to persecute the Macedonians.

25. *C. Th.* 16.5, 65 (428). Heretical sects were divided into four groups according to the degree of evil associated with each. First came the Arians, Macedonians, and Apollinarians; they were least harmful because they were only deceived (cf. the wording of Nestorius in the *Bazaar*, ed. Driver and Hodgson, p. 99). They might not have churches within any municipalities. Second came the Novatians and Sabbatians, who could not construct new churches; and third were a long list of heresies, the members of which were not to assemble anywhere within the empire and who could not make wills. Finally came the Manichaeans, the worst of all heretics; they were effectively deprived of all civic rights.

26. Cf. W. H. C. Frend's study, *The Donatist Church* (Oxford, 1952), pp. 76–111. He attempts to show how conversion—or lack of it—and the survival of pre-Christian ideas affected heretical developments.

27. The best treatment of this difficult topic is to be found in Aloys Grillmeier, *Christ in Christian Tradition*, trans. J. S. Bowden (New York, 1965), which is an amplification of his "Die theologische und sprachliche Vorbereitung der christologischen Formel von Chalkedon," in *Das Konzil von Chalkedon*, A. Grillmeier and H. Bacht, eds., vol. 1 (Würzburg, 1951), pp. 5–202. See also R. V. Sellers, *Two Ancient Christologies* (London, 1954).

28. Harry A. Wolfson, *The Philosophy of the Church Fathers*, 2nd ed. 1 vol. (Cambridge, Mass., 1956); see also Wolfson's article, "Philosophical Implications of Arianism and Apollinarianism," *DOP*, 12 (1958), 3–28.

29. G. Barielle, "Docetisme," *DTC*, vol. 4, part 2 (1920), 1484-1501; J. N. D. Kelly, *Early Christian Doctrines* (New York, 1958), pp. 140–42; Grillmeier, *Christ in Christian Tradition* pp. 93–101; 115–22.

30. Adolph von Harnack, *History of Dogma*, 3rd ed. vol. 3 (London, 1897), pp. 7–51, Kelly, *Early Christian Doctrines*, p. 140; Grillmeier, *Christ in Christian Tradition*, pp. 90–93; 134–71. It is interesting to note that Origen did not refer to those who minimized the divinity of Christ as heretics, but as "misled" or "simple" Christians (Harnack, *History of Dogma* p. 35).

31. Frend, *The Rise of the Monophysite Movement*, p. 104.

32. See, for example, the recent statement of Frend, *The Rise of the Monophysite Movement*, p. 119: "The ideas of Apollinarius coincided with those of a large proportion of the eastern episcopate and the people at large."

33. W. M. Calder, "Early Christian Epitaphs from Phrygia," *Anatolian Studies* 5 (1958), 27-31; Frend, *The Donatist Church*, pp. 110-11; and *Ibid., Martyrdom and Persecution in the Early Church* (Oxford, 1965), pp. 291-94. Charles E. Raven, *Apollinarianism* (Cambridge, 1923), p. 45, says that the simple faith of Syria was "very different from that of the Greek cities." Raven stresses the point that Paul was raised in the interior of Syria, where he might have been influenced by Judaism or Judaic Christianity (pp. 46-50). See also Frend's interesting comments about the negative influence of Manichaeanism on the shaping of Antiochene theology (*The Rise of the Monophysite Movement*, pp. 108-9).

34. Harry A. Wolfson, "Philosophical Implications," pp. 19-21, stresses the Biblicism and anti-paganism of Arius; Grillmeier, "Die Theological und Sprachliche Vorbereitung," pp. 68-77.

35. As an example of the complexity of this problem, Athanasius, who from such an analysis was a forerunner of Nestorius, was the primary source of much of the theology of Cyril, the foremost enemy of Nestorius. Grillmeier, *Christ in Christian Tradition*, pp. 329-33.

36. Eusebius said specifically that to the Arians Christ was a "second God." See also the letter of Alexander of Alexandria to Alexander of Constantinople in Theodoret *Hist. Eccl.* 1.3, and Athanasius *Oratio Contra Arianos* (*PG* 26, 3530), 2. 16.

37. C. E. Raven, *Apollinarianism, passim.*; H. de Reidmatten, O. P. "Some Neglected Aspects of Apollinarist Christology," *Dominican Studies* 1 (1948), 239-60, and "La Christologie d'Apollinaire de Laodicée," *Studia Patristica*, vol. 64, *TU* (Leipzig, 1957), pp. 28-34; Grillmeier, *Christ in Christian Tradition*, pp. 222-33. For the text of Apollinarius, see H. Leitzmann, *Apollinaris von Laodicea und seine Schule, Texte und Untersuchungen* (Tubingen, 1904).

38. *C. Th.* 16.5, 12-14; 33; Duchesne, *Early History of the Christian Church*, vol. 2, p. 475.

39. See, for example, Gregory of Nazianzus' complaint to Nectarius about them in Constantinople (Ep. 202).

40. J. Lebon, "Alteration dostrinale de la lettre à Epictète de Saint Anthanase," *Revue d'Histoire Ecclésiastique* 31 (1935), 713-61; and G. Bardy, "Faux et fraudes litteraires dans l'antiquité chrétienne," *RHE* 32 (1936), 5-23.

41. Apollinarius *ep. ad. Jovian* (ed. Leitzmann), pp. 250-53. Apollinarius was particularly fond of the term *theotokos* as applied to the Virgin.

42. Nestorius *Bazaar*, p. 99. For an excellent critical evaluation of the sources of the *Bazaar* and its usefulness as an historical and theological source, see L. Abramowski, *Untersuchungen zum Liber Heraclidis des Nestorius. Corpus Scriptorum Christianorum Orientalium* 242, Subsidia 22 (Louvain, 1962).

43. The people who approached Nestorius on this question may have been clerics or even theologians, but it is clear (if the account of Nestorius is reliable) they did not understand the theological issues at stake. Nestorius, whose own "theological means . . . were not adequate" (Grillmeier, *Christ in Christian Tradition*, pp. 373-74), managed to illuminate the problem for them. It is likely that these people differed only in that they were the products of theological "schools" established in Constantinople by students of earlier heretics. Lacking any firm understanding of the issues, they were reduced to the hurling of epithets and anathemas.

44. J. F. Bethune-Baker, *Nestorius and his Teaching* (Cambridge, 1908), pp. 13-14; 56-59, briefly discusses the use of the term; cf. G. Bardy, *Histoire*, p. 170. Much of the polemic of the Trinitarian controversy had concerned itself with the birth, generation, or creation of Christ, and the language used (e.g., *egeneto* ["begotten"], references to Mary) was a perfect preparation for the dispute over the *theotokos*: " . . . even as early as the first half of the fourth century Christology and Mariology went together" (Hilda Graef, *Mary, a History of*

Doctrine and Devotion [New York, 1973], p. 52). See also Grillmeier, *Christ in Christian Tradition*, pp. 74, 188n, 244, 256, 261, 364, 369-71, 272-74.

45. Socrates *Hist. Eccl.* 7. 29; Nestorius *Bazaar*, p. 99. Cf. the similar compromise attempted by Theodore of Mopsuestia.

46. Nestorius *Bazaar*, p. 99.

47. Friedrich Loofs, *Nestorius and His Place in the History of Christian Doctrine* (Cambridge, 1914), pp 28-32. Cf. Socrates *Hist. Eccl.*, speaking of the depositions at the time of the Arian controversy. See also N. H. Baynes, "Alexandria and Constantinople," pp. 97-115.

48. Socrates *Hist. Eccl.* 7.32: "Let no one call Mary *theotokos* for Mary was human and it is impossible for a human to give birth to God." Cyril, however, claimed that Dorotheus, possibly bishop of Marcianopolis, gave the sermon, saying: "if someone says that Mary is *theotokos*, he is anathema" (Letter to Pope Celestine, *ACO* I, i, 5, p. 11). It is, of course, possible that these references described different events. See Hefele-Leclercq, *Histoire des Conciles*, vol. 2, pp. 237 ff.

49. Socrates *Hist. Eccl.* 7.32: "Everywhere he forbade the word *theotokos*." The sermons are preserved in the contemporary, but probably inaccurate, Latin translations of Marius Mercator (*ACO* I, i, 5, pp. 26-46).

51. Socrates *Hist. Eccl.* 7.32: "Just as in a night battle, people said contradictory things."

52. Cyril's letter to the Egyptian monks, *ACO*, I, i, 1, p. 11: He complained that some people had come and disturbed the faith by saying that the Virgin should not be called *theotokos*. Who were these people who caused such a disturbance in the deserts of Egypt? Were they agents of Nestorius? It seems unlikely. Perhaps they were Egyptians who agreed with Nestorius, or those who had returned from Constantinople and reported the controversy factually. In any case, the teachings of Nestorius seem to have met with some success in the very heart of Cyril's domain.

53. Theophanes *Chronographia* (ed. de Boor), p. 88; *ACO*, I, i, 1, pp. 101-2. Note that de Boor's text says that Eusebius was "a lawyer of the Basilica of Constantinople." For the Basilica, see Janin, *Constantinople byzantine*, 2nd ed., pp. 157-60.

54. Theophanes *Chronographia* A.M. 5923 (ed. de Boor), p. 88.

55. Proclus had been consecrated bishop of Cyzicus by Sisinnius, but the inhabitants of that city refused to allow him to take possession of his see. An imperial law had required the election of the bishop of Cyzicus to be conducted under the supervision of the bishop of Constantinople, but the people of Cyzicus felt that this law was to apply only to the episcopate of Atticus (Socrates *Hist. Eccl.* 7.28). Whether this was the case or not, Proclus felt that it would be wiser to return to Constantinople rather than face the candidate who had already been elected in his stead. On the date of the sermon, and for all other dates, see the convenient table by Adolf Achonmetzer, "Zeittafel zur Geschichte der Konzil von Chalkedon," in *Das Konzil von Chalkedon*, ed. A. Grillmeier and H. Bacht, vol. 2 (Würzburg, 1953), pp. 942-67. There is no evidence to date this sermon securely, but the emphasis placed by Proclus on the conception and birth of Christ seems to indicate the Annunciation or, more probably, the Nativity (thus December of 428).

56. *ACO*, I, i, 1, pp. 103-7. The term ψιλὸς ἄνθρωπος was used no less than six times in this sermon. We should remember that this term was from a very early date associated (rightly or wrongly) with the heresy of Paul of Samosata. Representative of the sentiment of Proclus are the following statements:

"Salvation was not from a mere man" (p. 105, 25).

"The nature came together and the union remained unmixed . . . a mere man could not bring about salvation" (p. 107, 3-5).

"If Christ is one and God the Word is another, there is not a Trinity, but a Tetarty. Do not divide the heavenly garment of the economy [of salvation]. Do not learn from Arius" (p. 108, 23-24).

Note the alleged connection with Arianism.

57. Proclus did not say directly that the acceptance of the *theotokos* was a prerequisite for the acceptance of the divinity of Christ, but this was the implied point of the whole sermon: e.g., Mary was "the workshop of the unity of the natures."

58. *ACO* I, i, 1, p. 103. It is interesting that Proclus brings up the point of the virginity of Mary and seems to make this a condition of the divinity of Christ: "If the mother was not a virgin the child was a mere man and the birth was not miraculous." At two points in the sermon he insists on the conception of Christ through the ear of the Virgin! See my comments in "The Remarkable Christmas Homily of Kyros Panopolites," *GRBS*, 16, (1975), 317-24.

59. *ACO*, I, i, 1, p. 107.

60. *ACO*, I, i, p. 24.

61. *ACO*, I, 1, 5, p. 11.

62. *ACO*, I, i, 5, pp. 7-10. Nestorius probably had this document in mind when he said: "And you [Cyril] called up the hands of monks and bishops and sent [them] against me to the emperor and they accused me" (*Bazaar*, p. 102).

63. *ACO*, I, i, 5, p. 8. Was this perhaps the monastery of the Akoimetoi? Cf. Janin, *Constantinople byzantine*, 2nd ed., pp. 486-87, and *Géographie ecclésiastique*, pp. 109-11.

64. *ACO*, I, i, 5, p. 8. It is not certain exactly what the *dekanikon* was. Sophocles, *Greek Lexicon*, s.v., translates this as "ecclesiastical prison," but the *decanus* could be either a secular or an ecclesiastical figure. See G. J. M. Bartelink, *Vita Hypatii*, pp. 244-45, nn. 3 and 6.

65. Nestorius, *Bazaar*, p. 104.

66. Celestine's letter to Nestorius, *ACO*, I, i, 1, pp. 77-83.

67. *ACO*, I, i, 1, pp. 83-90; cf. *ACO*, I, i, 1, pp. 113-14.

68. This comparison appears to be a deliberate falsification since, as mentioned above, neither Atticus nor Sissinnius had been effective in dealing with heresy. This may be indicative of the respect many ecclesiastics had for the memories and intelligence of the faithful.

69. *ACO*, I, i, 1, pp. 113-14.

70. *ACO*, I, i, 1, pp. 110-12. Also see Loofs, *Nestorius*, pp. 33-41. The letter is given in an inaccurate Latin translation by Marius Mercator in *ACO* I, v, pp. 52-53.

71. Both of these statements imply that Nestorius realized his failure to win popular support for his teachings.

72. *ACO*, I, i, 1, p. 11: I have translated (κοπρίαι) as "dregs," although the meaning is a bit more precise.

73. Eduard Schwartz, "Cyril und der Monch Viktor," *Sitzungsberichte. Akademie der Wissenschaften in Wein, philosophische-historische Klasse*. 208, 4 (1928), 1-51.

74. *ACO*, I, v, pp. 29-44; 60-65; Socrates, *Hist. Eccl.* 7.32; Celestine *Epistulae*, 6 and 7.

75. *Commonitorium* of Marius Mercator, *ACO*, I, v, pp. 65-70.

76. Marcellinus Comes *Chronicon*, p. 78: "ignem in ecclesian ad comburendum altare dum infesti inaciunt, invicem sese resistente deo trucidant." See also Socrates *Hist. Eccl.* 7.33.

77. Socrates *Hist. Eccl.* 7.33 The identity of the poet is unknown.

78. Socrates *Hist. Eccl.* 7.33.

79. Of course, we do not know how many people, if any, simply sat at home wishing Nestorius well but taking no active part in his defense. Also, we cannot say anything about the numbers of those supporting either side, except to observe that the supporters of Cyril were apparently more numerous.

80. *ACO*, I, 1, 1, pp. 73-74. Nestorius claimed (*Bazaar*, pp. 96-97) that Pulcheria was exceedingly hostile to him throughout. She may have been won over to Cyril's side at this time—before the bribes.

82. Nestorius *Bazaar*, p. 96.

83. Socrates twice used οἱ πολλοί in a way which seems to indicate the lower classes rather than the Christian laity in general. One of these occasions (7.29) concerned the reaction of the first sermon of Nestorius; τινες τῶν πολλῶν thought that Nestorius' approach to the heretics was just right. On the second occasion (7.32), however, Nestorius was thought heretical παρὰ τοῖς πολλοῖς. If Socrates was precise in his terminology, this might indicate that between the arrival of Nestorius in Constantinople and his sermons against the *theotokos* the opinion of "the many" changed from approval to disapproval. In the first case, however, we should note that Socrates referred only to "some" of the many. Nestorius is also said to have referred to his concern for ἡμέτεροι δῆμοι (*ACO*, I, i, 1, p. 111). I am not certain of the significance of this statement, particularly since Nestorius said that the failure of the people to attain correct teachings was not ἔγκλημα τῶν λαῶν. It would be tempting, of course, especially since the term is in the plural, to connect the *demoi* with the circus factions, but there is no reason to do so here. Cf. Alan Cameron, "Demes and Factions," p. 80.

84. For aristocratic support of Nestorius, see *Bazaar*, p. 96; for aristocratic opposition to Nestorius, see *ACO*, I, i, 5, p. 11.

85. Bethune-Baker, *Nestorius and his Teaching*, pp. 56–59; E. Schwartz, "Zur Vorgeschichte des ephesinischen Konzils," *Historische Zeitschrift* 112 (1914), p. 249.

86. C. H. Roberts, *Catalogue of Greek and Latin Papyri in the John Rylands Library* vol. 3 (Manchester, 1938), pp. 46 ff; O. Stegmuller, "*Sub tecum Praesidium.* Bemerkungen zur altesten Uberlieferung," *Zeitschrift für katholische Theologie* 74 (1957), 76–82. The term was probably accepted by the council of Antioch in 325 (Grillmeier, *Christ in Christian Tradition*, pp. 188n; 244).

87. Chrysostom, of course, was raised in the tradition of Antiochene Christianity. It is interesting that his sermons which do little to increase the honor paid to the Virgin appear not to have diminished his popularity in Constantinople (assuming that those sermons were presented there, which is open to some doubt). See H. Graef, *Mary*, pp. 74–76.

88. See J. Hasse, "Die koptischen Quellen zum Konzil von Nicaea," *Studien zur Geschichte und Kultur des Altertums* 10, 4 (Pendenborn, 1920); A. Eberle, *Die Mariologie der H. Cyrillus von Alexandrien* (Freiburg, 1921); G. Soll, "Die Mariologie der Kappadozier in Lichte der Dogmengeschichte," *Theologische Quartalschrift*, 131 (1951), 178–88.

89. G. A. Wellen, *Theotokos* (Utrecht, 1961), pp. 14–29; 139. The feasts of the Nativity and the Epiphany probably originated during the fourth century; see B. Botte, *Les origines de la Noel et de l'Epiphanie: Etude historique. Textes et études liturgiques*, vol. 1 (Louvain, 1932); L. Fendt, "Der heutige Stand der Forschung über das Geburtsfest Jesu am 25 XII and über Epiphanias," *Theologische Literaturzeitung* 78 (1953), 1–10; and Massey H. Sheperd, Jr., "Liturgical Expressions of the Constantinian Triumph," *DOP* 21 (1967), 59–78. This might be taken as evidence of a growth of the importance of Mary, since she is generally assigned an important place in later celebrations of these feasts.

90. Epiphanius *Panarion* 79. 1.

91. It is interesting to note that Nestorius had earlier admitted the orthodoxy of the term: "If indistinguishably and without extension or denial of the divinity and the humanity, we accept what is said by them (*theotokos, authropotokos*), we sin not" (*Bazaar*, p. 99). But this was said in private and even some of Nestorius' enemies hestitated to use the term in public or in the liturgy. In his first letter to Celestine Nestorius said the same thing: "Ferri tamen potest hoc vocabulum," if it is understood correctly. (*ACO*, I, 2, p. 13, 30-31). See also his first sermon against the *theotokos* (*ACO*, I, 5, pp. 12–14; 132). After his deposition in Ephesus, Nestorius saw the conflict he had caused and said: "Let Mary be called *theotokos* and let the difficulties cease," but no one paid any attention to him (Socrates *Hist. Eccl.* 7.34). On this matter see Wolfson, *Philosophy of the Church Fathers*, vol. 1 pp. 451–63; and Grillmeier, *Christ in Christian Tradition*, pp. 369–99.

92. Nestorius' first sermon against the *theotokos* (in the translation of Marius Mercator), *ACO*, I, V, p. 30, 4–5; "Habet materm deus? Ergo excusabilis gentilitas matres diis subintroducens."

93. Nestorius' first letter to Celestine (trans Marius Mercator), *ACO*, I, ii, p. 13, 17–18: "Sed et virginem Christotoken ausi sunt cum deo quodam modo tractare divine."

94. F. Loofs, *Nestoriana* (Halle, 1905), p. 353, 17 ff., cf. *ACO*, I, V, pp. 37–38.

95. Socrates *Hist. Eccl.* 7.32.

96. Callinicus *Vita Hypatii* 32. 10, p. 212 (ed. Bartelink). Cf. Theophanes, *Chronographia*, A.M. 5923 (ed de Boor), p. 88: "he said that the Lord was a mere man." It might be possible to discount this evidence, since Hypatius and Theophanes reported what they thought Nestorious' theology was, not how it appeared to ordinary Christians. Socrates, however, said clearly that people regarded the bishop as a heretic.

97. Socrates *Hist. Eccl.* 7.32.

98. Nestorius *Bazaar*, p. 100.

99. *ACO*, I, i, 1, p. 24.

100. Nestorius *Bazaar*, pp. 100–101: "And many praised and gave glory and went away from me and remained in agreement until they fell into the snare of those who were seeking for the episcopate."

101. Syriac accounts of the life of Nestorius assert that he wished to close the games and the baths of Constantinople: Brière, "La légende syriaque," p. 19.

102. *ACO* I, i, 5, p. 10; I, i, 1, pp. 110–12; Duchesne, *Early History of the Christian Church*, vol. 3, pp. 239–40.

103. Malalas *Chronicon*, p. 365, ed. L. Dindorf.

104. *ACO*, I, i, 1, pp. 114–16; cf. his more harshly worded *sacra* sent to Cyril, ibid., pp. 73–74. Ephesus was chosen because, as the emperor said, it was easy of access to all of the bishops and it could provide all material necessities for the participants in the council.

105. Socrates *Hist. Eccl.* 7.34. These were probably the bishops from the diocese of Asia—perhaps the *synodos endemousa* of Ephesus—whom Memnon had assembled in great numbers. At least a hundred of these bishops eventually supported Cyril.

106. Socrates *Hist. Eccl.* 7.34.

107. *ACO*, I, i, 3, p. 46: οἱ τοῦ Ζευξίππου παραμένοντες.

108. *ACO*, I, i, 1, pp. 120–21. Candidianus was to take no part in the deliberations of the council, but was to deal with "the laymen and monks who have already assembled and to remove those who are now arriving from the city by any means." Appeal to any secular court except that of Constantinople was expressly forbidden. We know nothing about Candidianus except what we are told here. See O. Seeck, "Candidianus (no. 4)," *RE* (1899). The duties of the *comes domesticorum* are not fully known; he was, however, a military officer of high standing, a member of the *comitatus*, and he certainly had soldiers under his command (see Jones, *Later Roman Empire*, p. 372). We know something more about Ireneus. See A. Jülicher, "Eirenaios (no. 9)," *RE* (1905). He later became bishop of Tyre and died about 450. Theodoret's letters 3. 12 and 14 were probably addressed to him. In one of these he was stationed near the Euphrates and in another he was consoled for the death of his *gambros* (brother-in-law or other relative by marriage) who was from Antioch. There appears to be much to connect him with Antioch and possibly Antiochene theology. He was obviously a military officer and may have held the position of *comes rei militaris* or even *comes Orientis*. Thus, both Candidianus and Irenaeus were very important individuals.

109. The list of the Egyptian bishops is given in *ACO*, I, i, 3, pp. 6–7. See also Bardy, *Histoire*, pp. 177–78; J. Leipoldt, *Schenute*, pp. 42 and 90. Juvenal of Jerusalem arrived some time later; see Ernest Honigmann, "Juvenal of Jerusalem," *DOP* 5 (1950), 290–79. An invitation had been sent to St. Augustine, but it arrived just after his death. Pope Celestine sent his legates.

110. This was standard procedure before the opening of a council and its purpose was clearly to enlist popular support as well as to secure votes among the bishops. See Socrates, *Hist. Eccl.* 1.8, for similar events before the council of Nicaea.

111. In the council, Theodotus of Ankara reported that "he said that one should not speak of the suckling nor the birth of God from a virgin, and many times he said that one should not speak of God as a two-month-old or a three-month-old," and many persons heard him say these things at Ephesus: cf. Theophanes, A. M. 5925 (ed. de Boor), p. 90.

112. Nestorius *Bazaar*, p. 134.

113. Nestorius *Bazaar*, p. 134. All these charges came from the pen of Nestorius, who obviously wished to have himself pictured as the innocent victim of Cyril of Alexandria and his friends. Nevertheless, the evidence of Nestorius is in keeping with that given by Cyril himself and Candidianus.

114. Hefele-Leclercq, *Histoire des conciles*, vol. 2, pp. 296–97. Bardy, *Histoire*, pp. 180-81; Duchesne, *Early History of the Christian Church*, vol. 3, pp. 242–46; and P. Th. Camelot, *Ephèse et Chalcédoine* (Paris 1962), pp. 48–51.

115. Nestorius *Bazaar*, pp. 106–8; *ACO*, I, i, 5, pp. 119–24.

116. Nestorius *Bazaar*, pp. 108–16; *ACO*, I, i, 1, pp. 120–21; I, i, 5, pp. 119–24. These protests were not mentioned in the official *acta* of the council, drawn up by the notaries of Cyril and sent off to the emperor immediately after the close of the first session. We know of them only through the *Bazaar* and the testimony of Candidianus at the council of the easterners.

117. Nestorius *Bazaar*, p. 116; cf. *ACO*, I, i, 5, pp. 119–20.

118. *ACO*, I, i, 2, p. 9: ἐν τῇ ἁγίᾳ ἐκκλησίᾳ τῇ καλουμένῃ Μαρίᾳ. Some have questioned this name for the church, as it is unusual that the church should be called Mary, yet it seems undeniable that it was dedicated to the Virgin. See Duchesne, *Early History of the Christian Church*, vol. 3, p. 244n; *Forschungen in Ephesos*, vol. 4, part 1 (Vienna, 1932), pp. 51 ff; Herman Vetters, "Zum byzantinischen Ephesos," pp. 373–87; and Wilhelm Altzinger, "Ephesos, B," *RE* supplemental vol. 12 (1970). The church "called Mary" was the famous "double church" of Ephesus, located in the city of Lysymachus at the head of the old harbor, and built (probably in the middle of the fourth century) on the foundation of an older building (probably the museum, perhaps destroyed in the Gothic invasion of the third century). This first church was damaged, probably by an earthquake and rebuilt ("doubled") at the time of Justinian. An inscription of the sixth century confirms the dedication to the Virgin.

119. *ACO*, I, i, 2, p.10.

120. *ACO*, I, i, 2, pp. 11–12.

121. Nestorius *Bazaar*, pp. 134–35.

122. *ACO*, I, i, 2, p. 54. The letter of deposition sent to Nestorius is found at the same place.

123. *ACO*, I, i, 1, p. 118, 3–10.

124. Some of the inhabitants of Ephesus awaited the decision of the council in the agora of the city, just a short distance from the church of Mary. When the news of the deposition was brought to them, they formed a procession to show their support of the action of the council (*ACO*, I, i, 5, p. 120: the report of Candidianus given before the council of the easterners). The council met near the far western extremity of the ancient city; had the bishops wished to risk popular displeasure by exonerating Nestorius, they would not have been able to slip away unseen to their lodgings, which were probably to the east of the church.

125. *ACO*, I, i, 1, p. 118: εἷς κύριος, μία πίστις, ἓν βάπτισμα.

126. *ACO*, I, i, 5, p. 125.

127. *ACO*, I, i, 5, p. 121. This is from the *acta* of the council of the orientals. The purpose of this violence, according to the easterners, was to terrorize the supporters of Nestorius so that they would join Cyril's council. Later they said that they found "the holy synod full of Egyptian sailors and Asian peasants" (*ACO*, I, i, 5, p. 128: letter to the senate of Constantinople; cf. *ACO*, I, i, 5, p. 129, 11–24: letter to the faithful of the capital).

128. Nestorius *Bazaar*, pp. 266–67.

129. *ACO*, I, i, 2, pp. 70–104.

130. *ACO*, I, i, 2, p. 102.

131. *ACO*, I, i, 3, p. 4.

132. *ACO*, I, i, 3, p. 6.

133. *ACO*, I, i, 3, p. 7.

134. *ACO*, I, i, 5, pp. 119-20. They posted the notice of deposition on the wall of the theatre, something which suggests that they hoped for some popular support.

135. *ACO*, I, i, 3, pp. 46-47.

136. These countryfolk seem to have lived on the land owned by the church of Ephesus. If so, it is surprising that they opposed their bishop unless, as a landowner, he was less than popular with the rural population. It is possible that they were from the ecclesiastical property of the church of Constantinople, rather than Ephesus, and that they had been brought from the neighborhood of the capital, or wherever they lived (in Asia, perhaps?), by Nestorius. Remember, however, that the easterners claimed that "Asian farmers" and Egyptian sailors supported Cyril and Memnon (note 127 above).

137. Memnon says that the "orthodox" supported him. Perhaps the "heretics," if there were any, aided Irenaeus. An attempt to dethrone the bishop of Ephesus was hardly a novelty, as other bishops were not as popular as Memnon appears to have been. We will meet another attempt of this kind in chapter 6. If there was any local opposition to Memnon, we are unaware of it.

138. W. M. Ramsay, "The Worship of the Virgin Mary at Ephesus," *Pauline and Other Studies in Early Christianity* (London, 1906), pp 125-60; G. Jouassard, "Maria à travers la patristique. Maternité divine, verginité, sainté," in *Maria: Études sur la Sainte Vièrge*, ed. d'H du Manoir, (Paris, 1949), pp. 69-157. Much of Jouassard's argument is a modification of Ramsay's thesis. He seems correct in saying that the tradition of the death of the Virgin in Ephesus was a "popular" development which had not won official approval. Of particular interest is the terra-cotta image of Artemis as a mother (pictured opposite p. 160), which he discusses on p. 139. Workers who excavated the plaque at first thought it represented Mary. Cf. the third or fourth century painting of Isis suckling Harpocrates from Karanis (illustration published by André Grabar, *Byzantium from the Death of Theodosius to the Rise of Islam* (London, 1966), illustration 190. See also D. Knibbe, "Ephesos, A." *RE*, supplemental vol. 12 (1970).

139. Epiphanius *Panarion* 78, 11; cf. Ramsay, "Worship of the Virgin Mary," pp. 144-45.

140. *ACO*, I, i, 2, p. 70, 7-9: ἔνθα ὁ θεολόγος Ἰωάννης καὶ ἡ θεοτόκος παρθένος ἡ ἁγία Μαρία. "John" and "Mary" may refer to the two churches of the city, although the addition of *theotokos parthenos* makes this seem unlikely.

141. One could argue that the veneration of Mary (and John?) as the special protectress of the city and support for her against her detractors were really manifestations of local loyalty. See Jones, *The Greek City*, pp. 144-46; 182; 248-49; 251-52; 299-304. It is unfortunate that we do not hear anything specific about the sailors, longshoremen, and traders of Ephesus, who must have constituted an important element in the city. One would guess that their interest in trade might make them hesitant to encourage schism.

142. *ACO*, I, i, 5, pp. 13-15. This letter was signed by ten bishops besides Nestorius. Hefele-Leclercq, *Histoire des Conciles*, vol. 2, pp. 342-56, contains a good summary of events in Constantinople after the deposition of Nestorius.

143. The existence of this letter is known from the reply of the emperor, *ACO*, I, i, 3, p. 9.

144. *ACO*, I, i, 3, pp. 3-5. It is possible that Theodosius never received this letter, but this was probably not because of the "blockade" imposed by the emperor.

145. *ACO*, I, i, 3, pp. 9-10. Eventually Theodosius dispatched John, the *comes sacrarum largitionum*, to Ephesus to attempt to bring about a reconciliation. This ultimately resulted in the union of 433, in which the emperor agreed to the deposition of Nestorius.

146. *ACO*, I, i, 2, pp. 64-65. An *oikonomos* was an ecclesiastical official in charge of the financial administration of a church (Jones, *Later Roman Empire*, p. 902; cf. *ACO*, I, i, p. 359). Why the council warned the *oikonomoi* to watch over the ecclesiastical properties is not clear. Perhaps they feared that since Nestorius had been deposed, someone might appropriate ecclesiastical revenues on the grounds that there was no bishop.

147. Nestorius *Bazaar*, pp. 271-72.

148. In his French translation of the *Bazaar*, Nau calls them *les grands et les chefs* (p. 239); one would like to know what the original Greek was. These would presumably include some who had supported Nestorius earlier.

149. It will be remembered that Nestorius was an ardent persecutor of the heretics, but it is common to call one's enemies the "scum of the earth." Cf. Cyril's "dregs of the city" and the comments of Yavetz, *Plebs and Princeps*, pp. 146-49.

150. Dagron, "Le moines et la ville," pp. 253-68, especially p. 267.

151. On these visions, see F. Nau, "Jean Rufus, Évêque de Maoiuma, *Plérephories*," *Patrologia Orientalis* 8, 1 (Paris, 1912).

152. *ACO*, I, i, 2, pp. 66-68. The date of this letter is uncertain; it was probably written shortly after the other letter to the clergy of Constantinople (*ACO*, I, i, 2, pp. 64-65). A letter to the "fathers of the monks" (*ACO*, I, i, 2, pp. 69-70) and one addressed simply to "the reverend clergy and faithful" (*ACO*, I, i, 2, p.70) may have been sent to Constantinople as well, although their content makes this uncertain. We know nothing about Komarios and Potamon; presumably their sees were near Constantinople. In any case, from the *commonitorium* of the "bishops found in Constantinople" (*ACO*, I, i, 2, p. 65) we can tell that there was a large number of anti-Nestorian bishops in Constantinople immediately after the end of the first session of the council.

153. *ACO*, I, i, 2, p. 65. The clergy of Constantinople complained that before this they had received messages only from Nestorius.

154. Dalmatius had been a military officer when he was persuaded by St. Isaac to enter the monastic life. He had been married and had at least one son. He probably succeeded Isaac as abbot of the monastery which then bore his name—*Ta Dalmatou*, but see Janin *Constantinople byzantine*, 2nd ed., pp. 333-34. Interestingly, this monastery was located near the martyrion of St. Mokios, the site of the celebration over the emperor's capitulation. See Callinicus *Vita Hypatii* 1. 6, p. 74 (ed. Bartelink); A. Jülicher, "Delmatius" (no. 4), *RE* 4 (1901); and Dagron, "Les moines et la ville," pp. 266-70.

155. *ACO*, I, i, 2, pp. 65-66.

156. *ACO*, I, i, 2; Nestorius *Bazaar*, pp. 272-73.

157. Nestorius *Bazaar*, pp. 272-73.

158. The martyrion of St. Mokios was in the 12th region of the city, that is, in the southwestern corner. Janin's works, *Constantinople byzantine*, 2nd ed., p. 393, and *La géographic ecclésiastique de l'Empire Byzantine*, vol. 3, of *Les Églises et les Monastéres* (Paris, 1953), pp. 367-71.

159. Μονάζοντες μετὰ κηρίολων ψάλλοντες καὶ ὡς εἶδον τὰ πλήθη ... The subject of the second clause may be πλήθη, which would change the sense of the passage.

160. *ACO*, I, i, 2, pp. 65-66.

161. *ACO*, I, i, 2, pp. 66-67.

162. Nestorius *Bazaar*, p. 278-79.

163. Socrates *Hist. Eccl.* 7.34.

164. It is not certain that Theodosius gave up all hope that Nestorius might be saved since as late as August of 431 Cyril felt the need to bribe the imperial court (*ACO*, I, i, 5, pp. 135-36). The emperor was also obviously upset by the following Theodoret gained in Chalcedon a short time later.

165. *ACO*, I, i, 3, pp. 32-33; I, i, 7, pp. 67-68; 71; Duchesne, *Early History of the Christian Church*, vol. 3, pp. 252-70; Luibhéid, "Theodosius II and Heresy," pp. 20-27; cf. *C. Th.* 16, 6.2.

166. Socrates *Hist. Eccl.* 7. 35. At the time of this election Proclus was the popular candidate, but he was judged ineligible since he was nominally the bishop of Cyzicus. His support of the Cyrillians must have counted for much.

167. Theodoret's letter to Alexander of Hieropolis, *ACO*, I, i, 7, p. 80. Perhaps connected with this is the information that "long after the deposition of Nestorius, officers, clerics, and pious ascetics came frequently" to Hypatius and asked whether he would return to Constantinople. Hypatius answered that this would happen only if it was the "time of Antichrist." It is not certain whether these persons were Nestorians or (more likely) individuals who feared a return of the bishop. In any case it is interesting that this was still an issue. *Vita Hypatii* 39. 1-4, p. 232 (ed. Bartelink).

168. On the bribery of Cyril, see Duchesne, *Early History of the Christian Church*, vol. 3, p. 252, and the letter of Isidore of Pelusium (*PG* 78, 177-1646). See also Jones, *Later Roman Empire*, p. 1159, n. 65.

169. Nestorius noted that the monks "were very dear" to Theodosius and the Cyrillians undoubtedly wished to show the emperor that all the monks of the city were united in their opposition to Nestorius. Nevertheless, the support of a large number of laymen must have given weight to their demands.

170. See Jones, *Later Roman Empire*, pp. 430-32. The *collatio lustralis* was originally levied every five years, but "by the fifth century it was apparently demanded every four years," computed from the accession of the reigning emperor. It we use 408 as the beginning of the reign of Theodosius, the tax would have been due in 428, the year in which the controversy broke out. The *collatio glebalis* (abolished by Marcian, the successor of Theodosius) was collected annually, while the *aurum oblaticum* was probably payable in 428 as well (*C Th*. 6.2, 25).

171. *C. Th*. 13.5, 32; 14.16, 1 (cf. 12.1, 177). This reorganization had been carried out under some necessity, as the house of the *praefectus urbi* had just been burned at the time of a food shortage. (Marcellinus comes, s.a. 409; *Chron. Pasch.*, 407; cf. G.-I. Bratianu "La question de l'approvisionnement de Constantinople à l'époque byzantine et ottomane," *Byzantion* 5 (1929), 83-107; and J. L. Teall, "The Grain Supply of the Byzantine Empire, 330-1025," *DOP* 13 (1959), 87-139.

172. Marcellinus Comes, p. 78: "Hoc tempore dum ad horrea publica Theodosius processum celebrat, tritici in plebem ingruente imperator ab esuriente populo lapidibus inpetitur."

173. M. V. Anastos, "Nestorius was Orthodox," *DOP* 16 (1962), 119-40; cf. Grillmeier, *Christ in Christian Tradition*, pp. 496-505.

174. Socrates *Hist. Eccl*. 7.32. Socrates based his evaluation on a personal reading of the works of Nestorius and conversations with his supporters.

175. Heinrich Bacht, "Die Rolle des orientalischen Monchtums in der kirchenpolitischen Auseinandersetzungen um Chalkedon," in *Das Konzil von Chalkedon*, vol. 2, ed. A. Grillmeier and H. Bacht (Würzburg, 1953), pp. 193-314; Dagron, "Les moines et la ville."

V

THE LATROCINIUM: CONSTANTINOPLE AND EPHESUS

The Controversy Continued

The period from the deposition of Nestorius in 431 to the second Council of Ephesus in 449 produced a disturbing series of events in Constantinople.[1] In military affairs, these years were dominated by difficulties on three fronts: sporadic, but generally successful war against the Persians; two desultory campaigns against the Vandals in North Africa; and the increasing pressure brought by Attila in the north.[2] The latter difficulty was of the most immediate concern for residents of Constantinople, since the Huns threatened not only to attack the city itself, but managed to secure an immense tribute from the emperor: in 443, (or 447), for example, he demanded and received an immediate payment of 6,000 pounds of gold and an annual subsidy of 2,100 pounds.[3] The burden of taxation to support these payments was considerable, and it engendered much resentment:

> The Romans pretended that they made these payments voluntarily, but they really did so because of necessity and the overwhelming fear which oppressed their rulers.... And they sent the very heavy amount of tribute, even though their personal funds and the imperial treasuries had been exhausted—not for necessities, but for improper spectacles, unrestrained ambitions, pleasures, and uncontrolled feasts—things which no one in his right mind should do, even in normal times, unless he gives no thought to defense.... [The emperor] forced everyone to contribute to the sum of money which he sent to the Huns, both those who paid the tribute and those who for a time had been freed from the heavy burden of the land tax, either by the decision of the judges or by the liberality of the emperors. Those enrolled in the senate paid an amount of gold according to their rank. For many their outstanding fortune caused a change in their life; for after undergoing torture, they paid what those sent by the

emperor demanded of them. Thus, men who were formerly prosperous displayed their wives' jewelry and their furniture in the marketplace. After the war this misfortune fell upon the Romans, so that many either starved themselves to death or hanged themselves.[4]

Meanwhile, the forces of nature seem to have conspired against the empire, and earthquakes, plague, famine, and severe cold were unusually common during these years, especially in the period after 444.[5] Later writers, and undoubtedly many contemporaries, attributed these disasters to the wrath of God directed against blasphemy and heresy in the city. The mood of the city is well characterized by the actions of the bishop Proclus who reacted to a severe earthquake by assembling all of the faithful in the Campus of the Hebdomon to beseech God with the *Kyrie eleison*.[6]

In religious affairs, the situation was still confused. The Council of Ephesus had condemned Nestorius and any teaching which diminished the divinity of Christ, but it left many questions unanswered.[7] Exactly what role, for example, remained for Christ's humanity? Did he have a single nature—divine—or was it still possible to speak of a human nature joined in some way to the divine? Nestorius was still alive, and from his exile he continued to speak about the injustices he felt had been committed against him. Few people were willing to agree with the deposed bishop, but some thought that Cyril had gone too far in his emphasis on the divinity of Christ. Still the supporters of Cyril, especially the monk Eutyches—who had assumed the leadership of the monastic community of Constantinople after the death of Dalmatius—maintained an ascendency over Theodosius.[8] Thus, in 435 the emperor issued a law forbidding the Nestorians from calling themselves Christians and ordering all of their books to be burned.[9] The Nestorians, including both those who actually followed Nestorius and those who simply felt that Cyril and Eutyches had gone too far, resurrected the books of the older teachers of the school of Antioch, and the works of Diodore of Tarsus and Theodore of Mopsuestia began to circulate again with considerable effect.[10]

Reaction to this was not slow in coming. Proclus of Constantinople quickly condemned the revival of Nestorian tendencies, and Cyril of Alexandria followed with a treatise against Diodore and Theodore.[11] John of Antioch and the other oriental bishops agreed to subscribe to the definition of faith suggested by Proclus, but they refused to condemn the writings of the forerunners of Nestorius.[12] The diplomatic maneuverings were subtle and no schism emerged, but the underlying difference of opinion remained, ready to erupt at any moment.

Nor were these difficulties restricted to the theologians. At about this time, a small band of Armenian monks, fanatic supporters of the theology of Alexandria, again focused public attention on the complex theological problems left unsolved by the deposition of Nestorius.[13] They roamed the cities of the East, displaying quotations they alleged to have taken from the works of Theodore of Mopsuestia. In Constantinople they were particularly successful in causing a disturbance (*multorum sordidantes auditum calliditate sua omnia perturbabant*), and the emperor became concerned and requested Proclus to conduct an investigation into the matter.[14]

In response to these attacks on Antiochene theology, Theodoret, bishop of Cyrrhus, published his *Eranistes*, in 447.[15] Although this work did not mention his opponents by name, it clearly condemned the teachings which were then being accepted by the emperor and his court. At about the same time, Domnus, the new bishop of Antioch, wrote a letter to the emperor accusing the archimandrite Eutyches of Apollinarianism in attributing the sufferings of Christ to the divinity.[16] These attacks had little effect, however, and the emperor issued an edict in February of 448 which again condemned Nestorius and all his adherents, declaring them deprived of ecclesiastical rank and encouraging any person to denounce such heretics without fear of retaliation. Further, the new decree went beyond the law of 435 by ordering the destruction of all writings which in any way supported the teachings of the deposed bishop (meaning, of course, the works of Theodore of Mopsuestia and Diodore of Tarsus).[17]

The Council of 448

Matters finally came to a head at a local council called by Flavian, who had succeeded Proclus as bishop of Constantinople in 448.[18] Flavian had been a priest in Proclus' administration, but for one reason or another he encountered the antagonism of the eunuch Chrysaphius, an important adviser and confidant of the emperor.[19] Flavian had apparently taken an independent line in his dealings with Chrysaphius, and he had allied himself with Pulcheria against the eunuch's successful manipulation of court intrigue. This was important for the present issue since Chrysaphius was the godson of Eutyches and presumably a supporter of his theology from an early date.

On November 8, 448, Flavian summoned the bishops who happened to be in the capital to a meeting of the *syndos endemousa*. The reason for this council was a local dispute in the area of Sardis, about which we know almost nothing. This business was concluded quickly, but before Flavian could end the session Eusebius—the former accuser of Nestorius and now bishop of Dorylaeum in Phrygia—presented a written complaint against the teachings of Eutyches.[20] Regardless of Flavian's theological predilections, he was left with no choice but to investigate the matter. The members of the council decided to send the priest John and the deacon

Andreas to Eutyches to inform the archimandrite of the charges against him and to ask him to appear before the assembly. The synod then adjourned.[21]

The bishops met again to consider the issue on Monday, November 15. Eusebius opened the proceedings by remarking on the absence of Eutyches from the assembly. In reply, Flavian asked for the report of those sent to bring the archimandrite. The priest John told the synod that Eutyches had refused to accompany them, saying that he looked upon the monastery as his tomb. The deacon Andreas and another deacon, Athanasius, verified this report.[22] The synod then addressed a letter to Eutyches, again asking him to appear and make his apology. The task of delivering this summons was entrusted to the priests Mamas and Theophilus.[23]

While the bishops were awaiting the reply of Eutyches, Eusebius raised another matter for their consideration. He had received information that Eutyches sent a tract (*tomos*) to all the monasteries of the capital with the intention of raising insurrection (*stasis*) among the monks. To substantiate this charge, Eusebius brought forward the priest Abramios from a monastery in the Hebdomon, and he told how Eutyches had sent the tract to his archimandrite Manoulios and persuaded him to sign it. Not fully convinced by this evidence, Flavian ordered various clerics to go around to the monasteries in and near Constantinople to determine what harm Eutyches had actually done.[24]

Just at that moment, an official of the council announced the return of Mamas and Theophilus. The two priests presented a very interesting report. Upon their arrival at the monastery of Eutyches, they found several monks guarding the gate; these monks escorted the emissaries into the monastery. Once inside the precinct, they found themselves face to face with the archimandrite. After he had read the letter from the council, Eutyches replied that he could not possibly come since he had taken an oath not to leave his monastery "except for moral necessity." When Mamas and Theophilus pressed their demand, the monk protested that he was old and feeble.[25] Flavian heard this report and delegated three of his own clerics as a third and final embassy to Eutyches. The council addressed yet another summons to the archimandrite and set the following Tuesday—November 17—as the date by which Eutyches must make his appearance.[26]

When the synod met again, on November 16, an archimandrite and three monks from the monastery of Eutyches appeared before the doors of the *episkopeion*. They announced that Eutyches had sent them because he himself was sick. Flavian rejected this excuse and reminded the ambassadors that the archimandrite had managed to leave his cell at the time of the Nestorian controversy.[27] At the beginning of the session on the following day, Memnon, the leader of the most recent delegation sent to

Eutyches, reported that the archimandrite had finally agreed to appear personally on the following day, "God willing."[28] Flavian then proceeded to examine the clerics who had been sent to investigate the disturbances Eutyches had caused in the monasteries of Constantinople. They reported that they had found a general confusion among the monks. Some were disturbed by Eutyches' theology, some thought it was the same as that of Cyril of Alexandria and the Fathers at Ephesus, while still others had not received the tract. The clerics apparently found no evidence that Eutyches had resorted to violence and Eusebius' charge of insurrection was allowed to lapse.[29]

Finally the day of the confrontation arrived. An official of the council announced that the formidable party of Eutyches waited outside the doors of the episcopal residence. Along with the archimandrite were "a large number of soldiers and monks and dignitaries from the staff of the praetorian prefect."[30] At the head of the delegation was the *silentiarius* Magnus, who had undoubtedly been sent by the imperial court.[31] While Eutyches' other supporters waited outside, Magnus entered the assembly and read a letter from the emperor. In this letter, Theodosius reminded the bishops of his concern for the faith as established at Nicaea and Ephesus:

> Thus we wish no scandal to arise in the aforesaid orthodoxy. And since we know that the most honorable Patrician Florentius is a faithful man and one who bears witness to the correct position, we wish him to be present at the investigation of the synod, since the matter is one which concerns the faith.[32]

The bishops agreed that Florentius should be admitted to the debate, and they all cried out in praise of the emperor. From that time, Florentius assumed a leading role in the deliberations of the council.

Eutyches finally made his long-delayed appearance, and Flavian and Eusebius quickly brought the interrogation to the point where the two parties differed. Eutyches confessed that he held the person of Christ to be of the same substance (*homousios*) as the Father; and the Virgin was of the same substance as all mankind. But he denied that Christ was of the same substance as man. Flavian and Eusebius, along with Florentius, pressed the archimandrite concerning his belief in the two natures (φύσεις) of Christ. Eutyches replied: "I confess our Lord to have been born from two natures (ἐκ δύο φύσεων) before the union; but after the union I confess one nature."[33] Eutyches appealed to the writings of Athanasius and Cyril for support, but his fate was decided. Florentius cried out: "Do you confess two natures after the union? Speak! If you do not speak, you must be deposed!"[34] A formula had been devised—"one nature—or two—after the union"—which clearly separated the parties in the conflict. When Eutyches refused to admit the two natures after the union, Florentius declared that the archimandrite did not believe correctly. The bishops cried out in praise of the emperor. Flavian then prepared a formal statement declaring Eutyches guilty of the heresy of Apollinarius and Valentinian and announcing that he was deprived of all ecclesiastical rank.[35] Thirty bishops and twenty-three archimandrites signed this statement.[36]

The role of the court in this affair is not easy to understand. Chrysaphius, the godson of Eutyches, presumably controlled imperial policy at this time, and it is certain that he supported the archimandrite vigorously. The intervention of Magnus and the courtiers would seem to be an indication of imperial favor toward Eutyches, and Nestorius, from his distant exile, complained that the blasphemy of Eutyches was carried out with the support of the emperor.[37] But the position of Florentius is not at all clear. At first he appeared familiar with Eutyches, calling him *papa*, and as the representative of Theodosius he would presumably have reflected the will of the emperor. Yet he joined freely in the interrogation of Eutyches and eventually decreed that he must be declared a heretic; it would be surprising if this had been done in direct contradiction of the wishes of the emperor.[38]

We should probably expect Eutyches to have had the full support of the monastic community of Constantinople. He was the generally accepted leader of the monks and he had played an important part in the struggle against Nestorius. Moreover, the two events we have examined so far suggest that it was common for opposition to the bishop of Constantinople to center in the monasteries of the city.[39] Further, Eutyches had a large number of monks under his personal control, in his own house, and he went to some pains to disseminate his teachings among the other monasteries.

Nevertheless, the evidence suggests that the affair of Eutyches caused a significant division of opinion among the monks of Constantinople and that Eutyches was not able to mobilize the whole of the monastic *tagma* in his defense. In the first place, Eutyches apparently did not convince all the other archimandrites of his orthodoxy, as the testimony given at the Synod of 448 clearly shows. Whether this was a result of the weakness of Eutyches' propaganda or the actions of his enemies is unclear. Flavian certainly realized the importance of monastic opinion, and he did whatever he could to encourage differences among the monks. Eutyches, in a letter to Pope Leo written probably in the summer of 449, complained about the activities of the bishop, adding that such episcopal meddling in the affairs of the monasteries was unprecedented.[40]

Furthermore, twenty-three heads of monasteries, or their representatives, had signed the deposition of Eutyches in 448, and others were later encouraged to do the same.[41] One of the most important of these monastic opponents of Eutyches was the archimandrite Faustos, who was probably the son of Dalmatius born before the latter entered the monastic life.⁴² Dalmatius, it will be remembered, had been an important adversary of Nestorius, and his intervention had helped convince the emperor to abandon his support of the bishop. In 431, Dalmatius had worked closely with Eutyches, but by 448 his son Faustos had become an enemy of the archimandite. We do not know the reason for this development; it may simply have been that Faustos disagreed with the religious policy of his father or that he saw the teachings of Eutyches as an unreasonable extension of the doctrine of Ephesus. Political reasons might, however, have played a role in the disagreement. Eutyches had succeeded Dalmatius as leader of the monastic community, and Faustos may well have considered that position rightfully his own.

Even in his own monastery, it appears that Eutyches found some who disagreed with him. In 449, the monks of his house wrote to the council in Ephesus to complain about the injustice done to their archimandrite. Although the letter mentioned that there were three hundred monks in the monastery, the complaint was signed by only thirty-five. That some of the other two hundred sixty-five monks had agreed to the condemnation of Eutyches is confirmed by another passage in the letter where the monks who remained faithful to Eutyches reported that they had dealt with those who had participated in the "impious act."⁴³

Ultimately it seems impossible fully to disentangle the events and motives which characterized the monastic community during late 448 and early 449. It is clear, however, that the situation was in many ways a new one. During the past fifty years, monastic leaders had frequently opposed the bishop of Constantinople, usually with considerable success, but they had always relied on the unified support of the monks of the city. Now, for the first time, the monastic community was fragmented, and many archimandrites openly supported Flavian against their leader Eutyches. This was significant in itself, but it also must have had important repercussions for imperial policy and popular opinion, both of which were extremely sensitive to monastic leadership.

Unfortunately, we are poorly informed about crowd reaction to the deposition of Eutyches and the events subsequent to it. The testimony of Nestorius, however, suggests that the people of Constantinople were divided in their opinion and that, in fact, this division was the cause of Flavian's original involvement in the controversy:

> Flavian had heard that the churches were disturbed over these things and the monasteries were divided and the people were rising up in division, and that already the fire was kindling in all the world owing to those who were going and coming were preaching various things that were full of impiety.⁴⁴

During the course of the Synod of 448 Flavian, perhaps at that time an impartial observer, noted that both high and low had been offended by the teaching of Eutyches:

> Many heard [his doctrines] and were scandalized...and many of the important people were scandalized also.[45]

The most interesting evidence concerning popular feeling and involvement is supplied by the archimandrite himself. In a letter which he wrote to Pope Leo soon after his condemnation, Eutyches said:

> But when they had disregarded what I had said and closed the council with haste, they published the sentence of excommunication which had been drawn up against me before the trial. Relying on their faction (*sua factione confidentes*), they spread around so many lies that I was in danger of my life, had not some soldiers snatched me from the trap through the aid of God and your prayers.[46]

Later, in testimony before the Council of Ephesus in 449, Eutyches complained that Flavian had excommunicated him and forbade him from entering any monastery. Thus, he

> delivered me to the crowd (*plethos*) which had been prepared for this, both at the *episcopeion* and in the *agora*, to be killed as a heretic, a blasphemer, and a Manichaean, but the providence of God saved me.[47]

According to Eutyches, then, the supporters of Flavian made an attempt to influence public opinion against the archimandrite by calling him a Manichaean; recall from the testimony of Nestorius that supporters of the theology of Alexandria were frequently called Manichaeans by their enemies. They were so successful in this that on at least two occasions the crowd tried to lynch him, and he had to be rescued by imperial soldiers. The latter passage suggests that the followers of the bishop did not hestitate to organize a mob to set upon Eutyches, but we should suppose that in general they used more subtle means. Particularly significant was the attempt to separate the archimandrite from the rest of the monastic community and to close the churches of the city to his followers. The result was that any sermon given between the Synod of 448 and the meeting of Council in 449 must have reflected the theology of Flavian.

In his letter to Pope Leo, Eutyches provides further information about the attempts to influence public opinion by both sides of the controversy.

> And the *contestationes* which I wished to display as an explanation to the Christian people (*ad satisfactionem populi Christiani*), they would not permit to be published or brought to public attention. In short, those people who through faction (*factio*) and deliberate calumny wished everyone to think me a heretic by the removal of my defense took them down.[48]

Just what were these *contestationes* by which Eutyches hoped to convince the people of Constantinople of his orthodoxy? Generally speaking, the term refers to a statement or testimony, especially as given in a court of law.[49] But the *contestationes* of Eutyches can hardly have been prepared speeches; they must have been short statements of his beliefs and an explanation of their orthodoxy. These statements might have been read aloud in the streets—since the churches were closed to the archimandrite—but they were probably more generally posted in various public places, as was the public condemnation of Nestorius by Eusebius of Dorylaeum some years earlier. Remarkably, one of the *contestationes* of Eutyches has survived, unfortunately only in a Latin translation. It began:

> To the catholic and beloved Christian people (*populus*) of Constantinople, Eutyches the priest. That faction (*factio*) and calumny by which I am oppressed, I must think, know nothing at all about the people (*populi*) in Constantinople who honor God....[50]

The statement went on to affirm that Eutyches had received from his parents the faith of Nicaea which, as confirmed by the Council of Ephesus, he had maintained until the present moment. In particular, he said, he condemned those "who say that the flesh of our Lord Jesus Christ came down from heaven and was not made incarnate from the Virgin Mary and the Holy Spirit."[51] This latter statement gives us an important insight into the propaganda used by the supporters of Flavian. Obviously they had accused the archimandrite of believing that the humanity of Christ "came down from heaven," a doctrine which might be considered Manichaean or at best Apollinarian and which, notably, diminished the role of the Virgin in the economy of salvation.

Eutyches concluded his appeal:

> And I pray that their deceit and frauds and rumors will not cause the faithful to be scandalized in me—who have always worked for the catholic faith. Moreover, you religious people (*plebs*) should know that I brought these things forward once before as an explanation to you. But certain people from that faction (*factio*) took down the *contestationes* I had presented, so that they deprived you of the ability to learn the truth of my teachings.

This statement of Eutyches shows that his enemies not only deprived the archimandrite of an opportunity to speak in church, but that they went about the city tearing down the statements he had posted in his defense. All of this suggests that public opinion in Constantinople was generally against Eutyches. People must have accepted the "frauds and rumors" about him or he would not have taken the effort to deny them. Furthermore, the violence used against him may have been manipulated by his enemies, but if people had been convinced that he was a heretic, opposition to Eutyches may have been widespread.

Despite the canonical condemnation of his godfather, Chrysaphius did not abandon his support of Eutyches, and he appears only to have redoubled his efforts in his behalf. But, at about this time, the eunuch had other pressing matters to occupy him. In late 448 or early 449, Edeco, a lieutenant of Attila, arrived in Constantinople with a complaint that the Romans had violated the terms of the recent peace. While the Hunnic leader was being entertained by members of the court, Chrysaphius approached him with a proposal. Swearing Edeco to secrecy, the eunuch promised him a life of luxury and ease if he would return to the camp of the Huns and kill Attila. Edeco agreed willingly and Chrysaphius informed Theodosius and Martialis, the *magister officiorum*. The plot was set in motion and the embassy—which included the historian Priscus—set off for the Danube. Priscus described for us in remarkable detail the misfortunes of the venture, which resulted eventually in the betrayal of the plot to Attila by Edeco himself.[52]

The failure of this enterprise was disastrous for Chrysaphius, since he was rightly considered its instigator. Attila wrote an insulting letter to Theodosius, berating him for acting so treacherously toward his master (meaning himself). He promised to forgive the emperor only if Chrysaphius were handed over to the Huns for punishment.[53] It was improbable that Theodosius would have surrendered his adviser to Attila, but the position of the eunuch had become doubly insecure, since he had earned the emnity of Flavius Zeno, the powerful Isaurian commander, and he too demanded Chrysaphius' death.

Paul Goubert and, following him, Luibhéid suggest that these events had considerable effect on the development of the religious situation in Constantinople.[54] They maintain that Chrysaphius, in difficulty because of the failure of his plot against Attila, wished to do something to divert public attention away from himself. For this reason, the eunuch did not let the affair of Eutyches die, but, even after the condemnation of the archimandrite, he continued to press for his restoration, hoping that people would turn their attention from the recent diplomatic fiasco to doctrinal controversy. There is much to recommend this theory, and it would both explain why the decision of the *synodos endemousa* was subject to so much official opposition and provide another example of the importance of popular opinion.

Unfortunately, there are two fundamental objections to this interpretation. First, the reconstruction of Goubert implies that popular sentiment was already decidedly in favor of Eutyches—which we have seen it was not. Chrysaphius' connection with Eutyches was well known in Constantinople. If the position of the archimandrite was unpopular, it is difficult to understand why the eunuch would wish to use the religious controversy to divert public censure from himself. The unpopularity of Eutyches would hardly enhance the popularity of Chrysaphius.

An even more important objection is a fundamental chronological inconsistency in the theory of Goubert. The embassy of Edeco arrived in Constantinople at the earliest in the fall of 448 and made its return in late spring or early summer of the following year, long after the council of Ephesus had been summoned by Theodosius.[55] Considering the time involved in the trip to and from the camp of Attila and the long negotiations described by Priscus, it is all but impossible that news of the disaster could have been known in Constantinople before the assembly of the second Council of Ephesus in August of 449. It is much more likely that the discomfiture of Chrysaphius occurred later in 449 or even in early 450. This must lend support to the statement of Theophanes that in 450 Theodosius decided that he had been deceived by Chrysaphius and had him exiled to "a certain island."[56] Chrysaphius' opposition to the deposition of Eutyches was not a response to his other difficulties; it must be assigned to the more obvious motives already mentioned—his attachmennt to his godfather, enmity with Flavian, as well as probable sympathy for Alexandrian theology.

Meanwhile the archimandrite wrote several letters to the emperor, complaining of irregularity in the decision against him and calling for the meeting of a general council.[57] As already mentioned, Eutyches also wrote to Rome for support, and at this same time he sent a letter to Alexandria, hoping to involve the bishop of that city, Dioscorus, in the controversy.[58] Chrysaphius secured the support of Eudocia, and he importuned the emperor to summon a general council to deal with the controversy.[59]

As Easter of 449 (March 27) approached, expectations ran high among the monks devoted to Eutyches. During the Easter season, it was customary for the emperor to grant amnesty to condemned persons, and the monks hoped that Theodosius would take this opportunity to reverse the sentence against Eutyches. In anticipation of this, the supporters of the archimandrite said, "every house and every *agora* was filled with just pleasure," perhaps indicating some public support for Eutyches or even a demonstration in his behalf.[60] Nevertheless, Easter passed, and the emperor did not announce a suspension of the sentence against Eutyches.

Yet, perhaps in part because of this exhibition of support, Theodosius began to consider more active aid for the archimandrite. According to Nestorius, the emperor undertook a persecution of the clergy and nobility who had opposed the aged monk:

> And prelates were openly seized and rebuked before the crowds,[61] and every bishop who was not of the party of Eutyches was seized; and he commanded every tax upon the possessions of their churches which had been remitted unto them by him and by the emperors before him, even the tax of all these years, to be exacted of them at one time; and of those who were nobles or of the family of noble persons he exacted openly, in return for the honor which was theirs, a quantity of gold—by which every means he commanded vengeance to be exacted of Eusebius, the accuser of Eutyches, without mercy.[62]

Sometime during the Easter season[63] Theodosius visited Hagia Sophia, and Flavian approached him as though no difficulty existed. The emperor, however, acted insulted and, despite the protests of the assembled clergy and laity, he resolved to have no more communion with the bishop.[64] Then, on March 30, only three days after Easter, Theodosius dispatched a letter to Dioscorus, summoning him and twenty of his bishops, to appear on the first of August in Ephesus for the opening of an ecumenical council.[65] From the tone of the letter, it was clear that the emperor had already decided the issue in favor of Eutyches.[66]

Furthermore, on April 8, less than two weeks after Easter, the emperor decided to investigate Eutyches' charge that the proceedings taken against him were irregular. Macedonius, a *referendarius* and tribune of the notaries, brought this matter before a group of twenty-eight bishops assembled in the baptistry of Hagia Sophia, under the presidency of Thessalios of Caesarea in Cappadocia.[67] These bishops could not find anything amiss in the condemnation of Eutyches and so adjourned. On April 13, a greater assembly of bishops met under the direction of Flavian in the "greater stoa of the holy church" (Hagia Sophia), to investigate the charge that the records of the *synodos endemousa* had been falsified. The patrician Florentius and the *comes* Mamas accompanied Macedonius as representatives of the emperor.[68] Even more than in the earlier council, Florentius assumed the initiative in this investigation. Macedonius was decidedly committed to the acquittal of Eutyches.[69] Eutyches himself, as an excommunicated person, was not allowed to attend, but he was represented by three of his monks. The acts of the synod of November were read to the bishops, section by section, and the representatives of Eutyches duly registered their complaints.[70] Since the monks could not substantiate their points, however, Florentius declared the notaries of Flavian innocent of any wrongdoing.

Eutyches continued his protest, and he dispatched another letter to the emperor, complaining that Flavian had drawn up the sentence against him even before the proceedings had begun.[71] Theodosius instituted yet another commission to investigate this charge, this time under the direction of Martialis, the *magister officiorum*. The body met on April 27 in the presence of the *comes* Carterius, Macedonius, the *silentarius* Magnus, and Constantine, a monk of Eutyches' monastery.[72] Again, no basis for the charge could be found, and the accusation was allowed to lapse. Even after all this, the emperor forced Flavian to draw up a statement of his faith, sign it, and present it to the court for its inspection.[73]

One obvious question arises from the series of events which followed the deposition of Eutyches: why did the imperial court refuse to step in forcefully to insure the rehabilitation of the controversial archimandrite? Eudocia, Chrysaphius, and probably Theodosius himself favored such an outcome. The supporters of Eutyches presented the emperor with several occasions which would have been suitable for the renewal of the decree against Eutyches, and a careful selection of the members of the investigating bodies should have been enough to assure this. And even should "canonical" procedures fail, the emperor could easily have resorted to force to secure his will—as happened later in Ephesus. Why, then, did Theodosius display such hesitancy?

The answer, of course, may lie partly within the court itself. Not all of its members supported Eutyches with the ardor of Chrysaphius. Pulcheria harbored great resentment against Chrysaphius and Eutyches. She was, it was true, in temporary retirement in the Hebdomon, but her influence was undoubtedly still felt in the palace. Among the imperial officials who became directly involved in the controversy, too, there appears to have been some difference of feeling. While the *comes* Mamas and the tribune Macedonius supported Eutyches faithfully, Florentius, by far the most important dignitary commissioned by the emperor, remained properly neutral and pronounced the sentence against the archimandrite on two different occasions.

Although one must not underestimate the importance of this "domestic" disagreement in the indecision of Theodosius, it seems that there was another serious factor at work. As pointed out above, the situation in Constantinople in these years was all but calm. Court intrigues and earthquakes, storms and plagues combined with the threat of imminent attack by the Huns to produce a feeling of despair in the city. One need only cite the joyful reception of the Trisagion as the salvation of the city during an earthquake to realize how unstable the situation was.[74] As we have seen, heavy taxation, necessitated by the demands of Attila, angered the wealthy inhabitants of Constantinople, and restrictive measures against the Jews must have made this segment of the population unhappy with imperial policy.[75] In these circumstances, it is not surprising that Theodosius did not wish further to aggravate religious dissension in the city. Had all the people of Constantinople—or an overwhelming number of them—supported Eutyches, the emperor might have dealt with the matter quickly and firmly in whatever way was expedient. As it was, however, some people strongly opposed Eutyches, and the use of force to restore the hated archimandrite would have led to alienation and perhaps even violence in the capital. On the other hand, Theodosius had to satisfy Chrysaphius and the others demanding action in behalf of Eutyches. A vacillating policy and an ecumenical council in another city were the best ways to handle the difficulty.

As we have seen, the sources do not allow us to make clear distinctions between the supporters and the enemies of Eutyches. The latter were probably greater in number, or they were at least able to make their numbers more effectively felt, since the archimandrite went about in fear of his life.

There is, however, reason to think that some of the division of opinion may have run along economic or political lines. Perhaps some individuals or groups viewed the religious issues according to whether they approved or disapproved of the general policies of the government. Members of the imperial administration risked the displeasure of Chrysaphius for any support of Flavian, but the bishop himself tells us that many important people (πολλοὶ τῶν μεγάλων) were scandalized by Eutyches' teaching, and the testimony of Nestorius bears this out. Indeed, the direction of the government since the rise of Chrysaphius was bound to alienate the established members of society. Chrysaphius himself, as a eunuch and an individual who was ruthless in his treatment of the aristocracy—the fall of Cyrus of Panopolis is the best example—was certainly hated by many. And the wealthy were not pleased by the heavy taxes placed upon them to pay the tribute to the Huns. In fact, if we are to believe the testimony of Nestorius, the harsh measures used in collecting taxes from the rich were connected with the persecution of the followers of Flavian.

On the other hand, the poor of Constantinople must have appreciated a government which had expended huge sums in a series of building campaigns during the past ten years.[76] As mentioned earlier, construction projects, along with the bread dole, were an important source of income for the urban poor, and the popularity of the prefect Cyrus clearly shows the effect of such expenditures in shaping public opinion. Thus, some of the urban poor may have had reason to support the policy of the government on behalf of Eutyches. Further, as we would in any case expect, there is specific evidence that Eutyches' monastery devoted some of its wealth to the poor, and the archimandrite—along with the heads of other philanthropic houses—probably earned the devotion of some of the poor as a result of this.

After carefully studying the individual monks who were involved in this dispute, Heinrich Bacht concluded that a social or economic division lay behind the schism in the monastic community. The monks who supported Flavian represented a group with greater resources and social standing, while Eutyches maintained the loyalty of the more humble monks, especially those who lived outside the regular monastic houses, in the *martyria* and tombs of the city.[77]

In addition, it might be argued that the difference in religious policy was reflected in the division between the Green and the Blue circus factions. Theodosius II, and even more Chrysaphius, were ardent supporters of the Greens, and it would not be surprising if those who opposed the government—for political or religious reasons—grouped around the faction of the Blues. Nevertheless, as reasonable as this might be, there is no evidence that such an identification and alliance actually took place, and we must admit our ignorance of any involvement of the factions in this dispute.[78] In general, secular considerations probably played a role in the shaping of public opinion during the affair of Eutyches, but they were not the determining factor. Again, what seems to have been crucial was the control which the supporters of Flavian maintained over the churches and the pulpits of the city. Despite serious challenge and many defections, they remained the accepted spokesmen of orthodoxy, and their view of the controversy had the opportunity for greater public exposure.[79]

The Second Council of Ephesus

Theodosius had summoned the bishops of the empire to assemble in Ephesus at the end of the summer of 449. The emperor and his court obviously anticipated some difficulties at the council, and at an early date they began to take measures against any possible opposition. On May 14, Theodosius wrote to Barsumas, the famous Syrian archimandrite, inviting him to attend the forthcoming synod.[80] Some Eastern bishops, the emperor claimed, had been advocating Nestorian sentiments, and it was only right that one who had always opposed this heresy should join the council as the representative of oriental monasticism. Despite this official protestation, the real motive for Barsumas' invitation must have been clear to all, for he was already known throughout the East as leader of a band of terrorist monks who roamed Syria and Palestine burning synagogues and violently opposing all they thought guilty of corrupting the faith with pagan or Judaizing tendencies.[81] Barsumas could not have been expected to contribute to the theologial discussion: he had not been trained in the subtleties of current religious thought, and he could not even speak Greek.[82] But he and his monks would surely provide an intimidating force to the opponents of Eutyches.

On the day after writing to Barsumas, Theodosius sent a letter to Dioscorus of Alexandria, asking him to receive the archimandrite graciously and grant him a seat in the council,[83] thus showing that Theodosius had designated the bishop of Alexandria as president of the council.[84]

At about the same time, the emperor nominated Elpidius, the *comes sacri consistorii*, and Eulogius, the tribune and praetorian notary, as his representatives at the council. In a letter to Elpidius, the emperor outlined their duties. The previous council of Ephesus, he said, had condemned the heresy of Nestorius, but now these same teachings were appearing once again. The forthcoming synod would end this difficulty once and for all. Elpidius and Eulogius were to assist in this undertaking by seeing that all was done as the emperor wished and, most importantly, by taking care that no disturbance distract the deliberations of the bishops:

> You are to allow no disturbance (*thorybos*) to occur, but if you should see someone causing disruptions and disturbances (*tarachai kai thoryboi*) to the harm of the holy faith, you must report him to me.[85]

Furthermore, the imperial representatives were to prevent those who had participated in the *synodos endemousa* in Constantinople from voting at the council in Ephesus.

Because of the nature of their assignment, we should expect that

Elpidius and Eulogius were provided with soldiers. In fact, Theophanes said that Eudocia sent "a large army" to Ephesus and that this was put at the disposal of Dioscorus.[86] We know also that the emperor made further arrangements for the maintenance of order at the council. Immediately after he wrote to Elpidius, Theodosius sent a letter to Proclus, the proconsul of Asia who resided in Ephesus, ordering him to support the efforts to prevent insurrection at the synod.[87] This letter was typical in its recital of the reasons for the council, but it concluded with a thinly veiled threat. Apparently the emperor had reason to fear that Proclus, either through sloth—as he says—or for some more substantial reason, might be slow to suppress any disturbance in the city. Accordingly, he warned the proconsul that his actions would be closely watched by imperial representatives. Thus, when we encounter the soldiers of the proconsul of Asia, we should expect them to be under the effective command of Elpidius and acting in accord with the wishes of Dioscorus.[88]

It is not surprising that we are relatively poorly informed about the Robber Synod.[89] Its decisions were later reversed and its leaders deposed; it received only passing notice in the accounts of the ecclesiastical historians, and its acts almost perished. Fortunately, the desire for revenge on the part of the "orthodox" bishops at Chalcedon demanded that the compromising statements made by their opponents at Ephesus be read into the record of the later council. Accordingly, we have preserved—albeit imperfectly—large parts of the *acta* of the first session of the Robber Synod and various other extracts referring to what went on at the council. Syriac translators, who would be more interested in their contents, have preserved the records of the subsequent sessions of the council.[90]

Sometime during the spring, Flavian sent Pope Leo two letters which fully explained his position in the affair of Eutyches.[91] On May 21, Leo answered these letters, reversing his earlier stand against Flavian and promising to send him a full doctrinal statement in the future.[92] On May 13, Leo received the imperial summons to attend the council in Ephesus.[93] The pope, however, waited until June 13 to reply, stating that he would not come himself, but that he would send representatives to the council: Julius, the bishop of Puteoli, the priest Rentaus, and the deacon Hilarus, who was later to succeed Leo as pope.[94] At the same time, he dispatched a letter to Pulcheria and another to Flavian.[95] The latter was the famous "Tome" of Leo, in which the pope put forward his definitive dyophysite theology of the Incarnation, eventually accepted at the Council of Chalcedon. Thus, Flavian could count on whatever support the delegates of the pope could give.

In late summer of 449, the bishops began to arrive in Ephesus, and there is reason to believe that the city was once again the scene of party strife. For example, Eusebius of Dorylaeum later complained about the cortege of Dioscorus as it arrived in Ephesus:

> The goodly Dioscorus ... of the same opinion and mind as Eutyches, the empty-headed heretic, ignoring the majority of the people (λανθάνων δὲ τοὺς πολλοὺς) as he later showed himself to do ... gathering a number of the disorderly rabble (πλῆθος ἀτάκτων ὄχλων) and securing power for himself through money ... he enforced the evil doctrine of Eutyches.[96]

Other sources repeated the charge that many *parabalani* and monks accompanied the "Pharoah" to his new test of strength with the bishop of Constantinople.[97]

As soon as they arrived in Ephesus, the followers of Flavian went to the episcopal residence of Stephanos, the bishop of the city, to pay their respects. Stephanos received them warmly and held communion with them—or at least so he claimed at the Council of Chalcedon. His position, as bishop of the conciliar city, was an important one, for he controlled the local churches and had the opportunity to influence popular opinion greatly. One need only remember the role played by Memnon at the earlier Council of Ephesus.

At Chalcedon, Stephanos testified that violence had been used to secure his support of Eutyches in the summer of 449:

> Elpidius and Eulogius, soldiers, and the monks of Eutyches—three hundred in number—came upon me in the *episcopeion*. And they were about to kill me, saying that since I had received the enemies of the emperor, I was an enemy of the emperor. I replied, "But I am a hospitable man (ἐγὼ ξενοδόχος εἰμί) . I did not have communion over this matter [that is, Stephanos' reception of Flavian had nothing to do with the theological controversy]; I was not able to refuse communion to those coming in communion." And thus everything happened through force and necessity (καὶ οὕτω βίᾳ καὶ ἀνάγκῃ γέγονεν πάντα) .

The *archontes* at Chalcedon inquired whether Dioscorus had forced him to support Eutyches. Stephanos replied:

> All of his men and the *comites*. They did not permit me to leave the *secretum* of the church until I gave my consent to the opinions of Dioscorus....[98]

These protestations of Stephanos may be suspect because of the circumstances in which they were made, but they have a ring of truth about them. At the Council of Chalcedon, Dioscorus frequently interrupted his accusers to deny the truth of their testimony, but he allowed the statements of Stephanos to pass uncontested.

The position of Stephanos may be further clarified by testimony that was given during the twelfth session of the Council of Chalcedon.[99] At that time, Bassianos, an elderly member of the clergy of Ephesus, accused Stephanos of irregularity in his election and consecration as bishop.

Bassianos claimed that under the episcopacy of Memnon he had himself gained a certain amount of popularity because of his concern for the poor and sick.¹⁰⁰ In order to rid the city of a dangerous rival, Memnon had Bassianos consecrated bishop of Evagae. Bassianos refused to leave Ephesus, however, and Memnon had him beaten. Basil, the successor of Memnon, consecrated another bishop for Evagae and left Bassianos in his episcopal dignity. After the death of Basil, Bassianos said, "the faithful (*laos*) and the clergy and the bishops enthroned me, with much force and necessity, in the city of Ephesus."¹⁰¹

Later, Bassianos was suddenly interrupted while officiating at the Easter liturgy. "Certain people in the ranks of the clergy and certain others who were near-by" set upon him and dragged him to the *agora* where they beat him. Later they imprisoned him and threatened him with death; some of his supporters were killed, and his property was confiscated. Stephanos, who had been a priest of Bassianos, was the leader (ἀρχηγός) of this group, and he succeeded as bishop.¹⁰² Another priest who supported Bassianos substantiated this story. He told further how the enemies of Bassianos had tried to induce him to betray his master. He refused and so was forced to leave Ephesus. He told the council—in late October of 451—that he had been a beggar in Constantinople for four years.¹⁰³ Thus, we should place the deposition of Bassianos in the spring of 447.

Surely, we should keep these disturbances in mind when considering the situation in Ephesus in the summer of 449. In the best of conditions, the bishop of Ephesus could never be secure; but it is clear that the episcopacy of Stephanos was on particularly shaky ground. In 449, Stephanos had been bishop only two years, and Bassianos undoubtedly still had many friends in the city. His charity certainly would be remembered by the poor of the city, who had supported him enthusiastically in the past. Thus, when Stephanos was confronted with the controversy concerning Eutyches and the forthcoming council in his own city, he must have hesitated. Were he to take the side of one of the disputants, his enemies would surely use the occasion to sow dissension in the city and call for his deposition. On the other hand, Stephanos probably had real preferences in the doctrinal controversy, and he may have regarded Flavian, as bishop of Constantinople, with considerable suspicion.

On the whole, however, it appears that Stephanos remained largely neutral in the days preceding the second Council of Ephesus. Some of his clergy may have reminded the faithful that the "heresy" of Flavian was a revival of Nestorianism, and the followers of Dioscorus certainly seized the churches of Ephesus for this purpose after they imprisoned Stephanos. But the great assistance which Memnon gave to Cyril of Alexandria at the first Council of Ephesus was probably withheld from

Dioscorus at the second. It would be interesting to know how long Stephanos "held out" before he subscribed to the theology of Eutyches. If he did this immediately, and the council was still some time off, Dioscorus undoubtedly used the opportunity to have the bishop influence public opinion in favor of Eutyches. In any case, the absence of Stephanos from the forefront of the battle must have cost the supporters of Dioscorus some expected popular support.[104]

Finally, on August 8 the bishops assembled in the church of Mary to begin the second Council of Ephesus.[105] One hundred thirty-five bishops or their representatives (plus the two representatives of the pope who were below episcopal dignity) attended the opening of the first session of the council.[106] Dioscorus held the place of honor, while Julius, the emissary of Pope Leo, was second. Flavian was relegated to the fifth place.[107]

John, the *primicerius notariorum* and a priest of the church of Alexandria,[108] began the proceedings by reading the letter of invitation sent by Theodosius to Dioscorus. Julius and Hilarus explained—through an interpreter—the circumstances of their presence. Hilarus then gave to the notary John the letter which Leo had prepared to be read to the council, outlining his doctrinal position on the controversy. John received the communication, but ignored it completely, passing on to read the second letter of Theodosius to Dioscorus. After being invited by the president of the assembly, the *comes* Elpidius gave a short exhortation to the bishops and reminded them of his official position by reading his letter of commission from the emperor.[109]

These preliminaries completed, Dioscorus turned the attention of the fathers to a consideration of the matter at hand. Eutyches entered the church and gave his account of the synod in Constantinople, adding a summary of his theological position. Stephanos of Ephesus was one of the first to declare his theology orthodox.[110] When the archimandrite had concluded his defense, Flavian asked if Eusebius of Dorylaeum might also be heard, since he had been the primary accuser of Eutyches. The *comes* Elpidius replied that this was not possible because the emperor had declared that all those who had condemned Eutyches were now themselves to be judged. As Nestorius was to write: "And then the counts, who had been charged with this, restrained the bishops who were assembled and wanted to speak for him [Flavian]."[111]

Dioscorus suggested that they turn to a consideration of the sentence against Eutyches. Many of the bishops voiced their agreement.[112] The Roman legates, however, again asked that the letter of Pope Leo be read. Eutyches protested, saying that the representatives of the pope had been openly associating with Flavian so that their bias might prejudice the case against him.[113] The notary John began reading the *acta* of the synod in Constantinople of 448. This was carried out without incident, except for several exclamations from the bishops when a particular idea disturbed them: "No one says that the Lord is two after the union! Don't divide the indivisible! Nestorius thinks that way." At one point Dioscorus had to intervene: "Be quiet a little! We shall hear other impieties. Why do we blame Nestorius alone? There are many Nestorii! (πολλοὶ Νεστοριοί εἰσιν)."[114]

After reading the *acta* of the *synodos endemousa* and those of the imperial commissions established to investigate its decisions, Dioscorus requested that all the bishops give their opinion regarding the orthodoxy of Eutyches.[115] Seven or eight of the more important bishops, together with Barsumas, pronounced short statements, indicating their approval of Eutyches' theology. Another ninety-three bishops merely gave their assent without any additional comment. The notary John read the letter which the monks of Eutyches' monastery wrote to the council, and Dioscorus, after examining their faith, declared them all restored to communion.[116]

The work of the council seemed accomplished. The sentence of the council in Constantinople had been revoked—and Eutyches had recovered all of his ecclesiastical dignity. But Dioscorus had further plans in mind. He asked the bishops to give him their opinion of anyone who taught otherwise than the Council of Nicaea. Thalissius of Caesarea immediately exclaimed that anyone who went beyond the teachings of Nicaea could not be received as orthodox. Several bishops made similar statements, and finally an acclamation made the agreement universal.[117] The proposition seemed harmless enough in itself.

Dioscorus now had the mandate he wanted. Since Flavian and Eusebius—by insisting on the two natures after the union—had obviously taught things beyond the doctrine of Nicaea, he said, "we declare them deprived of every priestly and episcopal dignity."[118] He asked each of the bishops to communicate his opinion on this matter, and he added, as a threat, that all of this would quickly be made known to the emperor.

This proceeding came as a shock to many of the bishops. Flavian cried out in protest, and the deacon Hilarus, forgetting his need for an interpreter, shouted "*contradicitur!*"[119] The *acta* of the council, drawn up by the notaries of Dioscorus, told of no further disturbance at this point. They continued only with the vote on the condemnation of Flavian. Again, the more important bishops presented short statements agreeing with Dioscorus, while the less distinguished members of the council (about 140 in all) merely signed their names to the document drawn up by the Egyptian notaries.

Fortunately, we know something of the proceedings of the council from sources not dependent upon the good will of the bishop of Alexandria. From these, we see why few bishops openly opposed the actions of Dioscorus, although many later claimed that they really supported Flavian. In the words of Theodore of Claudiopolis, "What were we to do?

The Latrocinium 149

They made sport of murdering us." (τί εἴχομεν ποιῆσαι; εἰς τὸ αἷμα ἡμῶν ἔπαιξαν οὗτοι).[120]

Indeed, the violence which Dioscorus had at his disposal appears to have intimidated his opponents completely. Onesophoros of Iconium reported that when he and his fellow bishops heard Dioscorus announce the deposition of Flavian, they could hardly believe their ears:

> I, taking some other bishops with me, stood up and besought him [Dioscorus], saying, "Don't! I beg of you. He does not deserve to be deposed. But if he deserves to be censured, let him be censured." He [Dioscorus] rose from his throne and, standing on his footstool, he said, "Do you threaten me with violence? (στάσιν μοι κινεῖτε;) Bring in the counts!" And thus fearing we signed.[121]

Basil of Seleucia, attempting to justify his failure to defend Flavian at the Latrocinium, accused Dioscorus:

> You imposed much force (πολλὴ ἀνάγκη) upon us, both from outside [the church] and from inside, as well as from the church and the monks—both those with Barsumas and the *parabalani*—rose up, along with another great crowd.[123] After the deposition of the blessed Flavian you forced us into such a crime by the threats of the great crowd.[124]

Marianos of Sunadoi confirmed the story of Basil and Onesophoros:

> Thus a crowd assembled and we remained hanging on his [Dioscorus'] knees and beseeching him. And he shouted out, "Where are the counts?" I say this as a lover of the truth. The counts came in and brought along the proconsul who had with him chains and a great crowd. Finally, each one of us signed.[125]

Certainly, we must regard the testimony of these bishops with some suspicion. It was given at the Council of Chalcedon, and the prelates were anxious to explain their actions in the best possible light. Nevertheless, the agreement of their accounts suggests veracity, and they accurately reflect the situation in Ephesus as we know it to have been from other sources: Dioscorus was clearly in control, and he could rely on the soldiers of the *comites* and the *proconsul*, as well as the monks of Barsumas and the *parabalani*, for active support. The bishops, however, several times mentioned a great crowd (*plethos*) which participated in the intimidation of the supporters of Flavian. It is tempting to identify this as an angry group of laymen, such as had gathered in Ephesus during the council of 431. This suggestion is supported by the report of Nestorius that the people of Ephesus cooperated with the monks of Eutyches in a campaign of terrorism directed at their opponents:

> All of those with Eutyches—they were monks—were in the enjoyment of great liberty and authority ... so that they delivered unto the chiefs themselves and unto the inhabitants of the city all those who were indicated unto them. For

every man was made subject to them.... And they were carrying off men, some from the ships, some from the streets and houses, and others while they were praying from the churches. They pursued those who fled. And with all zeal they sought out and dug up those who were hiding in caves and in holes of the earth. And it was a matter of great fear and danger for a man to speak with the adherents of Flavian on account of those who were dwelling in the neighborhood and keeping watch as spies to see who entered in unto them.[126]

This graphic description is clear evidence that some of the people of Ephesus actively cooperated with the forces of Dioscorus: only natives could have acted as "spies" in the neighborhoods of the city. Further, by noting that the monks of Eutyches delivered their enemies to "the chiefs" and "the inhabitants of the city," we should infer that popular sentiment in Ephesus was generally opposed to Flavian and in accord with the teaching of Dioscorus. Finally, and perhaps most remarkably, this passage reveals something of the careful organization which the bishop of Alexandria had established in the city: contact was maintained with supporters at the local level to the point that no one could be certain he was not speaking with an agent of Dioscorus.

As a result of all this, the legates of Pope Leo fled from Ephesus in fear of their lives, leaving their property behind them. Obviously, they were considered men who spoke "with the adherents of Flavian."[127]

Flavian himself died a short time after his deposition. Most of the ancient sources say this happened on his way to exile, as a result of the ill treatment he had received at the council.[128] In this connection, the *acta* of the Council of Chalcedon preserve some interesting testimony. Diogenes, the bishop of Cyzicus, said: "Barsumas, who is among them, killed the blessed Flavian. He stood up and said, 'Kill him!'" (σφάξον) All the reverend bishops cried out: "Barsumas destroyed all Syria! (πᾶσαν Συρίαν Βαρσουμᾶς ἠφάνισεν). He brought down upon us a thousand monks.... Throw the murderer Barsumas out! To the stadium with the murderer! Anathema to Barsumas. Exile him!"[129] Scholars have doubted this testimony, unquestionably given in a moment of anger and emotion, and it is unlikely that Barsumas himself actually killed Flavian. But open violence obviously characterized the deposition of the bishop, and it is likely that the monks of Barsumas played a role in his death.

The second Council of Ephesus—less some of its more important members—assembled again on August 22. At this session, the bishops deposed Ibas, his nephew Daniel, Iraneus of Tyre (the former *comes* and friend of Nestorius), Aquilinios of Byblos, Theodoret, and Domnus of Antioch.[130] This session was conducted quietly and without incident, so it need not detain us further.

The Aftermath in Constantinople

The emperor Theodosius naturally was pleased with the outcome of the council, and he issued a law confirming its enactments.[131] He wrote to Valentinian III, Galla Placidia, and Licinia Eudoxia, saying that all was well in the East; ecclesiastical harmony had been restored with no damage to the faith.[132]

Yet, there is evidence that all was not as peaceful in the church of Constantinople as Theodosius claimed. The empress Pulcheria certainly opposed the action of the council, as she was soon to demonstrate,[133] and Pope Leo kept up a continuous correpondence with a wide range of people in the capital. In October of 449, he wrote to the "honorable clergy and people (*plebs*)[134] living in Constantinople." The pope advised his readers that he had good hope for the future. He realized, however, that at present their church was in difficulty through the impiety of treacherous men (*nunc quia ecclesiam vestram hac ratione cognovimus dissipatam . . . ut pro catholicae fidei defensione perfidorum nequitiae resistatis*).[135]

On the same day, the pope wrote another letter, similar in content, to the priests and archimandrites Faustus, Martinus, Petrus, and Emmanuel.[136] This letter shows that the same monastic sentiment which had favored Flavian before the Latrocinium continued after the council. This was all the more significant because the victors at the Latrocinium were surprisingly slow in following up their advantage in Constantinople. In particular, the emperor and his ecclesiastical advisers hesitated in the election of a new bishop, and the vacant see was not filled until March or April of 450, some seven or eight months after the deposition of Flavian. The new bishop Anatolius wrote to Pope Leo, indicating the confusion in the city which caused the long delay in his appointment:

> Thus there arose boundless division of opinion on these matters and all were divided there concerning many ideas.[137]

As a result of this situation, the supporters of Flavian must have maintained their control of the churches in Constantinople for a number of months after the Latrocinium. These priests and bishops undoubtedly lost no opportunity to condemn the council and praise the memory of Flavian. Further, the letters of Pope Leo and other similarly minded prelates were frequently read to the assembled crowds. In December of 449, Leo wrote again "to the citizens of Constantinople," this time congratulating them specifically for resisting heresy and maintaining the truth faith.[138]

A final indication that there was considerable, if passive, opposition to the second Council of Ephesus among the inhabitants of Constantinople is provided by another letter of Leo, addressed to Theodosius and dated October 17, 449.[139] This letter is remarkable in its apparent approval of the actions of the emperor and the decisions of the Robber Synod. Silva-Tarouca noted this divergence from the normal position taken by the pope, and he pointed to the similarities between this letter and another written to Theodosius on the same date. From this evidence, Silva-Tarouca suggested that the first letter—favorable to the Latrocinium—was a falsification of the second letter, carried out at the court under the direction of Chrysaphius.[140] As we have seen, letters were frequently used as propaganda to influence popular opinion one way or another. That Chrysaphius took the trouble to alter the letter of Leo to conform with the decisions of the Robber Synod suggests that there were people who needed to be convinced. Certainly there can have been little resistance to the decisions of the Latrocinium at the court, so opponents must have been found in the houses of the rich or throughout the city as a whole.

The Latrocinium, of all the events selected for discussion in this study, allows us the least certainty in attempting to define and understand popular feeling and action. In part, at least, this is a result of the nature of the sources. But it is possible that popular involvement, both in Constantinople and Ephesus, was much less intense than it had been in 431 or would be—at least in Egypt—in 451. We hear of few incidents of popular action, and these were generally not of a spontaneous nature.

Some differences in the reactions of the crowd in each city are, however, discernible. Support for Flavian was certainly greater in Constantinople than it was in Ephesus. At first this is surprising, since in 431 popular opinion in Constantinople almost universally condemned Nestorius. Flavian and Nestorius—as the latter frequently pointed out—adhered to similar theological positions. Why should people condemn Nestorius and support Flavian if both men taught the same doctrines?[141] The reason for this seems to lie in the differences in the ecclesiastical and political situations at the time of the two controversies.

Flavian was probably a native of Constantinople, and he had many friends among the clergy of the city. Nestorius, on the other hand, had been a stranger in the capital, and he quickly earned the enmity of his clerical subordinates. In 428, despite the support of the emperor, Nestorius gained the reputation of a heretic and a madman. His enemies controlled the pulpits of many churches, and from these they inveighed agianst the bishop, comparing his theology with that of known heretics. Flavian, although he was without favor at the court, had just presided over a local council which had condemned his opponent. Imperial investigations failed to reveal any impropriety in the bishop's actions, and he maintained control over all the churches of the city. The followers of Eutyches claimed that Flavian represented a revival of Nestorian sentiments, but they were not able to mount a successful campaign to convince people of that charge. Without a church from which to preach his doctrines, Eutyches tried to influence popular opinion by posting public notices, but these were torn down by the followers of Flavian, and the archimandrite himself was threatened with violence. Further, no emotional issue, such as the controversy over the *theotokos*, came to the surface to galvanize public opinion firmly on one side or another.

The attitude of the monastic community was crucial in both events. In 431, the solidarity of the monks had been an important factor in the overwhelming popular feeling against Nestorius. In 448-49, however, a considerable segment of the monastic community supported Flavian. This is important not only in its own right and in the history of Constantinopolitan monasticism, but it must have had a significant effect in the minds of simple believers. Had Eutyches been able to command the loyalty of all the monks of the capital, he might have been able to rally popular feeling on his behalf.

In both 431 and 449, the emperor espoused causes which might be called "unpopular" in Constantinople, and in both cases we have seen the emperor go to some lengths in an attempt to change that situation. In 448-49, this was represented by the several imperial investigations into the decisions of the *synodos endemousa*, which apparently had little effect.

It appears that many of the wealthier inhabitants of Constantinople, who were just then heavily burdened by the tribute paid to the Huns, opposed Eutyches—and thus the official religious policy of the emperor. This is not to suggest that these people had no interest in religious matters. Rather, since secular and religious concerns were inextricably bound together, the ill-treatment they received from the government was probably seen as a divine indication of the falseness of Eutyches' teaching.[142]

The situation in Ephesus is easier to understand, although we have much less information about crowd involvement there. In 431, the people of Ephesus had united to oppose the bishop of Constantinople (Nestorius) and in 449 they opposed Flavian. They consistently rejected the theology of Antioch for that of Alexandria, and they reacted strongly against the person of the bishop of Constantinople. But there were important differences between the circumstances in 431 and those in 449. While in 431 one has the impression that all the city rose up in anger against Nestorius, in 449 it is not clear that popular involvement was so widespread or so enthusiastic. In part this may have been a result of the position of the bishop of Ephesus. In 431, Memnon had been secure in his own see, and he stood firmly behind the actions of Cyril of Alexandria. In 449, Stephanos had just recently seized the episcopal throne from Bassianos, who continued in active opposition. Moreover, Stephanos was at best a reluctant supporter of Dioscorus. Memnon had closed the churches of Ephesus to the followers of Nestorius and allowed the Egyptian and his company to harangue the faithful concerning the importance of the doctrinal dispute. In 449, the bishop of Ephesus could not be used to rally the people behind any particular doctrinal position. Instead, organization, unity, and enthusiasm had to be imposed from without, by the monks of Eutyches and Barsumas and the cortege of Dioscorus of Alexandria. These were efficient in their work, and they enforced their views with a campaign of terrorism and violence.

In fact, violence was the most characteristic feature of the Latrocinium. While one cannot always draw firm conclusions about the role of the crowd in this controversy, it is easy to discern the part that violence played. In Constantinople, of course, we have seen that both sides resorted to violence, the emperor being restrained by popular support of Flavian. At Ephesus, however, careful plans were laid for the intimidation of the enemies of Eutyches, both in the city and in the conciliar church itself. This strategy was successful in that no popular support arose in behalf of Flavian, and the actual outcome of the second Council of Ephesus was determined by the soldiers and monks acting under the orders of Dioscorus.

1. On events during this period see Bury, *Later Roman Empire*, vol. 1, pp. 225-35; Stein, *Histoire*, vol. 1, pp. 285-98; Jones, *Later Roman Empire*, pp. 193-204; J. O. Maenchen-Helfen, *The World of the Huns*; E. A. Thompson, *A History of Attila and the Huns*. Unfortunately, the histories of Socrates and Sozomen, our primary sources for the two previous chapters and eyewitnesses to much of what they reported, end before most of the events discussed in this chapter. For ecclesiastical developments we must turn to the chronicles of Malalas and Theophanes, the so-called *Paschal Chronicle* and the sixth-century *Ecclesiastical History* of Evagrius. No secular history of the period survives, but the fragments of Priscus (*FHG*, IV, 71-110) illuminate several important areas. Of the greatest importance for this study are the letters and *acta* of the first session of the second Council of Ephesus, read into the proceedings at Chalcedon two years later (*Acta Conciliorum Oecumenicorum* [*ACO*] ed. Eduard Schwartz, vol. 2, i [Berlin, 1933]). The acts of subsequent sessions have survived in a Syriac translation (Samuel Perry, *The Second Synod of Ephesus* [Dartford, 1881]; J. Flemming, *Akten des ephesischen Synode vom Jahre 449* [Berlin, 1917]). The letters of Pope Leo are edited by Schwartz in *ACO* and by C. Silva-Tarouca, *S. Leonis Magni epistulae contra Eutychis haeresim* (Rome, 1934-35). On the ecclesiastical situation in general see P. Batiffol, *La siège apostolique*; Bardy, *Histoire*, pp. 211-24; Duchesne, *Early History of the Christian Church*, vol. 3; A. Grillmeier and H. Bacht, eds., *Das Konzil von Chalkedon*, 3 Vols. (Würzburg, 1951-54).

2. Bury, *Later Roman Empire*, vol. 1, pp. 247-48; 271-76; Stein, *Histoire*, vol. 1, pp. 291-93; Thompson, *Attila*, pp. 70-72; Maenchen-Helfen, *World of the Huns*, pp. 94-129.

3. Priscus, frg. 5, *FHG*, IV, p. 74-75; *cf*. Thompson, *Attila*, pp. 85-86; Maenchen-Helfen, *World of the Huns*, pp. 116-117 for a date in 447.

4. Priscus, frg. 5, *FHG*, IV, p. 74.

5. Evagrius, *Historia Ecclesiastica* 2.14 taken from Priscus, frg. 43 (earthquakes); Marcellinus Comes, pp. 81-82.

6. Theophanes, *Chronographia*, A.M. 5930 (ed. de Boor), p. 93; Th. Preger, ed., *Scriptores originum Constantinopolitanarum* (Leipzig, 1907), p. 150.

7. Thomas Camelot, "De Nestorius à Eutyches," in *Das Konzil von Chalkedon*, vol. 1 (Würzburg, 1951), pp. 213-47.

8. A. Jülicher, "Eutyches (no. 5)," *RE* 6 (1909). Nothing is known of his early life, except that he claimed in 448 to have been in his monastery for seventy years. If this is accurate, he entered the monastery in 378, undoubtedly at a very early age. To enter the monastery as a child or young man was unusual in this period; he thus had a different experience from the other great monastic leaders of the time. Jülicher suggests that he was dedicated to the monastic life at birth. In 448 he also claimed that he had been archimandrite of his monastery for thirty years. What monastery this was we do now know—certainly it could not have been Dalmatou or Rufianae, as these had been ruled by Dalmatius and Hypatius respectively during the previous thirty years.

9. *C. Th.* 16.5, 66. The Nestorians were to be called Simonians.

10. *Synodicon* 196-200; Liberatus *Breviarium* (*ACO*, II, v) 10. Much of the Nestorian agitation centered outside the empire, particularly in Persian Armenia. It is the central theme in the literature growing out of the affair of the Three Chapters. See the collections on the second Council of Constantinople in J. D. Mansi, *Sacrorum conciliorum nova et amplissima collectio*, 31 vols. [Florence and Venice, 1759-98], and Schwartz, *ACO* and L. Abramowski, "Der Streit um Diodor und Theodor zwichen den beiden ephesinischen Konzilen," *Zeitschrift für Kirchengeschichte* 57 (1956), 252-87.

11. See the "Tome" of Proclus, *ACO*, IV, ii, pp. 187-95; the treatise of Cyril is now lost. Cf. Liberatus, *Breviarium* (*ACO*, II, v, p. 111).

12. Duchesne, *Early History of the Christian Church*, vol. 3, p. 269.

13. Liberatus *Breviariuim* (*ACO*, II, v. p. 112). See also H. Bacht, "Die Rolle des orientalischen Mönchtums," *Das Konzil von Chalkedon*, vol. 2, p. 201.

14. Theophanes *Chronographia*, A.M. 5933 (ed. de Boor). According to this account Proclus wrote to the eastern bishops about the matter and when John of Antioch answered that Theodore was orthodox the matter was allowed to drop.

15. *Eranistes*, ed. Gerard H. Ettlinger (Oxford, 1975). Cf. R. V. Sellers, *The Council of Chalcedon* (London, 1961), pp. 37-41.

16. Facundus *pro defens.* (*PL* 67, 723 ff.) 7, 5; Hefele-Leclercq, *Histoire des conciles*, vol. 3, p. 188.

17. *ACO*, I, i, 4, pp. 66. The same decree commands Ireneus, the supporter of Nestorius at Ephesus, to relinquish his seat as bishop of Tyre. Cf. *Codex Justinianus* 1.1, 3.

18. Theophanes *Chronographia*, A.M. 5939 (ed. de Boor), p. 97, says that Flavian had been "priest and treasurer" of the Church of Constantinople; also he was "a most holy and virtuous man." The exact date of Flavian's accession is uncertain; Theophanes and the *Patria* imply that it was late in 447. Proclus had been preceded in death by Dalmatius (440), John of Antioch (441 or 442) and Cyril (444).

19. Theophanes *Chronographia*, A.M. 5940, (ed. de Boor), p. 98; Nicephorus Callistus Xanthopoulos *Historia Ecclesiastica* (*PG* 145-47), col. 1221. Evagrius says that Flavian sent Chrysaphius the sacred vessels of the church (*Historia Ecclesiastica* 3.3). Despite this explanation for the outbreak of the quarrel, it seems to me likely that the enmity between Flavian and Chrysaphius began even earlier and for more substantial reasons. If later events give any indication, the bond between Eutyches and Chrysaphius was very strong, and the eunuch may have had contact with Dioscorus—or at least Alexandrian theology—before 448. As an official in the administration of Proclus, Flavian would have had an opportunity to make known his theological leanings at an early date. Thus the enmity may have been theological, or at least ecclesiastical, from the beginning. Chrysaphius may even have opposed the election of Flavian. In this connection, it is possible that Chrysaphius had something to do with the "visit" of the monophysite Armenian monks to Constantinople. On Chrysaphius see the article by O. Seeck, *RE* 3, and P. Goubert, "Le rôle de Sainte Pulchérie et l'eunuque Chrysaphios," in *Das Konzil von Chalkedon*. On eunuchs and their place in the politics of the period, see J. E. Dunlap, *The Office of the Grand Chamberlain in the Later Roman and Byzantine Empires* (New York, 1929); R. Guilland, "Fonctions et dignité des eunuques," *Études Byzantines* 2 (1944), 185-244, and 3 (1945), 179-214; and Jones, *Later Roman Empire*, pp. 566-72. For an interesting approach to the phenomenon see K. Hopkins, "Eunuchs in Politics in the Later Roman Empire," *Proceedings of the Cambridge Philogical Society* 189 (1963), 62-80.

20. The record of this synod was read, in part, into the *acta* of the first session of the Robber Council of 449, which was in turn read into the *acta* of the first session of the Council of Chalcedon (*ACO*, II, i, 1, pp. 100 ff.). The accusations of Eusebius are found in *ACO*, II, i, 1, pp. 100–01. Cf. Liberatus *Breviarium* (*ACO*, II, v, pp. 113–17). The whole affair of Eutyches is discussed in detail by Eduard Schwartz, "Der Prozess des Eutyches," *Sitzungsberichte der bayerischen Akademie der Wissenschaften* 5 (1929), 1–93.

21. *ACO*, II, i, 1, p. 102.
22. *ACO*, II, i, 1, pp. 123–25.
23. *ACO*, II, i, 1, p. 126.
24. *ACO*, II, i, 1, pp. 126–27.
25. *ACO*, II, i, 1, pp. 127–28.
26. *ACO*, II, i, 1, p. 129.
27. *ACO*, II, i, 1, p. 129–31.
28. *ACO*, II, i, 1, pp. 131–32.
29. ACO, II, i, 1, pp. 132–34. It could be argued that Eusebius' charge of *stasis* referred only to Eutyches' obvious attempt to win supporters among the monastic community. Yet, if that had been the case, Eusebius would surely have pushed his point, since there was clear evidence that Eutyches had circulated his *tomos* among the monasteries of the capital. Instead, it seems that Eusebius had actually meant to accuse the archimandrite of stirring up open rebellion against Flavian. Another session of the council met on Saturday, the twentieth of November. It concerned itself with an investigation of the theology of Eutyches, as reported by the priest Mamas.

30. *ACO*, II, i, 1, p. 138: "Eutyches with a great crowd of soldiers and monks and officials of ... the praetorian prefect."

31. Later Eutyches wrote that Magnus came "for my protection." On the role of the *slientiarii* see Jones, *Later Roman Empire* pp. 571–72 and 1234. They were under the control of the *praepositus sacri cubiculi*, so Magnus was presumably an underling of Chrysaphius.

32. *ACO*, II, i, 1, p. 138, 21–24. On Flavius Florentius see Seeck's article *s.v.* "Florentius (13)" *RE* 6. He was praetorian prefect of the East in 428–29, consul in 429, praetorian prefect again in 438–39, and *praefectus urbi* in 442. Sometime between 444 and 448, he attained the rank of patrician. (He is to be distinguished from the Florentius who was a tribune in Ephesus in 431. Between 300 and 450, at least thirteen Florentii are known to have risen to prominence in the imperial service. Another Flavius Florentius, a *comes* of Constantius II, was a correspondent of Athanasius.) The role of Florentius at the *synodos endemousa* is particularly interesting and forms a striking contrast with the position of Candidianus at Ephesus. In 431, the representative of the emperor was not to participate in the discussion—and the council condemned the emperor's bishop. In 448, the representative of Theodosius was to dominate the discussion. This makes the condemnation of Eutyches despite imperial favor all the more difficult to understand.

33. *ACO*, II, i, 1, p. 143, 10–11.
34. *ACO*, II, i, 1, p. 144, 22–23.
35. *ACO*, II, i, 1, p. 145.
36. *ACO*, II, i, 1, pp. 145–47.
37. Nestorius *Bazaar*, pp. 336–40: "But apart (from this) he (Eutyches) was making use of the authority of the emperor ... Thus, while he was confirming and preparing these things by the authority and by the commands of (his) majesty, all the East was disturbed...."

38. E. Schwartz, "Prozess," 85 ff., suggests that Florentius was a supporter of the party of Eutyches and that he attempted to redeem himself at the *cognitio* the following April (*ACO*, II, i, 1, pp. 172–73): "I did not give this order for I am not one to speak out about theology." What then caused him not only to accept the deposition of Eutyches in 448 but actually to encourage it? With the soldiers near at hand he certainly cannot have feared to oppose the bishops. See Sellers, *Chalcedon*, p. 69, n.4.

39. Cf. Gilbert Dagron, "Les moines et la ville," 271–72.

40. Leo *Epistula* 21.

41. Zachariah of Mitylene *Hist. Eccl* 2.2, speaks of thirty-one bishops and twenty-two archimandrites and the Latin translation of the acts (*ACO* II, ii, 1, pp. 20–21) records 31 bishops and 18 archimandrites. See also Bacht, "Die Rolle," pp. 216, n. 107. Seven of the twenty-three in the Greek text signed through representatives. Marcellus, the last to sign, apparently noticed this and added that his signature was "in my own hand." It is possible that absent archimandrites supported Eutyches and that members of their houses were persuaded to sign for their leaders. Eutyches speaks of pressure being put upon the monks to sign statements condemning him, but it is unclear whether he meant at the synod or afterwards (probably the latter).

42. Bacht ("Die Rolle," 218), following U. Chevalier (*Répretoire des sources historiques du Moyen Age*, vol. 1 [Paris, 1905], p. 1464) points out that the sources make no mention of the connection between this Faustus and Dalmatius, so he suggests that there were two important monks of the same name. I find his reasoning on this point unconvincing. In fact, the subsequent action of Faustus seems very much in keeping with a son who had been deprived of his father's position.

43. *ACO*, II, i, 1, pp. 186–87. See H. Bacht, "Die Rolle," 210–21.

44. Nestorius *Bazaar*, pp. 336–37.

45. *ACO*, II, i, 1, p. 130.

46. *ACO*, II, ii, 1, pp. 33–35; cf. *ACO*, II, iv, p. 3.

47. *ACO*, II, i, 1, p. 95. Eutyches described how Flavian had published the sentence against him "in various chapels and in the monuments of the saints."

48. *ACO*, II, ii, 1, p. 35.

49. Cf. *Thesarus Lingaue Latinae*, vol. 4 (Leipzig, 1906-9), 687–88.

50. *ACO*, II, i, 1, p. 35, 15–32.

51. *anathematizans eos qui dicunt carnem domini nostri Iesu Christi de caelo descendisse et non ex Maria virgine et ex spiritu sancto incarnatum, et omnes haeresim usque Simonem magnum*.

52. Priscus, frg. 8, *FHG*, IV, pp. 77–95; Thompson, *Attila*, pp. 97–120.

53. Priscus, frg. 12–14, *FHG*, IV, pp. 96–98.

54. P. Goubert, "Pulchérie et Chrysaphios," in *Das Konzil von Chalkedon*, ed. A. Grillmeier and H. Bacht, vol. 1 (Würzburg, 1951), 304–21; Luibhéid, "Theodosius II and Heresy," 31–32.

55. Priscus, frg. 8; Thompson, *Attila*, pp. 98 and 102.

56. Theophanes. A. M. 5942, p. 101; Cedrenus *Historiae* (ed. Bonn, Leipzig 1838), p. 601B. See the discussion below at the beginning of chapter 6.

57. *ACO*, II, i, 1, pp. 152–53; 177–78; Liberatus *Breviarium* (*ACO*, II, v. p. 117).

58. Liberatus *Breviarium* (*ACO*, II, v, p. 117); Leo *Epistula* 24.

59. Theophanes, A.M. 5941, p. 100; Nicephorus Callistus 47, 1225.

60. *ACO*, II, i, 1, p. 187.18.

61. It is difficult to know what this evidence says about popular attitudes. If those crowds who witnessed the punishment of the bishops supported Flavian, the emperor's actions were meant to serve as a lesson and a warning. It is also possible, of course, that these crowds supported Eutyches and that they joined in the ridicule of the unfortunate churchmen.

62. Nestorius *Bazaar*, p. 341. Cf. Priscus, note 4 above. Nestorius may have confused the motivation for this increase in taxation; it may have been a result of the inreased tribute demanded by the Huns rather than a punishment for the supporters of Flavian. See note 64 below.

63. It was shortly after the service on Holy Saturday, since the newly-baptized were all assembled in their white garments.

64. Nestorius *Bazaar*, pp. 431–32. Nestorius then continued with a story which sounds very much like that related by Theophanes about the dispute between Chrysaphius and

Flavian over the *eulogiae*. Theophanes placed this incident at the beginning of Flavian's episcopate, but Nestorius set it early in 449 and he connected it with the heavy taxation placed upon the opponents of Eutyches. According to Nestorius, Theodosius said that "whatever was due" from the church of Constantinople would be exacted "with insult" and without respite. Flavian, then, because he was poor, sent word to the emperor that he could not send the required gold unless he melted down the gifts earlier emperors had made to the church. Theodosius paid no attention to this and Flavian "took out the vessels of the church and they were melted down openly, so that there was weeping and outcry among all those who took part in these exactions that were being made, as though (they were being) subject to persecution." It is difficult to know whether Theophanes or Nestorius is correct in his dating of the event, although Nestorius is the closest in time of any authority. But it is possible that Nestorius and the ecclesiastical historians have misplaced the motivation of the attack on the wealth of the church; it may have been a search for funds to pay the tribute demanded by the Huns, as Priscus says.

65. *ACO*, II, i, 1, pp. 68–69.

66. Theodosius made the attendance of Theodoret—a strong opponent of Eutyches—dependent upon a special invitation from the council.

67. *ACO*, II, i, 1, pp. 149–50.

68. *ACO*, II, i, 1, pp. 148–59.

69. Among other things, he demanded that all bishops who had participated in the deposition of Eutyches be made to swear an oath that they would tell the truth. Florentius did not approve this suggestion. *ACO*, II, i, 1, p. 152.

70. *ACO*, II, i, 1, pp. 156–76.

71. *ACO*, II, i, 1, pp. 177–78.

72. *ACO*, II, i, 1, p. 177.

73. Liberatus *Breviarium* ch. 11, *ACO*, v, pp. 113–17.

74. Theophanes, A.M. 5930 (ed. de Boor), p. 93.

75. Nestorius *Bazaar*, p. 341; *ACO*, II, i, 1, p. 130.

76. Besides his work on the walls of the city, the prefect Cyrus had carried out a restoration of much of the city. In 443, for example, the baths of Achilles, which had burned sometime earlier, were rededicated. See Demetrios J. Constantelos, "Kyros Panopolites, Rebuilder of Constantinople," *GRBS*, 12 (1971), 451–64.

77. Bacht, "Die Rolle," pp. 197–243.

78. The alliance of the court with the Greens seems to fall in with G. Manojlović's suggestion about the identification of the Greens with the poor and the Blues with the rich. On this, however, see the persuasive work of A. Cameron, *Circus Factions*, pp. 126–56.

79. It is unfortunate we know so little about the involvement of the Jews in this affair. Francois Nau suggests that the Roman government initiated restrictive measures against the Jews because of a prophecy that they were to assemble in Jerusaleum about 440 to form a separate state, "Deux épisodes de l'histoire juive sous Théodose II (432 et 438) d'après la vie de Barsauma le Syrien," *Revue des Études Juives* 83 (1927), 184–206. Affairs were then brought to a climax by the violence of Barsumas and his monks. It is interesting to note that Jewish hopes in 423 and afterward seem to have been encouraged by Eudocia and her uncle Asclepiodotus, and that the time of the new restrictive measures corresponded with the rise of Chrysaphius, who may be regarded as their instigator. It would thus be reasonable to assume that Jews joined the opposition to Eutyches for three reasons—a general dissatisfaction with recent imperial religious policy, hatred of Chrysaphius, who may have been a persecutor of the Jews, and the closer affinity of Antiochene theology to Jewish beliefs.

80. *ACO*, II, i, 1, p. 71.

81. See Nau, "Deux épisodes," pp 184–206, for an excellent account of some of his activities; see also, Bacht, "Die Rolle," pp. 225–26.

82. *ACO*, II, i, 1, p. 186. He had to address the council through an interpreter. It is, of course, true that he was not the only member of the council who had to resort to an

interpreter. The representatives of the pope could not speak Greek, and there were several Eastern bishops who also had had a language difficulty.

83. *ACO*, II, i, 1, p. 71.

84. *Cf.* Theophanes *Chronographia* A.M. 5940 (ed. de Boor), p. 100; Nicephorus Callistus, 47, 1225.

85. *ACO*, II, i, 1, p. 72.

86. Theophanes *Chronographic*, A.M. 5940, p. 100; Liberatus *Breviarium* (*ACO* II, v, p. 117): "Dioscorus vero habebat secum fortissimos milites rei publicae cum monachis Barsumae." Although Elpidius and Proclus must have retained their individual commands, it seemed to the supporters of Flavian that all was done at the instigation of Dioscorus.

87. *ACO*, II, i, 1, p. 73.

88. The soldiers of Proclus should not be confused with the regular troops of a province, which since the reforms of Diocletian and Constantine, were under the command of the *dux*. Nor were they probably *comitatenses*. Instead, they were probably the troops—perhaps "militia" is a better word—used by the governor of a province to preserve order in his capital city. See Jones, *Later Roman Empire*, p. 374.

89. The term *latrocinium* was first applied to the council by Pope Leo (*Epistula* 95) in 451.

90. S. Perry, *The Second Synod of Ephesus;* J. Flemming, *Akten des ephesischen Synode*.

91. Leo *Epistulae* 22 and 26 (*ACO*, II, ii, pp. 21–22, and 23–24).

92. Leo *Epistula* 27 (*ACO* II, iv, p. 9). C. Silva-Tarouca, *S. Leonis Magni Epistolae*, considers this letter suspect.

93. Leo *Epistula* 31 (*ACO*, II, iv, pp. 12–15).

94. Leo *Epistula* 29 (*ACO*, II, iv, pp. 9–10); also see *Epistula* 28.

95. Leo *Epistulae* 30 (or 31) and 28: (*ACO*, II, ii, pp. 24–33); Greek, II, i, 1, p. 10–11. The question as to which letter was actually sent to Pulcheria is disputed.

96. *ACO*, II, i, 1, pp. 66–67.

97. H. Leclerq, "parabalani," *Dictionnaire d'Archéologie chrétienne et de Liturgie*, 13 (Paris, 1938); A. Philipsborn, "La compagnie d'ambulanciers 'parabalani' d'Alexandrie," *Byzantion* 20 (1950), 185–90.

98. *ACO*, II, i, 1, p. 75.

99. *ACO*, II, i, 2, pp. 42–53.

100. *ACO*, II, i, 1, p. 46.

101. *ACO*, II, i, 1, p. 46.

102. *ACO*, II, i, 3, p. 45.

103. *ACO*, II, i, 3, p. 50. At the council of Chalcedon the bishops accepted the testimony of Bassianos and ordered that he be restored and Stephanos declared deposed. The reasoning for this was that Bassianos had been accepted by Proclus, who was then bishop of Constantinople. Too much weight should not be placed on the decision at Chalcedon, however, for the bishops there were undoubtedly more interested in punishing Stephanos for his alliance with Dioscorus than in establishing the truth about events in Ephesus four years earlier. The officials of the council, moreover, declared both now deposed.

104. It is significant that the notaries of Stephanos, who probably represented the views of their bishop, had to be forced to sign blank papers concerning the events at the council and the condemnation of Flavian. The notaries were kept locked in a church, guarded by soldiers and monks, and no relief was allowed when some of them became sick. Such actions would have been unnecessary had Stephanos supported Dioscorus completely (*ACO* II, i, 1, p. 88).

105. *ACO*, II, i, 1, p. 77. This was, of course, the same church in which the first Council of Ephesus had been held. On the Latrocinium in general, see Hefele-Leclercq, *Histoire des conciles*, vol. 2, pp. 584–606; Duchesne, *Early History of the Christian Church*, vol. 3, pp. 288–94; Bardy *Histoire* pp. 220–24.

106. There is some debate as to which of the papal legates were actually present at the council. The primary problem is that while Renatus was named by Leo as one of his ambassadors, his name does not appear in the acts. But Theodoret (*Epistula* 116) addressed a letter to him after the council, commending him for his actions there. See the discussion of this problem in Hefele-Leclercq, *Histoire des conciles*, vol. 2, pp. 617-21.

One hundred thirty-five was a small number of bishops to attend an ecumenical council. One hundred fifty-five bishops attended the first session of Ephesus I, excluding the large number of oriental bishops absent at the time; three hundred forty-three attended the first session at Chalcedon. The poor attendance at the Robber Synod may be explained partly by the exclusion of forty-two bishops who had participated in the synod of 448. There were some notable absences at the Latrocinium as well, including Anthemius of Thessalonica.

107. Flavian was seated fifth despite the decree of the Council of Constantinople (381) which placed the bishop of Constantinople second in honor only to the pope. When the list of bishops was read to the fathers at Chalcedon they cried out at this injustice. Stephanos of Ephesos was placed sixth (Memnon had been third at Ephesus I), a further indication that he was not as helpful to Dioscorus as he might have been.

108. The *notarii* of Dioscorus, of course, recorded the minutes of the council, and we may suspect them of suppressing things which did not redound to the glory of the bishop of Alexandria. They may also not have restricted their activities to note-taking. At the council of Chalcedon Theodorus, the bishop of Claudiopolis in Isauria, said: "The *notarii* of Dioscorus are crying out!" Dioscorus replied, "I have only two *notarii*. How can they cause a disturbance (θόρυβος)?" At Ephesus the *notarii* of Stephanos began to take notes for themselves. When the secretaries of Dioscorus saw this, they ran to the offenders and snatched away their tablets, almost breaking their fingers in the process.

109. *ACO*, II, i, 1, p. 85.

110. *ACO*, II, i, 1, pp. 85-86.

111. Nestorius *Bazaar*, p. 351.

112. *ACO*, II, i, 1, pp. 97-99.

113. *ACO*, II, i, 1, p. 99.

114. *ACO*, II, i, 1, p. 118.

115. *ACO*, II, i, 1, pp. 182-86. It is interesting that Basil of Seleucia, Aethericus of Smyrna, and Seleucus of Amasia were allowed to vote *for* Eutyches, even though they should have been excluded because they had participated in the council in Constantinople the previous fall.

116. *ACO*, II, i, 1, pp. 186-91. Hilarus, the papal legate, again asked that the letter of Leo be read and again his request was ignored.

117. *ACO*, II, i, 1, p. 191.

118. *ACO*, II, i, 1, p. 191.

119. *ACO*, II, i, 1, p. 191, 29-31; II, iii, 1, p. 238.

120. *ACO*, II, i, 1, p. 76. Theodore said that Dioscorus had a "crowd ... of disorderly individuals, many of them crying out and causing disturbance and condemning the council." He claimed that one hundred thirty-five bishops originally supported Flavian, while Dioscorus controlled only forty-two. After the disturbance, however, the supporters of Flavian numbered only fifteen.

121. *ACO*, II, i, 1, p. 180. The other bishops who cooperated with Onesophoros were Marianos of Synadoe, Nounechios of Laodicia "and others."

122. τὴν δὲ ἔνδοθεν does not occur in all of the manuscripts, but Schwartz puts it into his text. I understand τὴν δὲ ἀπὸ γλώσσης to refer to the threats of Dioscorus.

123. *ACO*, II, i, 1, p. 179. εἰσέτρεχον γὰρ εἰς τὴν ἐκκλησίαν στρατιῶται μετὰ ὅπλων καὶ εἰστήκεισαν οἱ μονάζοντες οἱ μετὰ Βαρσουμᾶ καὶ οἱ παραβαλανεῖς καὶ πλῆθος ἄλλο πολύ.

124. *ACO*, II, i, 1, p. 179: ταῖς ἀπελαῖς τοῦ πολλοῦ πλήθους.

125. *ACO*, II, i, 1, p. 180. εἰσῆλθον οἱ κόμητες καὶ εἰσήγαγον τὸν ἀνθύπατον μετὰ

κλοίων καὶ μετὰ πλήθους πολλοῦ. Cf. Liberatius Breviarium (*ACO*, II, v, p. 118): "quare surgentes quidam venerabiles episcopi teneurunt genua Dioscori et rogabant ne Flavianus innocens demnatur, qui nec diu petere poteurunt metu militum et monarchorum stantium cum gladiis et fustibus."

126. Nestorius *Bazaar*, pp. 352-53.

127. Prosper of Aquitaine (I, 304) says that Hilarus feared the military. Leo *Epistula* 50 (*ACO*, II, iv, p. 21): "*Hilarus . . . fugiens*"; Leo *Epistula* 46 (*ACO*, II, iv, pp. 27-28): "omnia in Epheso contra canones per tumultus et odia seculatia a Dioscoro episcopo gesta sunt."

128. Liberatus, *Breviarium* (*ACO*, II, vi, p. 118); Prosper says that the violence was done by those carrying him into exile; the *Breviculum Historiae Eutychianistarum* says that he died in Epipa and admits that it may have been from natural causes. Nicephorus Callistus dates his death three days after his condemnation (14, 47). Theophanes gives the same date and says that Dioscorus actually inflicted the wounds himself (A.M. 5941, p. 100). See, however, H. Chadwick, "The Exile and Death of Flavian of Constantinople: A Prologue to the Council of Chalcedon," *JTS* n.s. 6 (1955), 17-34.

129. *ACO*, II, i, 2, p. 116

130. Duchesne, *Early History of the Christian Church*, vol. 3, pp. 290-92; Perry, *Second Synod of Ephesus*; Flemming, *Akten*.

131. J. D. Mansi, *Sacrorum Conciliorum*, VII, 495-98; cf. Perry, *Second Synod of Ephesus*, pp. 364-70.

132. Leo *Epistulae* 55-58 (letters from the West); *Epistulae* 62-64 (replies of Theodosius).

133. Cf. Leo *Epistula* 60.

134. The Greek translation of this letter renders *plebs* as *laos*.

135. Leo *Epistula* 50 (*ACO*, II, iv, p. 21).

136. Leo *Epistula* 51 (*ACO*, II, iv, pp. 25-26); Greek translation in *ACO*, II, i, 1, pp. 51-52. The archimandrites never received this letter. Note that Faustus and Martianos had signed the condemnation of Eutyches at the council in Constantinople the preceding November (*ACO*, II, i, 1, p. 146, nos. 32 and 33). See Bacht, "Die Rolle," p. 233.

137. Leo *Epistula* 53 (*ACO*, II, iv, p. xxxvi).

138. Leo *Epistula* (*ACO*, II, iv, pp. 34-37).

139. C. Silva-Tarouca, *Textus et Documenta*, 15 (Rome, 1933), p. 30, and *Nuovi studi sulle antiche lettre dei Papi* (Rome, 1937), pp. 150 and 183.

141. Of course, the theological positions of Flavian and Nestorius were not identical; see A. Grillmeier, *Christ in Christian Tradition*, pp. 457-58. But nearly any of the charges made against Nestorius (with the important exception of the *theotokos*) could be made against Flavian, and we must presume that the supporters of Eutyches used these same arguments against Flavian.

142. The fact that Chrysaphius strongly supported Eutyches must have been known to all. This connection of the archimandrite with the powerful eunuch must not have endeared the former in the eyes of the upper classes in Constantinople. See K. Hopkins, "Eunuchs in Politics," pp. 62-80.

VI

THE COUNCIL OF CHALCEDON: CONSTANTINOPLE AND ALEXANDRIA

Toward a New Policy

The episcopal throne of Constantinople stood vacant for some time after the deposition and death of Flavian.[1] Probably in March or April of 450, Theodosius II called together a number of clerics who elected Anatolius, an Egyptian deacon and *apocrisiarius*, as bishop.[2] Someone less loyal to the decisions of the Latrocinium might not have been trusted to deal with affairs in the capital.

In the letter he sent to the pope, Anatolius made no profession of faith. In July of 450, Leo wrote to the orthodox archimandrites and clerics of Constantinople, saying that he was surprised by the lack of candor on the part of the new bishop. Not only had he failed to give an account of his own beliefs, but he had not even mentioned the scandal which had infected the church of Constantinople. Accordingly, Leo informed the archimandrites, he was sending the bishops Abundius and Aetius and the presbyters Basil and Senator to Constantinople, armed with a collection of appropriate texts from the Fathers. These men, together with the archimandrites themselves, would attempt to correct all those who had been led astray through force or their own simplicity.[3] The pope expressed similar sentiments in contemporary letters addressed to Pulcheria and Theodosius.[4]

The letter destined for the emperor was never delivered. For on July 26, 450, Theodosius fell from his horse while hunting near the River Lycus. He suffered a serious injury, and two days later he died.[5] Valentinian III was the sole living *augustus*, and in constitutional theory the rule of the entire empire should have devolved upon him. But Pulcheria, the elder sister of Theodosius, was in a position to seize power in Constantinople; according to one tradition, the emperor had entrusted the affairs of state to her just before he died.⁶ Realizing that she would need the aid of a man in maintaining her power, Pulcheria called upon Marcian, a distinguished Illyrian (or Thracian) army officer and senator.⁷ The empress agreed to marry him, on condition that he honor her vow of perpetual virginity, and on August 25 she crowned him *augustus* in the palace of Hebdomon.⁸

Not long after his succession, Marcian summoned the Council of Chalcedon, which ultimately reversed the decisions made at the Robber Synod. Scholars usually assign this drastic change in imperial religious policy to the sudden death of Theodosius and the coronation of Marcian: Theodosius was a monophysite while Marcian supported the theology of the two natures.⁹ There is undoubtedly some truth in this reconstruction, at least as it applies to Marcian. Yet, there is evidence which suggests that the change in imperial policy began even before the death of Theodosius and that Marcian only carried out a design that his predecessor had envisioned late in his life.

Our principal authority for this view is Theophanes. In 450, he reports that Theodosius "reconsidered" (ἐπιλογισάμενος) the events of the past few years and came to the conclusion that Chrysaphius had deceived him "concerning the impiety of Flavian." Accordingly, he had the eunuch exiled to a certain island. He further decided that Eudocia was the cause of all the evils besetting him, and especially of the disgrace of Pulcheria, and he ordered his wife to retire to Jerusalem.¹⁰ Theodosius then recalled Pulcheria from her retreat in the Hebdomon and she arranged a solemn procession to honor the remains of Flavian, which were deposited in the church of the Holy Apostles.¹¹

Paul Goubert has discussed at some length the evidence for these events. In the end, he concluded that the account of Theophanes is probably correct, although he was a little disturbed by the failure of any contemporary source (such as Leo or Liberatus) to mention the change in the emperor's theological position. Such a silence is, however, not surprising. Since the recall of Pulcheria occurred only a short time before the death of Theodosius, the pope probably did not hear of it until after the accession of Marcian. After that event, the wisest course for the orthodox was to impute the change to the ruling emperor. The story—which is found in Malalas and those who follow him—that Theodosius called his sister to his bedside indicates that an account of Pulcheria's early return (and hence a change in imperial religious policy) was known at least as early as the mid-sixth century.¹³

The recall of Pulcheria must be seen as part of a fundamental change in imperial policy, and we must ask ourselves what caused Theodosius to contemplate such a turnabout. In the first place, we should observe that this change was not unprecedented in the reign of Theodosius II—we have already discussed several similar examples which are usually interpreted as evidence of the weak will of the emperor. As Goubert observed, it is unlikely that the news of the scandalous activities at Ephesus and the death of Flavian were enough to change the emperor's mind. Several letters from the imperial chancery, still controlled by Chrysaphius, show that at least as late as spring of 450 Theodosius continued to support the actions of the Robber Synod. Goubert suggested that Pulcheria, strengthened by the resolve of the papacy and the Western court and encouraged by dissident army officers in Constantinople itself, forced her will upon the weak resolve of her brother.[14]

In fact, one need not refer to the weakness of Theodosius to explain his change of policy. He merely had to "reconsider"—Theophanes' ἐπιλογισάμενος—the ecclesiastical and political situation in Constantinople to arrive at this conclusion. For, in the months following the Latrocinium, the foreign and domestic situation of the Eastern empire had deteriorated dramatically. This, of course, strengthened the position of those who opposed imperial policy—both secular and religious—and it must have caused the emperor to review that policy. According to Theophanes, early in 450 the East was again seriously threatened by incursions of both the Huns and the Vandals.[15] In the spring of that year, the government of Theodosius negotiated a surprisingly favorable peace with Attila, and this danger seemed alleviated.[16]

But, at about the same time, a more serious threat arose to frighten the emperor. It will be remembered that the *magister militum* Zeno had joined with Attila in demanding the life of Chrysaphius. By 450 the ambitions of the Isaurian had reached a higher plane: Theodosius suspected him of seeking the throne for himself. As John of Antioch tells us, Theodosius was always willing to forgive any other fault, but he was an implacable enemy of anyone who plotted revolution. In his wrath against Zeno, the emperor dispatched land and sea forces to Isauria; unfortunately, we are ignorant of the outcome of this expedition, although Daniel and Baudon, otherwise unknown to us, were implicated in the revolt and killed by the agents of the emperor.[17] Finally, to complete the demoralizing picture, severe natural disasters again struck Constantinople in the twelve months following the Latrocinium.[18]

As we have seen, the dyophysite opposition in Constantinople was well organized around the clergy and monks of the capital, and it included many wealthy individuals. In the aggravated conditions of late spring and early summer of 450, Theodosius must have feared a repetition of the disturbances which had followed the deposition of Eutyches in 448, and he may have turned a more receptive ear to the followers of Flavian. As he had done two years earlier—and at many other times during his reign—the emperor undermined the coalition of his enemies by acceding to the demands of some of them. The opponents of the Robber Synod may not have favored the revolt of Zeno, but their resistance to imperial religious policy made them dangerous natural allies of the usurper.

The rehabilitation of Flavian eliminated one source of dissatisfaction and allowed Theodosius to devote his attention to other problems. Of course, it is impossible to be certain what the emperor would have done had he lived. But one might speculate that his policy would have included the "restoration" of Flavian to a place of honor and the condemnation of Eutyches—which most of the later monophysites accepted. However, he probably would not have called another ecumenical council and imposed a strict dyophysite theology. Nevertheless, it would seem that Theodosius did abandon his support of the decisions of the Robber Synod, and his characterization as a monophysite emperor must be seriously questioned.[19] Further, it is interesting to speculate on the changes in the fate of the empire had Theodosius been successful in imposing a compromise instead of the divisive theology of Chalcedon.

Marcian was well aware of the forces which had disturbed the reign of Theodosius, and immediately after his coronation he set about to deal with them. As indicated above, discontent in Constantinople—in both religious and secular matters—was greatest among the upper classes. The senators and wealthy landowners complained most bitterly about the financial exactions of the state, and they were most active in leading the opposition to the decrees of the Robber Synod. Marcian was himself of senatorial rank, and we should expect him naturally to sympathize with the interests of his peers, but the fear of opposition must also have induced the new emperor to follow a policy more consistently favorable to the wealthy of the empire.[20]

Marcian clearly realized what the heart of such a policy must be: a return to orthodoxy and a reduction of the huge tribute paid yearly to Attila. With the determination (or rashness?) which characterized his whole reign, Marcian dispatched a message to Attila, informing him that the empire would no longer pay any of the tribute demanded.[21] The removal of this huge drain on the imperial treasury made possible several other measures designed to win the support of the upper classes. Perhaps the most important of these were the remission of all tax arrears for the years 437–47[22] and the abolition of the tax on the property of senators (the *collatio glebalis* or *follis*), which had been collected since the time of Constantine.[23] The execution of Chrysaphius, which Marcian ordered almost immediately, also pleased these same individuals.[24]

As part of this general policy, Marcian openly demonstrated his opposition to the decisions of the Robber Synod. He recalled those who had been exiled for their support of Flavian, and Pulcheria prepared a grand reception for some of them in Constantinople.[25] Late in 450, both the emperor and the empress wrote to Pope Leo, reporting the arrival of his legates and offering to hold a new council in the East.[26] Pulcheria described the ceremonial return she had arranged for the remains of Flavian and informed the pope that Anatolius had finally agreed to sign the Tome and accept the theology of Leo.[27]

Efforts must have been made to convert the Eutychians, and in June of 451, Leo was able to write to Pulcheria rejoicing in the catholic faith of the priests and people of Constantinople.[28] In the same letter, the pope requested that Eutyches be removed from his position as archimandrite and that he be replaced by a monk of correct theological views. Given the ecclesiastical situation in Constantinople, this was a perfectly reasonable request, and one might wonder why this had not been done much earlier. But the reasons the pope gave for his request are particularly interesting, and they provide us with our first piece of evidence since the Latrocinium about the supporters of Eutyches.

> Concerning Eutyches, the author of all scandal and perversity, may your clemency [Pulcheria] order that he be taken away from that place [his monastery], which is too close to the city of Constantinople. For it is to be feared that he will make use (*utatur*) of his heretical disciples who come often to console him (*frequentioribus solatiis*).[29]

The meaning of this statement is clear. The pope feared that the supporters of Eutyches—presumably his monks—would spread heretical ideas throughout the city, nullifying the efforts he and the empress had been making among the inhabitants of the capital. In order to avoid such difficulties, the pope advised Pulcheria to remove Eutyches from his monastery, which was "too close to the city of Constantinople."

At about the same time eighteen orthodox archimandrites presented a petition to the emperor, requesting him to allow them to deal with the heretics in whatever way they should see fit.[30] Presumably the monks wished to use persuasion and argumentation in hopes of converting the ordinary adherents of the theology of Eutyches. But there was a class of heretics whom the archimandrites considered more dangerous. These were the *memoritai*—hermits who lived in the shrines of martyrs (*martyria*) rather than in regular coenobitic monasteries.[31] Either because the churches and monasteries of Constantinople had been closed to them, or because the hermits of the capital generally supported Eutyches, these *martyria* had become the centers of Eutychianism in Constantinople. In particular, there was one "cave" (σπηλαῖον) where these "savage men live and every day blaspheme Christ, the savior of all."[32] The monks asked the emperor to close this place immediately.

The Eutychian monks, in the meantime, had not been idle. They also presented a petition to the emperor, which was later read into the *acta* of the Council of Chalcedon.[33] In this document, they complained that while there was dissension among the Christians of Constantinople, Jews and pagans were left in peace. It was the duty of the emperor, they claimed, to secure harmony and agreement among all Christians. Such a solution would surely result from the forthcoming ecumenical council, but until that body met, the emperor should take measures against those who were persecuting the Eutychians. Their enemies, the monks contended, were inciting disturbances (*staseis*) and forcing them to sign anti-Eutychian statements. They closed their petition with an appeal that no one be driven "either from monastery, or church, or martyr's shrine" until the council could settle the matter once and for all.

Apparently, force was being used against the supporters of Eutyches in Constantinople. This petition, and that of the orthodox monks discussed above, provide us with no evidence with which to identify the persecutors. It is likely that the orthodox ecclesiastical party—made up primarily of monks, but by this time including the bishop of the city and the emissaries of the pope—would have been most concerned to secure signatures to an anti-Eutychian creed. And it is not impossible that the officials of the court had begun to persecute the "heretics." But the terrorism directed against the Eutychian monks may also have been a reaction on the part of the faithful of Constantinople. Most of the clergy of the city had remained loyal to Flavian and now, with the emperor and the bishop on their side, they were freely able to use their position to condemn the Eutychians. Spontaneous crowd action against the heretics may well have followed.

At Chalcedon, the Eutychian monks delivered their petition in person; they were accompanied by the eunuch Kalopodias and the Syrian archimandrite Barsumas. The fathers of the council had some doubt about the status of the Eutychians, and they called upon the orthodox monks to identify their adversaries. The orthodox agreed that three of the Eutychians were archimandrites as they had claimed. Seven of them they could not identify,[34] and another seven they declared to be *memoritai* rather than regular monks. The charge that these men were the inhabtants of *martyria* rather than ordinary monasteries was obviously meant to detract from the testimony of the Eutychians.

One must suppose from this testimony that monastic organization in Constantinople had become firm and regularized in the second quarter of the fifth century.[35] A certain number of would-be monks either refused to join the regular establishments or were excluded from them, and the regular monks looked with scorn on their more independent colleagues. It is significant that this split in the monastic movement corresponded to the division of opinion which we witnessed in the beginning of the Eutychian controversy. It is also interesting that the focus of this more independent monastic tradition was the *martyrium*. Tombs of the martyrs had, of course, been important points of Christian assembly from an early period, and great ascetics such as Hypatius and Daniel the Stylite had inhabited tombs in more recent times. Nevertheless, there was always the danger of excess, and Gregory of Nazianzus complained that the *martyria* had become places of banqueting and merrymaking:

> At one time those who wished to gain the favor of demons celebrated impure banquets for them. We Christians abolished this practice and established spiritual assemblies for our martyrs. But now a certain dread has seized me. Listen, you who love banquets! You desert us for the rites of demons.[36]
>
> I bear witness, prize-winners and martyrs, the belly-lovers (φιλογαστορίδαι) have converted your honors into licentiousness. You do not desire a sweet-smelling table or cooks; but they honor you with belching rather than righteousness.[37]

Thus those associated with the *martyria* were accused of excess and scandal; further, if one accepts the testimony of Gregory, the shrines of the martyrs had become centers for the continuation of openly pagan practices.[38]

H. Bacht has stressed a social distinction between the *memoritai* and the rest of the monastic community of the capital, suggesting that the *memoritai* were poor and generally of the lower classes. Certainly, the social status of the latter cannot be compared to that of the leaders of the regular monasteries, such as Faustos; one of the *memoritai* was identified as a former bear trainer—the same lowly occupation as that practiced by the empress Theodora's father.[39] Yet, we should be careful of such an assessment where there is simply very little evidence. Further, it is difficult to know what to make of the information that three of the *memoritai* had several "names," either in the Xylokerkos or in the Philippou, two of the racecourses in the city; thus, Hypses had "two or three 'names' in the Xylokerkos," while Kallinikos had "ten 'names' in a martyr's shrine in the Xylokerkos."[40] Hefele-Leclercq translated the former of these as "celui-ci habite au cirque de bois avec deux ou trois compagnons qui il appelle ses moines."[41] The names may therefore refer simply to the monks which each of these *memoritai* had under his authority. Even so, it is certainly surprising to find monks living in two of the racecourses of the capital, which were regarded as the centers of much of the disreputable activity in the city.[42]

Everything considered, no one would claim that popular opinion was the determining factor in the summoning of the Council of Chalcedon. Pulcheria and Marcian were both personally committed to a reversal of the decisions of the Latrocinium, and they acted accordingly. Nevertheless, the strong feelings which had divided the capital in 449 and 450 may well have played a role in the changes in policy made by Theodosius just before his death—changes which led to the recall of Pulcheria and the ultimate elevation of Marcian. Further, there was no popular outcry against the religious policies of the new emperor, and popular sentiment in Constantinople can only have strengthened Marcian in his resolve.

Supporters of Eutyches, and even the archimandrite himself, continued to live in the city, and there was some concern that they would spread their doctrines among the population. The leadership of Anatolius, however, was half-hearted, and the supporters of Flavian undoubtedly retained their positions within the urban hierarchy. This control of the public voice of the church and the opposition of the monasteries to the Latrocinium must have been important factors in the failure of the Eutychians to generate any favorable climate of opinion in Constantinople. Not only did the monasteries add prestige to the cause of Pulcheria and Marcian, but they and their supporters actively and violently persecuted the Eutychian monks whom they regarded not only as heretics, but also as renegades who had divorced themselves from the proper traditions of the monastic movement.

The Meeting of the Council

On May 23, 451, Marcian sent a letter to all the bishops of the empire, asking them to assemble before the first of September in Nicaea to attend an ecumenical council.[43] The emperor promised to appear in person unless the necessities of war prevented him from doing so.

During the late summer of 451, the bishops began to assemble in Nicaea, but the Hunnic raids in Illyria demanded the attention of the emperor and he did not appear on the appointed date. The bishops did not dare to begin the council without him—the papal legates were also still in Constantinople. But they wrote to him, complaining that the delay was difficult, especially for the aged and sickly among them. Marcian replied, asking them to wait until he should be able to come to Nicaea.[44]

Probably at about the same time Pulcheria wrote to a military commander in Bithynia, instructing him concerning the situation in Nicaea. It had come to the attention of the court, she remarked, that certain clerics, monks, and laymen intent on creating a disturbance (θορυβεῖν ἐπιχειροῦσι) were mingling with the bishops. Pulcheria ordered that

> with all firmness you shall cast out of the city, and all the area around it, those [who are there] without our summons or the permission of their own bishops, whether these be clerics who live there (αὐτόθι ἐνδημοῦντες κληρικοί),[45] both those of a regular rank and those who are not in communion with their bishops, or monks, or laymen who have no business at a council.[46]

In closing, the empress warned the imperial official that he would be held responsible should any of the local troublemakers (τὶς τοῦ λοιποῦ τῶν θορυβοποιῶν ἐνδημῶν) make an appearance.[47]

It seems reasonable to assume that those who were threatening to disturb the council were supporters of Dioscorus and Eutyches. It is interesting, therefore, to note that some of the lower clergy of Nicaea and the surrounding territory appear to have supported Eutyches. Remembering the care taken by Theodosius II to secure order at his councils, and anticipating the importance of the imperial officials at Chalcedon, it hardly seems likely that the letter of Pulcheria represents the first thought the court gave to security at the forthcoming council. It may be that the letter to the military official in Nicaea was either a "reminder" to him or an indication that events in the city had already progressed beyond a point at which an ordinary show of force was enough to control the discontented crowd. In fact, the unstable conditions in Nicaea may have had something to do with the emperor's decision not to come to the city and to move the council to nearby Chalcedon, where the unruly crowd might be controlled more easily.[48] Atticus, a deacon of the church of Constantinople, however, reported to the emperor that the bishops were unwilling to go to Chalcedon, since they feared some violence from the partisans of Eutyches:

> Those who agree with Eutyches, or some other person, are undertaking to carry out violence (*stasis*) or some other disturbance (*thorybos*).[49]

Marcian replied in a longer letter, pleading with the bishops and assuring them that they need fear no violence even though they would be close to Constantinople. "For we hope . . . that each of you will be able to return without any disturbance or riot" (*tarache* or *thorybos*).[50] Unfortunately, we have no information as to the identity of these supporters of Eutyches, whose reputation for violence reached even the bishops assembled in Nicaea. But it is probable that they were—or were led by—the monks and *memoritai* mentioned above.

On October 8, 451, the Council of Chalcedon opened in the church of St. Euphemia.[51] Representing the emperor were a large number of imperial officials (*archontes*), including the patrician and ex-consul Anatolius, the praetorian prefect Palladius, the prefect of the city Tatianos, Vincomalus the *magister officiorum*, and Sporacius the *comes domesticorum*. Representing the Senate were a number of other illustrious men, including the patricians Florentius and Nomus, several ex-prefects, and two former *praepositi sacri cubiculi*.[52] Bishop Paschasinus of Lilybaeum, in Sicily, represented Pope Leo and, together with the imperial officials, he presided over the council.

From the beginning, the assembly was divided into two hostile camps: those who supported Dioscorus, and those who accepted the theology of Leo and Flavian.[53] Since Marcian had made clear his own position, the Eutychians were on the defensive. At the first meeting, the opposing sides hurled violent invectives at one another, each side accusing the other of illegality, either at the Latrocinium or at the present council.[54] The reading of the minutes of the synod in Constantinople (448) and the Robber Council occupied most of the day. When the officials closed the assembly with the Trisagion, it was already dark.[55]

The second meeting of the council, held on October 10,[56] concerned itself more fully with matters of doctrine, but no agreement could be reached. The officials suggested that the council adjourn for five days, during which the more important bishops would gather in an attempt to find some grounds for reconciliation.[57]

The synod met again on October 13 in the *martyrion* of the church of St. Euphemia.[58] Dioscorus and the imperial representatives were absent. Aetius, the archdeacon of Constantinople, effectively directed the session, although Paschasinus still held the place of greatest honor. Eusebius of Dorylaeum, appearing in his familiar role of accuser, brought forward a complaint against Dioscorus. Although he mentioned the alleged heresy of the bishop's views, the emphasis of his statement concerned the violence and illegality Dioscorus had perpetrated at the second Council of Ephesus.[59] Eusebius demanded that he be allowed to confront Dioscorus personally, and Paschasinus sent clerics to summon the bishop. Dioscorus, however, had an excuse ready for every occasion, and he refused to make an appearance.[60]

When the canonical three summonses had failed to bring Dioscorus to the assembly, several of the bishops declared that he should be deposed because of his unjust and illegal actions.[61] The papal legates accordingly declared Dioscorus deprived of his ecclesiastical rank, and over three hundred bishops indicated their agreement by placing their signatures at the end of the minutes of the session.[62]

The council then sent a brief notice to Dioscorus, informing him that he had been deposed because of his action "against the divine canons" and his refusal to obey the summons to appear before the council. The bishops made no mention of his heretical theology.[63] They sent a similar note to the clergy of the church of Alexandria who were then in Chalcedon, mentioning by name the *oikonomos* Charmosynus who was presumably then regarded as the leader of the delegation. The council advised the Egyptians of the deposition of their bishop—again without mentioning any doctrinal difficulty—and warned them to take care of the property of the church, as they would be required to give account for it to a new bishop.[64]

Soon after this, the council learned that Dioscorus was spreading a rumor throughout Chalcedon and Constantinople. He claimed that his deposition was a mistake and predicted that he would soon be reinstated.[65] Dioscorus' purpose in circulating this rumor must have been to encourage his supporters and perhaps even to incite them to his active assistance. Although we do not hear of them at Chalcedon, there is no reason to think that the bishop failed to bring along his *parabalani* and other monastic attendants. Further, word of the presence of Eutychians in Chalcedon had reached the bishops of Nicaea, and the action of Dioscorus is probably an indication that he was prepared to repeat the violence he had perpetrated at Ephesus just two years earlier. The members of the council took this threat seriously and, to counter the rumors spread by Dioscorus, they drew up a number of public notices addressed to "all the Christ-loving faithful (*laos, populus* in the Latin translation) of Constantinople and Chalcedon."[66] In these documents, the bishops denied the truth of the rumor, but again they did not mention the heretical teachings of their deposed colleague, stating only that he had been deprived of office because of his misbehavior. Many members of the council undoubtedly hesitated to condemn Dioscorus for a theology which they themselves had been willing to accept at Ephesus only two years before, but perhaps the bishops also feared that any mention of the theology of Dioscorus would only serve to increase his popularity among the faithful.[67] In any case, it is significant that Dioscorus was concerned to create a rumor and that the fathers of the council took pains to counteract it. This incident is also a measure of the unreliability of "news" in the ancient world. Dioscorus was able simply to manufacture a statement which was directly contradicted by the facts, and many people undoubtedly believed him.

At the sixth session of the council, Marcian suggested that the bishops take measures against the monks who invaded the cities and caused disturbances in both ecclesiastical and secular matters.[68] When they formulated the canons of the council, the fathers included several regulations which contained and expanded the suggestions of the emperor. The fourth canon ran as follows:

> Some people have become monks only as a pretext and they confuse the matters of the church with those of the world, going about indiscriminately in the cities and wishing to found monasteries for themselves. No one shall build or set up a monastery or chapel without the consent of the bishop of the city. The monks in each city and territory shall be subject to the bishop and they shall strive after quiet (ἡσυχία), occupying themselves only with fasting and praying, remaining in the places to which they had been assigned. Nor should they concern themselves with ecclesiastical or secular affairs or take part in them, leaving their own monasteries only upon some necessity or at the order of the bishop of the city.[69]

The eighth canon was similar in content:

> The clergy of the poorhouses, monasteries, and *martyria* shall remain under the control of the bishop of each city . . . and they shall not act insolently or disobediently toward their own bishop.[70]

174   Vox Populi

The twenty-third canon is more specific in citing the reasons why the bishops were concerned about disobedient monks and clerics:

> It has come to the attention of the holy synod that certain clerics and monks, either without the consent of their own bishop or even after having been excommunicated by him, have descended upon the imperial city of Constantinople. They have remained there a long time and have stirred up disturbances (*tarachi*), throwing into confusion certain people, upsetting the ecclesiastical situation and even disturbing the houses of certain people (θορυβοῦντες τὴν ἐκκλησιαστικὴν κατάστασιν ἀνατρέπουσί τε οἴκους τινῶν).[71]

The council decreed that the *ekdikos* of the church of Constantinople should first warn these unruly clerics to leave the city. If they refused to obey, the official had the authority to expel them from the capital.

These canons were part of a larger program aimed at the control of disobedient clergy and the regularization of monasticism.[72] But these measures, and the knowledge that they were first proposed by the emperor, do indicate something of the danger posed by itinerant monks and other clerics. Constantinople was considered a haven for rebellious clergy, and the emperor, probably rightly, accused these fugitives of being responsible for many of the disturbances which upset the capital. We should suppose further that the individuals who frightened the fathers by gathering illegally at Nicaea and those who were rumored to be causing difficulties in Constantinople and Chalcedon during the council itself gave the bishops a specific incentive for the formulation of these canons. In addition, it is likely that many of these troublesome monks and clerics were Eutychian in sentiment; we have already seen that irregular monks were viewed as the core of Eutychianism in Constantinople.

Despite the action of the Council of Chalcedon and the strenuous opposition of the pope, the leadership of the Monophysite party in Constantinople after 451 remained much as it had been in the past. The fathers of the council allowed the Eutychian monks thirty days to reconsider their error.[73] Either because of the good will of the bishop Anatolius—who, it will be remembered, was from Alexandria—or because they finally gave their formal assent to the theology of Leo, many of their party managed to retain their ecclesiastical positions in the capital. Carosus and Dorotheus, leaders of the Eutychians at the council, retained control of their monasteries until at least 455.[74] If the distress of the pope is any measure, they continued their agitation for a Monophysite theology,[75] and even Eutyches himself still lived in the vicinity of Constantinople at least until 454.[76] We have no information concerning the less important supporters of Eutyches in these years, but, considering the generosity shown to their leaders, we may doubt that they—including the *memoritai* and the former bear trainers—were seriously threatened by the civil or ecclesiastical authorities.[77]

Throughout all this, however, popular opinion in Constantinople remained predominantly Chalcedonian in sentiment. The reason for this, as we have seen, was the success of Flavian and his followers in establishing and maintaining the view that their theology was orthodox, while the agreement of most of the monks of the capital counted for much. The threat of violence at the Council of Chalcedon was an ever-present concern—especially after the events at Ephesus two years earlier—but this was apparently a phenomenon without wide popular support, and the emperor was able to control the recalcitrant monks and other individuals with a proper show of force, for there is no evidence that the bishops of the council were ever subject to real physical danger.

Opposition to Dioscorus

Alexandria, long the "second city" of the empire, was notorious in antiquity for the unruliness of its inhabitants,[78] and many of the events we have already investigated had violent consequences there. The affair of the Tall Brothers, which played an important role in the difficulties of John Chrysostom, began when a body of Egyptian monks came to Alexandria intent on murdering Theophilus for his opposition to anthropomorphism.[79] Early in the episcopate of Cyril, open warfare broke out between Christians and Jews, which resulted in the expulsion of the latter from Alexandria and the expropriation of their property by the mob. This led to a confrontation between the bishop and the Augustal prefect, Orestes, and the brutal murder of the pagan philosopher Hypatia.[80] The death of Cyril and the elevation of Dioscorus appears also to have caused some disorder in the city.[81]

Dioscorus brought with him to the Council of Chalcedon nineteen Egyptian bishops and a large body of clerics and monks.[83] Of these nineteen bishops, four—Athanasius of Bousiris, Ausonius of Bebennytos, Nestorius of Phragonis, and Makarios of Kabasa—deserted Dioscorus during the first session and sat with his accusers.[83] It is unlikely that these bishops abandoned their superior out of fear of the power of the council, for the majority of their colleagues remained faithful to Dioscorus. Instead, it appears that these bishops represented a fairly large number of Egyptians who were, for one reason or another, displeased with the rule of Dioscorus. Nestorius of Phragonis had earlier disagreed with his bishop, and he was roughly treated by the agents of Dioscorus at the Robber Synod. It is possible that some of these discontented bishops had formed an alliance against their superior before they left Egypt for the council, and they may represent a larger movement of opposition to the episcopacy of Dioscorus.

At Chalcedon, while the fathers of the council were awaiting the response of Dioscorus to their summons, they heard the complaints of several members of the church of Alexandria. The first evidence was brought forward by the deacon Theodore, who must have been an old man at the time of the council.[84] He claimed that he had served for twenty-two years in the ranks of the *agentes in rebus* when Cyril—at about the time of the first Council of Ephesus—had made him a member of the clergy of Alexandria. When Dioscorus came to the episcopal throne, he dismissed Theodore, allegedly for no reason and without notice, and threatened to exile him from the city. The anger of Dioscorus was not capricious, however, since Theodore was an important man who had been associated with the administration of Cyril. When Dioscorus came to the episcopal throne, he ended the domination of the family of Theophilus, and he took particular care to purge the administration of the relatives and supporters of his predecessor. Theodore added that the new bishop did not hesitate to murder and exile some of these individuals.

In addition, Theodore accused Dioscorus of insulting the Holy Trinity and destroying the property of his enemies by fire and by cutting down their trees (δενδροκοπιῶν). When Dioscorus arrived in Chalcedon, Theodore charged, he forced the bishops who had come with him to sign a statement deposing Pope Leo. In explaining why only "ten bishops, more or less," had signed this document, Theodore said that many Egyptian bishops did not dare to come with Dioscorus to Chalcedon because they remembered the lawlessness he had perpetrated at Ephesus, evidence that the bishop's reputation for violence was resented and feared by some of his subordinates.[85] As proof of his allegations, Theodore suggested that the council call on Agorastos, Dorotheus, Eusebius, and the notary John.[86]

The second complaint was made by Ischyrion, another deacon of the church of Alexandria.[87] He also accused Dioscorus of ruining the estates of his enemies by cutting down their trees or destroying their homes. That the bishop was guilty of such crimes "not only the great and the famous men knew, but also the whole great city of Alexandria."[88] Everyone—clergy and laity alike—knew that Dioscorus had insulted the Trinity.[89] When the emperor sent grain to Alexandria, destined for the poor churches of Libya which did not even have bread for the Eucharist, Dioscorus seized the shipment so that he could resell it later, during a shortage, at higher prices.[90] No one, Ischyrion claimed, was ignorant of the affair of Peristeria. She gave a large amount of gold to be used in building monasteries and places of refuge for strangers and the poor of Egypt. Dioscorus, however, confiscated the money and spent it on people associated with the theatre.

Ischyrion complained further that "impious women" came often to the *episcopeion* and even to the bishop's private bath. A particularly frequent visitor was the notorious (περιβόητος) Pansophia Oreine. So well known was her relationship with Dioscorus that the common people of Alexandria made up a song about the couple, which they spread throughout the countryside.[91]

Ischyrion then turned to an elaboration of his own personal complaints against Dioscorus. He explained the animosity of the bishop toward him as a result of his own loyal service to Cyril. Dioscorus had, he alleged, "sent monks and some other people against our own humble possessions," so that by the destruction of his livelihood he might be reduced to penury. The monks burned his buildings and chopped down all of his fruit trees. On another occasion, Dioscorus sent against him an "ecclesiastical phalanx," directed by the deacon Peter, Harpokration, and the priest Mennas. They wanted to put Ischyrion to death, but he managed to escape. Harpokration, however, later seized him and kept him prisoner for some time in a *xenodocheion*. Harpokration and Peter, Ischyrion remarked, were the most violent supporters of Dioscorus, "as they demonstrated in Ephesus against Flavian . . . and many others, including Nestorius, who is now a bishop but was then *oikonomos* of the church of the great city of Alexandria."[92] Ischyrion closed his petition begging for mercy and asking that the council interrogate some of the confidants of Dioscorus, including the keeper of the episcopal bath.

The third complaint was made by the priest Athanasius, who was a nephew of Cyril.[93] According to him, Cyril had made a statement just before his death, requiring his successor to honor his family. But Dioscorus, in his general mismanagement of office, ignored the wish of the dead bishop and began a persecution of Cyril's family. This persecution later spread throughout the diocese. Athanasius and his brother Paul fled from Alexandria to Constantinople where they hoped to find protection and help. But Dioscorus wrote to Chrysaphius and Nomus and they had the fugitives beaten and tortured so that Paul died. For years, Athanasius wandered from place to place, not being permitted to stay even in churches or monasteries.[94] Finally, he returned to Metanoia, a suburb of Alexandria, which was formally called Kampos.[95] When Dioscorus learned of this, he decreed that the priest could not use the public bath there nor receive bread from the city dole, claiming that there was a shortage of space and a famine. All the money Athanasius was able to save or borrow—some 1,400 pounds gold—was confiscated by Nomus, who sent the *magistrianos* Severus to collect it. This reduced the priest to such poverty that he had only two or three slaves left in his possession.

The complaint of Sophronios was in many ways different from the three which had preceded it.[96] In the first place, Sophronios appears to have been a layman, as he identified himself simply as *Christianos*. He did not mention the reason why Dioscorus turned his anger against him, nor did he imply that he had any connection with the family or administration of Cyril. For apparently no reason, Dioscorus deprived him of all of his property and forced him to make his living as a teacher. When a certain Makarios[97] stole away his wife, Sophronios complained to the emperor and the prefects. The emperor responded by sending the venerable Theodorus to investigate the case.[98] Dioscorus protested that the affair was his concern rather than that of the "rulers," and he sent the wild-eyed deacon Isidorus and a band of country robbers against Sophronios. These ruffians drove Theodorus away and would have killed Sophronios had not a certain deacon disobeyed the orders of Dioscorus and helped him.

In the final plea to the council, Sophronios declared that Dioscorus had attempted to hinder the proclamation of Marcian's elevation in Alexandria.

> When the divine laurels,[99] after universal prayer, came to Alexandria, he [Dioscorus] did not hesitate to distribute bribes to the common people through the agency of Agorastos and Timotheos and some others. Thus he prepared to have them [those wishing to proclaim Marcian] driven away. For he was ill-disposed toward those who would proclaim such a ruler of the world, since he wished to rule Egypt himself.[100]

Affairs in Egypt, he assured the council, would have been in desperate condition had it not been for the efforts of Theodorus. In conclusion, Sophronios informed the fathers that he was not the only one with complaints against Dioscorus. There were many others who had experienced the wrath of the bishop, but who were prevented by poverty or fear from bringing their case before the council.

From these complaints, it appears that in Egypt there was already considerable opposition to Dioscorus before the Council of Chalcedon. All the complaints mentioned some heretical teaching of the bishop, usually an "insult" to the Trinity—probably a reference to his monophysite theology, which may be viewed as a denial of the Trinity. But it is clear that the primary concern of each individual was some physical or financial injustice suffered at the hands of Dioscorus.

The family of Theophilus had controlled the church of Alexandria for over fifty years, and it is not surprising that many relatives of the bishop found their way into important offices. Further, it was not uncommon for a new bishop to mistreat the friends and relatives of his predecessor, especially if he considered them hostile or incompetent. Indeed, more than one of those who complained against Dioscorus claimed that they had earned the bishop's displeasure simply because of their connection with Cyril. Yet, there seems to be more behind the actions of Dioscorus than simple antagonism toward the family and friends of Cyril. All of those who complained about Dioscorus—including Sophronios, who was apparently not connected with Cyril—were very wealthy men. The deacon Ischyrion complained that Dioscorus had destroyed his buildings and "all his fruit trees." We can only speculate what kind of trees Dioscorus is alleged to have cut down, but they were undoubtedly designed to produce a cash crop. Perhaps they were grown on land which had once belonged to the church of Alexandria. The priest Athanasius alleged that he had been robbed of 1,400 pounds of gold. This amount was thirty-five times the annual salary of the *dux* and Augustal prefect of Egypt in the sixth century and roughly equal to the amount Cyril is supposed to have spent on bribes in the affair of Nestorius.[101] Athanasius complained that after Dioscorus had finished with him, he had only two or three slaves left—hardly an indication of extreme poverty even then.

Thus, the "persecution" of Dioscorus appears directed as much against the wealthy of Alexandria as against the friends and relatives of Cyril. Perhaps the actions of Dioscorus were the result of a general reform of the episcopal administration—such as that carried out by John Chrysostom: those who had taken over the wealth of the church through graft or nepotism had to be dispossessed. It is possible, also, that the bishop's actions may be assigned to simple rapacity, either to increase his own fortune or that of the church of Alexandria.[102] In any case, Dioscorus used excessive force in this program, and he earned considerable enmity long before the Council of Chalcedon.

As is often the case, we have little information as to how the poor people of the city felt about their bishop. It is true that Sophronois assured the fathers of the council that more people would have presented their complaints against Dioscorus had they not been hindered by poverty. If the allegation of Ischyrion was true—that Dioscorus had stolen money destined to build places of refuge for the poor—one might expect these people to join in opposition to the bishop. But the complainants do not present any positive evidence that the ordinary inhabitants of Alexandria were personally ill treated by Dioscorus, and they seem to try too hard to convince the fathers of the council that they (the wealthy) were not the only ones who disliked the bishop. Indeed, the inhabitants of Alexandria seem rather to have enjoyed the affair of the bishop with the notorious Pansophia. If one attributes the persecution and confiscations of Dioscorus to an attempt to attain justice or punish wrongdoers, one may suspect that he enjoyed a greater popularity than his enemies would imply.

As we have mentioned, four Egyptian bishops deserted Dioscorus almost at the beginning of the council. During the fourth session, after the deposition of Dioscorus, the officials of the council announced that a group of thirteen Egyptian bishops had presented a statement of faith to the emperor. These bishops, who had not agreed to the condemnation of their superior, asked that this be read before the full council. The synod gave its approval and a secretary read the short statement in which the

Egyptians affirmed their orthodoxy and denounced all heretics from Arius to Nestorius.[103] As they made no mention of Eutyches and the current controversy, several bishops demanded that they explain their position more fully, and the papal legates asked whether they would subscribe to the Tome of Leo. Ierakis, the leader of the Egyptians, answered evasively, saying that anyone who disagreed with what they had stated should be anathema. As for the Tome of Leo, he replied that the Council of Nicaea had placed all of Egypt under the authority of the bishop of Alexandria and no single bishop could speak without his approval. Accordingly, he besought the council to allow the bishops to await the decision of their archbishop.[104]

When the other bishops refused to accept this statement, the Egyptians finally agreed to condemn Eutyches specifically. But they still balked at the prospect of signing the Tome. They reminded the council that there were "very many bishops in Egypt," and they could not speak for all of them—even though they had earlier claimed to do so. If they should act without the approval of their archbishop, all of Egypt would oppose them as having done something uncanonical.[105] They appealed to the council to have mercy on their old age and not force them to endanger their lives.

Kekropios of Sebastopolis demanded that the Egyptians give their assent to the doctrine of Leo. They objected:

> Then we shall no longer be able to live in the province! Have mercy on us!

Lucentius, the papal envoy, again tried to persuade them, but they cried out:

> We shall be murdered! Have mercy on us. We shall die. We would rather die by your hands, and not there. Let a new archbishop be appointed now and we shall sign and agree . . . Anatolius [the bishop of Constantinople] knows that in Egypt all the bishops must obey the archbishop of Alexandria.[106]

Finally, the officials of the council suggested that the Egyptians remain in Constantinople for some time, since they could not act without the approval of their superior. Paschasinus agreed to this, with the stipulation that they give some security that they would not leave the city until a new bishop was chosen.

Why did the Egyptian bishops so strongly refuse to accept the dyophysite theology of Leo and the deposition of Dioscorus? The primary reason may have been theological—they may simply have believed that the theology of the council was in error. But this was not the reason they gave their opponents.[107] Instead, they claimed that they would face real physical danger in Egypt if they acted without the approval of their ecclesiastical superior—who, of course, had been deposed. But why was this? Whom did they fear in Egypt? One finds it hard to believe that it was the other bishops of Egypt. According to the deacon Theodore, many

Egyptians disliked Dioscorus and had refused to come with him to the council. Further, had the thirteen bishops agreed to subscribe the Tome—as did four of their colleagues—they would have found themselves in control of the ecclesiastical situation in Alexandria and in a position to help select the new bishop. As we have seen, it is unlikely that the bishops would have experienced any opposition from the wealthy of Alexandria had they approved of the deposition of Dioscorus.

If we are to accept the statement of the Egyptian bishops, we must conclude that their betrayal of Dioscorus would meet with the disapproval of an important and violent segment of the population of Alexandria and all Egypt. Presumably this included members of the ecclesiastical "establishment" built up by Dioscorus and the monastic community, but it probably also referred to the ordinary inhabitants of Alexandria and the Egyptian countryside. Also, it is particularly revealing that the bishops said nothing about the theological issue. Apparently they felt that, in the eyes of their countrymen, the betrayal of Dioscorus and the contravention of long-standing local tradition—acting without the approval of the bishop of Alexandria—were more serious than the abandonment of Eutychian theology. Events were to confirm their judgment.

Revolt in Alexandria

After the Council of Chalcedon, Dioscorus went into exile—first to Cyzicus, then to Heraclea, and finally to Gangra in Paphlagonia, where he died.[108] Proterius, the archpriest left in charge of the city during the council, succeeded him as bishop of Alexandria.[109] Despite the requirement that the Egyptians not leave Constantinople until a new bishop was selected, the election and consecration seems to have taken place in Alexandria.[110] In the words of Liberatus:

> Those bishops and clerics who had come with him [Dioscorus], but who had sat together in Chalcedon and by signing the letter of Leo agreed to the condemnation of Eutyches and Dioscorus—Athanasius... Nestorius... Ausonius... and Makarios—returned to Alexandria. According to the wish of all the citizens (*cum omnium civium voluntate*), they set about the election of a new archbishop to be ordained. Letters from the emperor (*sacrae litterae*) had already been sent to the *Augustalis* Theodorus for this purpose. Accordingly, the *nobiles* of the city gathered together to select him whose life and speech were worthy of a bishop. This, indeed, had been ordered by the imperial commands. Much uncertainty (*multa dubitatio*) developed about this, as the citizens (*cives*) did not wish to ordain anyone at all, lest they appear as patricides (*volentibus civibus neminem penitus ordinare, ne patralyae videntur*) since Dioscorus was still alive. Finally, the opinion of all (*universorum setentia*) settled upon Proterius... Proterius was therefore consecrated in the presence of the aforementioned bishops.[111]

The distinction between the wishes of the *nobiles* and those of the *cives* is noteworthy. From the account of Liberatus, it is clear that the *nobiles*, together with the four "orthodox" bishops, actually selected Proterius, while the rest of the population felt that no election should be held while Dioscorus still lived.[112] This is not surprising in view of what we have suggested about the attitude of many wealthy individuals in Alexandria: they were more than happy to provide a replacement for the hated bishop. Among the majority of the inhabitants of the city, however, Dioscorus had developed a fanatical following, and this was not diminished by his deposition. Indeed, the council lost authority in the eyes of the Alexandrians when it condemned the bishop; its actions and decisions were suspect because of its treatment of Dioscorus, who was the standard of correct belief and practice. This is further confirmation of the view of the Egyptian bishops at Chalcedon: in Alexandria, at least, the issue was not so much theological as it was canonical or, more accurately, personal. To accept a new bishop while Dioscorus still lived was tantamount to parracide.[113]

So it is not surprising that Proterius had difficulty in establishing himself as bishop of Alexandria. In the words of Liberatus:

> When he had been installed on the episcopal throne, there arose division and disagreement among the people (*divisio et discissio populi facta est*), because Dioscorus still lived and was in exile. Proterius, therefore, endured considerable danger, so that during much of his episcopate he was in need of protection from the military.[114]

Evagrius drew his information for these difficuilties from the eyewitness account of Priscus of Panium, who had just come into Alexandria from the Thebaid when the violence erupted. Both Liberatus and Evagrius (Priscus) agree that there were two sides in the confrontation and that Proterius had some support, but the Dioscorans were apparently very much the stronger, and they were restrained only by the military intervention of the government. According to Evagrius:

> When he had seized his throne a great and irresistable disturbance (*tarachos*) arose among the people (*demos*) who were swept along like a wave by different opinions. As is usual in such situations, some supported Dioscorus, while others valiantly held out in behalf of Proterius. The result was much irreparable damage.

Apparently the followers of Dioscorus had the better of the situation and just as Priscus came into the city he saw

> the people (*demos*) advancing together against the officials (*archontes*). When the soldiers tried to put a stop to the insurrection (*stasis*) they threw stones at them.[115]

The officials and the soldiers took to flight and secured themselves in the old temple of Serapis.[116] This provided only a temporary respite, however, for the crowd besieged the building and finally set fire to it. All within were burned alive.

The Serapeum was in the quarter of Rhakotis, an area of Alexandria traditionally regarded as "Egyptian"—as opposed to those quarters inhabited by Greeks and Jews—and it had been the scene of embattled conflict between Christians and pagans some half a century before.[117] That the officials and soldiers encountered difficulty in this area suggests that resistance to the election of Proterius was strong among the native population. Indeed, this resistance was greater than the officials had expected, and they lost their lives as a result.

One should view this event in its simplest terms as the violent rejection of the deposition of Dioscorus, yet it is tempting to find larger ramifications. Was this perhaps a reflection of growing hostility between Greeks and Egyptians or a symptom of Egyptian nationalism? Tensions were always present among the various ethnic groups in Alexandria, but there is no evidence that nationalism was in any way an issue in this event. Instead, we might suggest that the historical growth of Christianity in Egypt and, more recently, the influence of the monks, particularly such figures as Schenute of Atripe, had led to a focus on the distinction between pagan and Christian and a general identification of the local aristocracy and the officials sent from Constantinople as pagans.[118] This was demonstrably not always true, and the theologians of the church of Alexandria were every bit as steeped in Hellenic culture as were the philosophers and sophists. Nevertheless, recent events such as the brutal murder of Hypatia had hardened the line between pagan and Christian in Alexandria. And, if we are to read anything more than simple opposition to Proterius into the violence at the Serapeum, we must view this as popular opposition to the wealthy *archontes*, who revealed their true sympathies by taking refuge in the old pagan sanctuary, just as their "pagan predecessors" had done in 391.

The leaders of the disturbance—whoever they may have been—apparently were unprepared for their success. As a result of the confrontation, they had the city at their disposal for a period of at least two weeks, but they made no attempt to oust Proterius or to establish any kind of ecclesiastical or political autonomy. Perhaps the authority of Proterius—he was, after all, a priest of Alexandria, and he must have had strong local connections—saved the situation; but the indecision of the rioters who probably had no firm program or organization must have played a part. One is reminded of the sudden collapse of the riot in Antioch (A.D. 387) just when the demonstrators had gained a tactical victory.

When the emperor learned of the massacre in Alexandria, he immediately dispatched 2,000 newly enlisted soldiers for Egypt.[119] They made such a good voyage that they arrived in Alexandria on the sixth day. This show of force subdued the Alexandrians for a time; but when the soldiers began to molest the wives and daughters of the citizens, "even greater violence" broke out.

> Later, the people (*demos*) assembled in the hippodrome and petitioned Florus, who was both the military commander[120] and the civil governor. They asked him to restore to them the distribution of grain, of which he had deprived them, as well as the baths and the spectacles and other such things as had been denied them because of the disturbance (*ataxia*). And thus at his own suggestion, Florus appeared before the people (*demos*) and, by promising them these things, he quickly put a stop to the insurrection (*stasis*).[121]

According to Evagrius, the dispute began because of different "opinions." This may be the only reference we have to the role of the doctrinal dispute in the violence in Alexandria, although these "opinions" may have referred simply to the question of who should be bishop of Alexandria. In any case, Evagrius, too, stressed the importance of the person of Dioscorus. Each party used its bishop as symbol and focus, and even if a theological question lay at the heart of the dispute, the combatants openly disagreed only about the correctness of the consecration of Proterius.

From the account of Evagrius (or Priscus), we can see that the military force at the disposal of the officials of Alexandria, even when increased by reinforcements, was quite unequal to the violence of the crowd. We hear nothing about any violence carried out by the supporters of Proterius, and Evagrius implies that the Alexandrian *demos* was virtually united in its loyalty to Dioscorus. Another interesting aspect of the report concerns the soldiers sent to Alexandria. The troops were "newly enlisted," and it is likely that they were barbarians. Marcian probably selected them to deal with the explosive situation in Egypt because they had not formed opinions concerning the decisions of the Council of Chalcedon and because they had no ties to the people of Alexandria. Thus, they would obey the orders of Florus and the emperor without question, just as newly enlisted barbarians had been used to deal with the troublesome supporters of John Chrysostom. Nevertheless, these soldiers only worsened the situation, as their treatment of the women of Alexandria brought on further violence. Brutality or overreaction increased the polarization of the community and may have brought many into the camp of Dioscorus who had no quarrel with the theology or canonical standing of Proterius.

During the violence, the prefect Florus suspended the distribution of bread, the use of the public baths, and the spectacles. This achieved what military force could not, and the city was temporarily pacified. One might be tempted to call the Alexandrians fickle in their attachment to a religious cause when they agreed to abandon their opposition to Proterius in exchange for the notorious "bread and circuses." Yet, we should remember that the supporters of Dioscorus were the *cives* of Alexandria (as opposed to the *nobiles*). Closure of the public baths and spectacles may have been only an inconvenience to the Alexandrians, but the suspension of the bread dole would mean hunger and starvation for many. In this measure, the state had a weapon whose power should not be underestimated.

The account of these events written by Zachariah of Mitylene is in many ways similar to that of Evagrius. In tone, however—for Zachariah was a monophysite—as well as in several details, it is quite different. In the first place, Zachariah informs us that some time elapsed between the enthronement of Proterius and the outbreak of violence.[122] Originally, he claimed, Proterius vigorously opposed the decisions of the council, but he quickly changed his position when he found he might seize the episcopal throne for himself.[123] After his consecration, he persecuted those who opposed him, exiling some and confiscating their property "by means of the 'governors' who obeyed him in consequence of the emperor's command."

> Whereupon, indeed, the priests and the monks and many of the people, perceiving that the faith had been polluted both by the unjust deposition of Dioscorus and the oppressive conduct of Proterius and his wickedness, assembled themselves in the monasteries and severed themselves from his communion. And they proclaimed Dioscorus and wrote his name in the book of life as a chosen and faithful priest of God. And Proterius was very indignant and he gave gifts into the hands of the Romans,[124] and he armed them against the people and he filled their hands with the blood of believers, who were slain; for they also strengthened themselves and made war. And many died at the very altar and in the baptistry, who had fled and taken refuge there.[125]

According to Zachariah, opposition to Proterius developed for three reasons: pollution of the faith, the deposition of Dioscorus, and the ill treatment accorded many Alexandrians by the new bishop. Zachariah placed considerable emphasis on this last factor, and it is unfortunate that we do not know more about it. We do not know exactly who was persecuted, although they presumably included some of those involved in the episcopal administration of Dioscorus. Zachariah also stressed the simple loyalty of many people to their deposed bishop, and he mentions no theological motivation for this. By "pollution" of the faith, Zachariah may have meant the doctrinal decisions of Chalcedon, although the text seems to confuse this with the deposition of Dioscorus and the bishop's mistreatment of his subjects. In another passage, however, Zachariah made himself a little clearer: "The whole city of Alexandria hated Proterius, some in consequence of their zeal for the faith, others, because they had been plundered and persecuted by him."[126] This "zeal for the faith" must refer to the theological decisions of Chalcedon, although we might be surprised that a Monophysite author cannot clearly stress the doctrinal nature of the conflict. We should probably conclude that even Zachariah realized that concern for Monophysite theology was not the primary motivation for most of the supporters of Dioscorus.

We have seen that the soldiers stationed in or near Alexandria—at first perhaps only the city guard under the command of the prefect Theodorus—had received orders to assist Proterius in his attempt to defend his see. From the account of Zachariah, we learn—what we did not find in the orthodox sources—that the soldiers inflicted some casualties on the people of Alexandria before they found themselves besieged in the Serapaeum. It is, however, difficult to understand why Proterius gave gifts to the soldiers and armed them against the crowd—unless this testimony represents only an attempt by the author to discredit the bishop. As Zachariah had said earlier, the soldiers were under the emperor's order to defend Proterius. Perhaps the soldiers shared some of the sentiments of the Alexandrians, and the bishop used the wealth of the church to encourage them in the performance of their duty.

According to Zachariah, the supporters of Dioscorus gathered in the monasteries to decide what action they should take.[127] The protest focused on the uncanonical consecration of Proterius while Dioscorus was still alive. Whatever their disagreements with Proterius might have been—theological, personal, financial—all were able to embrace a program whose basis was the simple "illegal" action of the new bishop.[128] The monks of Alexandria, perhaps already under the influence of Timothy Aelurus[129] and Peter Mongus,[130] were in the forefront of the opposition, and it was probably under monastic leadership that many of the inhabitants of the city demonstrated their disapproval of Proterius.

Theophanes has preserved further information concerning events in Egypt after the Council of Chalcedon:

> Dioscorus then went into exile and Proterius was put forward [as bishop]. Those who agreed with Dioscorus and Eutyches made a great insurrection and threatened to prevent the transport of grain [to Constantinople]. Marcian learned of this and gave orders for the grain of Egypt to be brought down the Nile to Pelusium, rather than to Alexandria. From there it was conveyed by ship to the imperial city. The people of Alexandria then, suffering from famine, asked Proterius to intercede for them with the emperor. And thus they refrained from the disturbance.[131]

The significance of this account lies in the reference to the interference with the shipment of grain from Egypt. Certainly, one must question the reliability of Theophenes' story, but there is some circumstantial evidence which suggests its plausibility.[132] In the first place, we know from Evagrius that about this time there was a drought, with attendant destruction of crops and famine, throughout Asia Minor and in other areas of the East.[133] The loss of grain from these areas certainly had important repercussions in Constantinople, which must then have become almost totally dependent upon the grain of Egypt.[134] This would account for the hasty action of Marcian in rerouting the grain transport when it was threatened by disturbances in Alexandria. It may also help to explain the action of those who wished to halt the shipment; they realized that this was a critical time in which such action would have the greatest effect.

Although one must assume that the grain supply of Alexandria came from the same sources as that destined for Constantinople, it is surprising that the diversion of the grain transport away from the city would cause a famine there—unless food was already in short supply in Alexandria. The testimony of the priest Athanasius at the Council of Chalcedon indicated that this was indeed the case. He complained that Dioscorus had not allowed him to participate in the free distribution of bread because there was a famine in the city.[135]

It is unclear how the supporters of Dioscorus were able to disrupt the grain shipment from Egypt. Since all the evidence we have suggests that the wealthy landowners were prominent among the enemies of the deposed bishop, and since they would in any case have been unwilling to injure themselves financially, it is unlikely that the grain was withheld by the producers. Perhaps the violence and unrest in Alexandria prevented the regular shipments; it is improbable that there was a strike at the docks.[136]

Sometime shortly after his consecration, Proterius wrote to Pope Leo, including a short profession of faith. The pope did not consider this statement satisfactory, and he demanded another from the new bishop. Proterius complied and sent another letter by the hands of Bishop Nestorius of Phragonis. At the same time, probably late in 453, Proterius sent a petition to the emperor. These letters have been lost, but their contents can be inferred from the surviving letters of the pope.[137] The concern of Proterius was twofold: he wanted the emperor to continue to send him military support, so that he could deal with his enemies; and he asked the pope to grant him official recognition, so that he could maintain the support of the Chalcedonian bishops of Egypt.

The supporters of Dioscorus, he informed Leo, had made a translation of the Tome. This translation, Proterius alleged, was intentionally incorrect, and it was designed to prove that the Chalcedonians were really Nestorians who divided the person of Christ. The Dioscorans took great care to circulate this forgery and to point out the difficulties in the theology of Leo; one of their primary points was that Proterius and his followers were introducing something new into the faith.[138] From all we can tell, this campaign was successful in eliciting popular support and introducing real doctrinal differences into the controversy.

Leo replied to Proterius that he must guard against those who deceived simple people (*simplex plebs*) by a teaching which, while heretical, contained some semblance of truth. The error of the Dioscorans, he observed, lay hidden in very small corruptions and changes in the faith, and this was not evident to all. He encouraged Proterius to show the people and clergy (*plebs et clerus*) that he was not teaching anything new. He should try to do this by reading extracts from the Fathers which agreed with the teaching of Chalcedon:

> Wherefore, after the statements of the above-mentioned prelates have been read, let also my letter be read, so that the ears of the faithful may believe that we teach nothing other than that which we received from our predecessors. And let those who are less experienced in understanding these matters (*qui ad haec discernenda minus exercitatos habeant sensus*) at least learn from the Fathers' words how ancient is this evil . . . .[139]

Leo further advised Proterius to make use of the traditional power of the bishop of Alexandria to maintain his authority over the provincial bishops of Egypt. He assured Proterius that he would not attempt to interfere with his authority at home.

The pope sent a similar letter to Marcian. In this, he asked the emperor to help Proterius against the "ignorant disagreement (*imperita dissensio*) of those whom stupidity and the instigation of a few heretics have made harmful (*quos paucorum haereticorum instigationibus ignorantia facit obnoxios*)." He advised "that which they are unable to understand through their own efforts should be suggested within their hearing at appropriate times."[140] Leo then requested that the emperor use his authority to order the appropriate readings in Alexandria, so that no one would think that Proterius had introduced anything new into orthodox theology.

From these letters we can see that reports of conditions in Alexandria reaching Rome described the followers of Dioscorus as simple, ignorant people who had been deceived into opposition to the decision of Chalcedon. If they were presented with a correct picture of Chalcedonian belief, the pope thought, the faithful of Alexandria would quickly see the error of their ways and abandon their support of Dioscorus. As events were to show, Leo was much mistaken in his expectations. Nevertheless, it is interesting to note the methods proposed by the pope: *florilegia* were to be prepared and read to the people. This acknowledged the centrality of the theological controversy, although even here the dispute was to be settled by appeal to authority rather than argumentation.

On September 4, 454, Dioscorus died in exile in Gangra. Immediately upon the arrival of this news, disturbances broke out once again in Alexandria.

> On account of the love that they had for him [Dioscorus], they [the Alexandrians] proclaimed him as a living man, and his name was set in the diptych . . . but the believing party [the supporters of Dioscorus] were desirous of appointing a bishop in place of Dioscorus. However, they were afraid of the threats of Marcian the emperor; for he was sending letters in every direction and fulminating against all who would not agree to the Synod and receive the Tome. For so it was that when he heard the men of Alexandria and of their intention to appoint a new bishop for themselves after the death of Dioscorus, he sent John, the chief of the *silentiarii*, with a letter from himself exhorting the Alexandrians to be united to Proterius.[141]

In this letter to the inhabitants of Alexandria, the emperor followed the advice of Leo and identified the faith of Chalcedon with that of the Fathers and that of Dioscorus with the heretic Eutyches.[142] He also accused the monks of Egypt of being responsible for the disorders in Alexandria. The *silentiarius* John returned to Constantinople with a petition in behalf of the Dioscorans. Nevertheless, his mission must have been at least a partial success, for the schismatics did not at that time elect a rival to Proterius.[143]

This was not the end of difficulties in Alexandria. If anything, the situation became worse in the years which followed the death of the emperor Marcian. In 457, the supporters of Timothy Aelurus took advantage of the change of imperial administration and the absence of the military governor to consecrate their leader as bishop. They murdered the hapless Proterius and dragged his body through the streets.[144] The government finally managed to oust Timothy, after a great massacre, and the Proterians again elected an orthodox bishop.[145] During the troubles surrounding the revolt of Basiliscus, Timothy once again ascended the throne of St. Mark, amid great popular rejoicing.[146]

Despite the intrinsic interest of these events and their importance in ecclesiastical and political history, we need not proceed further in our study of the urban crowd at Alexandria. By 454 the division of the population into "parties" was already set and fixed. A small, but important, section of the populace supported the successors of Proterius and accepted Chalcedonian theology. These were, in general, the *potentiores*, who possessed some wealth and who often had interests outside Egypt. The majority of the population, however, strongly supported the party of Dioscorus and violently opposed the efforts of the government to impose orthodoxy on Alexandria. From the time of the death of Dioscorus, theology clearly divided the two parties: the Dioscorans were Monophysites, and the Proeterians were Chalcedonians.[147]

Scholars have adduced various reasons for the violent cleavage of religious sentiment in Alexandria following the Council of Chalcedon.

Some have seen these disturbances as evidence of a growing Egyptian nationalism, which regarded Chalcedonian orthodoxy as an "excuse" for opposing the hated Roman government.[148] Others have argued that the situation can be explained only in religious terms: the supporters of Dioscorus were not Egyptian nationalists, they merely regarded his Monophysite theology as correct.[149] Our study of the evidence for this question does not support either of these hypotheses.

There is almost nothing in the sources which would lead one to believe that the supporters of Dioscorus regarded themselves as Egyptian nationalists. It is true that they resented and opposed the efforts of the Roman government to impose orthodoxy in Alexandria. But, so far as we are able to tell, this opposition was concerned only with ecclesiastical matters. It was a direct result of the armed support the emperor gave to Proterius. The evidence nowhere suggests that, at this time at least the Dioscorans had any political program.[150]

The population of Alexandria was, however, divided roughly along class lines. The rich of the city generally supported Proterius, while the majority of the population remained loyal to Dioscorus. One might see this as evidence of Egyptian nationalism, since the rich of Alexandria were presumably Greeks who had interests throughout the empire, while the poor were largely native Egyptians. This may be true, but the preponderance of "foreigners" among the upper classes in Alexandria at this time must be proven rather than assumed. In fact, we know that many native Egyptians had risen to positions of great importance under the later empire.[151] In any case, there still is no evidence that the poor of Alexandria supported Dioscorus because of enmity toward the Roman state.

If the division of the population of Alexandria was not nationalist in origin, might it not be described as a kind of economic or social struggle? We can say almost certainly that such was not the case. In the first place, as with the other incidents we have studied, the sources have not recorded any indication of class consciousness or action on the part of the poor. The supporters of Dioscorus did not, so far as we know, direct any violence against the persons or property of the rich. The wealthy of Alexandria, it is true, may have supported Proterius as the representative of the faith of the emperor. Some of them were imperial officials and many depended upon trade with other parts of the empire. Their interests were in the wider world, and they could be expected to oppose a bishop officially deposed by a council called and presided over by the emperor. But the motive of these individuals was probably not so simple. Their disagreement with Dioscorus dated from the very beginning of his episcopate, and the persecutions and confiscations carried out by the bishop presumably made the wealthy willing to support a rival candidate at any time. The rich may have acted to protect their economic standing, but simple hatred for Dioscorus undoubtedly influenced their position.

Thus, the division of the population of Alexandria was not primarily political or social. On the other hand, the disturbances in Egypt cannot be explained simply by theological considerations. As we have seen, the sources say nothing certain about theological differences in the early stages of the violence in Alexandria. It was not until just before, and especially after, the death of Dioscorus that the theological question came to the forefront of the controversy. Until then, the sources tell us, the issue dividing the two sides was canonical: the deposition of Dioscorus, and the consecration of Proterius while the former bishop was still alive.

Many people who did not understand the subtle distinctions between the conflicting theologies realized only that their bishop had been deposed and another put in his place. This was undoubtedly connected with the unique position of the bishop of Alexandria: probably more than any other prelate of the ancient church, he exercised absolute control over the ecclesiastical establishment of his diocese; local priests were closely supervised; and the people of Egypt came to look upon their archbishop as the embodiment of the will of God. Furthermore, a bishop of Alexandria was rarely deposed. The most notorious example, other than that of Dioscorus, was that of Athanasius. In the fourth century, as in the fifth, the inhabitants of Alexandria reacted violently to the interference of the government in the affairs of the church of Egypt. Loyalty—and enmity—to Dioscorus is probably the best explanation for the initial division of the population of Alexandria and the violence which followed the Council of Chalcedon.

This is not to say that theological considerations were unimportant, but they were clearly not the crux of the matter at the outset. As time went on, and especially after 454, the anti-Chalcedonian faction needed more than the memory of the unfortunate bishop to hold their party together. Timothy Aelurus and his followers lost one opportunity when they failed to consecrate a successor to Dioscorus in 454. From that point, however, the canonical distinction became less of an issue, since the episcopal succession of the Dioscorans had been broken.

From at least as early as 453, each side of the controversy began to make a concerted effort to convince the Alexandrians of the correctness of their position. They did this in a way which has become familiar from earlier examples. Both the Monophysites and the Chalcedonians sought to convince the faithful that their theology was identical with that of the Fathers. The doctrine of their enemies was either a complete innovation or was identified with that of some notorious heretic. The leaders of both parties devised elaborate procedures to convey this point. The Monophysites mistranslated and falsified the Tome of Leo so that the Chalcedonians would appear to be Nestorians. The Chalcedonians, on the other hand, with the help of the emperor, staged public readings of excerpts from the works of the Fathers. The faithful were then to see for themselves that the theology of the council was that which the church had always taught. The Chalcedonians thought that the majority of the Monophysites—"who [in Pope Leo's words] are less experienced in understanding these matters"—had been deceived into opposition to the council. The Monophysite leadership, however, controlled most of the churches of Alexandria, and the memory of Dioscorus remained strong among the faithful, who never accepted the decisions of the Council of Chalcedon.

As usual, it is difficult to assess the ultimate significance of popular feeling in Alexandria. Clearly these events were different in many respects from the others we have examined. In part, this is because the political and religious decisions had already been made, and the lines were clearly drawn at the council in distant Chalcedon. Yet, we have seen how the decisions of the Latrocinium—and some would argue those of the first Council of Ephesus—were set aside, and years of wrangling over Monophysitism and Monotheletism were in store for the church of the East. It is true that the overwhelming Dioscoranism of the people of Alexandria had little immediate effect on the political or ecclesiastical situation in Constantinople or in Egypt. Marcian and Leo I did not waver significantly in their Chalcedonianism, and a bishop of Alexandria continued to be appointed with the approval of the court for many years.

Nevertheless, the division of opinion which developed in Alexandria after the deposition of Dioscorus remained the primary fact of life for the church of Alexndria until the Arab conquest and beyond. The population of Alexandria, with some notable exceptions, agreed with the inhabitants of the Egyptian countryside in opposing the decisions of the Council of Chalcedon—again, first in personal terms and later in theological terms. Against such unanimity of opinion fixed and hardened into a system of belief, the Chalcedonian prelates could make but little headway. This was symbolized by the fate of the unfortunate Proterius.

Such acts of violence, however, were not the ultimate weapons of the supporters of Dioscorus in Alexandria. In fact, throughout the fifth century, the government was generally able to impose its will by means of superior force. But violence only served to drive the opposition underground. When used early in a controversy to intimidate minority groups and deny them access to media for the expression of their views, violence could be effective. But more frequently violence, especially that organized by the state, was simply a last resort and a sign of failure: when confronted with sizeable and well-organized public opinion, as it was in Egypt, violence as a basis of policy was doomed to failure.

1. The date of the election of Anatolius is controversial. See R. V. Sellers, *The Council of Chalcedon*, p. 94, n. 4. The bibliography on the Council of Chalcedon and attendant events is much the same as that for the Latrocinium. For political events, see Bury, *Later Roman Empire*, vol. 1, pp. 235-29; Stein, *Histoire*, vol. 1, pp. 311-15; Jones, *Later Roman Empire*, pp. 217-21; Thompson, *Attila*; and O. Seeck, *Geschichte des Untergangs*, vol. 6. The Council of Chalcedon itself has been the subject of numerous works, especially at the time of the fifteen-hundredth anniversary of the event. Most important of these is A. Grillmeier and H. Bacht, eds., *Das Konzil von Chalcedon*, which besides learned articles on the history and theology of Chalcedon contains a bibliography of 922 items. This work also examines the influence of the theology of Chalcedon on modern Christianity. In addition, see R. V. Sellers, *The Council of Chalcedon*; Hefele-Leclercq, *Histoire des conciles*, vol. 2, pp. 649-880; Duchesne, *Early History of the Christian Church*, vol. 3, pp. 299-315; and Bardy, *Histoire*, vol. 4, pp. 228-67. The theology is discussed by Grillmeier, *Christ in Christian Tradition*, pp. 479-95. The most important collection of primary material is edited by E. Schwartz in the *Acta Conciliorum Oecumenicorum* [*ACO*], vol. 2, which contains the *acta* of the council and many letters and other documents pertaining to it. Also important are the letters of Pope Leo (*ACO* and *S. Leonis Magni Epistulae*, ed. C. Silva-Tarouca). The fragments of Priscus contain some significant materials for this period, but we must rely on the ecclesiastical history of Evagrius and the later chronicles of Theophanes, Malalas, Prosper, and the author of the *Paschal Chronicle*. Zachariah of Mytilene presents the Monophysite's point of view of these events, and his chronicle (*Historia Ecclesiastica*) has survived in a Syriac translation (ed. and trans., E. W. Brooks, *CSCO*, Scriptores Syri III, 5 and 6 [Paris/Louvain, 1919-24]; Eng. trans., F. J. Hamilton and E. W. Brooks [London, 1899]).

2. Liberatus *Breviarium* (*ACO*, II, v, p. 118). The Robber Synod may have recommended that Anatolius be the next bishop of Constantinople and the opposition may have been to that decision. See Zachariah of Mytilene *Historia Ecclesiastica*. Anatolius says specifically that he was elected by the *synodos endemousa* of Constantinople.

3. Leo *Epistulae* 71 (*ACO*, II, iv, pp. 31-32). The *florilegium* is found in *ACO*, II, i, 1, pp. 22-25. Cf. P. Mouterde, "St. Abundius de Come et ses trois compagnons à un synode de Constantinople en 450," *Anal. Bolland.* 48 (1930), 124-29.

4. Leo *Epistulae* 69-70 (*ACO*, II, iv, pp. 29-31).

5. Liberatus *Breviarium* (*ACO*, II, v, p. 119); Theophanes p. 103 (de Boor); Malalas, p. 366 (Bonn); *Chronicon Paschale*, p. 589 (Bonn); Theodore Lector, *PG* 86, 1, p. 165.

6. Malalas, pp. 336-37; *Chronicon Paschale*, p. 589.

7. Bury, *Later Roman Empire*, vol. 1, p. 236; Stein, *Histoire*, vol. 1, pp. 311; Evagrius *Historica Ecclesiastica* 2.1 (from Priscus).

8. Theophanes *Chronographia*, A.M. 5942 (ed. de Boor), p. 103. He implies that the patriarch took part in the ceremony of coronation: Pulcheria "summoned the patriarch and the Senate and she named him king of the Romans." See W. Sickel, "Das byzantinische Kronungsrecht bis zum 10. Jahrhundert," *BZ* 7 (1898), 517. But W. Ensslin, "Zur Frage nach der ersten Kaiserkrönung durch den Patriarchen und zur Bedeutung dieser Akten im Wahlzeremoniell," *BZ* 42 (1942), 101-15 and 369-72, argues that Pulcheria actually crowned Marcian and the first coronation of an emperor by the bishop of Constantinople was that of Leo I in 454. See also Peter Charanis, "Coronation and its Constitutional Significance in the Later Roman Empire," *Byzantion* 15 (140-41), 49-66.

9. See, for example, Stein, *Histoire*, vol. 1, p. 311: "Sa mort subite va mener dans le gouvernement de l'orient un revirement total en faveur de la papauté"; Seeck, *Geschichte des Untergangs*, vol. 6, pp. 267-69; Duchesne, *Early History of the Christian Church*, vol. 3, pp. 295-96.

10. Theophanes *Chronographia*, A.M. 5942 (ed. de Boor), pp. 101-02; Zonaras *Epitome Historiarum* III, p. 242 (ed. Dindorf); Nicephorus Callistus *Historia Eclesiastica PG* 145, 1232 (14, 49). See the discussion in Maenchen-Helfen, *The World of the Huns*, pp. 112-16.

11. Theophanes *Chronographia*, A.M. 5942 (ed. de Boor), p. 102.

12. P. Goubert, "Pulchérie et Chrysaphios," *Chalkedon*, I, pp. 313-15. Malalas (p. 336)

reports that Theodosius went to Ephesus, to the church of St. John the Theologian, to learn who was to succeed him. Goubert suggests that this journey was intended to announce a return to orthodoxy, but that the emperor died on the way and the announcement was never made. This reconstruction is ingenious and it is tempting to see something significant in Theodosius' visit to the city where the previous two councils had been held, but the Lycus is not on the way to Ephesus. Further, Malalas says specifically that Theodosius reached his destination in Ephesus and learned the name of his successor in a dream.

13. Malalas, pp. 366–67; *Chronicon Paschale*, pp. 589–90. Malalas may have taken this account of these events from a source he calls "the most wise Nestorian the chronographer [who wrote] up to the reign of Leo II" (p. 324, 12 and 376, 19). Presumably this indicates that the source presented Nestorian views.

14. Goubert, "Pulchérie et Chrysaphios," p. 314.

15. Theophanes *Chronographia*, A.M. 5942 (ed. de Boor), p. 102. Cf. Nestorius *Bazaar*, p. 363.

16. Priscus, frg. 14; E. A. Thompson, *Attila*, pp. 123–24. That Nomos was a member of the embassy to Attila shows that the supporters of Chrysaphius and the Robber Synod were still in power at that date. It might be argued that the favorable settlement of this matter would relieve the pressure on the government of Theodosius and thus counteract the other disturbing events at that time. This may be true, but one should remember how unstable a truce with the Huns might be, especially one which did not grant them all they desired. The attempt of Theodosius to secure more favorable terms from the Huns is probably an indication of the pressure put on his government by those who opposed his policies. Thus it is parallel to his restoration of Flavian just before his death.

17. John of Antioch, fr. 199, *FHG*, IV, p. 613.

18. *Chronicon Paschale*, p. 589; Nestorius *Bazaar*, pp. 363–65.

19. The traditional evaluation of Theodosius clearly needs to be revised (see Thompson, *Attila*, pp. 200–203 and Luibhéid, "Theodosius II," p. 39). Theodosius may have been a weak man personally, but some of his apparent weakness was really a vacillation made necessary by the conflict of goals.

20. Whereas the policies of Theodosius changed to suit the political situation, Marcian appears to have "believed" in one position, which he maintained throughout his reign. Thus, he is much more understandable to us—and to the later Byzantine historians—than the "unstable" Theodosius II. Stein suggests that the dominant concern of the new emperor was the desire to be recognized by the court of Valentinian III—and thus by the papacy, which had considerable influence in Ravenna (*Histoire*, vol. 1, p. 312).

21. Priscus, frg. 15.

22. Novella of Marcian, 2 (*Codex Theodosianus*, ed. Theodore Mommsen and Paul Meyer, vol. 2 [Berlin, 1905]), issued sometime between October 11, 450, and January 18, 451. Although the novel is issued in the names of the two *augusti*, it is significant that it was directed to Palladius, the praetorian prefect of the East. The effect of the remission of overdue taxes was felt primarily in the East.

23. C. J. 12.2, 2. In 450 Marcian confined the burdens of the praetorship to senators actually residing in Constantinople (C. J. 12.2, 1). In 452 the emperor declared that the various consuls of the year should contribute to the repair of the aqueducts of the city instead of distributing money to the poor of the capital (Marcellinus Comes, *s.a.* 452, p. 84). He also annulled the law forbidding the marriage of a senator and a woman of low estate; from this time on, a senator could marry any woman of good character (Novella of Marcian, 4). See Bury, *Later Roman Empire*, vol. 1, pp. 236–27.

24. Marcellinus Comes, *s.a.* 450, p. 83; Prosper, p. 481; Theodore Lector, *PG* 86, 1, 165; *Chronicon Paschale*, p. 590; Theophanes *Chronographia*, A.M. 5942 (ed. de Boor), p. 101. The place and the circumstances of the death of Chrysaphius are obscure. Some of the sources say that Pulcheria actually gave the order. This may reflect confusion regarding the time of her return to power. See P. Goubert, "Pulchérie et Chrysaphios," pp. 315–18.

25. Theophanes *Chronographia*, A.M. 5942 (ed. de Boor), p. 103. Of course, as many authorities have pointed out, Marcian had considerable interest in the West and this

required that he please the papacy. Cf. E. A. Thompson, "The Foreign Policies of Theodosius II and Marcian," *Hermathena*, 76 (1950), 58–75.

26. Leo *Epistulae* 76–77. The pope was naturally not anxious to have another council. With the accession of Marcian, if not before, his theology was accepted in the East and he had all he wanted. Another council might only raise new issues of difficulty (which it did). However, if another council were to be held, he wished it to meet in Italy.

27. The official acceptance of the theology of Leo probably took place at a local synod held in Constantinople late in 450. See Leo *Epistula* 80; P. Mouterde, "Fragmentes d'actes d'un synode tenu à Constantinople en 450," *Mélanges de l'Université St. Joseph Beyrouth* 15 (1930), 35–50. This is another indication that many of the clergy of Constantinople still supported Flavian.

28. Leo *Epistula* 84 (*ACO*, II, iv, p. 43): "sacerdos et populos catholicae puritatis fidem iam tenere cognoscitur."

29. Leo *Epistula* 84 (*ACO*, II, iv, p. 44). *Frequentioribus solatiis* may mean "who came in droves to console him," rather than "who came often . . . ."

30. *ACO*, II, i, 2, pp. 119–20. See also Bacht, "Die Rolle," pp. 237–43; Hefele–Leclercq, *Histoire des conciles* vol 2, pp. 704–11.

31. E. A. Sophocles *Greek Lexicon of the Roman and Byzantine Periods* (New York, 1887), p. 743, translates this term as "anchorites living in tombs," while Hefele-Leclercq renders them "garden de tombeaux" (*Histoires des conciles* vol. 2, 707). Bacht says they were "caretakers" (*Hüter*) of the *Martyria* ("Die Rolle," p. 238, n. 46). See also André Grabar, *Martyrium: Récherches sur le culte des reliques et l'art chrétien antique* 2 vols. (Paris, 1946).

32. *ACO*, II, i, 2, p. 120.

33. *ACO* II, i, 2, pp. 115–16. The petition was from eighteen monks (listed by name) and "the entire synod in Christ and the rest of the clergy and monks and laity." One might wish further information about these people, especially the laymen, and how many supporters Eutyches could then claim in Constantinople.

34. It is difficult to interpret this piece of evidence. The orthodox monks obviously meant to imply that these men were either strangers in Constantinople or that they were completely unknown to the monastic community there. We might expect some dishonesty here, except that the Eutychians presumably had ample time to prove their identity to the council; apparently they could not do so.

35. See H. Bacht, "Die Rolle," p. 250; J. Pagoire, "Les débuts du monachisme," pp. 67–132; and G. Dagron, "Les moines et la ville," pp. 229–76.

36. *Palatine Anthology* 8.175. Edited by F. Dubner, vol. 1 (Paris, 1864).

37. *Palatine Anthology* 8.269. Poems 166–70 and 174 repeat the same sentiment. Poem 172 suggests that those who feasted in the tombs of martyrs constructed the shrines from the stones of older tombs. Poem 170 says that some martyrs were buried alongside pagan priests.

38. It is interesting that the *memoritai* were Eutychians (thus protomonophysites). Those who see Monophysitism as a survival of paganism might make much of this.

39. *ACO* II, i, 2, p. 115.

40. A third monk had five "names" in the Philippou.

41. Hefele-Leclercq, *Histoire des conciles*, vol. 2, p. 707, n.

42. It may be significant that the adherents of John Chrysostom, when they met in open opposition to the court, assembled in the Xylokerkos. Perhaps it was a safe place to meet. It was located just outside the old walls of Constantine and may not have been used as a circus at this time. The site of the Philippou is unknown. Janin, *Constantinople byzantine*, 2nd ed., pp. 410–11. It is possible, of course, that the *martyria* of these monks were not located in the structures of the circus; they may have only been in the locality.

43. *ACO* II, i, 1, p. 27–28; *ACO* II, iii, 1, pp. 19–20 (Latin). In some copies, the letter is dated May 17.

44. *ACO* II, iii, 1, pp. 20–21 (preserved only in Latin).

196   Vox Populi

45. The Latin text reads only *clericos*, without indicating where they were from.
46. *ACO* II, i, 1, p. 29; *ACO* II, iii, 1, p. 21 (Latin).
47. Again, the Latin text makes no mention of where the troublemakers lived.
48. *ACO* II, i, 1, pp. 28–29.
49. *ACO* II, i, 1, pp. 30, 24–25.
50. *ACO* II, i, 1, p. 30.
51. On the site of the council, see the description in Evagrius *Historia Ecclesiastica* 2. 3, and Alfons M. Schneider, "Sankt Euphemia and das Konzil von Chalkedon," in *Das Konzil von Chalkedon*, ed. A. Grillmeier and H. Bacht, vol. 1 (Würzburg, 1951), pp. 291–302.
52. There were nineteen of these *archontes* in all. The *acta* list them before the bishops (*ACO*, II, i, 1, pp. 55–56). For their role in the council, see Hefele-Leclercq, *Histoire des conciles*, vol. 2, pp. 650–51.
53. The bishops of Palestine and Illyricum, besides those of Egypt, originally supported Dioscorus. Why was this? One might understand Egyptian influence in Palestine, but how can we explain the action of the bishops of Illyricum, whose leader, the bishop of Thessalonica, was a staunch supporter of Flavian (he did not attend the council of 449)? Perhaps political and ecclesiastical disputes concerning Illyricum may explain this. Illyricum had, for the previous fifty years, been disputed between the Eastern and the Western empires, and the contention of the pope and the patriarch of Constantinople over this territory was to last much longer. Perhaps the bishops of Illyricum wished to assert their own independence and used the theological issue to dramatize this.
54. At one point the *archontes* had to remind the bishops that such "vulgar outcries" were not appropriate for men of their station (*ACO* II, i, 1, p. 70, 29–30).
55. *ACO* II, i, 1, pp. 195–96.
56. The numbering of the sessions of the Council of Chalcedon is a notorious problem. At question here is the reversal of the second and third sessions in some manuscripts. See Hefele–Leclercq, *Histoire des conciles*, vol. 2, pp. 649–58, for a discussion of this difficulty. Each important bishop—as well as the imperial officials—probably had his own staff of notaries. This would explain why there is no official text of the *acta*. Latin translations were made very early (some items, e.g., imperial letters, were composed in Latin)—some by the council itself. Only the records concerning the affair of Carosus and Dorotheus (Fourth Session) remained to be translated in 1608 by the Roman editors. Julian of Cos (?) may have been responsible for some of the early translations; others were made in the sixth century during the controversy over the Three Chapters. See Hefele–Leclercq, *Histoire des conciles*, vol. 2, pp. 658–65, and E. Schwartz, "Über die Reichskonzilien von Theodosius bis Justinian," *Gesammelte Schriften*, vol. 2 (Berlin, 1960), pp. 111–58.
57. *ACO* II, i, 2, pp. 69–84.
58. *ACO* II, i, 2, pp. 3–42.
59. *ACO* II, i, 2, pp. 8–9.
60. *ACO* II, i, 2, pp. 10–14, 26–27. Dioscorus at first claimed that he was willing to come to the council, but that he was being kept prisoner and that the *magistriani* (*agentes in rebus*) and the *scholarii* prevented his appearance. The emissaries from the council were carrying this report back to the bishops when they encountered Eleusinios, the assistant of the *magister officiorum*, who commanded the functionaries by whom Dioscorus claimed he was imprisoned. Eleusinios denied that his men were in any way hindering the movement of the bishop of Alexandria. The emissaries then returned to Dioscorus, who changed his story and made other protestations. It is probable that some of the forces of the *magister officiorum* were guarding the quarters of Dioscorus (see the discussion in Chapter 4 regarding the soldiers who were guarding Nestorius' house in Ephesus in 431), but it is unlikely that they prevented his reponse to the summons of the council.
61. *ACO* II, i, 2, pp. 27–28.
62. *ACO* II, i, 2, pp. 28–41. The Latin acts (*ACO*, II, iii, 2, pp. 45–83) are probably correct when they report that 192 bishops gave vocal approval to the sentence, followed by the signature of 308 bishops. About 350 bishops attended the first session of the council; the

supporters of Dioscorus apparently did not attend the session in which he was deposed. On the names and number of bishops at the council see E. Honigmann, "The Original Lists of the Members of the Council of Nicaea, the Robber Synod and the Council of Chalcedon," *Byzantion* 16 (1944), 20-80; and V. Laurent, "Le nombér des Pères au concile de Chalcédoine 451," *Academia Romana Bulletin, Setiunea istorica* 26 (1945), pp. 33-46.

63. *ACO* II, i, 2, pp. 41-42.

64. *ACO* II, i, 2, p. 42. Dioscorus thus had, as we might expect, a large number of clerics with him in Chalcedon and the vicinity. We can only speculate on their activities. They may have cooperated with the followers of Eutyches to spread rumors about their bishop's reinstatment. Or perhaps Dioscorus had lost his influence over some of them. When it became clear that Dioscorus was doomed, they may have thrown their lot in with the supporters of Proterius in hope of future rewards.

65. *ACO* II, i, 2, p. 42, 27: Dioscorus prepared "to spread a report that he had recovered his priesthood."

66. *ACO* II, i, 2, p. 42.

67. In their letters to Marcian (*ACO*, II, iii, 2, pp. 83-84) and Pulcheria (*ACO*, II, iii, 2, pp. 86-87), preserved only in Latin, the bishops were also hesitant to mention any doctrinal error on the part of Dioscorus. In fact, in the letter to Pulcheria they cited Dioscorus' refusal to read the *Tome* of Leo at Ephesus as the only reason for his deposition.

68. *ACO* II, i, 2, p. 157.

69. *ACO* II, i, 2, p. 159. This is taken almost verbatim from the text proposed by Marcian (cited above, note 68). On the significance of the canons of Chalcedon for clerics, see Leo Ueding, "Die Kanones von Chalkedon in ihrer Bedeuntg für Mönchtum und Klerus," in *Das Konzil von Chalkdeon*, ed. A. Grillmeier and H. Bacht, vol. 2 (Würzburg, 1953), pp. 569-76.

70. *ACO* II, i, 2, pp. 159-60.

71. *ACO* II, i, 2, p. 162.

72. G. Dagron, "Les moines et la ville."

73. *ACO* II, i, 2, p. 120.

74. Part of the difficulty in this whole affair lay in the disagreement between the pope and the bishop of Constantinople over the twenty-eighth canon. Leo had never liked Anatolius and he always suspected him of Monophysite sympathies. The affair of the twenty-eighth canon and the presence of Carosus and Dorotheus in Constantinople confirmed his enmity. Cf. Leo *Epistulae* 132 and 135.

75. Leo *Epistulae* 136, 141-43 (*ACO*, II, iv, pp. 87, 94-95).

76. Leo *Epistulae* 134 (*ACO*, II, iv, pp. 87-88).

77. See, however, the law of July 8, 453, which was directed largely against the monastic supporters of Eutyches: *ACO*, II, i, 3, pp. 122. There is no evidence that it was ever effectively enforced.

78. As mentioned in chapter two, there is no fully satisfactory study of Alexandria in this period. The most recent survey is the article by W. Schubert, *s.v.* "Alexandria," *RAC*, vol. 1 (1950). H. I. Bell, *Jews and Christians*, illustrates the conflict among the various groups in the city. See also E. L. Woodward, *Christianity and Nationalism*; E. R. Hardy, *Christian Egypt*; and H. Musurillo, *The Acts of the Pagan Martyrs: Acta Alexandrinorum* (Oxford, 1954), which illustrates the anti-Roman feeling in Alexandria during the first and second centuries. For an earlier period see P. M. Fraser, *Ptolemaic Alexandria*. Perhaps the best insight into the working of the church of Alexandria is to be found in the *Vita Johannis Eleemosynarii*, *Anal. Bolland.* 45 (1927), 19-73.

79. See above, chapter 3.

80. Socrates *Hist. Eccl.* 7.4; Philostorgius *Historia Ecclesiastica* 8.9; Bury, *Later Roman Empire*, vol. 1, pp. 216-19; Seeck, *Geschichte des Untergangs*, vol. 6, p. 404; Stein, *Histoire* vol. 1, pp. 276-77; Bell, *Jews and Christians*, pp. 10-21.

81. Theophanes *Chronographia*, A.M. 5940 (ed. de Boor), p. 98; Liberatus *Breviarium* (*ACO*, II, v, p. 113).

82. *ACO* II, i, 1, pp. 59–60, numbers 140–58. Most commentators, for some reason, ignore the bishops of Tisilas and Hermopolis. See also Honigmann, "The Original Lists," *Byzantion* 16 (1944), pp. 20–80.

83. *ACO* II, i, 1, p. 116; cf. Liberatus *Breviarium*, p. 123.

84. *ACO* II, i, 2, pp. 15–16. See Hefele–Leclercq, *Histoire des conciles*, vol. 2, pp. 693–97.

85. οὐδὲ γὰρ πλείους τετολμήκασιν ἐξελθεῖν ἅμα διὰ τὰ παρ' αὐτοῦ· κατὰ τὴν Ἐφεσίων παρανομηθέντα.

86. These men were apparently officials of the church of Alexandria. Because their names are common and Theodore gives us no further information, it is impossible to identify Dorotheus and Eusebius. Agorastos was a *syncellus* of Dioscorus (*ACO*, II, i, 2, p. 24, 22) and Sophronios accused him and Timotheos of carrying out violence against him. John was presumably the notary who presided at the Latrocinium. The other complainants also called upon the clergy of Dioscorus to support their statements.

87. *ACO* II, i, 2, pp. 17–18.

88. τοῦτο μεγάλοι τε καὶ περιφανεῖς ἄνδρες ἴασιν, οὐ μὴν δὲ ἀλλὰ καὶ πᾶσα ἐκείνη ἡ μεγάλη πόλις Ἀλεξανδρεία. This statement suggests that the hostility of the "great and famous men" toward Dioscorus was well known; Ischyrion, however, alleged that "the whole city" knew of the bishop's misdeeds.

89. ἅπας μὲν ὁ τῆς περιωνύμου πόλεως ἐκείνης λαὸς οὐ μὴν δὲ ἀλλὰ καὶ ὁ . . . κλῆρος καὶ οἱ . . . μονάζοντες ἐπίστανται.

90. It is probable that this grain was originally from Egypt and was diverted by the emperor from Constantinople or its regular market to the disaster area in Libya. Perhaps the grain was grown or transported by the agents of the bishop of Alexandria, a practice seen later in the *Vita Johannis of Eleemosynarii*. See also J. L. Teall, "Grain Supply of the Byzantine Empire," pp. 87–139, for a general treatment of this question.

91. Cf. Hefele–Leclercq, *Histoire des Conciles*, vol. 2, p. 695.

92. *ACO* II, i, 2, p. 17. The text is confusing here. The Greek manuscript reads προτερίου. but this is clearly impossible, since Dioscorus was still the bishop when Ischyrion delivered this statement. Προτερίου must be the interpolation of a later reader who thought the reference was to the successor of Dioscorus. The Latin text (certainly translated before the corruption in the Greek text) gives Νεστορίου, and this would seem to be the original reading, since he was then (νῦν μὲν) bishop of Phragonis, but in any case we must still wonder why Dioscorus made Nestorius a bishop shortly after their disagreement at Ephesus and then brought him along to Chalcedon.

93. *ACO* II, i, 2, pp. 20–21.

94. He claimed that Dioscorus had converted all the houses of Cyril's relatives into churches.

95. This was probably Canopus, which possessed a monastery called Metanoia. Paul van Cauwenbergh, *Étude sur les moines d'Égypte* (Paris, 1914), p. 77, n. 8.

96. *ACO* II, i, 2, pp. 23–24.

97. Sophronius called Makarios ὁ πολιτευόμενος τῆς μεγάλης Ἀλεξανδρείας, "a *decurio* of the great city of Alexandria." Πολιτευόμενος can in this period mean πολίτης, i.e., "citizen." But I think it is more likely that Makarios was a member of the *curia* of Alexandria and thus an important citizen.

98. Theodorus was the *Augustalis praefectus Aegypti*. Almost nothing else is known of him. See W. Ensslin, *s.v.* "Theodorus (81)," *RE*, series 2, vol. 5, part 2 (1934). Sophronios suggests that Theodorus arrived in Alexandria only to deal with this case, but this seems unlikely. Is it possible that the arrival of Theodorus was a result of the accession of Marcian? The previous prefect, perhaps an appointee of Chrysaphius, might not fit in with the new emperor's policies.

99. *Theia laurata*. This was the *imago laureata*, the official presence of the emperor outside of the imperial court. See E. Kitzinger, "The Cult of Images in the Age before Iconoclasm," *DOP* 7 (1954), 83–150.

100. *ACO* II, i, 2, p. 24.

101. A. H. M. Jones, *Later Roman Empire* pp. 904–6 and 1159, n. 65.

102. In these persecutions Chrysaphius and Nomos had been the accomplices of Dioscorus, and Nomus sent his agents to deprive Athanasius of his property. We cannot be certain of the chronology of these events, but Dioscorus and Chrysaphius appear to have been in league before 448. Then, too, it is possible that Dioscorus was cooperating with Chrysaphius and his agents in an attempt to secure the full revenue from Egypt that was necessary to make the heavy payments due to the Huns. If this was the case, the attitude of the wealthy of Alexandria toward Marcian and his policies would be more easily understandable.

103. *ACO* II, i, 2, p. 110. They claimed to represent "all the bishops of your diocese of Egypt."

104. *ACO* II, i, 2, p. 111. Did he mean the new bishop who would shortly be selected or Dioscorus? Eusebius of Dorylaeum listened to the statement of Ierakis and the protestations of the Egyptians and replied simply, "they're lying."

105. *ACO* II, i, 2, pp. 112–13.

106. *ACO* II, i, 2, p. 113.

107. Of course they could hardly have been expected to say that they supported Eutyches' theology, condemned by nearly everyone.

108. Timothy Aelurus, in *Patrologia Orientalis* 13 (1919), ed. and trans., F. Nau, p. 210; Zachariah of Mitylene *Historia Ecclesiastica* 22; Evagrius *Historica Ecclesiastica* 25; Leo *Epistula* 140 (*ACO* II, iv, pp. 93–94).

109. See H. Engberding, *s.v.* "Proterius," *Dictionary of Christian Biography* 4.

110. Evagrius *Historia Ecclesiastica* 2.5. Zachariah of Mitylene *Hist. Eccl.* 3.2, and Theophanes *Chronographia*, A.M. 5945 (ed. de Boor), p. 106.

111. Liberatus *Breviarium* (*ACO* II, v, p. 123).

112. The local aristocracy normally played an important role in the episcopal elections by the fifth century. See Jones, *Later Roman Empire*, pp. 918 and 1384. Evagrius says that Proterius "was chosen as bishop by the common vote of the synod of Alexandria." This presumably relates to an "election" conducted by the four orthodox bishops after their return to Egypt.

113. This does not explain Liberatus' statement that the election was held *cum omnium civium voluntate*. Perhaps this is an error, or it may reflect confusion when news of the actions of the council first reached Alexandria. Presumably this came by means of the emperor's letters or through the four "orthodox" Egyptian bishops, who would have made a one-sided case for the election of a new bishop. When the followers of Dioscorus returned to Egypt, however, they would have had a different tale to tell and this may have turned popular opinion against the election.

114. *ACO* II, v, p. 123.

115. Evagrius *Historia Ecclesiastica* 2.5; *FHG* IV, p. 101. See also Theophanes, p. 106.

116. The Serapaeum had been destroyed in 391, but was quickly converted into a church and named after the emperor Arcadius (Sozomen *Hist. Eccl* 7.15; Socrates *Hist. Eccl.* 5. 16).

117. P. M. Fraser, *Ptolemaic Alexandria*, pp. 267–71 and the map following p. 8.

118. J. Leipolt, *Scheunte von Atripe*, pp. 24–26, and 177.

119. Evagrius *Hist. Eccl.* 2. 5.

120. On the position of *praefectus Augustalis* see M. Gelzer, *Studien*, pp. 17–19; O. Seeck, "Florus (6)," *RE*, vol. 6, col. 2761. Theodorus, the Augustal prefect as late as the time of the election of Proterius, was perhaps still in office, but if so, he was unable to deal with the violence. Florus may have come along with the delegates returning from the council or, more likely, he may have been the commander of the two thousand fresh troops sent by the emperor. In any case, he appears to have been dispatched with extraordinary powers to deal specifically with these difficulties in Alexandria, although he later commanded maneuvers against the Blemmyes and Nobadi in Upper Egypt.

121. Evagrius *Hist. Eccl.* 2.5.

122. This does not explicitly contradict Evagrius, who says nothing of the time elapsed between the consecration of Proterius and the eruption of violence. But most modern accounts have assumed that Priscus arrived in Alexandria about the same time as the consecration of Proterius, while from Zachariah's account it would appear that he came sometime later when opposition to the new bishop had had time to develop.

123. Zachariah *Hist. Eccl.* 3. 2. Unfortunately, we do not know Zachariah's source for these events. As mentioned earlier, Zachariah's work represents a Monophysite's point of view, but his account of the course of events does not deviate drastically from that of the orthodox historians. It is possible that he drew on orthodox sources and does not here reflect a Monophysitic tradition.

124. By "Romans" Zachariah clearly means Roman soldiers (see *Hist. Eccl.* 3. 9).

125. Zachariah *Hist. Eccl.* 3. 2.

126. Zachariah *Hist. Eccl.* 3. 10.

127. Zachariah *Hist. Eccl.* 3. 2. On the monasteries of Alexandria see Paul Van Cauwenbergh, *Étude sur les Moines d'Égypte*, pp. 72–76. We do not know which monasteries Zachariah had in mind in this passage and indeed we know little about the role of the monasteries of the city itself during the christological controversy. We have more information about the monasteries a short distance west; in this area most of the monks, led by Longinus of the Ennaton (i.e., the monks of the Oktokaidekaton and the Eikoston), strongly opposed Chalcedon and Proterius. See Cauwenbergh *Étude*, pp. 66–69; 78–80.

128. As we have seen, it was common to accuse an enemy of uncanonical action instead of theological error. A person whose enmity toward Proterius was personal or financial might not have participated in a program whose orientation was strictly theological. John Chrysostom, Nestorius, and Dioscorus himself were all deposed for violating canons rather than for holding any heretical opinions.

129. On this very interesting figure, see H. G. Opitz, *s.v.* "Timotheos (24)," *RE*, series 2, vol. 6, part 2; J. Lebon, *Le monophysitisme sévérien* (Louvain, 1909), pp. 16 ff. Little is known of Timotheos' life before 451.

130. See Thomas Niggl, *s.v.* "Petrus III Mongus," *Lexikon fur Theologie und Kirche*, vol. 8, (1963), pp. 370–371; Wm Bright, *s.v.* "Petrus (6)," *Dictionary of Christian Biography*, vol. 4 (1887). He had been ordained deacon by Dioscorus and was reputed to have been a leader in the violence against Flavian at Ephesus (Mansi, VI, 1017). See also Liberatus *Breviarium* (*ACO*, II, v, pp. 123–24).

131. Theophanes *Chronographia*, A.M. 5945 (ed. de Boor), pp. 106–7.

132. It had become customary to accuse one's enemies in Alexandria of plotting to shut off the grain supply from Egypt; the Arians, for example, accused Athanasius of attempting this (Socrates *Hist. Eccl.* 1. 35).

133. Evagrius *Historia Ecclesiastica* 2. 6. The drought struck Phrygia, Galatia, Cappodocia, Cilicia, and "many other areas." I have been unable to ascertain whether such conditions in Asia Minor and Palestine would indicate a drought in the Abyssinian plateau—and thus a low Nile and famine in Egypt. See H. G. Lyons, *The Physiography of the River Nile and its Basin* (Cairo, 1906), pp. 350–87, who discusses the variation of the Nile flood and its causes. From his data it would appear that a long period of drought in Egypt (e.g., seven years—or the period from the return of the priest Athanasius to Metanoia to 453) was very unlikely.

134. See G. Richard, "Le problème du blé à Byzance," *L'information Historique* 19 (1957), 93–99; G.-I. Bratianu, "La question," pp. 83–107; J. L. Teall, "The Grain Supply of the Byzantine Empire," pp. 87–139.

135. *ACO* II, i, 2, p. 20.

136. See W. H. Buckler, "Labour Disputes in the Province of Asia," in *Anatolian Studies Presented to Sir William Mitchell Ramsay* (Manchester, 1923), pp. 27–50; Ramsay MacMullen, "A Note on Roman Strikes," *Classical Journal* 58 (1963), 269–71. Of course, it is also possible that the shipment of grain was hindered by rural supporters of Dioscorus, before it ever reached Alexandria.

137. Leo *Epistulae* 127 (*ACO* II, iv, pp. 82–83 [January 9, 454]).

138. Leo *Epistulae* 129 (*ACO* II, iv, pp. 84–86), and 130 (pp. 83–84), dated March 10, 454.

139. Leo *Epistulae* 129 (*ACO* II, iv, p. 85). There may be some rationale behind Leo's use of *plebs* rather than *populus* in this context. He believed that only the simple people of Alexandria were being deceived by the propaganda of the Dioscorans.

140. Leo *Epistulae* 130 (*ACO* II, iv, p. 83).

141. Zachariah *Hist. Eccl.* 3. 2.

142. *ACO* II, i, 3, pp. 129–30; the Latin text of this letter (*ACO* II, v, pp. 3–4) is more complete than the Greek and mentions the mission of John.

143. Zachariah *Hist. Eccl.* 3. 5. See also Duchesne *Early History of the Christian Church*, vol. 3, p. 330.

144. Zachariah *Hist. Eccl.* 4. 1–3; Evagrius *Hist. Eccl.* 2. 8; *ACO*, II, v, pp. 11–22; Duchesne *Early History of the Christian Church*, vol. 3, pp. 221–33; Bardy, *Histoire*, p. 280.

145. Zachariah *Hist. Eccl.* 4. 9, claims that ten thousand perished, and the Proterians aided the forces of the government.

146. Zachariah *Hist. Eccl.* 5.2–4; Evagrius *Hist. Eccl.* 3.4–5.

147. On events in Egypt after this period the best study is Jean Maspero, *Histoire des patriarches d'Alexandrie* (Paris, 1923). W. H. C. Frend, *The Rise of the Monophysite Movement*, says all too little about Egypt.

148. See especially, E. L. Woodward, *Christianity and Nationalism*; and E. R. Hardy, "The Patriarchate of Alexandria: A Study in National Christianity," *Church History* 15 (1946), 81–100, and *Christian Egypt*.

149. A. H. M. Jones, "Ancient Heresies," pp. 280–96.

150. For an excellent discussion of this question, again see A. H. M. Jones, "Ancient Heresies."

151. See, for example, the Egyptian family Apion, which attained consular dignity in the fifth and sixth centuries, in Oxyrhynchus. E. R. Hardy, *The Large Estates of Byzantine Egypt* (New York, 1931), pp. 25–38.

VII

CONCLUSIONS

The religious controversies of the fifth century A.D. were complicated disputes which strained the capacities of the greatest minds of the age. Despite their complexity, the controversies affected every stratum of society, and the streets and the markets of the cities of the empire were filled with dispute. Often this popular involvement led to violence, perpetrated by the monks, by the soldiers of the state, or by anonymous members of the crowd. This study has sought to investigate and explain these interrelated phenomena by examining each in a series of specific events.

Throughout, a primary concern has been the question of motivation: why did the people of the late Roman East behave as they did in these controversies? As we have seen, the ancient sources are almost universal in their explanation of this. Each authority, according to his own religious position, pictured those who agreed with his view as moved by a love of truth and justice, while those who acted differently were wicked heretics and schismatics—or, often, pagans and Jews. Modern historians, on the other hand, have frequently doubted the simple religious explanations of the ancient authorities and sought social, economic, and political causes.

Since the sources say almost nothing about secular motivation, the historian has had to read between the lines to find such factors at work. Perhaps the most attractive approach to this problem is to see if religious and secular concerns correlate in any specific way, and throughout our investigation we have been particularly sensitive to any indication of divisions of the population along secular lines. On a number of occasions, such distinctions did in fact appear. Thus, the poor of Constantinople enthusiastically supported John Chrysostom, while most of his enemies were rich and powerful. Likewise, the wealthy of Constantinople opposed the deposition of Flavian, and the poor of Alexandria remained loyal to Dioscorus while the rich supported his successor.

Nevertheless, reference to such simple social or economic distinctions does not fully explain the evidence as we have it.[1] Thus, while it is true that the most important enemies of Chrysostom were from the upper classes of Constantinople, some of his most devoted followers were also wealthy, and they willingly associated with the poor who defended the popular bishop. In this case, the apparent social and economic considerations were merely the result of the "accident" of Chrysostom's preaching and manner of life: because he was outspoken in his criticism of the rich and powerful, he earned the enmity of many of them, while others, including most of the poor, were attracted by his eloquence and asceticism.

The situation in Alexandria seems more to have resembled a social conflict, since the division of opinion followed economic and social lines. The reason for this, however, is simple and applies only to the situation as it existed then in Alexandria. That is, there is no reason to think that the rich opposed Dioscorus because of any class issue, but simply because he had persecuted many of them and threatened their economic well-being. The poor, on the other hand, supported the deposed bishop, not because the rich opposed him, but because of certain religious considerations. There is no evidence that these controversies in any way represented class conflicts, and the poor, in particular, do not seem generally to have been influenced by economic or social factors. Further, nowhere was there any indication of hostility of the poor toward the rich or of action taken against their persons or property.

Incipient nationalism is another general secular consideration which has been discussed in connection with the late Roman religious controversies. Certainly the term "nationalism" is incorrect and misleading as applied to this period, but one might reasonably still ask about the importance of regional cultural unity and opposition to Roman control as a factor in the religious disputes. This question is naturally very difficult, and the sources provide exceptionally little information with which to answer it. On the surface, one should probably expect that the apparent resurgence of native language and art—or perhaps their acceptance as part of the growth of Christianity—contributed to an increase in regional identification. But such a conclusion does not necessarily follow. It is true that Alexandria and Ephesus, in the events discussed above, appear to have rejected the theology of Constantinople. Yet, it is misleading to see this as simple opposition to Constantinople, since both cities accepted the theology of the capital in 449. The importance of regional loyalty should not be summarily dismissed, but the conclusion of this study is that it did not play a significant role in the events considered.

Local patriotism should probably be clearly distinguished from the nationalism or regionalism discussed above: local patriotism would lead the inhabitants of one city to oppose those of another, neighboring city, even if they belonged to the same regional group. By the fifth century, the wars and athletic contests which had served as the outlet for local patriotism in an earlier period had long passed away. A city might, however, still be proud of the beauty of its buildings or the reputation of a native orator or imperial official, and with the rise of Christianity, local patriotism might naturally focus on a native saint or bishop. Such a phenomenon is difficult to detect, as it would be carefully concealed in the sources. But it is at least reasonable to suggest that the inhabitants of Ephesus and Alexandria felt a kind of local patriotism and that this had some effect in the development of popular attitudes. The encroachments of the bishop of Constantinople in the affairs of the churches of Ephesus and Alexandria were well known, and the faithful may have seen their bishops as the champions of local interests in their struggles with the capital. As we have seen, however, there is no direct evidence to support such a hypothesis; so far as we know, the crowd never shouted slogans hailing their bishop as the leader of the city against outside forces. Further, only when the inhabitants of the city were solidly in support of the bishop could he be regarded as the representative of the community, and on several occasions public opinion was so divided that this cannot have been the case.

The *nobiles* of Alexandria are a case in point because their concern for trade and their involvement in the affairs of the empire as a whole separated them from local concerns. Thus, the aristocracy of Alexandria did not support Dioscorus; other more pressing concerns prevented them. Likewise, in Ephesus the people seem generally to have supported Memnon, but internal schism had divided the loyalty of the citizens before 449 and Stephanos could not command such devoted assistance. In Constantinople, the situation was much more complex, perhaps because of the cosmopolitan character of the city and the fact that it was recently founded and expanded. The inhabitants had not yet had time to develop a consciousness as Constantinopolitans. However, it may well be that the episcopacy of Flavian represented a turning point and that from 449 onward the people came more and more to look upon their bishop as a representative and symbol of their civic identity and importance.

Only rarely did popular religious feeling directly involve the emperor. Perhaps this was because the imperial throne, in the East at least, was relatively secure in the first half of the fifth century. Particularly instructive is the slogan which the opponents of Nestorius shouted in Constantinople: "We have an emperor; we don't have a bishop." Even though Theodosius had openly supported Nestorius, the crowd was unwilling to blame him. Once again, we should probably distinguish between politics as a general behavioral explanation and politics as a particular factor affecting the actions of certain individuals in specific situations. Thus, while political factors do not appear to have been significant in the general division of the populace into opposing religious positions, political concerns were not always insignificant, especially in the motivation of the powerful and presumably more politically conscious segments of the population. The wealthy of Constantinople, for example, may have opposed Eutyches for political reasons, since the archimandrite was clearly identified with imperial policy as determined by Chrysaphius.

All in all, then, it seems impossible to postulate a general secular explanation of popular opinion and action. In certain instances, economic or political considerations—usually opposition to imperial policy—probably affected certain people. But such factors influenced only a small segment of the population, and the effect of this changed from event to event. Further, it is significant that whatever secular concerns may have been involved were expressed only in religious terms. At no time, so far as we know, did anyone publicly involve secular considerations in the theological disputes. Even if the leaders may occasionally have been cynical in their manipulation of the religious sensibilities of ordinary people, the constant reference to theological questions must have submerged secular concerns in the minds of all but the most hardened. It is possible that the poor inhabitant of Ephesus or Alexandria unconsciously regarded his bishop as the champion of his political or economic interests, but, were we to ask him about this, he would probably deny it and proceed to explain the controversy in simple religious terms.

In fact, it is unlikely that the inhabitants of the cities of the later empire could have made the distinctions we have been discussing. Secular and religious concerns were not separate, and both were expressed in religious terms. Thus, from the time of Constantine, the keystone of successful imperial policy was the maintenance of correct religious doctrine. Conversely, oppressive and ill-directed policy—as well as natural disaster—was regarded as an obvious sign of God's displeasure with the religious views of the emperor and his court. Since secular and religious concerns could not be fully separated, we should not wonder if economic and political dissatisfaction was expressed in religious terms and that religious disputes reflected society, in a general rather than a specific way. It is important to see that any secular motivation would have been at most unconscious; the Johannite who set fire to Hagia Sophia and the Monophysite who tore Proterius limb from limb undoubtedly felt they were acting in defense of religious principle.

Nevertheless, it is not enough to say that the motivation of the urban crowd was primarily religious. This does not explain why, for example, the inhabitants of different cities supported different religious positions One approach to this problem is to investigate the nature and role of "popular Christianity," as opposed to the Christianity of the theologians, during this period. This is a particularly difficult question, but one which is crucial to the present study.

Clearly, our analysis has shown that one cannot simply equate popular Christianity with a particular set of beliefs; it did not by necessity lean either toward Monophysitism or Nestorianism. This question has frequently been connected with the idea that in the later empire "oriental" or "native" elements, long submerged beneath a veneer of Hellenistic culture and Roman political control, began to reassert themselves. There is considerable disagreement about what this may have meant, but generally this "native" renaissance is assumed to have favored Monophysitism, in part because an emphasis on the majesty and unity of the Godhead presumably appealed to simple "oriental" preconceptions.

At first sight, the result of our study, and the development of the Monophysite controversy in general, seem to support this analysis: the inhabitants of both Ephesus and Alexandria supported proto-Monophysite theology as, ultimately, did most of the East; Constantinople, on the other hand, maintained a Dyophisite position. The situation as it developed, however, was not nearly as simple as it might appear. Even in Egypt one can argue that Monophysite theology was not originally the issue; it became crucial only after the death of Dioscorus, three years after the lines of division had been finally drawn. Earlier, in the days of Cyril, many of the monks—who must be taken to represent the mainstream of popular native religion—opposed the Origenism of the bishop and insisted on an anthropomorphic God, certainly a far cry from Monophysitism.

A further difficulty lies in distinguishing between the Romanized and the native elements in the population of the cities of the later empire. One might equate the rich with the Romanized inhabitants and the poor with the native population, but the danger of this should be obvious. Of course, it is interesting to note that the inhabitants of Constantinople, who were presumably less oriental—whatever that may ultimately mean—did accept the Council of Chalcedon, but we must be careful in rushing to a conclusion in this regard. In the first place, Alexandria had a long history of division along ethnic and cultural lines, and we should not suppose that the cosmopolitan Greeks had totally lost their dominance by the middle of the fifth century; in most respects it remained a Hellenistic city. Ephesus also presents a problem in this regard, for it had been a thoroughly Greek city for nearly all of its existence. Moreover, the inhabitants of Constantinople, who were presumably Hellenized and who supported Flavian and Chalcedon in 448 and 451, cried relentlessly for the deposition of Nestorius, who represented an extreme form of that same theology. This is particularly significant, for it shows conclusively that popular Christianity was not a static fixed system of beliefs, but that it might change according to the situation and the personalities involved.

One must be careful, however, not to dismiss the importance of popular religion entirely. Within a given area an undercurrent of theological assumptions may have tended in one direction rather than another, but this is generally impossible to prove, and it must not be made the basis of any overall interpretation of religious developments. Viewed from another angle, however, the concept of popular Christianity may be of value in our assessment of the dynamics of these controversies. Looking at a slightly earlier period in the history of the church, H. J. Carpenter observed that popular Christianity could be characterized by three general considerations: a concern with moral questions, an interest in institutional organization, and a focus on theology that was practical and historical in orientation.[2] The latter two points are particularly interesting and relevant to the present study. Specifically, Carpenter argued that "... the average Christian was more ready to respond to aspersions cast on the lives of individuals than on arguments of a theological nature." He contrasted such practical concerns with the speculative theology of the intellectuals, but admitted that as time went on, in the East at least, theological considerations became more important. This last point is certainly true, and no one can doubt that popular Christianity in the fifth century had a theological orientation, although some of the old tendencies still remained and played a dominant role in the evolution of popular opinion.

An important consideration in the analysis of the religious controversies of the fifth century is the nature and role of leadership. On numerous occasions it can be shown that leaders influenced popular opinion and directed the actions of the crowd. Normally, such leaders were local in origin and they had a personal or institutional base of power from which they could operate, but at times outside agitators were brought in expressly to encourage unrest among the crowd. Epiphanius, the bishop of Salamis, was such an agitator, as were the monks and sailors of Egypt. This is not to say that urban unrest was "caused" by agitators—or leaders, to use a more neutral term—as they could not direct a crowd against its will—witness the failure of Epiphanius. But leaders normally played a crucial role in the development of popular opinion and its canalization into action.

For the most part, we may assume that the leaders were concerned with their own ecclesiastical or political careers, and they saw the manipulation of the crowd as a means to that end. Thus, we should probably be prepared to distinguish the motives of the leaders from those of the crowd. This is not to say that all popular leaders were ruthlessly cynical and dishonest. While presumably interested in practical politics, many were also moved by a concern for correct doctrine and practice. Nestorius found himself in difficulty because he refused to countenance the public use of the *theotokos*, a term, he admitted privately, which was perfectly orthodox but might lead the simple Christian into heresy. Similarly, John Chrysostom was an unwilling leader of the crowd; he went into exile rather than provoke sedition on his behalf.

The personality, public life, and institutional position of leading figures frequently played a significant role in the development of the loyalty which determined the direction of popular opinion. In part, this was a factor of the nature and organization of fifth-century Christian society, which produced a remarkable variety of popular leaders. Chief among these was the bishop, an individual who owed his position partly to the institutional structure in which he found himself.

By the early fifth century, of course, the bishop had come to be universally recognized as the legitimate head of the local Christian community. In his control over the church, its personnel, and its finances, the bishop had ample opportunity to earn popular support as an accepted leader and secular patron. Moreover, in its homiletic and liturgical aspects, the episcopal office presented the bishop as the intermediary between God and the Christian people. Every time he performed the sacraments or proclaimed the word of God, the bishop demonstrated his legitimacy and advanced his doctrinal position. It is almost a truism that loyalty toward a bishop increased as the years went by; one never hears of a bishop suddenly becoming unpopular after years of successful rule. Popular opposition developed early, or it never developed at all. As we have seen, the affection felt for John Chrysostom increased from year to year, while Dioscorus overcame initial difficulties to engender unshakable loyalty among the majority of his subjects. Nestorius, on the other hand, encountered opposition as soon as he ascended the episcopal throne, and he was never able to establish his position firmly nor to develop personal loyalty toward himself.

How much loyalty toward a leader was affected by popular religious sentiment is difficult to say. This question is of fundamental importance, for it asks whether a leader was successful because he advocated a popular cause—or was a cause popular because a successful leader supported it? To cite a specific example, one may wonder whether Nestorius' difficulty was a result of his failure to appreciate and agree with popular doctrinal sentiments. It is not easy to answer this question with certainty, but it appears that preexisting popular belief played a minor, but limiting, role, Thus, the problems faced by Nestorius were not initially or fundamentally popular or even theological in nature. Had he been able to overcome these, the issue of the *theotokos* might never have been raised, or, if it had, he might well have been able to win popular opinion to his side.

This is not to suggest that popular opinion, when once fixed, was easily swayed. During the early stage of a controversy, issues were more fluid and personalities undoubtedly counted for much. Against established public opinion, however, no bishop could hope for any significant success, as Proterius and his followers learned to their dismay.

The abilities of an individual as an orator apparently were important in influencing popular opinion, but this should probably not be overly stressed. Thus, the oratorical skill of Chrysostom had considerable effect, as the sources clearly show, but Nestorius was also an accomplished public speaker and he was unable to translate that ability into effective popular support for reasons quite beyond his individual control. Perhaps more to the point was the experience of Severianus of Gabala, one of Chrysostom's opponents and an orator of some distinction. He had spoken openly against John just after his first exile. Not only did he fail to convince the people of John's guilt, but he set off the demonstration that ultimately resulted in the bishop's recall to the city.

The personality and religiosity of a public figure appear to have played a somewhat larger part. In particular, the ascetic, especially one renowned for extraordinary self-denial, was likely to possess considerable authority with the crowd. In part, this was because of the ascetic's ability to act as a "spiritual patron" for man before the court of God. When a bishop—with his considerable institutional legitimation—was also a famous ascetic, his leadership of the crowd was virtually unshakable, unless it could be clearly shown that he was a heretic. Not infrequently, however, there was a conflict between these two different kinds of popular legitimation, when the personal sanctity of the holy man contested the authority of the bishop. These two forces could be very evenly matched and individual circumstances and personalities played a crucial role in determining the outcome of such a conflict. Chrysostom was opposed by the monks of Constantinople, but he was himself an ascetic, and the monastic community of the capital could not effectively compete against him. In the case of Nestorius, however, the monks were eminently successful in their leadership of the opposition, and they later provided important support for Marcian and the time of Chalcedon. In Alexandria the situation was different because of the unique position of the bishop and his relationship to the monastic communities of Egypt, but we have seen how popular opinion in the days after the Council of Chalcedon, both for and against Proterius, formed around the monasteries.

From the events we have examined, it would appear that the leadership of the emperor counted for almost nothing in determining popular

Conclusions 211

religious feeling. Such a conclusion may be slightly misleading, for neither Arcadius nor Theodosius II were very popular or dynamic leaders, but it must be significant that in nearly every incident popular sentiment ran decidedly counter to the wishes of the emperor. This is all the more interesting in view of the exalted position of the emperor and the close relationship between emperor and the church in this period. It would seem, from these examples at least, that Constantine's claim to be "equal to the apostles" had fallen on deaf ears among the people of the cities.

From a discussion of the nature of popular leadership, it is necessary to move to a consideration of the means used to influence popular opinion. What methods were used and how effective were they? In many instances, popular opinion was controlled simply by whoever had effective possession of the church of a city. The faithful had long been accustomed to hear theological truth from their local priest, and the sermon was a most effective weapon in the arsenal of those who wished to sway public opinion. The bishop of the city, who was normally able to monitor the actions of his clergy, most often profited from the influence of the sermon, and on only one occasion did a bishop fail utterly to control popular opinion. Nestorius, as we have said, was an accomplished public speaker—this was a primary reason for his choice as bishop—and he clearly realized the importance of the sermon in influencing the minds of the faithful. But the new bishop was never in control of the situation in Constantinople; his election had been hotly contested, and his opponents did not accept his elevation graciously. They spoke openly in the churches condemning his teachings, and Nestorius was not able to command the monopoly of propaganda that was the prerogative of most bishops.

Another vehicle frequently used to influence popular opinion was the public notice: a document set up in a prominent place to explain and defend a particular theological position. Examples of this are provided by the denunciation of Nestorius tacked up by Eusebius of Dorylaeum in the church of Hagia Sophia, and the various notices set up by Eutyches and his followers. That the enemies of the archimandrite went about systematically tearing down the notices suggests that the notices were felt to be effective in achieving their purpose. Yet, as a means by which to sway popular opinion, the public notice had several disadvantages. As we have seen, one's enemies or the agents of the government could easily remove them. Perhaps more importantly, only a fairly limited number of people could read such a notice at one time, and many of the inhabitants of the cities could not read at all. As a result, would-be popular leaders frequently had important documents read to assembled crowds throughout the city. Imperial orders and letters from important ecclesiastical dignitaries were often treated in this manner. Proponents of one position or another organized elaborate processions, replete with the chanting of psalms and the ringing of bells, which wound their way through the quarters of the city. As the procession gathered attention and a crowd began to form, the leaders called a halt at an appropriate spot—perhaps a martyr's shrine—and they read the document in question, presumably with some explanation.

Such processions and other organized gatherings were important in their own right. One of the most serious problems faced by a popular leader is that individuals rarely support a cause for exactly the same reasons. In order to be successful, the leader must present the issue at the lowest common level to invite support from as wide a group as possible. Elementary justification has to be provided, to encourage the indifferent and convince the doubtful, but this cannot be too specific, lest this alienate some potential support. Ceremonial processions often fulfilled this function in the most economical way. Their form and, one might almost say, entertainment value, attracted attention while keeping the theological and canonical issues simple. Thus, one person might join in a demonstration praising the restoration of John Chrysostom or protesting the views of Nestorius simply because certain leaders had organized a good show. Others who had some deep theological or spiritual reason for taking part could join in the demonstration without hesitation and without arguing over incidentals.

Slogans and songs often served the same function. They expressed the complaints and the demands of the crowd on a fairly elementary level. No opponent of Nestorius, regardless of why he disliked the bishop, could object to the cry βασιλέα ἔχομεν, ἐπίσκοπον οὐκ ἔχομεν. Similarly, in another context, the slogan "One is the incarnate nature of God the Word" concisely expressed the position of the Monophysites, just as "*Nika*" unified the Greens and the Blues in 532. The rhythmical chanting of a slogan undoubtedly attracted the uncommitted and emotionally bound together those whose motives were very dissimilar. The evidence that slogans were frequently shouted further indicates at least a modicum of organization.

From a consideration of the vehicles by which spokesmen attempted to encourage and direct popular opinion, we should turn to the content of these vehicles: what arguments did popular leaders make in their sermons and public notices and which of these were more successful in eliciting popular support?

By far the most common argument was the appeal to tradition. In almost every sermon and other public statement, the protagonists claimed that their opponents had espoused a position which had long ago been condemned by all right-thinking men. The most frequent means of doing this was to assert, usually over and over, that one's opponent represented nothing less than the reappearance of some particularly notorious heresy.

Thus, the opponents of Nestorius equated him with Paul of Samosata, while Nestorius called his adversaries Manichaeans. After the condemnation of Nestorius, Eutyches labeled Flavian a Nestorian, and the Eutychians were called Apollinarians. This kind of appeal was undoubtedly a reflection of the conservative and exclusivist aspect of Christian thought. Even the ordinary believers felt that the truth had been revealed once and for all and that present ideology was to be judged against the standards of past decisions.

Obviously, it was not sufficient merely to assert that one's enemies were heretics. In order to prove this allegation, the protagonists brought forward statements attributed to condemned heretics and compared them with the views of their opponents. The point was obvious: anyone who said the same things as Paul of Samosata must be a heretic and therefore deserving of condemnation.

A defense could be made against these charges. Those accused of heresy or innovation prepared *florilegia* of quotations from the Fathers showing that their views had been held by orthodox theologians in earlier years. Again, like the letters and other documents, these statements were frequently paraded through the streets and read to the faithful amid much ceremony.

Other arguments, of course, were used. One might make frequent reference to the Bible or explain how one's opponent had acted illegally or immorally. As the historian Socrates remarked, when it was impossible or inconvenient to accuse an enemy of heresy, it was always possible to discover something which he had done against the canons. The Council of Chalcedon deposed Dioscorus not for his Monophysite theology, but because of his uncanonical actions at the Latrocinium and because he refused to reply to the three summonses to appear at the council. His supporters, meanwhile, deplored what they considered his illegal condemnation. Public sermons and letters frequently mentioned illegalities as important considerations, and the best example was probably the case of Chrysostom, where his enemies tried to found their argument on the bishop's uncanonical behavior. In this instance they had a good case, but it had little effect on the people of Constantinople, who might have been moved only if a theological objection to the bishop had been established. In this connection, a distinction should be made between charges of illegality of an abstract or political nature—such as Chrysostom's returning to his duties too early or his interference in the affairs of Asia—and those which might immediately be perceived by the crowd (e.g., charges which involved moral culpability). In addition, the deposition of a bishop (for example, Chrysostom, Dioscorus and possibly Flavian) might itself be regarded as illegal, and opposition to such an action often lay at the basis of popular opposition. But this involved sentiments of personal loyalty, and the issue is quite distinct from accusations against an official for dishonest or uncanonical behavior. In other words, although the issue in Alexandria in 451 was the deposition of Dioscorus, this canonical concern was not the primary reason why individuals supported or opposed the bishop.

Frequently, theological arguments were made in a way that the crowd could understand and appreciate. The problems involved in the christological controversy were complicated, and we should suspect that the protagonists might have met with popular indifference had they attempted to explain their views in technical theological language. Instead, whenever possible, they clearly explained the practical consequences of their theology for the salvation of the individual. And, of course, this was the central question of the controversy: was the Christ preached by the theologians able to save mankind? As we have seen, popular Christianity did not provide any "natural" answer to this question, although the school of Alexandria probably had the slightly simpler case: when the issue is the ability of Christ to save mankind, it is easier to emphasize his divinity rather than his humanity.

Theologians on both sides did not hestitate to simplify their theological arguments and often to distort the views of their opponents. A crucial point was the use of key words and phrases to define and characterize theological positions. Cyril of Alexandria realized, for example, that if people believed that the Christ of Nestorius was a mere man (ψιλὸς ἄνθρωπος), few would support him. A similar and even more crucial role was played by the *theotokos* in the same controversy. One of Nestorius' main difficulties was his inability to express his theology simply in a way that was persuasive and acceptable to the people of Constantinople.

Appeals to faith, tradition, and justice were the most common means used to influence popular opinion throughout this period, but violence was often resorted to and the phenomenon should be viewed in the same context. Violence—or the threat of it—was most frequently employed by the state to deal with religious dissidents or a hostile crowd. Such officially directed violence might occur at two different stages in the development of a controversy. The most spectacular forms of violence took place once popular opinion had formed and there was considerable opposition to official religious policy. Persuasion had failed, and an attempt was made to neutralize popular opinion by force. Examples of this were the attacks on the Johannites and the military action taken in support of Proterius. In all such cases, the state used the army to suppress the crowd, and special measures were often taken to secure soldiers who had no interests in the controversy and who might be expected to deal harshly with civilians. The confrontations were bloody, and excesses on the part of the soldiers were far from rare. Because of the overwhelming military superiority of the state, the short-term outcome was always the same: the soldiers secured order and frustrated the wishes of the crowd. On the other hand, this use of violence did nothing to change men's minds, and the brutality of the soldiers often encouraged sympathy for the demonstrators. Opposition to the religious policy of the state continued and had to be controlled by the continuous presence of the army. In the end, of course, such a program could not be successful. It is difficult to see what else the state could have done in the situation; certainly it could not tolerate open defiance of official religious policy. But we must conclude that—as a means to influence popular opinion (as opposed simply to controlling it)—violence was a failure once a particular view had been accepted by a substantial number of people.

In an earlier stage of a controversy, however, the situation might be different. As we have seen, individuals in a conflict, including those opposed to the policy of the emperor, did not hesitate to use violence to intimidate their enemies. Much of this may have been simple harassment designed to discomfort individuals, but some of it had a significant effect on the formation of popular opinion. Thus, when the supporters of one view closed the churches to their enemies or kept them shut up in their homes or monasteries, they deprived them of an opportunity to present their side to the people. In such a situation, it is obvious that popular opinion would tend in one direction rather than the other. Nestorius and Eutyches both seem to have been particularly hampered by the intimidating tactics of their enemies. In this way, when applied at an early or crucial stage in the development of a controversy, violence might play a significant, although secondary, role in the formation of popular opinion.

The state and the various individual protagonists were not the only ones who used violence to express their views; occasionally the crowd itself resorted to open demonstrations and acts of violence. Such crowd violence, in the events we have studied, was surprisingly rare, but several examples did occur. The most significant of these were the destruction of Hagia Sophia by the Johannites and the opposition to Proterius in Alexandria after the Council of Chalcedon. Note that both of these events involved not only crowd violence, but also violence directed by the state. Much more frequent were demonstrations of popular sentiment where, so far as we know, no violence occurred. These demonstrations, which ranged from a few angry individuals shouting at an unpopular cleric to a well-organized group chanting their demands before the palace of the emperor, characterized all of the events we have examined. From all of the evidence, the religious controversies of the fifth century, just as those in the time of Gregory of Nyssa, commanded the passionate interest of most of the people of the late Roman East—interest which was expressed vocally in demonstrations and occasional acts of violence.

216   *Vox Populi*

Such expression of popular views seems out of place in the "corporate state" of the later empire, under which the individual is supposed to have been all but submerged in the rigid economic, religious, and political structures which surrounded him. The emperor, in the seclusion of the sacred bedchamber or in the *sacrum consistorium*, made all important decisions of policy, and a complicated bureaucracy enforced these decisions on a population firmly regimented and long accustomed only to passive obedience.

Nevertheless, in the events examined above, the crowd never waited passively to be told how it should react to the religious questions of the time. It often took action, sometimes violently opposing the wishes of its bishop and emperor. Likewise, as we have seen, the crowd did not seem to have acted irrationally, but pursued reasonable, well-defined goals.

Ironically, the structure of late Roman society seems to have been responsible for the frequent outbursts of popular feeling. Life and property were never secure in an ancient city, but through the second century, at least, the Roman government—or the various municipal governments—seriously undertook the maintenance of public order. In the later empire, however, life was notoriously dangerous, as the state progressively withdrew its protection from the private citizen. In part this was probably connected with the barbarian invasions, which threatened nearly every city in the empire, and it involved the general shifts in priorities occasioned by the near collapse of the empire in the third century. The maintenance of peace within the cities was not as important as the protection of the frontier or the collection of taxes.

We cannot follow this process in any detail, especially in the smaller cities, but in Rome, and to a lesser extent Constantinople, the decline in public order is clear. The praetorian guards and urban cohorts, which had maintained peace since the time of Augustus, were disbanded by Constantine. There were replaced for the most part by a kind of amateur night watch, which was of little value in controlling mass insurrection. The *praefectus urbi* in Rome and the provincial governors and municipal officials in smaller cities had normally to meet the actions of the crowd supported only by the members of their *officium*, who were trained for secretarial rather than police duty.

When a disturbance first broke out, an appropriate official attempted to deal with the rioters himself, either appealing to reason or sympathy or holding out threats of ultimate punishment. Not surprisingly, these methods were rarely successful. At this point, the disturbance evolved in one of several directions. In some cases, perhaps because the issue was not serious enough, enthusiasm dwindled and the crowd melted away. More frequently the disturbance continued until the government yielded to the demands of the insurgents or called for the use of armed troops against the crowd.

This failure of the Roman state to develop a really workable police system probably encouraged the outbreak of urban violence, which was rarely stopped in its initial phase. But this does not fully answer the question. The government, which at this time did not hesitate to attempt to control the economy of the empire and the minds of its citizens, surely could have provided a more effective police force. Indeed, when the state chose to employ force against the crowd, it never failed to quell the disturbance, at least temporarily. The massacre of thousands of people in Thessalonica under Theodosius I and in Constantinople under Justinian are the best examples of what the government could do against a rebellious crowd if it so desired. Instead, at the onset of trouble, the emperors took little action against the expression of popular opinion. Only when the disturbance continued for some time, and especially when it erupted into open violence, did the government intervene, almost always effectively, with the use of force.

Shortages of manpower may have played a role in the hesitancy of the state to act quickly and decisively, but other reasons may be sought. Not even the most autocratic of governments can for long ignore the demands and interests of its subjects, and it is unlikely that the later emperors attempted to do this. In many states, popular opinion can be effected, or at least discerned, through constitutional means; but by the time of Constantine, the popular assemblies of the Roman Republic had long passed out of existence and the provincial and city councils—which might have served as a bridge between ruler and subject—were collapsing under new political and economic strains. Emperors of this period had to devise new means or adapt old institutions in order to ascertain the needs and desires of their subjects. For this purpose, public demonstrations—based partly on the old Roman practice of *acclamatio*—probably attained a quasi-constitutional position.[3]

The circus had long been recognized as a place where the inhabitants of Rome could petition the emperor and otherwise freely express their sentiments. The almost inevitable consequence of this "customary liberty" was that this right of free speech would be exercised in the streets and the marketplaces, as well as at the spectacles. Such a practice, assuming that it could be properly controlled, had several advantages for the state as well as for the people. As Ramsay MacMullen has said, "It is in the nature of aloof and authoritarian governments to communicate with their subjects from some royal box or palace balcony . . . and to respond not only to mass acclaim but to mass abuse."[4]

The Codex Theodosianus preserves several statutes which suggest that

218   *Vox Populi*

the emperor listened with interest to the vociferous shouts of the urban crowd, whether they praised good provincial governors or condemned official imperial policy. In 331, Constantine guaranteed

> to all persons the privilege of praising by public acclamations the most just and vigilant judges, so that We may grant increased accessions of honor to them. On the contrary, the unjust and evil-doers must be accused by cries of complaint, in order that the forces of Our censure may destroy them. For We shall carefully investigate whether such utterances are truthful and are not poured forth effusively and wantonly by clients (*clientelae*). The praetorian prefect and the counts who are stationed throughout the provinces shall refer to Our Wisdom the utterances of Our provincials.[5]

Nor did the provincials have to depend upon the praetorian prefect alone to relay their wishes to the emperor: a law of 371 shows that they had the right to use the *cursus publicus* to bring local acclamations to the attention of the emperor.[6] But most important for our purposes, and most remarkable in view of the exalted position of the emperor in the later empire, is a statute of 393. It deserves quotation in full:

> If any person, insensible to decency and ignorant of propriety, should suppose that Our name should be assailed with wicked and imprudent maledictions, and if, riotous with drunkenness, he should disparage Our time, it is Our will that he should not be subjected to punishment or sustain any harsh or severe treatment, since, if such conduct should proceed from levity, it must be treated with contempt; if from insanity, it is most worthy of pity; if from a desire to injure, it should be pardoned. Wherefore, the case shall be referred to Our knowledge with all its details unchanged, so that We may consider the words on the basis of the character of the man and that We may decide whether the offense should be punished or not.[7]

In this law, the government hedged against undue criticism: all who spoke against the emperor were foolish, insane, or malicious. Yet, it is remarkable that such persons were not always to be punished. Instead, the primary function of the law was to require that all public complaints against the emperor be brought directly to his attention "with all the details unchanged," thus allowing him to escape for a moment the flattery of the court and learn what people were saying about him. This is not to suggest that the emperor openly encouraged public opposition, merely that statements critical of the government might be tolerated. Despite the rigid structure of society—or perhaps because of it—the emperor needed to know what his subjects were thinking.

Some of the laws of the Code do forbid gatherings and demonstrations. But all of these were concerned with religious disputes, particularly the Arian controversy after 381 and the intransigence of the Johannites after 404—both incidents in which the emperor took an unpopular position after some hesitation. Obviously, once an emperor had made up his mind about an issue and refused to reconsider it, demonstrations against his decision were only irritating and dangerous.

One of these laws which restricted assembly and protest plainly implies that such a right was normally a very real one, appreciated by the populace as a whole:

> If those persons who suppose that the right of assembly (*collegendi copiam*) has been granted to them alone should attempt to provoke any agitation against the regulation of Our tranquility, as authors of sedition (*seditionis auctores*) and as disturbers of the peace of the church (*pacisque turbatae ecclesiae*), they shall pay the penalty of high treason with their lives and blood.[8]

After the first exile of Chrysostom, the crowd beseiged the palace demanding the recall of the bishop. Although the wishes of Arcadius were clear, no measures were taken against the demonstrators. Even more significant was the inaction of the emperor during the episcopate of Nestorius. Theodosius openly supported the bishop, but he did nothing against those who loudly called for his deposition. After the Council of Ephesus, he tried to prevent news of its decisions from reaching Constantinople, but the enemies of Nestorius were at work in the city, "rousing up a disturbance and discord among the people with an outcry, as though the emperor were opposed to God."[9] So far as we can tell, Theodosius took no action to discourage this expression of popular sentiment. In fact, Nestorius complained that "the emperor allowed everything to take place." Similarly, Theodosius and Chrysaphius supported Eutyches against Flavian, yet they took little action against those persons who spread rumors against the archimandrite and tore down the notices he had posted in his own defense. Only when the crowd threatened Eutyches' life did the emperor intervene by sending troops for the monk's protection. Again, in Alexandria after the Council of Chalcedon, the imperial forces appear to have been completely unprepared for the violence which suddenly broke out, and the emperor could respond only by sending soldiers from Constantinople.

The hypothesis that the government did not always wish to discourage popular demonstrations will help to explain the frequency of the phenomenon. But why did the autocratic emperors of late antiquity concern themselves with popular opinion in the first place? One reason for this is obvious: the inhabitants of the cities of the empire posed a serious threat to the stability of the state. The high degree of centralization heightened the danger since a serious disturbance in the capital might disrupt the whole functioning of government. Thus, demonstrations and even minor rioting might be accepted as a warning against more serious dangers to come. The government apparently heeded these warnings and took appropriate measures against popular revolution, for, although the number of demonstrations and minor riots in the later empire was large, the number of disturbances which seriously threatened the government was surprisingly small.

Nevertheless, the line between a nonviolent demonstration and a violent riot is very fine. In the cases we have studied, the distinction seems to depend most frequently upon the attitude of the government. On several occasions, there was violence between the supporters of two different causes, such as the battle between the inhabitants of Constantinople and the groups of Egyptians after the recall of John, and the various incidents preceeding the first Council of Ephesus. But more often violence erupted when the government attempted to suppress the expression of popular opinion by force. The supporters of Chrysostom in 404 acted no differently from the way they had at the time of the first exile of their bishop; they wished to defend him, and they protested the action of the emperor. At the time of the first exile, the situation was potentially violent; bloodshed was averted when Arcadius acceded to the demands of the crowd. At the time of John's second exile, the emperor and his advisers were prepared to accept confrontation and violence as the price of being rid of Chrysostom. They escalated the conflict by refusing to yield to the demands of the Johannites. The attitude of the latter was not different from what it had been before, but now they met armed resistance. The result was the destruction of Hagia Sophia and the violent persecution of the Johannites. Theodosius II, on the other hand, averted bloodshed and serious sedition in the affair of Nestorius by abandoning the bishop when he discerned the magnitude of popular opposition. In Alexandria after 451, Marcian was determined to enforce the decisions of Chalcedon at any cost; from the outset there was massive popular resistance to Proterius and the Chalcedonians, and the inflexibility of the emperor made bloodshed inevitable.

We have suggested that the reason that the emperor was prepared to tolerate the expression of popular sentiment was primarily practical: he wished to learn what his subjects were thinking and thus avoid serious political difficulties. Another reason may have been ideological. It is true that in the later empire the political philosophy which underlay the imperial throne was more and more "oriental"—or, perhaps better, Hellenistic—in character. Monarchy was praised as the best form of government, and the power of the emperor was regarded as coming directly from God. In such a scheme, one would think that there was little place for the common people. Yet, a spark of the old Roman "democratic" tradition survived, and it is interesting to note that it frequently found expression in exactly the way we have been discussing. For example, upon the accession of a new emperor, it remained customary for his subjects to "approve" his election by shouted acclamations. Of course, the common people had no say in the choice of an emperor, and their role

Conclusions 221

had become little more than ritual. Yet, the idea which lay behind that ritual—that power came ultimately from the governed—was not entirely dead, and the reality of political revolution made any ruler realize his dependence on the goodwill of his subjects.[10]

A modification of this idea and its adaption to fit the new conception of monarchy was the belief that in a special way the actions and feelings of the crowd represented the will of God—the familiar *vox populi voluntas dei*. The considerable attention paid by the ecclesiastical historians to popular opinion is probably a reflection of this view.

Everything we know about the structure of the late Roman city leads us to expect that popular demonstrations and violence would be organized and led by the various organizations through which the state dealt collectively with its citizens: the guilds, the circus factions, even the theatrical claques. Urban dwellers must have been accustomed to approach the government through these groups, many of which had special weapons they could use in any confrontation: the circus factions were presumably armed, and the guilds could withhold essential goods and services. Each group also had an organization which could give unity to popular demands. Nevertheless, a close study of popular involvement in the religious controversies of the early fifth century provides little evidence that these groups played any role at all in the formation or direction of popular feeling. There is an occasional mention of the circus factions, but their role is impossible to assess. The sailors of Egypt, who were presumably closely organized, took part in the violence in Constantinople, but their role as outsiders was a special one, and they cannot be seen in the same category as local groups. It is dangerous, of course, to argue *a silentio* that the urban organizations could have played no role in these controversies—as they clearly appear to have done in later events— but it is noteworthy that we hear almost nothing about them. The reason probably is that the disputes were exclusively religious, while the organizations were—at this time at least—predominantly secular in orientation and function. Religious divisions probably cut across the membership of many of the groups.

Up to this point we have been examining the question of why individuals accepted one theological position rather than another. It is appropriate now to investigate the more general question as to why the inhabitants of the late Roman cities became involved in these controversies in the first place. Cyril of Alexandria and Nestorius agreed that Christ was both human and divine; they further agreed that there were two natures in the person of Christ. The difference in their theologies involved the definition of the unity present in the person of Christ: Cyril held a close association of the divine and human elements (ἕνωσις ὑποστατική), while Nestorius taught a looser connection (κατὰ συνάφειαν). The uneducated people of Constantinople cannot have fully understood this controversy, but they all realized its importance to them personally. A sailor and a shopkeeper might decide to support Cyril or Nestorius for reasons which had little to do with the theological issues as such—they might be persuaded by whoever was the best speaker or had the most appealing personality—but a deep identification with Christianity as they understood it would force both a sailor and a shopkeeper to become seriously involved in the controversy. In this period, as throughout the history of the Christian Roman empire, a person identified himself as a Christian first and as a Roman, an Egyptian, or a citizen of Constantinople second. His very existence, and his relationship with his environment, was determined by his Christianity. Christianity, whether correctly understood or not, was the center of his existence, and it defined him as a person.

This intense personal concern for Christianity and its theological system was largely responsible for the involvement of the urban crowd in the religious controversies. The application of the methods of Greek philosophical inquiry to Christian doctrines may have given rise to the controversies on an intellectual plane, but the participation of ordinary believers was not primarily due to any "Greek love of disputation." Dockmen and laborers in Constantinople may have enjoyed a good argument, just as their descendants in Athens do today, but that can hardly explain the massive and passionate outbursts of popular sentiment. Those who supported Chrysostom and Dioscorus did so, not because they liked to quarrel, but because they understood that their personal salvation depended upon the successful resolution of the controversy. Further, since nearly every aspect of life had been connected, in one way or another, with Christianity, all kinds of personal loyalties and interests were inseparably involved with the controversies. As argued above, economic, social, and political concerns must be rejected as the overt motivation of the crowd, but the ability of Christianity to subsume all secular concerns into itself must have contributed greatly to the passionate concern shown by the urban crowd.

A.H.M. Jones has proposed various criteria for determining whether ancient heresies were really nationalist or social movements "in disguise."[11] Among these is the proposition that the heretic or schismatic had to realize that his opposition to orthodoxy was really disguised secular concern. Clearly, such was normally not the case. Yet, as Jones seems to have realized, this is not nearly enough. The Johannites, Nestorians, and Monophysites—at least in the early stages—did not represent nationalist or social movements, partly because they did not all share a common motive. The only bond which held each group together was religion and opposition to the religious policy of the emperor. Yet, the individual is complex, and it is unlikely that the motivation of any person was a simple matter. Secular concerns, personal loyalties, and psychological factors, about which we will never know, contributed in a unique way to determine the action of each individual. This is difficult to understand fully, even in a modern situation where there is much more information and evidence.

Life in a late Roman city must have been filled with tension, frustration, and insecurity. Population was probably increasing, and the barbarian threat was greatest in the East during the first half of the fifth century. The rigid and stultifying effects of the post-Constantinian social, economic, and political structure have certainly been exaggerated, but there can be little doubt that regimentation and control were characteristic features of contemporary life. On the other hand, no vital social structure can survive without some institutional means of relieving its pressures, and the spectacles in the hippodrome have long been recognized as fulfilling such a function: as we have seen, they provided an opportunity for the ordinary people of the great cities to express their feelings openly. The religious controversies probably served a similar function as a kind of social safety valve. Correct Christian doctrine was a matter which interested everyone and, as we have seen, the state took little decisive action to discourage the public discussion of these issues. In this way, the religious controversies provided a nearly unique opportunity for the expression of popular opinion, which would otherwise have been suppressed.[12]

At very least, popular involvement in the religious controversies reflected some of the basic characteristics of contemporary society and culture. Thus, any familiarity with this period will show the central place of religion, especially Christianity. This concern with religion was shared not only by bishops and theologians, but it was deeply and personally felt at all levels of society, and it is no wonder that even the least educated people took an extraordinary interest in religious questions. One rarely hears of such religious disturbances in the earlier empire simply because the nature of the religious experience was essentially different: it was not personal, doctrinally oriented, and exclusivist, as Christianity was to be. In addition, the expression of popular religious attitudes in the fifth century reflected the contemporary organization of society. Thus, there was little in the way of popular or revolutionary leadership; leaders, instead, were members of preexisting groups (bishops, monks) whose authority was already legitimate. These leaders were absolutely crucial in the formulation and expression of popular religious ideas, something which undoubtedly derives from the traditionally structured character of late Roman society, where emperors, bishops, senators, and generals were acknowledged as leaders and separated from the mass of humanity not only by the power at their disposal, but also the visible symbols of that power, such as distinctive dress, the numerous members of their entourage, and specific kinds of portrait iconography. It is no wonder that, in the East at least, religious division in such a society never denied traditional values and approaches and that Johannites, Nestorians, Eutychians, and Chalcedonians all maintained their affection for ritual and a strict hierarchical church.

In a very real sense, popular involvement in the religious controversies is proof of the vitality of contemporary urban life. On the intellectual level, it has long been recognized that the religious controversies represented a continuation of the Greek philosophical tradition which was kept alive by the intellectual and academic institutions of the late Roman city. It was no accident that the Western part of the empire, where urban life was failing, made little substantial contribution to the theological debate. The same can be said of popular involvement in the controversies. In the East, popular preachers were trained in theology, and the cities provided an intangible stimulus for curiosity and a relatively high level of popular consciousness. The result was that in the West, where this stimulus was absent, theological controversy met with general popular indifference, while in the East, as we have seen, there was overwhelming popular concern and participation, not only in jurisdictional or disciplinary disputes, but also in controversies involving the most difficult theological issues.[13]

The popular debate, of course, did not always use the complex language and reasoning of the intellectual debate, and personalities and simplification played important roles. But popular argument never departed very far from the learned controversy, and it would be fair to say that in any popular demonstration or movement, most participants understood at least the fundamentals of the theology involved.

We need finally to consider the effect of popular involvement on the eventual resolution of the religious controversies of the early fifth century: exactly how important was popular sentiment in the larger context? In the first place, we should note that this question may be improperly put. As seen on several occasions, popular religious opinion was not something fixed and determined; it evolved and changed according to local events and circumstances. Therefore, it should always be seen in a dynamic relationship with various official and nonofficial views and positions. In most cases, popular opinion was determined as the controversy was being resolved, and it is not always easy to know which movement affected the other. Nevertheless, on several occasions popular opinion had to contend with considerable opposition, usually from the emperor, and it is remarkable that the final solution of every controversy reflected popular opinion as it prevailed in each city.

Conclusions 225

The urban crowd of the late Roman empire had several means by which it might force its will upon the emperor or his representative. The most important of these, of course, was violence or the threat of it. Ever since the early days of the empire, the population of the great cities had posed a very real danger to the rulers of the Roman world. When any sizable portion of the urban population united for a specific purpose, it could do great damage, especially in one of the important administrative centers of the empire. A violent uprising, particularly in Constantinople, might disrupt the normal functions of state and could even threaten the person of the emperor. In a great economic center such as Alexandria, popular violence could—and did—disrupt the flow of goods, not only to the commercial market, but also for the critical needs of the state. Fire, a frequent weapon of the angry urban crowd, was potentially devastating in the tightly packed cities of the ancient world, and the destruction of important buildings and monuments was disturbing to rulers who used these structures as evidence of the munificence and general excellence of their reign. Perhaps most important, the politics—secular and religious alike—of the later empire often turned on very fine points. Opposing forces were normally well-balanced and, even after the demise of the ancient popular assemblies, the inhabitants of Roman cities could often turn the tide of events by allying with one side or another. Such power must always have given the rulers practical reason to listen to popular opinion with interest.

On most occasions, however, the crowd did not have to resort to violence in order to make its wishes known: emperors and bishops were normally prepared at least to listen to peaceful protest. It is true that almost all demonstrations of popular opinion were potentially violent, and a fear of violence might ultimately force those in power to consider the demands of the crowd. Yet, as we have argued, there is good reason to think that the expression of popular opinion was in some way regarded as an indication of the will of God. In the Byzantine view, success was its own justification: since God actively rules the world, any important policy which is in accord with the will of God must succeed. In the case of religious dispute, it was the duty of the emperor and the bishops to define and defend the truth and maintain the unity of the faith. The refusal of large numbers of people to accept official religious policy was a sign of its failure and an indication of the anger of God.[14]

Ultimately, for both practical and ideological reasons, the late Roman emperors had to come to terms with the religious opinions of their subjects. By the latter part of the fifth century, these had hardened into at least two mutually hostile camps and, although a succession of emperors attempted to respond to this problem, they were ultimately unsuccessful, and only the partition of the empire by the Arabs could put an end to the difficulty. In the early fifth century, however, the situation was different, and the emperor could deal with the problem of popular opposition by yielding to it once it was clearly established. This is not to say that the urban crowd determined the solution of the christological controversies; there were clearly many forces at work, including politics at court, bribery, and the interests of important individuals. Nevertheless, the action and influence of the urban crowd was certainly a significant ingredient which cannot be ignored in any reconstruction of these events.

---

1. In this regard I would accept the ideas of Mary Douglas (in *Natural Symbols*) against those of many sociologists who wish to see specific changes in society or specific reactions of individual groups as the motivating factor in religious change. Instead, it would seem to be more useful to examine the social (and ideological) system as a whole, and place religious movements in that broader context. This is perhaps a historian's prejudice.

2. H. J. Carpenter, "Popular Christianity and the Theologians in the Early Centuries," *JTS*, n.s. 14 (1963), 294–310, esp. 296–300. On the question of popular religion see the interesting comments of A. Momigliano, "Popular Religious Beliefs and the Late Roman Historians," and W. H. C. Frend, "Popular Religion and Christological Controversy in the Fifth Century." Both articles may be found in *Popular Belief and Practice*, ed. G. J. Cuming and Derek Baker (Cambridge, 1972).

3. See Theodor Klauser, *s. v.* "Akklamation," *RAC*, vol. 1. There were various kinds of acclamations, from the obsequious and tiresome shouts of senators in support of an imperial edict (for example, see the minutes of the Senate usually appended to the text of the *Codex Theodosianus*) to the approval given an *imperator* by his troops. On the political significance of popular acclamations see Milton V. Anastos, "*Vox Populi Voluntas Dei* and the Election of the Byzantine Emperor," in *Christianity, Judaism and Other Greco-Roman Cults*, part 2, ed. Jacob Neusner, (Leiden, 1975), pp. 181–207. In the later Empire acclamations became more and more stereotyped and formal: "die Akklamation wird mehr und mehr zum Hymnus, der von Dichtrn und Musikern, auf Geheiss vor allem der Zirkusparteien, vorbereitet und von eigenen Sägern vortragen wird" (Otto Treitinger, *Die oströmische Kaiser und Reichsidee nach ihrer Gestaltung im höfischen Zeremoniell* [Jena, 1938], p. 72; see also P. Petit, *Libanius et la vie municipale*, pp. 224–25). This stylization did not, however, rob the acclamation of its effect or even its spontaneity so long as the compositions remained outside the control of the state (i.e., until about the seventh century). For until then acclamations might be "hymns" in honor of the government, but they might also be popular, rhythmic solgans against imperial policy. We have already stressed the importance of such slogans in unifying an angry crowd.

4. *Enemies of the Roman Order*, pp. 178–79. In the famous passage describing the visit of Constantius II to Rome in 357, Ammianus speaks of the *libertas coalita* of the *plebs* at the spectacles (*Res Gestae* 16. 10, 13). The evidence for this customary liberty in the early Empire is collected by Yavetz, *Plebs and Princeps*, pp. 18–24, and there is considerable evidence that in the later Empire the rulers were at least willing to listen to the statements of the crowd. Cf. P. Petit, *Libanius*, p. 225: Constantine and Julian "en un mot considère comme efficace ce moyen de connaître l'opinion."

5. *C. Th.* 1.16, 6 (November 1, 331, Constantinople), translation Pharr.

6. *Ch. Th.* 8.5, 32 (December 11, 371, Trier). In this statute the right to use the public post is granted to senators, but from the text it is clear that the *plebs urbana* and the provincials (presumably through the provincial councils?) already had that right.

7. *C. Th.* 9.4, 1 (August 9, 393, Constantinople).

8. *C. Th.* 16.4, 1. (January 23, 386, Constantinople). This law was published at a time

when the government of Theodosius was threatened by the revolt of Maximus in the West (see Stein, *Histoire*, vol. 1, pp. 202–7) and it is possible that the emperor made concessions to those who might have harmed him in order to undermine Maximus' support or to appease such people as the Arians, whom he had recently persecuted.

9. Nestorius *Bazaar*, pp. 271–72.

10. Milton V. Anastos, "*Vox Populi Voluntas Dei* and the Election of the Byzantine Emperor."

11. A. H. M. Jones, "Ancient Heresies," pp. 280–96.

12. For a modern theoretical analysis of some of these ideas see Ted Robert Gurr, *Why Men Rebel* (Princeton, 1970).

13. For a stimulating discussion of differences between East and West in this period, see Peter Brown, "Eastern and Western Christendom in Late Antiquity," in *The Orthodox Churches and the West*, ed. Derek Baker (Oxford, 1976), pp. 1–24.

14. Cf. the interesting suggestion of Paul J. Alexander, "Religious Persecution and Resistance in the Byzantine Empire of the Eighth and Ninth Centuries," *Speculum* 52 (1977), 238–64.

BIBLIOGRAPHY

Primary Sources

Ammianus Marcellinus. *Res Gestae*. Edited by V. Gardthausen. Leipzig, 1874. Translated by J. C. Rolfe. 3 vols., London, 1935-39.

Callinicus. *Vita Sancti Hypatii*. Edited and translated by G. J. M. Bartelink. Sources chrétiennes no. 177. Paris, 1971.

Chronicon Paschale. Edited by Ludwig Dindorf. 2 vols. Bonn, 1832.

Chronographus anni 354. Edited by Theodor Mommsen. *MGH. Auctores Antiquissimi*, 9. Berlin, 1892, pp. 13-196.

John Chrysostom. *Epistulae*. PG 52, 529–742.

———. *Homilia contra Ludos et Theatra*. PG 56, 263–70.

———. *Homilae de Statuis ad Populum Antiochenum*. PG 49, 15–222.

———. *De Sacerdotio*. PG 48, 623–92.

———. *Sermo post Reditum ab Exsilio*. PG 52, 444–48.

Codex Theodosianus. Edited by Theodor Mommsen and Paul M. Meyer. 2 vols. Berlin, 1905. Translated by Clyde Pharr. Princeton, 1952.

Cyril of Scythopolis. *Vita Euthymii*. Edited by Eduard Schwartz. *TU*, Vol. 49, part 2, 1939.

Epiphanius. *Adversus Haereses (Panarion)*. Edited by K. Holl. *GCS*, Vols. 25, 31, 37, 1915–33.

Evagrius Scholasticus. *Historia Ecclesiastica*. Edited by J. Bidez and L. Parmentier. London, 1898.

Hierocles, *Synecdemus*. Edited by Ernest Honigmann. *Corpus Bruxellense Historiae Byzantinae, Forma Imperii Byzantini*. Brussels, 1939.

John of Antioch. *Fragmenta*. *FHG*. IV, 1868, pp. 535–622.

Leo. *Epistulae*. Edited by C. Silva-Tarouca. Rome, 1932–35.
Libanius. *Opera*. Edited by R. Forster. 12 vols. in 13. Revised edition Hildesheim, 1963.
Liberatus. *Breviarium*. *ACO*, II, v, 98–141.
Malalas. *Chronicon*. Edited by Ludwig Dindorf. Bonn, 1831.
Mansi, J. D. *Sacrorum conciliorum nova et amplissima collectio*. 31 vols. Florence and Venice, 1759–98.
Marcellinus Comes. *Chronicon*. Edited by Theodor Mommsen. *MGH, Auctores Antiquissimi*, 11. Berlin, 1894, pp. 60–104.
Marcus Diaconus. *Vita Porphyrii*. Edited by H. Grégoire and M.-A. Kugener. Paris, 1930.
Marius Mercator. *Commonitorium*. *ACO*, II, v.
Michael the Syrian. *Chronique*. Edited and translated by J.-B. Chabot. 3 vols. Paris, 1899–1905.
Nestorius, *The Bazaar of Heracleides*. Edited and translated by C. R. Driver and Leonard Hodgson. Oxford, 1925. Also edited and translated by F. Nau. *Le Livre d'Héraclide de Damas*. Paris, 1910. Reprinted 1969.
———. *Nestoriana*. Edited by F. Loofs. Halle, 1905.
Nicephorus Callistus Xanthopoulos. *Historia Ecclesiastica*. *PG* 145–47.
Notitia Dignitatum. Edited by Otto Seeck. Berlin, 1876.
Olympiodorus of Thebes. *Fragmenta*. *FHG*, IV, 1868, pp. 58–68.
Palatine Anthology. Edited by F. Dubner, Vol. 1. Paris, 1864.
Palladius. *Dialogus de vita S. Johannis Chrysostomi*. Edited by P. R. Coleman–Norton. Cambridge, 1928. Translated by Herbert Moore. London, 1921.
———. *The Lausiac History*. Edited by Dom C. Butler. Cambridge, 1904.
Philostorgius. *Historia Ecclesiastica* (abridged by Photius). Edited by J. Bidez. *GCS*, vol. 21. Berlin, 1913.
Photius. *Bibliotheca*. Edited by René Henry. 7 vols. Paris, 1959–74.
Priscus. *Fragmenta*. *FHG*, IV, 1868, pp. 71–110.
Prosper of Tiro. *Chronicon*. Edited by Theodor Mommsen. *MGH Auctores Antiquissimi*, 9. Berlin, 1892, pp. 341–500.
John Rufus. *Vita Petri Iberi*. Edited by R. Raabe. Leipzig, 1895.
Schwartz, Eduard. ed. *Acta Conciliorum Oecumenicorum*. 4 vols. in 14. Berlin, 1914–74 (to date).
Scriptores originum constantinopolitanarum. Edited by Theodor Preger. Leipzig, 1907.

Socrates. *Historia Ecclesiastica*. *PG* 67, 33–841.

Sozomen. *Historia Ecclesiastica*. Edited by J. Bidez. *GCS* vol. 50. Berlin, 1960.

Suidas. *Lexicon*. Edited by A. Adler. 5 vols. Leipzig, 1928–38.

Theodore Anagnostes. *Historia Ecclesiastica*. Edited by G. C. Hansen. *GCS*. Berlin, 1971.

Theodoret. *Epistulae*. Edited by Y. Asema. Paris, 1955.

———. *Historia Ecclesiastica*. Edited by L. Parmentier. 2nd ed. *GCS* vol. 84. Berlin, 1954.

Theophanes. *Chronographia*. Edited by Karl de Boor. 2 vols. Leipzig, 1883–85.

Vita S. Danielis Stylitae. *Anal. Bolland*. 32 (1913), pp. 121–24.

Vita Johannes Eleemosynarii. *Anal. Bolland*. 45 (1927), 19–73. Translated by Elizabeth Dawes and Norman H. Baynes. Oxford, 1948.

Zachariah of Mitylene. *Historia Ecclesiastica*. Edited by E. W. Brooks. *CSCO, Scriptores Syri*. Vols. 38–39. Louvain, 1953. Translated by F. J. Hamilton and E. W. Brooks. London, 1899.

Zonaras. *Epitome Historiarum*. Edited by L. Dindorf. 4 vols. Leipzig, 1868–75.

Zosimus. *Historia Nova*. Edited by Ludwig Mendelssohn. Leipzig, 1887.

Secondary Sources

Abramowski, L. *Untersuchungen zum Liber Heraclidis des Nestorius*. CSCO 242, 22. Louvain, 1962.

Adams, Jeremy Duquesnay. *The Populus of Augustine and Jerome*. New Haven, 1971.

Alexander, Paul J. *The Oracle of Baalbek*. Dumbarton Oaks Studies, 10. Washington, D.C., 1967.

———. "Religious Persecution and Resistance in the Byzantine Empire of the Eighth and Ninth Centuries: Methods and Justifications." *Speculum* 52 (1977), 238–464.

Altheim, Franz. *Attila und die Hunnen*. Baden-Baden, 1951.

Anastos, Milton V. "Nestorius Was Orthodox," *DOP* 16 (1962), 119–40.

———. "*Vox Populi Voluntas Dei* and the Election of the Byzantine Emperor." *Christianity, Judaism and Other Greco-Roman Cults*. Part 2. Studies in Judaism in Late Antiquity, 12. Edited by Jacob Neusner. Leiden, 1975, pp. 181–207.

Arendt, Hannah. *On Violence*. New York, 1969.

Arnheim, M. T. W. *The Senatorial Aristocracy in the Later Roman Empire*. Oxford, 1972.

Bacht, Heinrich. "Die Rolle des orientalischen Mönchtums in den kirchenpoltischen Auseinandersetzungen um Chalkedon." In *Das Konzil von Chalkedon*. Edited by A. Grillmeier and H. Bacht. Vol. 2. Würzburg, 1953, pp. 193–314.

Baillie, P. K. *The Vigiles of Imperial Rome*. Oxford, 1926.

Ball, John. *Egypt in the Classical Geographers*. Cairo, 1942.

Bardy, G. *La conversion au Christianisme durant les première siècles*. Paris, 1949.

———. *Paul de Samosate*. Louvain, 1929.

———. *Recherches sur saint Lucien d'Antioche et son école*. Paris, 1936.

Bardy, G.; Labriolle, P. de; Brehier, L.; and Plinval, G. de. *Histoire de L'Église de la mort de Théodose à l'élection de Grégoire le Grand*. Vol. 3 of *Histoire de l'Église depuis les origines jusqu'à nos jours*. Edited by Augustin Fliché and Victor Martin. 21 vols. Paris, 1948.

Batiffol, Pierre. *La siège apostolique (359–451)*. 3rd ed. Paris, 1924.

Baur, Chrysostomus. *Der heilige Johannes Chrysostomus und seine Zeit*. 2 vols. Munich, 1929–30. Translated as *John Chrysostom and His Time*. Translated by M. Gonzaga. 2 vols. Westminster, Maryland, 1959.

Baynes, Norman H. "Alexandria and Constantinople: A Study in Ecclesiastical Diplomacy." *JEA* 12 (1926), 145–56. Reprinted in his *Byzantine Studies and Other Essays*. London, 1955, pp. 97–115.

———. *Constantine the Great and the Establishment of the Christian Church*. Proceedings of the British Academy, 15 (1929). Reprinted London, 1930.

Beck, H.-G. *Kirche und theologische Literatur im byzantinischen Reich*. Handbuch der Altertumswissenschaft XII, 2, 1: Byzantinisches Handbuch II, 1. Münich, 1959.

———. "Konstantinopel: Zur Sozialgeschichte einer frühmittelalterlichen Hauptstadt," *BZ* 58 (1965), 11–45.

———. "Senat und Volk von Konstantinopel," *Sitzungsberichte der bayerischen Akademie der Wissenschaften*. Munich, 1966.

———, ed. *Studien zur Frühgeschichte Konstantinopels*. Miscellanea Byzantina Monacensia, 14. Munich, 1973.

Bell, H. I. "Alexandria." *JEA* 13 (1927), 171–78.

———. "The Byzantine Servile State in Egypt," *JEA* 4 (1917), 86–98.

———. *Egypt from Alexander the Great to the Arab conquest*. Oxford, 1948.

———. *Jews and Christians in Egypt*. London, 1924.

Beloch, Julius. *Die Bevölkerung der griechischerömischen Welt.* Leipzig, 1886.

Besevliev, Veslin; and Seyfarth, Wolfgang, eds. *Die Rolle der Plebs im spätrömischen Reich.* Berlin, 1969.

Bethune–Baker, J. F. *Nestorius and His Teaching.* Cambridge, 1908.

Boyce, A. A. "Eudoxia, Eudocia, Eudoxia: Dated Solidi of the Fifth Century," *Museum Notes* (American Numismatic Society) 6 (1954), 131–41.

Braaten, C. E. "Modern Interpretations of Nestorius," *Church History* 32 (1963), 251–67.

Bratianu, G.-I. "La question de l'approvisionnement de Constantinople à l'époque byzantine et ottomane," *Byzantion* 5 (1929), 83–107.

Brière, M. "La légende syriaque de Nestorius," *Revue de l'orient chrétien* 15 (1910), 1–25.

Brockhoff, W. *Studien zur Geschichte der Stadt Ephesos vom 4. nachchristlichen Jahrhundert bis zu ihrem Untergang in der ersten Halfte des 15. Jahrhunderts.* Dissertation, Jena, 1905.

Brown, Peter. "Eastern and Western Christendom in Late Antiquity: A Parting of the Ways." *The Orthodox Churches and the West.* Edited by Derek Baker. Studies in Church History, 13. Oxford, 1976, pp. 1–24.

———. "Religious Dissent in the Later Roman Empire: The Case of North Africa," *History* 46 (1961), 83–101.

———. "The Rise and Function of the Holy Man in Late Antiquity." *JRS* 61 (1971), 80–101.

Browning, Robert. "The Riot of A.D. 387 in Antioch: The Role of the Theatrical Claques in the Later Empire," *JRS* 42 (1952), 13–20.

Brunt, P. A. "The Roman Mob." *Past and Present* 35 (December, 1966), 3–27.

Buckler, W. H. "Labour Disputes in the Province of Asia." In *Anatolian Studies Presented to Sir Wm. Mitchell Ramsay.* Edited by W. H. Buckler and W. M. Calder. Manchester, 1923, pp. 27–50.

Bury, J. B. *History of the Later Roman Empire, from the Death of Theodosius I to the Death of Justinian (395–565).* 2nd ed. 2 vols. London, 1923.

Camelot, Thomas. "De Nestorius à Eutyches: L'opposition de deux christologies." In *Das Konzil von Chalkedon.* Edited by A. Grillmeier and H. Bacht. Vol. 1. Würzburg, 1951, pp. 213–47.

———. *Ephèse et Chalcédoine.* Paris, 1961.

Cameron, Alan. *Circus Factions: Blues and Greens at Rome and*

Byzantium. Oxford, 1976.

———. "The Date of Zosimus' New History." *Philologus*, 113 (1969), 106–110.

———. "Demes and factions." *BZ* 67 (1974), 74–91.

———. *Porphyrius the Charioteer*. Oxford, 1972.

Carpenter, H. J. "Popular Christianity and the Theologians in the Early Centuries." *JTS* n.s. 14 (1963), 294–310.

Ceran, W. "Stagnation or Fluctuation in Early Byzantine Society." *Byzantinoslavica* 31 (1970), 192–203.

Chastagnol, A. *La Préfecture urbaine à Rome sous le Bas-Empire*. Paris, 1960.

Chitty D. J. *The Desert a City: An Introduction to the Study of Egyptian and Palestinian Monasticism under the Christian Empire*. Oxford, 1966.

Claude, Dietrich. *Die byzantinische Stadt im 6. Jahrhundert*. Byzantinisches Archiv, 13. Munich, 1969.

Colin, Jean. *Les villes libres de l'Orient greco–romain et l'envoi au supplice par acclamations populaires*. Collection Latomus, 82. Brussels, 1965.

Constantelos, Demetrios J. *Byzantine Philanthropy and Social Welfare*. New Brunswick, New Jersey, 1968.

———. "Kyros Panopolites, Rebuilder of Constantinople." *GRBS* 12 (1971), 451–64.

Courtois, C. *Les Vandales et l'Afrique*. Paris, 1965.

Cuming, G. J. eds. *Popular Belief and Practice*. Studies in Church History, 8. Cambridge, 1972.

Cuming, G. J.; and Baker, Derek, eds. *Councils and Assemblies*. Studies in Church History, 7. Cambridge, 1971.

Dagron, G. "Les moines et la ville: Le monachisme à Constantinople jusqu'au concile de Chalcédoine (451)." *Traveaux et Mémoires* 4 (1970), 229–76.

———. *Naissance d'une capital: Constantinople et ses institutions de 330 à 451*. Bibliothèque byzantine, 7. Paris, 1973.

Daube, David. *Civil Disobedience in Antiquity*. Edinburgh, 1973.

Delehaye, H. *Les Origines du cults des martyrs*. Brussels, 1912.

Démougeot, E. *De L'unité à la division de l'empire Romain (395–410). Essai sur le gouvernement imperial*. Paris, 1951.

Diakonov, A. "Vizantiiskie dimy i fackii v V-VII vv" [Byzantine demes and factions in the fifth through seventh centuries], *Vizantiskii sbornik* (1945), 144–227.

Dolger, Franz. "Die frühbyzantinische und byzantinische beeinflusse Stadt (V-VIII Jahrhundert)." In *Atti del 3° Congresso Internationale di Studi sull'alto Medioevo* (1956). Spoleto, 1959, pp. 65–100.

Douglas, Mary. *Natural Symbols: Explorations in Cosmology.* London, 1970.

Downey, Glanville. *A History of Antioch in Syria from Seleucus to the Arab Conquest.* Princeton, 1961.

———. "The Size of the Population of Antioch." *Transactions and Proceedings of the American Philological Society* 89 (1958), 84–91.

Draguet, R. "La Christologie d'Eutyches d'après les actes du synode de Flavien (448)." *Byzantion* 6 (1931), 441–57.

Dunlap, J. E. *The Office of the Grand Chamberlain in the Later Roman and Byzantine Empires.* New York, 1929.

Dvornik, Francis. "The Circus Parties in Byzantium: Their Evolution and their Suppression." *Byzantina-Metabyzantina* 1 (1946), 119–33.

———. *Early Christian and Byzantine Political Philosophy.* Dumbarton Oaks Studies, 9. 2 vols. Washington, D. C., 1966.

———. *The Idea of Apostolicity in Byzantium and the Legend of the Apostle Andrew.* Dumbarton Oaks Studies, 4. Cambridge, Massachusetts, 1958.

Echols, Edward. "The Roman City Police: Origin and Development," *Classical Journal* 53 (1958), 377–85.

Festiguière, A. J. *Antioche paienne et chrétienne.* Paris, 1959.

———. *Les Moines d'Orient.* 4 vols. Paris, 1961–64.

Fine, John V. A., Jr. "Two Contributions on the Demes and Factions in Byzantium in the Sixth and Seventh Century." *Recueil des travaux de l'Institut d'Études Byzantines* (Belgrade) 10 (1967), 29–37.

Flemming, J. *Akten des ephesischen Synode vom Jahre 449.* Gesellschaft der Wissenschaften zu Göttingen, philosophisch-historiche Klasse, 15. Berlin, 1917.

Forschungen in Ephesos. Edited by the Österreichisches archäologisches Institut. 6 vols. Vienna, 1906–51.

Foss, Clive. "Byzantine Cities of Western Asia Minor." Ph.D. dissertation, Harvard University, 1972.

Frank, R. I. *Scholae Palatinae: The Palace Guards of the Later Roman Empire.* Papers and Monographs of the American Academy in Rome, 23. Rome, 1969.

Fraser, P. M. *Ptolemaic Alexandria.* 3 vols. Oxford, 1972.

Frend, W. H. C. *The Donatist Church.* Oxford, 1952.

———. "Popular Religion and Christological Controversy in the Fifth

Century." *Popular Belief and Practice.* Edited by G. J. Cuming and Derek Baker. Studies in Church History, 8. Cambridge, 1972, pp. 19–30.

———. "Religion and Social Change in the Late Roman Empire." *Cambridge Journal* 2 (1949), 487–97.

———. *The Rise of the Monophysite Movement: Chapters in the History of the Church in the Fifth and Sixth Centuries.* Cambridge, 1972.

Friedlaender, Ludwig. *Darstellungen aus Sittengeschichte Roms in der Zeit von Augustus bis Ausgang der Antonine.* 10th ed. 4 vols. Leipzig, 1921–22.

Gage, Jean. *Les classes sociales dans l'empire romain.* Paris, 1964.

Le Gall, J. "Rome, ville de fainéants?" *Revue des Études Latines* 49 (1971), 266–77.

Garnsey, Peter. *Social Status and Legal Privilege in the Roman Empire.* Oxford, 1970.

Gaudemet, J. "L'étranger au Bas-Empire." *Recueils de la société Jean Bodin* 9 (1958), 209–35.

Geffcken, J. *Der Ausgang des griechisch-römischen Heidentums.* Religionswissenschaftlich Bibliothek, 6. Heidelberg, 1920.

Gelzer, M. *Studien zur byzantinischen Verwaltung Ägyptens.* Leipziger historische Abhandlungen, 13. Leipzig, 1909.

Goossens, R. "Note sur les factions du cirque à Rome." *Byzantion* 14 (1939), 205–9.

Goubert, Paul. "Le rôle de Sainte Pulchérie et de l'eunuque Chrysaphios," in *Das Konzil von Chalkedon.* Edited by A. Grillmeier and H. Bacht. Vol. 1. Würzburg, 1951, pp. 302–21.

Graef, Hilda. *Mary, a History of Doctrine and Devotion.* Vol. 1. New York, 1963.

Gregorovius, F. *Athenais: Geschichte einer byzantinischer Kaiserin.* Leipzig, 1887.

Grillmeier, Aloys. *Christ in Christian Tradition.* Translated by J. S. Bowden. New York, 1965.

Grillmeier, Aloys; and Bacht, H., eds. *Das Konzil von Chalkedon.* 3 vols. Würzburg, 1951–54.

Grosse, R. *Römische Militargeschichte von Gallienus biz zum Beginn der byzantinischen Themenverfassung.* Berlin, 1920.

Guilland, R. "Fonctions et dignités des eunuques." *Études Byzantines* 2 (1944), 185–225, and 3 (1945), 179–21.

Güldenpenning, Albert. *Geschichte des oströmischen Reiches unter den Kaisern Arcadius und Thodosius II.* Halle, 1885.

Gurr, Ted Robert. *Why Men Rebel.* Princeton, 1970.

Gwatkin, H. M. *Studies of Arianism.* 2nd ed. Cambridge, 1900.

Hardy, E. R. *Christian Egypt: Church and People.* New York, 1952.

———. *The Large Estates of Byzantine Egypt.* Columbia Studies, 354. New York, 1931.

Harnack, Adolph von. *Mission und Ausbereitung des Christentums in den ersetn drei Jahrhunderten.* 4th ed. 2 vols. Freiburg, 1924.

Heaton, J. W. *Mob Violence in the Late Roman Republic.* Illinois Studies in the Social Sciences 23, no. 4. Urbana, 1939.

Heckel, A. *Die Kirche von Alexandria.* Dissertation, Strassburg, 1918.

Hefele, Karl Joseph von. *Histoire des conciles.* Translated by Henri Leclercq. 2nd ed. 2 vols. Paris, 1907–49.

Hengel, Martin. *Property and Riches in the Early Church.* A translation of *Eigentum und Reichtum in der frühen Kirche.* Philadelphia, 1974.

Hirschfeld, O. "Die Sicherheitspolizei im romischen Kaissereich." *Sitzungsberichte der könglichen preussischen Akademie der Wissenschaften zu Berlin* (1891), 845–77.

Hobsbawm, E. J. *Primitive Rebels: Studies in Archaic Forms of Social Movements in the 18th and 20th Centuries.* Manchester, 1959.

Holum, Kenneth G. "Aelia Pulcheria and the Eastern Roman Empire." Ph.D. dissertation, University of Chicago, 1973.

Honigmann, Ernest. "Juvenal of Jerusalem." *DOP* 5 (1950), 209–79.

———. "The Original Lists of the Members of the Council of Nicaea, the Robber Synod and the Council of Chalcedon," *Byzantion* 16 (1944), 20–80.

Hopkins, Keith. "Eunuchs in Politics in the Later Roman Empire." *Proceedings of the Cambridge Philological Society* 189 (1963), 62–80.

Janin, R. *Constantinople byzantine.* 2nd ed. Paris, 1964.

———. *La géographie ecclésiastique de l'Empire Byzantin.* vol. 3, *Les Églises et les monastères.* Paris, 1953.

Jarry, Jacques. "Hérésies et factions à Constantinople du Ve au VIIe siècle." *Syria* 37 (1960), 348–71.

———. *Hérésies et factions dans l'Empire byzantine du IVe au VIIe siècle.* Publications de l'institut francais d'archéologie orientale du Caire: recherches d'archéologie, de philologie et d'histoire, 142. Cairo, 1968.

Johnson, Allan Chester. *Roman Egypt. An Economic Survey of Ancient Rome.* Edited by Tenney Frank. Vol. 2. Baltimore, 1936.

———, and West. Louis C. *Byzantine Egypt: Economic Studies.* Princeton, 1949.

Jones. A. H. M. *The Cities of the Eastern Roman Provinces.* Rev. ed. Oxford, 1971.

———. *Constantine and the Conversion of Europe.* Rev. ed. New York, 1962.

———. *The Greek City from Alexander to Justinian.* Oxford, 1940.

———. *The Later Roman Empire, 284–602: A Social, Economic and Administrative Survey.* 2 vols. Oxford, 1964.

———. "Were Ancient Heresies National or Social Movements in Disguise?" *JTS* 10 (1959), 280–96.

Jugie, M. *Nestorius et la controverse nestorienne.* Paris, 1912.

Kaegi, Walter E., Jr. *Byzantium and the Decline of Rome.* Princeton, 1968.

Keil, Josef. *Führer durch Ephesos.* Vienna, 1964.

Kitzinger, Ernst. "The Cult of Images in the Age before Iconoclasm." *DOP* 7 (1954), pp. 83–150.

Kleberg, T. *Hôtels, restaurants et cabarets, dans l'antiquité romaine: Étude historique et philologique.* Upsala, 1957.

Kohns, Hans Peter. *Versorgunskrisen und Hungerrevolten im spätantiken Rom. Antiquitas.* Vol. 6. Bonn, 1961.

Kopek, Thomas A. "The Social Class of the Cappadocian Fathers," *Church History* 42 (1973), 555–66.

Laistner, M. J. W. *Christianity and Pagan Culture in the Later Roman Empire.* New York, 1951.

LeBon, G. *The Crowd: A Study of the Popular Mind.* London, 1709.

Lebon, J. *Le monophysitisme sévérien: Étude historique, litteraire et théologique sur la resistance monophysite au concile de Chalcédoine.* Louvain, 1909.

Leipoldt, J. *Scheunte von Atripe und die Enstehung des national-ägyptischen christentums. TU,* vol. 25. Leipzig, 1903.

Leitzmann, H. *Apollinaris von Laodicea und seine Schüle: Texte, und Untersuchungen.* Tubingen, 1904.

Lexikon für Theologie und Kirche. Edited by J. Hofer and K. Rahner. 10 vols. 2nd ed. Freiburg, 1957–65.

Lichtheim, Miriam. "Autonomy versus Unity in the Christian East," *The Transformation of the Roman World.* Edited by Lynn White, Jr. Los Angeles, 1966, pp. 119–46.

Liebeschuetz, J. H. W. G. *Antioch: City and Imperial Administration in the Later Roman Empire.* Oxford, 1972.

———. "Did the Pelagian Movement Have Social Aims?" *Historia* 12 (1963), 227–41.
Lintcott, A. W. *Violence in Republican Rome.* Oxford, 1968.
Loofs, Fredrich. *Nestorius and his Place in the History of Christian Doctrine.* Cambridge, 1914.
L'Orange, H. P. *Art Forms and Civic Life in the late Roman Empire.* Princeton, 1965.
Lot, Ferdinand. *The End of the Ancient World and the Beginning of the Middle Ages.* Edited by Glanville Downey. Revised edition. New York, 1961.
Luibhéid, Colm. "Theodosius II and Heresy." *Journal of Ecclesiastical History* 16 (1965), 13–38.
MacMullen, Ramsay. *Enemies of the Roman Order.* Cambridge, Massachusetts, 1966.
———. *Roman Social Relations 50 B.C. to A.D. 284.* New Haven, 1974.
———. "Social Mobility and the Theodosian Code," *JRS* 54 (1964), 49–53.
———. *Soldier and Civilian in the Later Roman Empire.* Cambridge, Massachusetts, 1963.
McNamara, J. "Theodore of Mopsuestia and the Nestorian Heresy." *Irish Theological Quarterly.* 19 (1952), 254–68 and 20 (1953), pp. 172–91.
Maenchen-Helfen, J. Otto. *The World of the Huns.* Berkeley, 1973.
Magie, David. *Roman Rule in Asia Minor to the End of the Third Century after Christ.* 2 vols. Princeton, 1950.
Mango, Cyril. *The Brazen House.* Copenhagen, 1959.
Manojlović, G. "Le Peuple de Constantinople." Translated by H. Grégoire. *Byzantion* 11 (1936), 617–716.
Maricq, A. "Factions du cirque et partis populaires." *Bulletin de l'Academie royale de Belgique, Classe des Lettres,* 5th ser. 36 (1950), 396–421.
Martindale, J. R. "Public Disorders in the Late Roman Empire, Their Causes and Character." B. A. Thesis, Oxford, 1960.
Maspero Jean. *Histoire des partiarches d'Alexandrie depuis la mort de l'empéreur Anastase jusqu'à la reconciliation des églises jacobites, 528–616.* Paris, 1923.
———. *Organization militaire de l'Égypte byzantine.* Paris, 1912.
Matthews, John. *Western Aristocracies and Imperial Court, A.D. 364–425.* Oxford, 1975.
Mazzarino, S. *Aspetti sociale del quarto secolo.* Rome, 1951.
Milne, J. G. "Egyptian Nationalism under Greek and Roman Rule." *JEA*

14 (1928), 226-34.

———. *A History of Egypt under Roman Rule.* 3rd ed. London, 1924.

Miltner, Franz. *Ephesos: Stadt der Artemis und des Johannes.* Vienna, 1958.

Momigliano, Arnaldo. "Popular Religious Beliefs and the Late Roman Historians." *Popular Belief and Practice.* Edited by G. J. Cuming and Derek Baker. Studies in Church History, 8. Cambridge, 1972, pp. 1–18.

Monks, George R. "The Church of Alexandria and the City's Economic Life in the Sixth Century." *Speculum* 28 (1953), 359–62.

Moravcsik, Gyula. *Byzantinoturcica.* 2nd ed. 2 vols. Berlin, 1958.

Musurillo, Herbert. *The Acts of the Pagan Martyrs.* Oxford, 1954.

Nau, Francois. "Deux épisodes de l'histoire juive sous Théodose II (423 et 438) d'après la vie de Barsauma le Syrien." *Revue des Études Juives* 83 (1927), 184–206.

Norman, A. F. "Gradations in Later Municipal Society." *JRS* 48 (1958), pp. 79–85.

Norris, R. A., Jr. *Manhood and Christ: A Study in the Christology of Theodore of Mopsuestia.* Oxford, 1963.

Oost, Stewart Irvin. *Galla Placidia Augusta.* Chicago, 1968.

Ostrogorsky, George. *History of the Byzantine State.* Translated by Joan Hussey. Rev. ed. New Brunswick, N. J., 1969.

Pargoire, J. "Les débuts du monachisme à Constantinople." *Revue des questiones historique* 65 (1899), 67–143.

Perry, Samuel. *The Second Synod of Ephesus.* Dartford, 1881.

Petit, Paul. *Libanius et la vie municipale à Antioche au IVe siècle après J.-C.* Paris, 1955.

Philipsborn, A. "La compagnie d'ambulanciers 'parabalani' d'Alexandrie." *Byzantion* 20 (1950), 185–90.

Quasten, Johannes. *Patrology.* 3 vols. Utrecht, 1950–60.

Ramsay, William M. *Pauline and Other Studies in Early Christian History.* London, 1906.

Raven, Charles E. *Apollinarianism.* Cambridge, 1923.

Rostovtzeff, Michael. *Social and Economic History of the Roman Empire.* 2nd ed. 2 vols. Oxford, 1957.

Rouillard, Germaine. *L'Administration civile de l'Égypte byzantine.* 2nd ed. Paris, 1928.

———. "The Study of Popular Disturbances in the 'Pre-Industrial' Age." *Historical Studies* (Melbourne) (1963) 457–69.

Russell, J. C. *Late Ancient and Medieval Populations. Transactions of the American Philosophical Society* n.s., 48, 3. Philadelphia, 1958.

Schubert, W. "Alexandria." *RAC* 1.

Schwartz, Eduard. "Cyril und der Mönch Viktor." *Sitzungsberichte Akademie der Wissenschaften in Wien, philosophisch-historische Klasse.* 208, 4 (1928) 1-51.

———. "Der Prozess des Eutyches." Sitzungsberichte der bayerischen Academie der Wissenschaften 5 (1929), 1–93.

———. "Über die Reichskonzilien von Theodosius bis Justinian." *Gesammelte Schriften.* Vol. 2. Berlin, 1960, pp. 111–58.

———. "Zur Vorgeschicthe des ephesinischen Konzils: Ein Fragment." *Historische Zeitschrift* 112 (1914), 237–63.

Seeck, Otto. *Geschichte des Untergangs der antiken Welt.* 6 vols. Berlin, 1895–1921.

———. *Regesten der Kaiser und Päpste.* Stuttgart, 1919.

Sellers, R. V. *The Council of Chalcedon.* London, 1961.

———. *Two Ancient Christologies.* London, 1954.

Seyfarth, Wolfgang. "Von der Bedeutung der Plebs in der Spätantike." *Die Rolle der Plebs im spätromischen Reich.* Edited by Veslin Besevliev and Wolfgang Seyfarth. Berlin, 1969, pp. 7–18.

———. *Sociale Fragen der spätrömischen Kaiserzeit im Spiegel des Theodosianus.* Berlin, 1963.

Sinnigen, William G. *The Officium of the Urban Prefect during the Later Roman Empire.* Papers and Monographs of the American Academy in Rome, 17. Rome, 1957.

Smelser, N. J. *Theory of Collective Behavior.* New York, 1963.

Sophocles, E. A. *Greek Lexicon of the Roman and Byzantine Periods.* 2 vols. New York, 1887.

Starr, Chester G. *Civilization and the Caesars.* Ithaca. N.Y., 1954.

Stein, Ernst. "L'Administration de l'Égypte byzantine." *Gnomon* 6 (1930), 401–7.

———. *Histoire du Bas-Empire.* Edited and translated by Jean-Remy Planque. Vol. 1. Paris, 1959.

Steinwenter, A. "Die Stellung der Bischöfe in der byzantinischen Verwaltung Ägyptens." *Studi in onore di P. Francisci.* Vol. 1 Milan, 1954, pp. 77–99.

Stockle, A. *Spätrömische und byzantinische Zünfte.* Leipzig, 1911.

Teall, J. L. "The Grain Supply of the Byzantine Empire, 330–1025." *DOP* 13 (1959), 87–139.

Thompson, E. A. "The Foreign Policies of Theodosius II and Marcian."

Hermathena 76 (1950), 58–75.

———. *A History of Attila and the Huns.* Oxford, 1948.

———. "Peasant Revolts in Late Roman Gaul and Spain." *Past and Present* 2 (1952), 11-23.

———. *The Visigoths in the Time of Ulfila.* Oxford, 1966.

Thompson, Homer A. "Athenian Twilight: A.D. 267–600." *JRS* 49 (1959), 61–75.

Tillemont, Le Nain de. *Mémoires pour servir à l'histoire ecclésiastique des six premiers siècles.* Paris, 1693–1712.

Tinnefeld, Franz. *Die frühbyzantinische Gesellschaft: Strukturen-Gegensätze-Spannungen.* München, 1977.

Treitinger, Otto. *Die oströmische Kaiser- und Reichsidee nach ihrer Gestaltung im höfischen Zerimoniell.* Jena, 1938.

Van Cauwenburgh, Paul. *Etude sur les moines d'Egypte.* Paris, 1914.

Vetters, Hermann. "Zum byzantinischen Ephesos." *Jahrbuch der Österreichischen byzantinischen Gesellschaft* 15 (1966), 273–87.

Vries, W. de. "Das Konzil von Ephesus 449, eine 'Raubersynode'?" *Orientalia Christiana Periodica* 41 (1975), 357–98.

Walbank, F. E. *The Awful Revolution.* Toronto, 1969.

Wallace-Hadrill, J. M. *The Barbarian West.* London, 1962.

Weiacher, Franz. *Recht und Gesellschaft im der Spätantike.* Stuttgart, 1964.

Wellen, G. A. *Theotokos: Eine ikonographische Abhandlung über das Gottesmutterbild im frühchrisliche Zeit.* Utrecht, 1961.

Wilson, Bryan R. "An Analysis of Sect Development." *Patterns of Sectarianism.* London, 1967, pp. 22–45.

Wolfson, Harry A. "Philosophical Implications of Arianism and Apollinarianism," *DOP* 12 (1958), 3–28.

———. *The Philosophy of the Church Fathers.* 2nd. ed. Vol. 1. Cambridge, Massachusetts, 1956.

Wood, J. T. *Discoveries at Ephesus.* London, 1877.

Woodward, E. L. *Christianity and Nationalism in the Later Roman Empire.* London, 1916.

Yavetz, Z. *Plebs and Princeps.* Oxford, 1969.

INDEX

Acacius, bishop of Beroea, 59–60
Acclamations, 217–20, 226 n. 3
Alexandria, 19, 30, 34, 181–92
Anastasius, priest of Constantinpole, 89, 90, 96
Anatolius, bishop of Constantinople, 151, 163, 167, 170, 174, 180
Anatolius, patrician, 171
Anthemius, *praetorian prefect*, 81, 114
Antioch, 20–21, 29, 31, 41–45, 81–82
Antropotokos, 89
Apollinarius of Laodicea, 87–88, 98
Arcadius, emperor, 53, 61, 81, 211, 219–20
Arians, Arianism, 43–44, 46, 51, 71 n. 37, 83–84, 86–88, 98, 100
Arsacius, bishop of Constantinople, 64–65, 83
Athanasius, bishop of Alexandria, 5, 191
Athanasius, priest of Alexandria, 177, 179, 181, 187
Athens, 20
Atticus, bishop of Constantinople, 65–66, 83, 93-94
Attila, 129, 137–38, 141, 165–66

Barsumas, monk, 143, 148–50, 154, 168
Bassianos, bishop of Ephesus, 145–46, 153
Bribery, 113, 226

Candidianus, *comes domesticorum*, 101–3, 105–8, 123 n. 108
Celestine, bishop of Rome, 91, 93, 95, 100–102
Christological controversy, 85–88, 97
Christokos, 89
Chrysaphius, 131, 137–42, 152, 155 n. 19, 164–66, 177, 206, 219
Chrysostom, John, bishop of Constantinople, 12, 30, 41–69, 81, 83, 89, 96, 98, 102, 175, 179, 203–4, 209–10, 212–13, 219–20, 222
Circus factions, 9, 11, 27–29, 142, 221
Cities: and bread dole, 17, 25, 36 n. 9, 142, 184–85; police in, 29–30, 216; populations of, 19–21, 31, 34–35; social conditions in, 15–19, 22–26; spectacles in, 15–16, 42, 49, 223; walls of, 20, 21, 29
Claque, theatre, 27, 29, 221
Collegia (guilds), 9, 27, 65, 67, 221
Collyridions, 98, 107
Constantinople, 31, 34–35; Hagia Sophia, 62–63, 65, 67, 139–40; Senate of, 62–63; Xylokerkos, 63, 169
Council of Chalcedon (451), 12, 28, 170–81, 184, 186, 213
Council of Ephesus (431), 12, 94, 98, 100–108, 129–30
Council of the Oak, 53, 57–59, 101
"Crowd, the": as term, 9–11
Curiales, 18–19, 23

243

244 Index

Cyril, bishop of Alexandria, 66, 89, 91–96, 99–108, 112–13, 115, 130, 133, 146, 153, 175–79, 207, 214, 221–22

Dalmatius, monk, 81, 110–11, 113, 126 n. 154, 130, 134–35
Diodore of Tarsus, 130–31
Dioscorus, bishop of Alexandria, 12, 139–40, 143–50, 154, 171–73, 175–82, 184–92, 204–5, 209, 213–14, 222
Douglas, Mary, 6–7

Elpidius, *comes sacri consistorii*, 143–45, 147
Ephesus, 31–32, 75 n. 90, 105–7
Epiphanius, bishop of Salamis, 52–53, 98, 107, 208
Eudocia, empress, 21, 81, 96, 139–40, 144, 164
Eudoxia, empress, 51, 53–55, 58–60, 64
Eulogius, tribune, 143–45
Eusebius of Dorylaeum, 90, 93, 100, 131–33, 137, 145, 147, 172, 211
Eutropius, eunuch, 44, 50–51
Eutyches, monk, 12, 130–36, 138–43, 145–50, 153–54, 155 n. 8

Faustos, monk, 134–35, 151, 157 n. 42, 169
Flavian, bishop of Constantinople, 94, 131–37, 139–40, 142, 144–54, 163–68, 170–71, 175, 177, 204–5, 208, 213, 219
Florentius, patrician, 133–34, 140–41, 156 n. 32, 171
Florus, Agustal prefect of Alexandria, 184
Frend, W. H. C., 5

Gainas, 50–51
Gibbon, Edward, 4–5
Gregory of Nazianzus, 43, 97, 169
Gregory of Nyssa, 3, 217

Heraclides, bishop of Ephesus, 57
Hilarus, emissary of Pope Leo, 147–48
Holy men, 26, 49
Honestiores and *humiliores*, 22–23
Huns, 29, 81, 114, 129, 137–38, 141–42, 153, 165–66, 170
Hypatius, monk, 82, 96, 99, 110

Ireneus, *comes*, 101, 105–7, 123 n. 108, 150

Isaac, monk, 46, 53, 56–57, 72 n. 42
Ischyrion, deacon of Alexandria, 176–79

Jews, 33–34, 61–62, 67–68, 109, 141, 143, 158 n. 79, 168, 175
Johannites, 61–69, 214–15, 218, 222–23
John, bishop of Antioch, 102, 104–6, 130, 165
Jones, A. H. M., 6, 222
Julius, emissary of Pope Leo, 147

Latrocinium (second Council of Ephesus, 449), 12, 143–52, 154, 163, 165, 167, 169–70, 172, 192, 213
Leo, bishop of Rome, 134, 136, 144, 151–52, 163, 166, 171, 187–88
Leontius, bishop of Ancyra, 59
Lucius, *tribunus*, 60, 62

Macedonius, *referendarius* and *tribunus notariorum*, 140–41
Magnus, *silentiarius*, 133–34, 140
Mamas, *comes*, 140–41
Manichaeans, Manichaeanism, 88, 136–37
Marcian, 12, 164, 166, 169–71, 173, 178, 186–87, 189, 192, 210, 220
Mary, mother of Jesus, 31, 88–91, 97–99, 105, 107, 137
Memnon, bishop of Ephesus, 102–8, 112, 114, 145–46, 153, 205
Memoritai, 167–69, 171, 174
Monks, 8–9, 26, 46–47, 56, 82, 92, 98, 109, 116, 134–35, 149–51, 153, 165, 167–70, 173, 185–86, 189, 210

Nectarius, bishop of Constantinople, 43, 45, 47, 64
Nestorius, bishop of Constantinople, 12, 66, 81–85, 87–116, 129–31, 134–35, 137, 139, 142–43, 147–48, 152–53, 179, 205, 208–13, 215, 219–20, 222
Nestorius of Phragonis, 175, 177, 187
Notices, public, 90, 100, 125 n. 134, 136–37, 152, 173
Novatians, 43, 46, 79 n. 152, 84, 100

Optatus, *praefectus urbi*, 63
Origen, Origenism, 51–52, 55, 66, 84–85, 89

Pagans, paganism, 34, 46, 60–62, 68, 85–86,

Index 245

98, 109, 168
Pelagians, Pelagianism, 94–95
Panis aedium, 25
Parabalani, 145, 149, 159 n. 97, 173
Paschanius, bishop of Lilybaeum, 171–72, 180
Patronage, 24–26
Paul of Samosata, 88, 92–93, 100, 115, 213
Poor: concern for (*philanthropia*), 17–18, 142
Popular Christianity, 86–87, 207–8, 214, 226 n. 2
Popular opinion and action: attitudes of the ancient sources, 4, 11, 115
Praefectus urbi, 17, 30, 216
Procession(s), 46, 104, 109–12
Proclus, bishop of Cyzicus and Constantinople, 81–82, 90–91, 98, 100–101, 105, 115, 130–31
Proclus, proconsul of Asia, 144
Proterius, bishop of Alexandria, 181–91, 206, 210, 214–15, 220
Pulcheria, 81, 96, 131, 141, 144, 151, 163–67, 169–71

Rude, George, 7–8

Schenute of Atripe, 183
Serapion, deacon, 45, 52
Severianus, bishop of Gabala, 54, 210
Sisinnius, bishop of Constantinople, 81–83, 93
Slogans, 55, 71 n. 38, 88, 92, 97, 104, 205, 212
Social classes, 22–24
Sophronios, layman of Alexandria, 177–79

Stephanos, bishop of Ephesus, 145–47, 153, 205
Synodos endemousa, 96, 131, 138, 140, 143, 148, 153, 193 n. 3

Tall Brothers, 51–53, 55, 175
Theodore, deacon of Alexandria, 176, 180–81
Theodore of Mopsuestia, 82, 130–31
Theodoret, bishop of Cyrrhus, 112–13, 131, 150
Theodosius I, 32, 217
Theodosius II, 33, 66, 81–82, 84, 93, 95–96, 101, 108, 110–11, 113–16, 116 n. 2, 118 n. 20, 130, 133–34, 138–44, 147, 150, 152, 163–66, 169, 171, 205, 211, 219–20
Theophilus, bishop of Alexandria, 44–45, 51–58, 66, 89, 175–76, 178
Theotokos, 88–91, 97–100, 105, 115, 209–10, 214
Timothy Aelurus, monk, 186, 189, 191
Tome of Leo, 167, 180–81, 187, 189, 191

Valentinian III, 151, 163
Vandals, 29, 129, 165
Violence, 3, 11, 67, 97, 102, 105–6, 145, 149–50, 154, 176, 192, 214–15, 220, 225

Women, 60, 64, 98, 104, 107
Woodward, E. L., 5

Xylokerketes, 63

Zeno, *magister militune*, 138, 165–66